MSU LIBRARIES
3 2109 00158 1363

D0984706

ARCHAEOLOGY AND THE LANDSCAPE

Leslie Grinsell at the Museu Regional d'Arta, Mallorca, Christmas, 1970.

ARCHAEOLOGY AND THE LANDSCAPE

Essays for

L. V. Grinsell

Edited by

P. J. Fowler

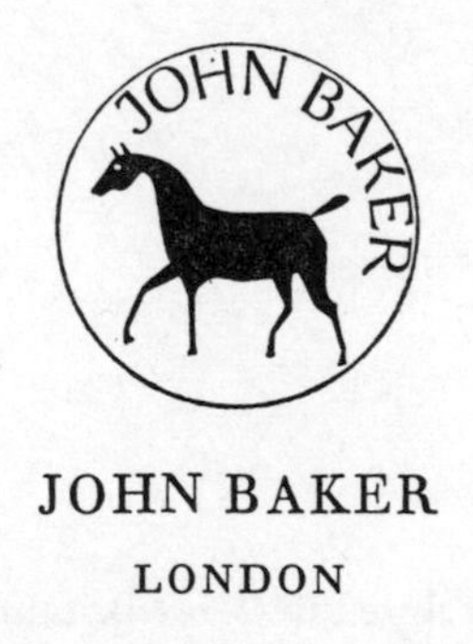

JOHN BAKER

LONDON

First published in 1972 by
John Baker (Publishers) Ltd
4, 5 & 6 Soho Sq
London WIV 6AD

ISBN 0 212 98398 9

Printed in Great Britain
by W & J Mackay Limited, Chatham

Contents

List of Illustrations

PLATES

FIGURES IN THE TEXT

PART I

Fieldwork Reviewed

Preface

Fieldwork which does not involve excavation is one of the peculiar and distinctive merits of British archaeology. One of its most persistent and consistent practitioners for the last forty years has been L. V. Grinsell and we offer him this book of essays in admiration of his achievement and in gratitude for his example.

The essays deliberately concentrate on field archaeology in England because it seemed better to produce a book on various aspects of one subject, able to stand without its dedication if necessary, rather than to try to reflect the many interests of Leslie Grinsell. The Bibliography of his publications (below pp 250–56) indicates those clearly enough and suggests what a diverse (and unsatisfactory?) book it would have been had we tried to range from Egypt through folklore to late Saxon coins. We suspect, however, that field archaeology is his first love and that it is in this that he has made his greatest single contribution to knowledge.

Since we are concerned here mainly with field archaeology, however, in fairness to LVG a further word or two on his work is called for, if only because he has never been a narrow-minded specialist, and some aspects of the man are not mentioned at all in the following pages. In addition to the range of his original studies and his published output, nearly all carried out in his spare time, he has become a dedicated and painstaking museum curator as the recently displayed galleries at Bristol City Museum show. He has always linked his own work to teaching, at the Literary and Philosophical Society in London and, more recently in museum studies and as a part-time tutor for Bristol University's Department of Extra-Mural Studies and for the W.E.A. And he has taken his enthusiasm to teach into his life-long association with the Youth Hostels Association and into many a school.

Despite the solitary nature of so much of his work, he has given himself unstintingly in corporate effort, in supporting, indeed in activating, the essential work of institutional archaeology. For twenty-two years he was the meticulous Honorary Treasurer of the Prehistoric Society, an achievement for which the Society gratefully made him a Life Member; he saw to it that the South Western Group of the Council for British Archaeology functioned and was well represented; and locally his many services, which include being a founder member and mainstay of the Bristol Archaeological Research Group, have recently been simultaneously acknowledged by his election as a vice-president of the Bristol & Gloucester Archaeological Society and President of the Somerset Archaeological and Natural History Society. At the same time, he has served in various roles in the councils of museologists, numismatists and folklorists.

In such a life so fully dedicated to archaeology, there could perhaps be little time for other interests; yet LVG somehow has managed to read voluminously, to cultivate and enjoy a love of music to the extent of being no mean pianist himself, to sketch sparingly and to photograph plentifully. As he approaches his formal retirement from the museum, he can hardly wait to start writing those books he knows he has in him; one of the greatest pleasures to his friends is to see him like this, fully recovered from the serious illness of a few years ago which threatened to impede his work and his publications, the latter of which reached such a climax in 1969–70. The following pages were all written towards the end of that period and, with the exceptions of the editor's essays (!), take no account of views or discoveries after December, 1970.

Spring, 1971 *University of Bristol*

CHAPTER I

Leslie Valentine Grinsell, Field Archaeologist

Nicholas Thomas

'In the following study, the region dealt with is bounded on the north by the Thames, and on the west by the Avebury and Stonehenge area. It consists, therefore, of Wiltshire, Hampshire, Berkshire, Surrey, Sussex and Kent, and a small portion of Dorset. The area contains about 5,000 barrows, or ancient burial mounds, about seven-eighths of which I have seen; it is believed, therefore, that the following details are fairly complete.'

L. V. Grinsell in *Proceedings of the Prehistoric Society of East Anglia*, 7 (1932–34), 203

In the year 1932, the achievement of this young, dedicated amateur archaeologist was probably without parallel even among professional workers like Crawford and the circle of such established antiquarians as Williams-Freeman, Allcroft and Eliot Curwen, from whose work and writings Grinsell had drawn his own inspiration. In 1941, the introduction to LVG's paper on The Bronze Age round barrows of Wessex (1941b, 73–75) makes even clearer the pre-eminent position in which he stood in his chosen field of study. This paper epitomizes his work on Wessex since 1929. Now the area on which he had tramped has increased, particularly westwards; over 6,100 barrows had been taken into account, of which LVG had visited at least 5,750 personally. His distribution maps presented a distinctive settlement pattern in a geological setting, his tables of barrow details offered a massive corpus of information for other scholars to synthesize (e.g. Ashbee 1960 and 1970). The typology of Wessex barrows as earthworks had also been fully worked out and was presented in a series of assured diagrams. All this had happened in little more than ten years: yet the bulk of his work was still to come and his long career as a professional archaeologist lay ahead, beyond a world war and a period of interest in the pyramids of Egypt, to whose study he brought a technique self-taught on the chalk downlands of England.

THE BACKGROUND

Leslie Grinsell and his family moved to Brighton shortly after the First World War and his interest in British archaeology dates from this time. H. S. Toms (1874–1940), Curator of the Brighton Museum and formerly chief assistant, with H. St George Gray, to General Pitt-Rivers, took up and encouraged the young enquirer and nurtured his interest. By about 1927 LVG had embarked upon his first career in Barclays Bank and had moved to London. He had learned, from Toms chiefly and also from his own reading, that of all the classes of ancient earthwork surviving so incredibly upon the downs of southern England, only the barrows, or burial mounds, had escaped the close scrutiny of the Curwens, Allcroft and the rest. So it was that Grinsell decided to devote himself to their study, feeling, as he did, that here alone an amateur could make a contribution to British archaeology. Forty years and more on, and now for long a professional, he is still giving all his spare time to the same study in the same belief.

LVG came into archaeology at a period when a number of British antiquarians of consequence were active in southern England. These were members of the country-dwelling professional middle class who did so much to foster prehistory, especially its field antiquities, as Stuart Piggott has pointed out in his Presidential Address to the Prehistoric Society (Piggott, 1963, 2). He eagerly sought their help and advice and it was given freely. In the late twenties it was Dr Eliot Curwen (1865–1951), father of Dr E. Cecil Curwen, who, after Toms, next offered him much personal encouragement. About 1928, LVG was present at a lecture on the excavations of White Hawk given by Dr E. C. Curwen, at which Hadrian Allcroft (1865–1929) proposed the vote of thanks. LVG followed up this first meeting with Allcroft, whose book on earthworks (Allcroft, 1908) he already knew, by corresponding with him. Whatever benefit he might have derived from knowing Allcroft was, however, short-lived, for soon afterwards Allcroft died tragically, within a few hours of his wife, from a kind of diphtheria epidemic spread, it was said, by germs in milk from Hole's Farm, Preston Park (Sussex), near where they lived.

The surveys of barrows in Sussex and Surrey were behind LVG by about 1934 and he had begun walking over the chalk downs of Wiltshire. He has recalled to the writer how, following the work on Surrey, he had developed an interest in bell-barrows as a specialized type, and this had led to his first tramping holiday in Wiltshire. The year was probably 1931; with knapsack loaded with clothes, note-book, maps and reel-tape, he worked his way by train, bus and on foot from Alton (Hants) to Salisbury Plain at a cost of about three pounds. Yet the next area chosen for barrow survey was Berkshire, not Wiltshire, and here Harold Peake (1867–1946) wielded a considerable influence over him. Grinsell freely acknowledges his debt to Peake, through his writings on Berkshire archaeology and by his personal support, and, fittingly, it was LVG who first lectured to the Newbury Field Club after Peake's death, the proceedings beginning with a minute's silence in memory of a considerable figure.

The First International Prehistoric Congress was held in London in 1932, and it marked an important stage in the progress of a number of young British archaeologists. Leslie Grinsell shared, also, in the inspiration which such an international gathering of scholars can give. First, he met A. E. van Giffen, to whom he showed plans of Sussex bell-barrows and with whom he discussed their possible connection with the Dutch palisade barrows which van Giffen was excavating at that time. This meeting led to Grinsell's only excavation, a section across the berm and ditch of one of the bell-barrows called the Devil's Humps on Bow Hill (Sussex), in search of timber uprights on the berm which would have helped to associate this special form of barrow with those in Holland. The work was carried out in April, 1933, with the help of two members of the Brighton and Hove Archaeological Society and it was published, after an uncharacteristic delay, in 1942 (1942b).

At the 1932 Congress, LVG was introduced to O. G. S. Crawford (1886–1957). Grinsell's work in the field was dependent upon maps, and from this moment he enjoyed a close acquaintance with Crawford and, particularly, with the growing accumulation of archaeological information which Crawford was gathering together at the Ordnance Survey office in Southampton. The writer has enjoyed hearing how, at their first meeting at the Survey office, Crawford talked so much that LVG was almost completely frustrated in the primary purpose of his visit, to look at maps. Throughout his writings, the debt to Crawford is freely acknowledged: though they differed widely in character and in style of scholarship, in their fieldwork they came close, Grinsell working steadily through his self-appointed task mainly on foot, with knapsack, Crawford preferring a bicycle loaded with carrier bags (Crawford, 1955, pl 10). Their annotations on maps in the field are curiously similar and, in retrospect, it is astonishing that one small country should have seen two such field archaeologists at work in the same general area at one time. British pre-eminence in archaeological fieldwork, which today is beyond doubt, was being forged then by scholars like Crawford and Grinsell.

LVG first met Heywood Sumner (1853–1940) about 1937 when at work on the barrow survey of Hampshire. By then Sumner was in his eighties. He was, however, readily disposed to encourage the eager young archaeologist, who called at his house unannounced (apparently Sumner had no telephone at Cuckoo Hill, his home outside Fordingbridge) and whom he took walking in the New Forest. Heywood Sumner, an architect, also drew and painted with great beauty and a strange intensity, much influenced by the leading British artists of the later nineteenth century and by the *art nouveau* style. Grinsell had come to know Sumner's archaeological books, illustrated with his unmistakable plans and drawings (Pl VIII), long before he met him in Hampshire, and his great debt to the artist is apparent in his early plans of barrows. The *art nouveau* feeling in LVG's survey of the Longstone, Mottestone, Isle of Wight (1941c, Pl v), with its Sumner-like vignette, seen again in his plan of the Lambourn, Berks., long barrow (1936d, opp p 59) and in the survey of Wayland's Smithy (1939e, II, opp p 15; fig 2), owes an undeniable debt to the illustrations of Heywood Sumner, in the way that Stuart Piggott's early draughtsmanship also acknowledges him. Piggott's survey of the barrows on Petersfield Heath in 1939, published in Grinsell's second paper on the barrows of Hampshire (1939c, fig 7), clearly has the same stylistic source.

Youthful impetuosity prompted Grinsell to telephone Dr Williams-Freeman (1858–1943) in 1938 while he was near Southampton working on barrows for the Hampshire survey, and, with the courtesy of his generation, the older man gave him much consideration. By that time, Grinsell's book *Ancient Burial-Mounds of England* had been published (1936b) and talk on barrows and other earthworks must have come easily to both when they met for dinner at Williams-Freeman's home in Curdridge.

Williams-Freeman exerted influence upon LVG, as upon Crawford and others, mainly through his writings, particularly *An Introduction to Field Archaeology as Illustrated by Hampshire* (1915). He was, after all, the first to draw distributions of sites using a map showing vegetation plotted on a geological basis. His archaeological symbols also established a style followed by LVG: long barrows, for example, were portrayed by a pear-shaped symbol which indicated their orientation and 'business end', while disc-barrows appeared as the now familar dot within a circle.

About the time of the outbreak of the Second World War, Grinsell had been influenced by two other established British archaeologists, R. F. Jessup and R. Rainbird Clarke (1914–1963) and had surveyed barrows in the field with both of them. This aspect of his work is still not widely known, however, because the results remain unpublished. With Jessup, LVG prepared a survey of the barrows of Kent, and during the war the notes were sent to England from his Royal Air Force station in Egypt for editing and publication as a joint paper. Unhappily, they were destroyed during an air-raid, along with Jessup's contribution, and the project has never been resuscitated. Grinsell and Rainbird Clarke planned a similar joint paper on the barrows of Norfolk, and here the service of members of the Norfolk Research Committee was enrolled in a combined operation of a kind that LVG has not since attempted. The county was divided into areas by Rainbird Clarke, who assigned pairs of fieldworkers to each, with instructions to prepare draft surveys which would be checked by the joint authors as a second phase of the operation. A card catalogue was built up and is still preserved at the Norwich Castle Museum. Though unpublished, it is of crucial importance to the area, for the barrows of Norfolk, like those of so many other counties surveyed by Grinsell, have since suffered irreparable damage from deep ploughing, and the authors' corpus of measurements constitutes a record which cannot be compiled again.

In his work as a field archaeologist, Grinsell began early to seek additional information from written sources of all kinds. Study of his published barrow lists shows how wide is his reading and how unusual his acquaintance with obscure publications and documents. Here, the library of the Society of Antiquaries of London has been of great value: until he was elected a Fellow, in 1947, LVG obtained access to it through membership of the Royal Archaeological Institute. Yet before 1930 he had been introduced to the Librarian by Dr Eliot Curwen and had been allowed, as a young man, to use it for brief visits taken out of his rigidly controlled lunch-hour at Barclays. This aspect of LVG's scholarship owes much, also, to L. F. Salzman the medieval historian who was then editor of the *Victoria County History* and who also supervised the publication of the Sussex Archaeological Society's *Collections* for fifty years. Grinsell met Salzman when working on the Sussex barrow survey and by him was shown an unpublished reference to the Hove barrow in the manuscripts of the Reverend John Skinner (1772–1839), housed in the library at the British Museum. The Skinner manuscripts, whose study LVG has made his own, have proved a priceless source of reference for barrow research throughout southern England, and in all his surveys since 1935 Grinsell has drawn heavily upon the wealth of information they contain. Probably the value he has placed throughout his work on tithe maps, eighteenth-century perambulations and other early documentary sources for the location of barrows now destroyed must owe much to this chance reference by Salzman to the existence of the Skinner manuscripts.

Early written sources were not the only ones searched through by LVG in his quest for completeness in field surveys. Before 1935, he had recognized in aerial photographs an important new source for the location of lost sites and for the portrayal of upstanding barrows in publication. Although Crawford must take the major credit for developing air photography as an instrument of archaeological research in Britain, Grinsell's place in this field should not be overlooked, and here, too, his interest owes much to personal contact: through a friend who was an amateur flier, LVG had been introduced to Major G. W. Allen (1891–1940) early in the nineteen thirties. Allen had first realized the archaeological possibilities of air photography through chance perusal of one of the Ordnance Survey monographs, as Crawford himself has related (Crawford, 1955, 46), but it was Grinsell who really fired his interest and persuaded him to take photographs of barrow groups for the surveys then being undertaken. Those for Surrey, Berkshire and Hampshire include superb photographs taken by Allen especially for Grinsell and published with the surveys for the first time. Grinsell himself flew at this period, particularly when working on the Berkshire barrows, 'to get air-minded' (1935a, 191).

Mention has already been made of the value to Grinsell of the Skinner manuscripts in the British Museum, but he owes much also to certain members of the Museum's staff who played an important part in his development as a field archaeologist. These include the late R. A. Skelton, Superintendent of the Map Room (1906–1970), Sir Thomas Kendrick and Professor C. F. C. Hawkes. Like many scholars in the British Museum, Skelton and Hawkes banked at the branch of Barclays where LVG worked, and it was during one such transaction in 1949 that Hawkes by chance mentioned to Grinsell his need for an assistant to work on the archaeological volumes of the *Victoria County History of Wiltshire* which he and Professor Stuart Piggott had just been commissioned to write. Within a few days, LVG had decided to throw up his career in banking and join the staff of the Victoria County History as their assistant. He moved to Devizes as soon as he could, and his new career as a professional archaeologist had begun.

It is, however, in the character of the man himself that an explanation can best be found for the unquenchable urge to pursue the study of barrows in the field, year after year and in almost all weathers, just as it is his own unusual mental approach which enables him to tabulate great masses of information with complete reliability. Possibly his training as a banker has been of value here, or else he took to the banking profession because his mind already worked naturally in this way. Whatever the priority, his bank work and his particular way of listing archaeological information are linked and help to explain his success in both fields. Moreover, Grinsell, like Crawford before him, is a bachelor and one doubts if a married man could ever have achieved a comparable volume of work; nor, in all probability, would a man with a family be prepared to undertake the sort of single-handed fieldwork to which the study of barrows is peculiarly suited.

THE INTENTIONS AND THE FIELDWORK

From the first, one intention behind Grinsell's lifetime study of barrows has been to throw light upon their distribution and to establish the chronology of the rarer types. Implicit in his first published surveys, it was expressly stated in the introductions to those for Hampshire (1938), the Isle of Wight (1941), Dorset (1959) and Gloucestershire (1960). Only in the last two has his concern with general typology also been included in the pre-amble to the published survey, but from the Sussex survey of 1934 onwards an invaluable product of his published fieldwork has been the gradual emergence of a comprehensive typology for round barrows in the south of England. These endeavours, however, are all secondary to the main part of his work, which on its own constitutes a project of daunting proportions—the total recording of round barrows, extant or destroyed, for southern England: the analysis is secondary to the records, although in every survey the whole study has been carried through.

Perhaps more than any of his contemporary fieldworkers and predecessors, Grinsell has studied 'the totality of phenomena in field archaeology' (Daniel, 1950, 294): alongside the inventory of barrows he has set the folklore and the early place-names. References in early literature, contents of graves and the whereabouts of finds have been compiled meticulously. Invariably, the need to indicate certain unprotected sites which ought to be scheduled under the Ancient Monuments acts has been borne in mind; and frequently LVG has added suggestions for future research and for selective excavation to settle problems of relative chronology or of structure which his personal fieldwork has shown to be of particular importance and interest.

The listing of work undone, so that his successors may know where best to follow his lead in a particular area, has been an important part of LVG's research; so in Devon, in a new survey recently published, LVG has stressed the need to search for unrecorded barrows, despite his own exhaustive work, and he has reminded us that the N.E. Devon area of Exmoor should be examined after the periodical burning of undergrowth which occurs there every seven years (1969e, 107). Turning to the field surveys themselves, detailed inventories have been prepared and published for the counties of Sussex (1934–1942), Surrey (1934), Berkshire (1935–1939), Hampshire (1938–1940), Isle of Wight (1941), Wiltshire (1957), Dorset (1959), Gloucestershire (1960), Somerset (1969–1971) and North Devon (1969). In 1952, an examination of the barrows around the Thornborough Circles (Yorks. N.R.) was carried out for the writer as part of the excavations of the central circle and published in 1955 (Thomas, 1955, opp p 442). These surveys, which constitute the bulk of LVG's fieldwork, have resulted in the detailed inventorying and, in the majority of sites, the personal examination, at least once, of the following approximate numbers of long and round barrows:

County or area	Numbers of long barrows	Numbers of round barrows
Sussex	3	479
Surrey	1	110
Berkshire	3	209
Hampshire and Isle of Wight	38	1,171
Yorks (N.R.) around Ripon	—	28
Wiltshire	113	2,204
Dorset	52	1,800
Gloucestershire	75	350
Somerset	15	750
N. Devon	—	340
Totals:	300	7,441

No account is taken here of the many barrows in Kent and Norfolk which were studied and listed in the same detailed way but never published, nor of the hundreds more for the north of England and the extreme south-west, which LVG has also examined. It is clear, however, that taking into account the large number of sites which have been visited on more than one occasion, he has probably carried out between 10,000 and 12,000 detailed barrow-visits. The magnitude of this achievement becomes the more astonishing when it is remembered that only for Wiltshire was he acting in a full-time professional capacity. Even then, his barrow-work was only part of the documentation: his gazetteer for the county included all earthworks and finds until the end of the Pagan Saxon period. The other work has been carried out at week-ends and on holiday. Nor can the fieldwork always have been just for personal pleasure. In 1941 he wrote (1941b, 115)

> The interminable nature of the study of the barrows of a county is shown by the work of R. N. Worth and his son, T. H. Worth, who have between them published nearly 60 annual reports on the barrows of Devon . . .

Nevertheless, the quest for completeness in the county surveys at moments brings the kind of triumph in discovery which must be one of his chief spurs. Recently the writer encountered LVG after such a success: during the previous week-end he had discovered Palmer's Barrow, on the parish boundary of Chewton Mendip, in Somerset (Emborough 1a/1b) at the third attempt. He knew the barrow was in that area, because he had located it first on an eighteenth-century boundary map. It had been obscured by a hedge and dense undergrowth, but in the autumn of 1970 it had yielded itself up to the man whose persistence was too strong and whose knowledge was too sure to be put off by two previous failures in the field.

From this basic work of recording the position, form, size and other details of the surviving barrows in southern England, Grinsell has established certain patterns of distribution. The most obvious aspect of these, the massive concentration on the chalk, has, of course, long been realized, but LVG's work has confirmed it positively; thus, for Sussex, about 95% of barrows are on the chalk. From Hampshire came evidence that in the early Middle Bronze Age chalk country was overwhelmingly favoured, whereas in the Middle/Late Bronze Ages there was a noticeable spread of barrows on to the heath. This spread, observed in Hampshire, led him to re-examine the Sussex heathlands when he had completed the former, and it accounts for his second Sussex barrows paper (1940e) in which his new heathland discoveries are detailed. While the Sussex clays, as in other counties, failed to yield barrows, he also noticed that the Tunbridge Wells sands are equally barren, perhaps because they are surrounded by claylands. In the Isle of Wight we can see a concentration in the west, opposite the massed barrows on Beaulieu Heath (Hampshire), as if there had been close cultural ties between the two areas.

On a more detailed scale, the position of Stonehenge at the centre of a series of large nucleated and linear cemeteries has emerged from his work for the *Victoria County History of Wiltshire*, while we can also observe an impressive spread of barrows and major cemeteries like Snail Down across the Avon, towards the north-east. Around Avebury, the concentration appears equally marked, but large cemeteries of the Salisbury Plain kind are not present. Grinsell's work in Dorset has emphasized the extraordinary importance of the Dorset Ridgeway as a burial ground in early Bronze Age times: and his interest in heathland had led to his establishment of the Dorset heath in the south-east of the county as a notable secondary area for barrows.

Grinsell's work on the barrows of Dorset was, indeed, so thorough and reliable that, when the Royal Commission on Historical Monuments began their own series of volumes on the county, they accepted that for a general list of barrows they could not surpass his survey. Instead, they concentrated upon detailed plans of cemeteries, an aspect in which LVG's work was weak, and thus made their own contribution to the study of burial mounds in Dorset (RCHM 1970).

In Gloucestershire, LVG's recent survey has emphasized in detail the observation made earlier by W. F. Grimes (Grimes, 1960, 39–40, 111–112), that round barrows are almost always located near long barrows, as if there was a cultural link between the two types. He has also been able to show the exceptionally high proportion of long to round barrows here, suggesting that construction of the former may have continued longer than elsewhere, at the expense of round barrow-building in the earlier Bronze Age.

Grinsell, more than anyone, has concentrated upon the specialized forms of Wessex barrow as individual types, and much information has emerged from his topographical and typological studies of bell, disc, saucer and pond-barrows. The Sussex survey first showed that bell and disc-barrows have a peculiar distribution. They tend to occur west of the River Arun, although over 700 bowls occur to the east; and most bells occur on hill-tops. He has also shown that around Avebury bell-barrows tend to have narrower berms than those on Salisbury Plain and that in Surrey they are below average in height. The Dorset survey has revealed that there is a distinctive type of disc-barrow here which occurs in the south of the county, west of Dorchester.

It is impossible to know what influenced Neolithic and Bronze Age men in their choice of setting for a burial mound or a cemetery. Study of the burial practices of modern primitive peoples has established that the location need not be selected for any obvious topographical or aesthetic reasons which spring to mind when considering the situation of a Bronze Age barrow. Yet Grinsell has attempted to answer the problem, as must anyone who is concerned with barrow studies. His suggestions throw light on one aspect of his own enthusiasm for the subject, and, for all we know, his sensitive feeling for the countryside may echo the delight of certain prehistoric barrow-builders, even if it only accounts for the location of *some* of their mounds. Grinsell believes that the concentration of barrows along the Dorset Ridgeway reflects a choice of high ground overlooking the sea. In Berkshire, also, the fine views commanded by the Downs and the bracing air are, for him among the chief factors in the choice of ground for barrows. In 1940 this thesis was set out in lyrical terms and, whether we agree or not, it gives us an important key to LVG's sustained enthusiasm: '. . . and, perhaps above all, the many benefits which nearly everyone experiences when walking over the Downs, including a sense of safety and freedom, and also the tonic properties of the air' (1940e, 212).

Through the work of Grinsell, a typology has now been established for upstanding round barrows in the south of England. The descriptive names *bowl*, *bell*, *disc*, *saucer* and *pond* had, of course, already become part of archaeological terminology. Grinsell gave more precise meaning to these terms, particularly in his paper of 1941, where he reproduced the final version of his well-known diagram of typical cross-sections (1941b, 77, fig 1). He has also established the convention of placing a hyphen between the descriptive word ('pond, bell, disc, saucer') and 'barrow' and has led us to accept the spelling of disc with a *c* not a *k* (The Oxford University Press, however, insists upon spelling disc with a *k*, and so it appears as *disk-barrow* in LVG's contribution to the *Victoria County History of Wiltshire*). For bell and disc-barrows, LVG has fully defined the types with their variants in detail, taking account of the significance of their contents to suggest that, while the first had usually been built over the remains of men, disc-barrows generally covered female burials. He was also able to disprove the assertion of Crawford that many bells had an outer bank (Crawford and Keiller, 1928, 13). Important details have been established for bowl-barrows including, for example, the hitherto unrecognized fact that the early Beaker bowl-barrows are as a rule very small, while necked Beakers are usually found in large examples of this generalized type of mound.

Grinsell's early surveys, particularly of Surrey and Sussex, began to suggest the existence of a series of special barrow types whose terminology he, himself, never used consistently and which he has subsequently largely abandoned. The terms *ring mounds*, *circular ring-works* and *earth circles* are commonly encountered in writings of the nineteen thirties, but even in 1934 C. F. C. Hawkes pointed out that Grinsell was being inconsistent in their use and that they had not been sufficiently standardized (Hawkes, 1934, 315). As early as 1931, however, LVG had published a typological scheme for Sussex barrows, in which his criteria for distinguishing these specialized disc-like earthworks were set out with the help of a diagram and examples (1931a; fig 1), and later he described similar special types in Somerset (1939f). Excluding long barrows, bowls and bells, he distinguished eight types akin to disc-barrows to which terms like *platform*, *ringwork* and the like were given. Many of these structures LVG now believes to be relatively recent and to include tree-plantation banks.

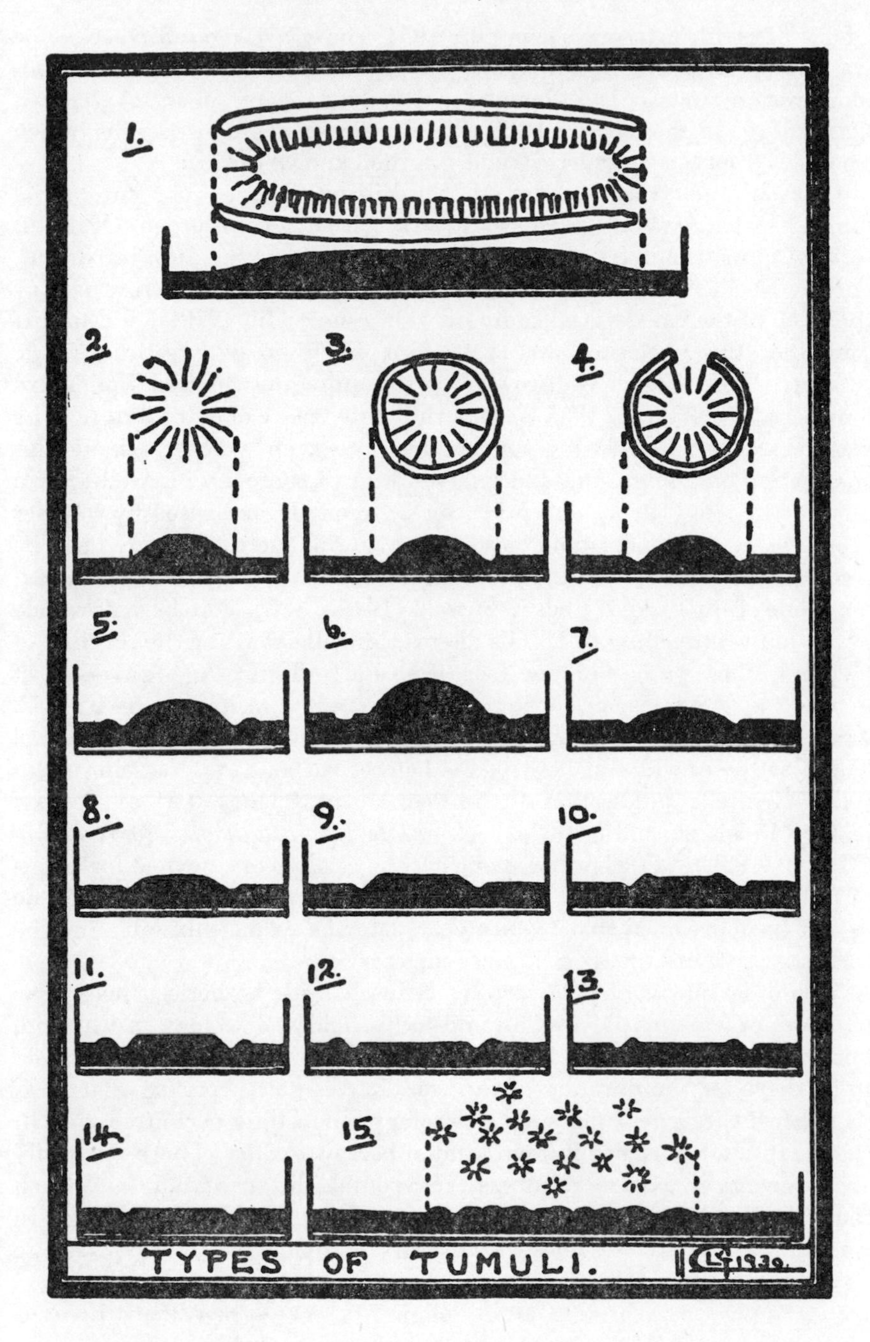

1. 'Types of Tumuli' as defined in Grinsell, 1931a (reproduction of original illustration).

Of his fifteenth category set out in 1931, the grave-mound clusters, he was, however, never in doubt, despite the criticism of some of his contemporaries; and in the November (1931) issue of *Sussex Notes and Queries* (1931b) he described the type in greater detail, listing the fifteen examples from Sussex, Surrey and Kent then known to him.

Grinsell's fieldwork has led to the discovery of a very substantial number of barrows and other earthworks hitherto unrecorded. Of all his services to British archaeology, this is probably one of the most important. For the Neolithic period, LVG was the first to note that a barrow overlay the ditch of the causewayed camp on Whitesheet Hill (Wilts) and to surmise that this enclosure was, therefore, likely to be pre-Bronze Age (Piggott, 1952, 404). His discovery of the quite unsuspected Lambourn long barrow (Berks.) in 1935 was another noted piece of detection; here he was helped by Allen with a superb air-photograph which confirmed his observation on the ground and enabled him to complete his well-known plan of the site (1936d, opp p 59; fig 2), recently excavated by Wymer (1966). We can understand, also, the triumphant terms in which he recorded the discovery of another long barrow, at Up Marden in Sussex: '. . . one of my luckiest finds in Sussex' (1942b, 123). For the writer, one of the most compelling of LVG's discoveries will always be the carvings of feet and other symbols on one face of an Early Bronze Age grave-slab at Pool Farm, West Harptree (Somerset), as strange in its way as R. J. C. Atkinson's finding of carvings at Stonehenge, because so many people had looked at the carvings at both places before, without ever noticing them (pl I). Grinsell's publication of the Pool Farm carvings (1957a) recalls a passage in his charming little book *White Horse Hill and Surrounding Country* (1939e, 21) where he describes the folklore of supposed footprints of feet and hands on stones like the Heelstone at Stonehenge: in 1939 he cannot have dreamed that twenty years later he would, himself, find the earliest known instance in Britain of such carvings.

Two other pieces of fieldwork by Grinsell must be noticed here. The outbreak of war in 1939 saw an end to his field archaeology in England, and in 1942 he was in the Royal Air Force, stationed in Egypt and likely to be there for the duration of the war. It was not surprising that LVG should feel the urge to pursue archaeology when time permitted and, in the pyramids, Egypt had its own kind of barrow to offer. There were only about seventy in existence, none an insuperable distance from Cairo: each could be visited easily and repeatedly in the manner of LVG's technique in English barrow study. These four years of fieldwork in Egypt led to *Egyptian Pyramids* (1947a) which he published at his own expense, and are an episode in Grinsell's archaeological career extraordinary in itself but wholly explicable in the light of his unquenchable enthusiasm for ancient burial monuments. LVG is the first to admit that the bulk of his book is based upon the plans and surveys of earlier Egyptologists. Yet it made a contribution to Egyptology: the air photographs in it, which he obtained through the special circumstances of his service in the R.A.F., were new and valuable; and his eye for details, developed over many years on the chalk downs of southern England, detected a number of hitherto unrecorded features in certain pyramids, like the quarry marks of Khnmw-knuf on core-stones of the Great Pyramid. The book, however, was not well received in Britain: though supported by Crawford, it was snubbed by Egyptologists, partly, perhaps, because Grinsell was an amateur in a scholarly and restricted field where amateurism had little place. Probably for the same reason *Pyramids* was more enthusiastically received in the United States of America. Of course, its scholarship left much to be desired: nobody could expect a member of the Armed Forces, in the short time at his disposal, to become fully acquainted with the literature on which proper study of the pyramids must depend, and one who, before 1942, had no knowledge of hieroglyphics. Grinsell never set out to write an original study on the pyramids: he simply attempted to fill a gap in the literature on these monuments, as his words in its preface make clear:

> It is designed to provide a short but adequate account of the pyramids of Lower Egypt, in plain language, for all who are interested, including Egyptologists and intelligent sightseers. Although largely a synthesis based on the labours and writings of others, it embodies a good deal of personal investigation and study through repeatedly visiting the monuments themselves.

In the tradition of his barrow research methods, he followed up his work on pyramids by writing a paper on the folklore of these monuments soon afterwards (1947b). He has not, however, abandoned his interest in the Mediterranean since returning to England at the end of the Second World War. His appointment to the Curatorship of Anthropology and Archaeology at the Bristol City Museum in 1952 enabled him to maintain his interest in this region through the richness of its Egyptian and other foreign collections, and during the last few years he has devoted his holidays to visiting the main islands in the Mediterranean systematically to study their tombs. In due course, we shall see the fruit of his foreign studies in a book on the surviving prehistoric tombs of this part of the Old World.

For one whose contribution to British archaeology is so outstanding it is, perhaps, invidious to single out particular pieces of work, for his barrow surveys and his other archaeological research are closely related and it is their overall results on which he must be judged. Two of his projects are, nevertheless, of special interest since in the writer's view they combine all that is best and most admirable in LVG's approach to archaeology. The Gazetteer of field monuments and finds from prehistoric times down to the end of the Pagan Saxon period, which LVG compiled for the *Victoria*

County History of Wiltshire (1957c), represents the high point in his combined powers of fieldwork, grasp of secondary sources and handling of a great volume of detailed information. No less valuable is *The Archaeology of Wessex*, LVG's handbook to this area (1958a), which is largely based upon the work he carried out on the Wiltshire gazetteer. It forms an incomparable source book for those working and lecturing on Wessex, and these two volumes can stand as a fitting twentieth-century tribute to this region of unsurpassed archaeological richness.

The second project, published in 1964, constitutes LVG's most remarkable piece of research involving detailed fieldwork related to study of documents (1964d, 1966g). It concerned the collection of flint implements assembled from the area around Lower Swell (Gloucestershire) by the Reverend David Royce (1817–1902), rector of that parish from 1850 until his death. Of the 2,508 barbed and tanged arrowheads in the collection, 555 of them bore the names of fields in which they had been picked up. There were also 504 leaf arrowheads; and, like the juxtaposition of round and long barrows in Gloucestershire which we have already discussed, it was clear that hardly a field producing leaf arrows had failed to yield also its quota of barbed and tanged heads. Grinsell set out to locate the relevant fields over a three-year period of intensive study, using the Tithe Maps of *c.* 1840, questioning modern owners and tenants and tramping endlessly over the fields in the region. The result is an extraordinary distribution map covering an area of about 14 square miles, on which the 500-odd localized arrowheads have been plotted by quantities per field against surface geology and a land utilization map of 1932–36. From this most persistent piece of work, which combined LVG's love of antiquities with his techniques for barrow-searching, a nineteenth-century collection of surface implements has been used to re-create a Neolithic/Early Bronze Age pattern of settlement (or perhaps of hunting grounds) in an area which he has shown to have been well drained, well watered and relatively clear of vegetation at the time when the arrowheads were lost. LVG himself characteristically will not admit to the remarkable nature of this piece of research, explaining it simply by saying that it took him to a lovely stretch of countryside at week-ends.

FIELDWORK TECHNIQUE AND PUBLICATION

Grinsell's field technique for finding and recording barrows was entirely self-taught. He has told the writer that he was so completely on his own to begin with that, when he bought his first reel-tape, several months elapsed before he discovered that it possessed a retractable metal winding-handle. Apart from this tape (33 ft to begin with, 100 ft added when he could afford it) LVG's equipment from the first has been the relevant Ordnance Survey map (usually 6 ins but on occasion 25 ins) and a 5 ft folding ruler.

The rucksack which he always wears is useful as an anchor for one end of the tape when measuring single-handed.

Grinsell does not drive a car. Almost all his fieldwork has been carried out using trains and buses and on foot, and for him the favoured time of year is Spring to Autumn. A series of train and bus timetables has also been an essential part of his travelling equipment: before the Second World War, public transport was much more frequent than it is today, yet LVG's methods of travel have not altered, except that in recent years pressure of work and contraction of public transport have made him on occasion seek the help of friends with cars (1970c, 5). Before 1939, he usually worked at week-ends, making use of bed-and-breakfast accommodation which gave him at least two full days in the field. Since 1946, he has relied heavily upon Youth Hostels as bases for walking. His personal needs while out on fieldwork are simple, yet it has to be remarked that Grinsell's daily programme is rigidly devised so that by about 4 o'clock in the afternoon he is close to a hotel or café where a really good, rich, preferably cream, tea is available. Those who have shared a day in the field with him can vouch for his extensive knowledge of the whereabouts of fine places for afternoon tea.

Field notes have always been recorded directly on to the map, and at the end of each day they are transferred to a slip catalogue (fig 3). LVG has evolved a series of conventions for ease in recording, for example:

H/C = Hollow at centre
D = ditched
28/5 = 28 paces in diameter, 5 ft high.

He tries to visit every barrow in an area at least twice a year, at widely separated intervals, so that the effect of changes in vegetation can be recorded: on second visits, the slip catalogue cards (which are nowadays printed) are taken into the field, so that the original entry can be checked against the state of the barrow as he next finds it. Some of his published field entries emphasize the value of this aspect of his work:— Shapwick 3 (Dorset), 'Very small (1935); gone (1954)'; Alton 17 (Wilts) 'Measured LVG when under grass before 1939: since then ploughed and type features obscured'; Milton Lilbourne I (Wilts) 'Measured before 1939, since when it has been greatly reduced by ploughing.' A less tragic entry for Ashwith 2 (Somerset), typical of his fully evolved recording and publication method using abbreviations, shows how much information for the present and for posterity is contained in his published records: 'LVG Aug. 1964: rough grazing. H/C with evidence of incursion from the N' (it is valuable to include, as here, the initials of the recorder). The care with which repeated visits to the same site are noted is shown, for example, in his published entry for Bisley-with-Lypiatt 2 (Glos) . . . 'long barrow, seen 17-IV-31 and 21-VI-59.'

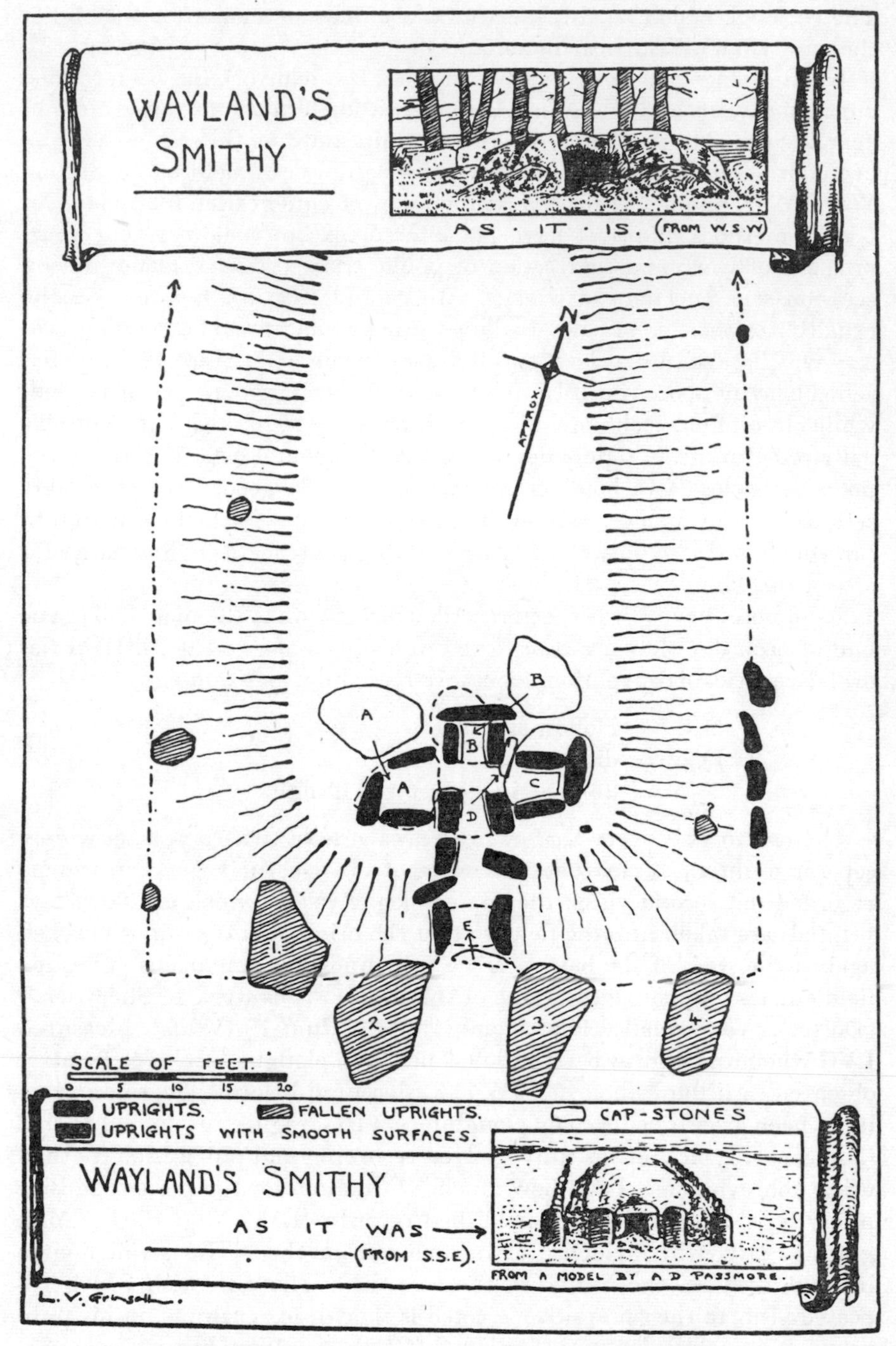

II. PLAN OF WAYLAND'S SMITHY

2. Wayland's Smithy, Berkshire, as illustrated by Grinsell, 1936.

The measuring technique used in the field has been described in the introduction to several of the surveys. In the Gloucestershire account (1960c, 66–67) it is set out thus:

> It will be noticed that the length and width of long barrows are given in feet and measured by reel tape, while the diameter of all round barrows is given in paces. LVG has used this method for some 30 years and finds it has many advantages. Pacing over a high barrow can be stretched to counteract the error that would otherwise be introduced by the height; it is easier to pace across a barrow covered with brambles or other obstructive vegetation than to measure it with reel tape; pacing has obvious advantages in muddy or rainy weather; and in any case LVG checks his pace over a stretch of 100 ft, with a reel-tape every day of field-work.

Grinsell's 33 paces usually cover about 98 ft. His eye-level is 5 ft 8 ins above the ground and, using his folding rule, the heights of barrows are easily calculated. Long barrows have always been measured in feet, and he tends to use a reel tape for any barrow sufficiently clearly preserved to justify its precise measurement. All these dimensions are, then, to a degree rough-and-ready, but, through constant checking, they have an overall reliability and are consistent: by their means LVG has managed to record several thousand barrows, many of which are now no longer available for accurate survey by the more scientific methods of field teams like those of the Royal Commission.

As a self-taught amateur, LVG had also to learn to understand the significance of changes in vegetation colour or pattern and the other clues which sometimes indicate the presence of a buried archaeological feature. On an early visit to Wiltshire, he discovered for himself that the Winterslow Great Barrow has a berm as wide as 14 yards, because the levelled ditch beyond it showed beneath a conspicuous growth of weeds. During the Sussex survey, one of his earliest, he discovered that the ditch around Patching 35 was indicated by a ring of mole-hills. Again, at Sparsholt (Hants), the disc-barrow was visible in September, 1937, only as a ring of slightly browner stubble. LVG could not see it clearly when standing within it, but he *could* do so when stationed on a bowl-barrow to the south. The method he adopted to record it, single-handed, was to mark its outer circumference with a series of objects, using repeated observations from the bowl, and then to measure these. As he worked he noted, once again, the presence of mole-heaps over the site of the ditch.

Grinsell publishes his fieldwork, county by county, as soon as each survey has been completed; his bibliography bears witness to this essential part of his research. His method of publication has also developed gradually, like his field technique. The field surveys have always been published promptly in the appropriate county journal, and, where additional information has accumulated subsequently, it has been described in succeeding numbers of the journal concerned; the series of supplements for Berkshire and Sussex, listed in the bibliography, shows well the continuous process of LVG's work and the heavy emphasis he has always placed upon publication of the evidence. On occasion, a series of surveys has led to a more general paper in a national journal or a book, but the primary evidence obtained in the field has been published in a local journal, with the exception of his Wiltshire survey which was commissioned for the *Victoria County History*.

In an earlier section of this essay, mention has been made of the various aspects of barrow study which are included in the published surveys, ranging from a brief history of previous fieldwork in that county to lists of sites for future scheduling or excavation, references in charters and perambulations, finds in museums and private collections and the like. LVG's thoroughness in exploration of these secondary sources has, over the years, yielded an important corpus of detailed and sometimes bizarre information. Thus, we learn that an urn from Challacombe 3 (N. Devon) was given to the North Devon Athenaeum, Barnstaple, where it was smashed by a drunken porter about 1914. Obscure resting-places of finds from Gloucestershire barrows include the porch of the church at Winchcombe; while a skull from barrow (b) on Arreton Down (Isle of Wight) was left at the Hare and Hounds Inn nearby. More seriously, the lengthy bibliography for the Sunninghill barrows (Berks), for example (1936a, 55), shows the high degree of detail in which Grinsell has always pursued his barrow research.

The main part of each survey comprises a detailed inventory which is tabulated. In the earliest surveys, like that for Surrey (1934b), this information was arranged in an open layout without columns. By 1940, a tabulated arrangement in vertical columns had been arrived at and this lay-out has continued to the present day. Information thus categorized has varied only a little between the first published survey of 1932 and the latest and has included the following particulars:

1932, *Surrey*

Map position	Local situation	Parish	Soil	Dates seen and photographed	Description	Literature

1934, *Sussex*

6 in O.S.	Inches from inner left margin	Inches from bottom inner margin	Parish	Type	Ditch	Diam in paces	Ht in ft	Other details

1940, *Isle of Wight*

6 in O.S.	Lat	Long	Parish	Diam (paces)	Ht (ft)	Other details

1957, *Wiltshire*

Parish	No	Locality	N.G.R.	Dimensions D in paces: Ht in ft	Other details

The Wiltshire survey, his first since the Second World War, has become the model for all subsequent tables of barrow details.

Publication has also included distribution maps which, through the influence of Williams-Freeman in particular, have comprised a geological base with indications of surface vegetation and find spots superimposed. Since the last war, a colour-system of two or more colours has usually been used. Grinsell's maps have become well known in the realm of archaeological scholarship and for these alone he has established an enviable reputation which can only be enhanced by the beautiful visual effect of his latest barrow map (1969e, fig 1). Essentially without artistic embellishment, they show clearly the pattern of occupation represented by barrows and provide a general but comprehensive basis for assessing the significance of barrow distribution in southern England.

More detailed plans, particularly of cemeteries, have never formed an important part of the published surveys, and attention has been paid to such an obvious point of criticism earlier in this essay. LVG has included a few plans from time to time, however, which only serve to emphasize this gap in his work. In Gloucestershire, his plan of the barrows in Hull Plantation (Longborough ii and 1–9) (1960c, 122) is of great importance, since this is now the only barrow cemetery in this county which survives intact, while his survey of the barrows on Bloxworth Down, Dorset (1959a, fig 4), shows a group subsequently destroyed by ploughing except for the mounds in the wood. Those on Wyke Down in the same county have also been heavily damaged since LVG drew their plan (1959a, fig 5). So, too, the diagram comparing the plans of a group of barrows on Farthing Down (Surrey: 1934b, 46, fig. 2) as shown on Ordnance Survey maps of three different periods together with his own survey is of value for many reasons, as is the group of plans for Gloucestershire, illustrating the siting of some long and round barrows (1960c, 15, fig 1); it is to be regretted that he has not illustrated his papers more fully in this way.

Grinsell has to some extent compensated for the general lack of plans in his published work by including fine photographs, both his own and, particularly, the aerial views so often commissioned from G. W. Allen. Like those in his *Egyptian Pyramids*, they have added positively and often aesthetically to his surveys (e.g. 1959a, pls I–III).

THE ACHIEVEMENT

Leslie Grinsell's astonishing volume of published fieldwork has assured for him a place without equal in the history of British archaeological studies.

ROUND BARROW County:

Parish:	No.	Locality:	Nat. Grid ref.

Diameter:

Height:

Composition (from surface indications):

Whether ditched:

Type of subsoil:

Other details:

References to Publications:

Date visited and by whom: Land usage at time of visit:

3. Grinsell's printed Round Barrow record card, approx. (above, p 27).

Setting aside the maps, the secondary sources for barrow studies and the analyses which have been included in his surveys, the basic listing of barrows with their location, measurements and other details of structure is a feat of which the value cannot now be over-estimated. A striking impression of the volume of fieldwork which LVG has got through in some forty-five years of part-time outdoor recording can best be gained by comparing the area he has covered with that which the Royal Commission has examined using full-time teams of archaeologists over a longer period of time (*cf* figs 4; 126). Grinsell began his self-appointed task before deep-ploughing and land development had started to make their savage inroads upon the ancient earthworks which survived, miraculously, on the heaths and downlands of southern Britain—'a circumstance uniquc in Europe' (Piggott, 1970, 79). Without his work, detailed knowledge of our prehistoric funerary monuments would now be totally inadequate for statistical study and for the application of the kind of techniques which are being employed by modern geographers. In these circumstances it is fortunate that the recording has been so thorough. While Grinsell has made it a point of his field technique to re-visit sites, the time has arrived when further checking ceases to be possible; the rate of destruction is now so high. Together with the recording of what has been visible during the last forty to fifty years, much of it unaltered since Bronze Age times except through natural erosion and change, there has accumulated an immense list of newly discovered sites, from a causewayed camp and long barrows to almost invisible bell-beaker barrows and carvings on a long-known cist slab in Somerset. This enormous inventory of prehistoric funerary monuments is Grinsell's great achievement.

There is reason to believe, too, that unlike areas such as Cornwall, where destruction of barrows in early times has been so great, LVG's surveys for southern England give a fairly complete picture of the original quantity of our Neolithic and Bronze Age burial mounds, whereas along many of our rivers in central England each new sortie by the aerial photographer brings to light more sites, and it is still too early to begin to estimate the original number of barrows on the river gravels. It seems reasonably likely that, for the regions of southern England over which he has worked, Grinsell has recorded a very high proportion of the number of barrows which formerly existed (*cf* pp 87, 119 below).

Another valuable aspect of the barrow surveys has been the assembling of the whole volume of the evidence. Here, Grinsell would readily acknowledge the lead set by Sir Cyril Fox; but Grinsell's output has been much greater and his pursuit of secondary sources, including folklore, more persistent. The interests of Fox were wider, perhaps more scholarly: yet Grinsell's singleness of purpose in pursuing barrows alone will enable him to complete and publish surveys for almost the whole of southern England by the time this volume of essays is presented to him.

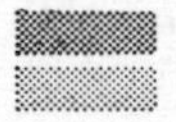

Areas with many round barrows or crop-mark circles
Areas with scattered round barrows or crop-mark circles

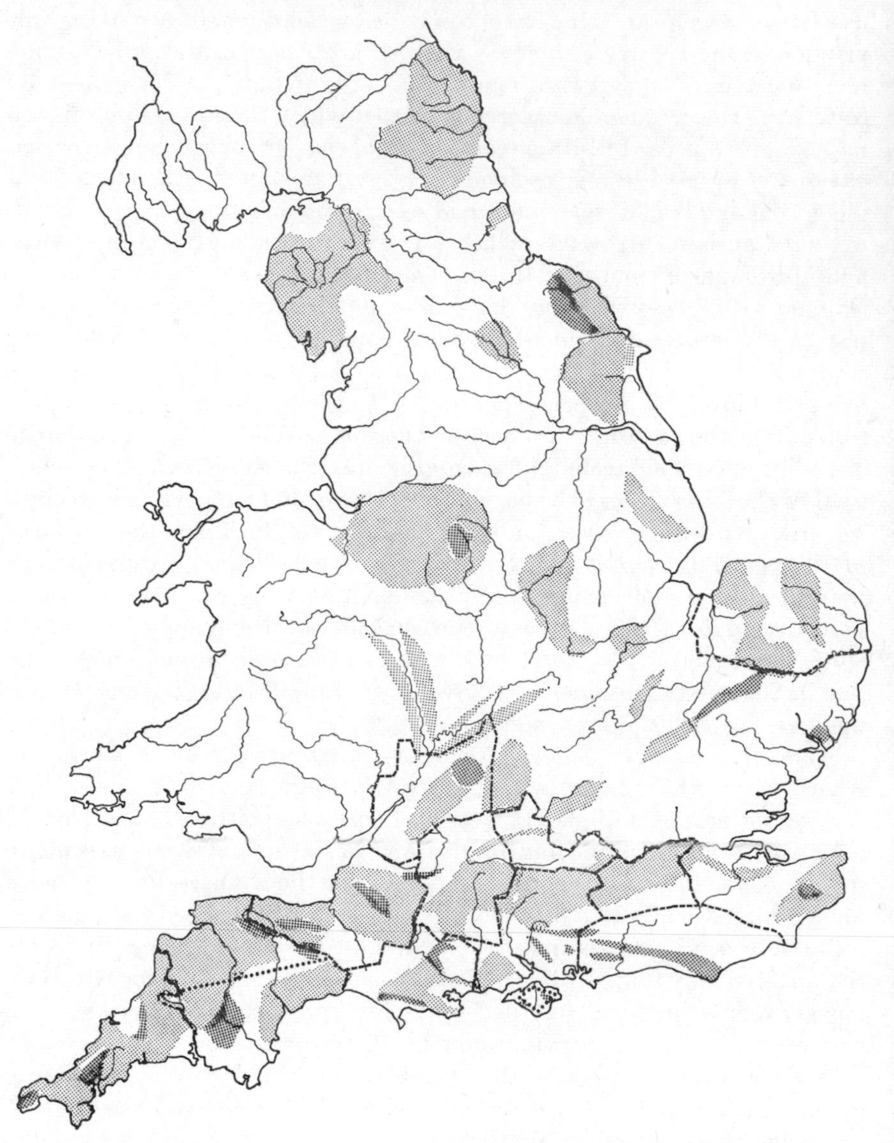

4. The density of round barrows in England. Counties surveyed by Grinsell are outlined (*cf* p 19 above).

Of course, there have been points to criticize in LVG's work, and attention has been drawn to some of them in this essay. To these can be added the fact that interest in barrows, at the expense of their surroundings, has on occasion led LVG to miss details which are sometimes of great importance: characteristically, he himself has pointed out to the writer that, for example, because of his preoccupation with the mound of Handley 19 (Dorset), he failed to notice its surrounding ditch: this was obscured by associated earthworks, but it was also square (the barrow was proved subsequently to be of Iron Age date: White, 1970), and since LVG had assumed that the barrow's ditch would have been circular in plan, he failed to appreciate the character of this highly complicated site.

Nevertheless, LVG has developed a skill in assessing the characteristics of barrows in the field which has made his work increasingly reliable and from which future field workers will be able to learn much. The fine distinction between disc-barrows and plantation rings, or bowl-barrows and mine-shafts; between long barrows and confluent bowl-barrows, genuine burial mounds and windmill steadings or spoil heaps—these difficulties LVG has gradually learned to resolve and, in so doing, has made it easier for those who follow.

At the beginning of this essay, we described Grinsell's debt to his predecessors: we end by recording that, during his lifetime, Grinsell has inspired few followers in barrow studies. In his survey of barrows in the Chilterns, James Dyer followed LVG's method exactly (Dyer, 1959), and Antony Gunstone has deliberately based his gazetteer of sites and finds from Staffordshire upon the model of Grinsell's volume for the *Victoria County History of Wiltshire* (Gunstone, 1964, 1965). For east Kent, Ashbee and Dunning have published a survey of round barrows (1960) which, strangely, makes no attempt to do what LVG would have done. The writer is glad to acknowledge that his own survey of Neolithic and Bronze Age sites and antiquities in Bedfordshire (Thomas, 1964) was at least in part inspired by the work of his old friend Grinsell although, to its detriment, the manner of its presentation little resembles that for Wiltshire. Otherwise, no archaeologists have undertaken and published similar field surveys, although large areas of the British Isles remain to be examined, with great profit, in this manner. Perhaps this is an unwitting tribute to Grinsell's possession of certain qualities of mind which have enabled him to restrict and pursue his interest. Few British archaeologists today are prepared to ignore excavation completely in the way that Grinsell has done: and interest in documentary sources, place-names, folklore and antiquities, which help to relieve what might otherwise, surely, become too monotonous a type of earthwork, is very seldom found combined in one person.

In his Presidential address to the Council for British Archaeology in 1970, Professor Stuart Piggott urged 'a return, in modern terms, to what has been in the past one of the peculiar and distinctive merits of British archaeology—fieldwork which does not involve excavation.' (Piggott, 1970, 79). Here, for almost half a century, Leslie Grinsell has set us a great example: he has shown that fieldwork can achieve results comparable in value to any excavation, that the amateur still has a valued place in the ranks of practising archaeologists and, above all, that whatever is discovered only becomes significant when it is published. Much remains to be done, and time is not on the side of field archaeology. In making his contribution in honour of one of the greatest of field archaeologists, the writer hopes that Leslie Grinsell may long continue in the field. The flow of such priceless information must continue, although it leaves us ever more deeply in his debt.

REFERENCES

Allcroft, A. Hadrian, 1908. *Earthwork of England* (Macmillan).
Ashbee, P., 1960. *The Bronze Age Round Barrow in Britain* (Phoenix House).
Ashbee, P., 1970. *The Earthen Long Barrow in Britain* (Dent).
Ashbee, P. and Dunning, G. C., 1960. 'The Round Barrows of East Kent', *Archaeol. Cantiana* **74**, 48–57.

Crawford, O. G. S., 1953. *Archaeology in the Field* (Phoenix House).
Crawford, O. G. S., 1955. *Said and Done* (Weidenfeld and Nicolson).
Crawford, O. G. S. and Keiller, A., 1928. *Wessex from the Air* (Clarendon Press).

Daniel, G. E., 1950. *A Hundred Years of Archaeology* (Duckworth).
Dyer, J. F., 1959. 'Barrows of the Chilterns', *Archaeol. J.* **116**, 1–24.

Grimes, W. F., 1960. *Excavations on Defence Sites, 1939–45, I. Mainly Neolithic to Bronze Age* (Ministry of Works, Archaeological Reports No. 3. HMSO).
Gunstone, A. J. H., 1964, 1965. 'An Archaeological Gazetteer of Staffordshire. Pt. 1 (1964), Chance finds and sites excluding barrows and contents; Pt. 2 (1965), barrows', *N. Staffordshire J. Fld. Stud.* **4**, 11–45; **5**, 20–63.

Hawkes, J. and C., 1934. 'Prehistoric Britain in 1934', *Archaeol. J.* **91**, 301–329.

Piggott, S., 1952. 'The Neolithic Camp on Whitesheet Hill, Kilmington Parish', *Wiltshire Archaeol. Natur. Hist. Mag.* **55**, 404–410.
Piggott, S., 1963. 'Archaeology and Prehistory', *Proc. Prehist. Soc.* **29**, 1–16.
Piggott, S., 1970. 'British Archaeology and the Enemy', *Council for British Archaeology, Report No. 20 for the year ended 30 June, 1970*, 74–85.

RCHM, 1970. *Royal Commission on Historical Monuments: Dorset*, II (HMSO).

Thomas, N., 1955. 'The Thornborough Circles, near Ripon, North Riding,' *Yorkshire Archaeol. J.* **38**, 425–445.
Thomas, N., 1964. 'A Gazetteer of Neolithic and Bronze Age Sites and Antiquities in Bedfordshire', *Bedfordshire Archaeol. J.* **2**, 16–33.

White, D. A., 1970. 'The Excavation of an Iron Age Round Barrow near Handley, Dorset, 1969', *Antiq. J.* **50**, 26–36.
Wymer, J., 1966. 'Excavation of the Lambourn Long Barrow, 1964,' *Berkshire Archaeol. J.* **62**, 1–16.

NOTES:

(i) textual references in the above paper to L. V. Grinsell's publications correlate with his Bibliography, *below* pp 250–56.
(ii) abbreviations in the References at the end of each paper follow the Council for British Archaeology's *Standard List of Abbreviated Titles of Current Periodicals* (May, 1971).

CHAPTER II

Field Archaeology: Its Origins and Development

Paul Ashbee

The term 'field archaeology' was coined by J. P. Williams-Freeman in 1915. He told O. G. S. Crawford (1953, 36) that he was struck by the term 'field naturalist', which was used to distinguish those who studied plants and other living things in the open air as contrasted with such pursuits in laboratory or museum. Field archaeology was thus defined as an outdoor occupation and, in a discussion of methodology, it was said that the best way to visit ancient earthworks was by the prehistoric methods of walking, riding or driving. The bicycle was not entirely dismissed while the motor-car was reserved for 'the lame and the lazy, the old or the hurried', as a means for making all places accessible. Presciently, air observation was left as a subject for the future.

Yet field archaeology, that is pure fieldwork and survey carried out in the open air, has roots, in Britain and Ireland, that strike back to the topographers of the sixteenth-century totalitarian Tudor state. Now four centuries later we are in an age of absolute land use by persons possessed of powers of destruction against which the bodies, official and otherwise, responsible for the recording and preservation of our national heritage enshrined in barrows and other field monuments are powerless.

Foreboding of difficulties as the prospect of our future field archaeological studies may be, it is apposite to offer this essay as a tribute to Leslie Grinsell who, for a lifetime, has, in the best traditions of British field archaeology, walked the length and breadth of much of England recording the barrows that our Tom Robinsons would destroy. His application of the principles and disciplines of field archaeology, together with his publication of detailed results and records, presents an enduring monument to our age, and it must be said that unless Leslie Grinsell's methods and mode of work be extended, without delay, to other areas of our islands, we may never begin to comprehend the palimpsest that, part by part, is British prehistory.

In terms of the men whose efforts helped to establish the modes of procedure that we consider as field archaeology, every age has had its giants and heroes (fig 5). Some of these have received a measure of biographical treatment. Well-documented works depict tireless, melancholic John Leland (Kendrick, 1950), magistral William Camden (Piggott, 1951), whimsical John Aubrey (Powell, 1948), our exquisite antiquary Mr Lhuyd of Oxford (Gunther, 1945; Daniel, 1966), and lovable William Stukeley (Piggott, 1950), to chart the formative period. Recently a biography has appeared of Sir Richard Colt Hoare (Woodbridge, 1970) which pays some attention to his relationship with William Cunnington.

A brief biography of Lt.-General Pitt-Rivers by his assistant H. St George Gray (1905) accompanied the *Index* to *Excavations in Cranborne Chase*, issued in 1905. For the present century we have the charming individualistic autobiography of O. G. S. Crawford (1955). Were one to take the achievements of these men alone, and set them together, much of what comprises field archaeology would be seen to be contained in their labours. However, no man being an island, each, separated though he is by the conditioning of time and perception, is the product of his age; so that, while much of what these men thought and did was new and innovatory, their investigations were carried out within the framework of a tradition, an inheritance into which they entered and which, modified by their efforts, they transmitted to be subsequently redefined by their successors. This, crudely, is the manner in which the advancement of knowledge operates within society—the gradual modification of ideas previously held. Thus, if one seeks the development of a particular aspect one should consider these giants and heroes in terms of their associates, ideally inquiring after patterns of inter-connection rather than catalogues of individual achievements. Such an approach does not in any way detract from the value of the particular contributions that put them to the fore in a given age. Seen against the backcloth of time and circumstance their work gains in substance and purpose.

The interest in prehistoric monuments, which is a manifestation of Tudor times, would appear to have had its basis in a number of factors. In terms of politics and religion, king, queen, statesman, scholar and churchman were adventuring on to uncharted waters but, at the same time, were concerned with establishing their new world upon the firm foundation of respectable antecedent. In practice the foundation had to be a compound of recognisable elements of classical or biblical antiquity. Yet there were recognisable antiquities that had to be accounted for. Inevitably much of the 'field archaeology' was concerned with mediaeval monuments; the erstwhile feudal nobility were impotent and had moved out of their castles, while many of the monasteries at the dissolution, became, at a blow, like our railway stations, historical monuments. Prehistoric field monuments were another matter. There was a niche left empty by the loss of faith in mythical British history. It was to be infilled by an amalgam: by the earthen monuments dimly perceived as pertaining to a remote era, by comparative ethnography, made possible by the discovery of America and its aboriginal inhabitants, and the remains of Roman Britain which served to forge a link between England and the respectability of the classical world, the contemporary civilized European norm.

It is one of the ironies of history that the king who brought about the destruction of the monasteries was prepared to be the patron of a man who studied and described their remains. John Leland (Kendrick, 1950, 45–64), a genius shadowed by melancholic madness, was in 1546 able to sign his 'New Year's Gift to King Henry VIII' as Joannes Lelandus Antiquarius.

Leland, who has probably been more extensively quoted in subsequent topographical works than any other writer of his age, was an omnivorous topographer-antiquary who commented upon all that excited his attention. His travels, which led ultimately to the *Itinerary*, edited by Thomas Hearne (Douglas, 1939, 226–48) and by Toulmin Smith (1907–10) in this century, seem to have begun early in 1534. He collected monastic books for the King's library and secured manuscripts of chronicles with a view to their publication. At first his interests were those of the documentary historian. As his travels led him further afield, he embraced descriptive topography and field monuments.

To early field monuments he paid no more than ordinary interest. He visited the Roman Wall and the Vallum, Offa's Dyke and the Devil's Arrows, near Boroughbridge in Yorkshire. Oddly enough, neither Silbury Hill nor Stonehenge is mentioned, although he passed close by the latter and knew its legend (Kendrick, 1950, 55). The Iron Age camp at South Cadbury (Alcock, 1967–1970) seemed of special significance as associated with Arthur and thus had a direct bearing upon the veracity of history. Indeed, he took a marked interest in hill-forts as they were the camps of the men of war, and he realised that some of them had to be pre-Roman. Barrows were referred to in like terms, the 'sepultures of men of warre . . . in dyvers places of the playne' (Salisbury Plain) (Toulmin Smith, 1907–1910, Pt X, 81). Barrows in Anglesey were brought to Leland's notice by one of his correspondents and he wrote of them thus: 'Mr. Roulande Griffith tolde me that . . . in tyme of myned menne usid not in Termone (i.e. Anglesey) to separate thyr groundes, but now stille more and more they digge stony hillokkes yn thyre groundes, and with the stones of them rudely congestid they divide theyre groundes after Devonshire fascion, Yn digging of these (they) digge up yn many places yerthen pottes with the mouthes turnid douneward, conteyning (cineres et ossa mortuorum).'

Whatever the ultimate purpose of Leland's labours—and the expulsion of 'the crafty coloured doctrine of a rout of Roman Bishops' was one intention of our arch-patriot—his example stimulated others. Two men, one in Kent and one in Cornwall, are outstanding in this period as field archaeologists. Indeed, their work was hardly equalled for at least a century.

John Twine was headmaster of King's School, Canterbury, for twenty years, was Mayor of Canterbury in 1554 and, for a time, member of Parliament. However his book, *De Rebus Albionicus Britannicus atque Anglis*, published in 1590 by his son Thomas, was written before 1550 (Kendrick, 1950, 105). He claimed that earthworks and chamber tombs were the works of erstwhile 'Albionic' inhabitants, while Phoenicians, seeking Cornish tin, were colonisers. He knew of a great camp near Chilham (presumably Bigberry at Harbledown) as well as Danebury, Kingsclere, Highclere and others. Kits Coty House, the Rollright stones and Stonehenge were also familiar to him. He assembled a collection of Romano-British antiquities which must have made an impression upon the contemporary Canterbury scene. His measure as a field archaeologist is that he used his material to a specific theme. Significantly, he was held in high esteem by both Leland and Camden.

John Norden (Graham, 1966) conceived of himself as a map-maker and he laboured long and in poverty towards the realisation of a detailed survey of England. His *Survey of Cornwall* was compiled in about 1584 but not published until 1728. The volume contains a map of the county and detailed engravings of the separate hundreds, with places and antiquities arranged and designated according to their hundred locations. For the first time in such a work illustrations of field monuments are used to press home matters deployed in his text. Of particular note are the accounts, and their accompanying drawings, of St Michael's Mount, the stone circle called the Nine Sisters, an early stone-bordered enclosure called 'Arthur's Hall', Tintagel and Trethewy Quoit (the remains of a stone-chambered tomb of the portal dolmen class). These are innovations and match his new cartographical devices such as the use of conventional signs to depict towns. In his work can be seen the qualities of field archaeology; good maps—their excellence was recognised by his contemporaries—coupled with detailed description and depiction.

William Camden represents the fulfilment of embryonic archaeology in terms of Tudor antiquarian activity. He planned his career, studying antiquities as a schoolboy, and trained himself as an antiquary by his travels. There were few precedents—'it was a sort of learning that was then but appearing in the world'—but he recognised the need to know Welsh and Anglo-Saxon for place-names, and considered that he should see monuments with his own eyes if he was to put them into their historical framework. Thus armed he set about *Britannia* 'sive florentissimorum regnorum Angliae, Scotiae, Hiberniae Chorographica descriptio' with the aim to establish Britain as a member of those nations who drew their strength from Roman roots.

Stuart Piggott (1951, 208) assessed the *Britannia* in his memorable Reckitt lecture delivered upon the quartercentenary of Camden's birth, suggesting that:

> the framework of the Britannia, persisting through every edition is that of the Celtic tribal areas of Britain as recorded by the classical geographers, with the English shires grouped within their accomodatingly vague boundaries. In such a scheme, too, the descriptions of British

and Roman coins, and the recording of Roman inscriptions in growing numbers in each edition, so that by 1607 nearly eighty are included, would have significance, and not least of all, Camden's famous first-hand account of the Roman Wall, the most considerable monument in the province, would form an appropriate climax, between the tribal area of the Brigantes and that of the Ottadini, the last tribe named before he reaches the remote regions of Scotia and the outer Ocean.

The *Britannia*, that first published in 1586 being of coat-pocket size, was a best-seller. Six editions appeared in Camden's lifetime, all in Latin, except the last, that of 1610, which was translated by Philemon Holland. To begin with, the work was addressed to the European world of scholarship. Successive editions catered for a new class of readers anxious to read antiquarian literature—a genre that the *Britannia* had gone a long way to create.

Camden's field-work was undertaken on a series of antiquarian tours. As early as 1578 he was abroad in East Anglia and he continued to travel collecting material which was included in subsequent editions of the *Britannia*. Between 1589 and 1596 he went into Wales, the West Country and Wiltshire. In 1599 he was on the Roman Wall with Sir Robert Bruce Cotton, though he had been there already in earlier years. A factor that emerges from his work is that he was a practical and efficient man, marshalling material from tours which were put to good account.

Although Norden compiled his *Survey* in about 1584, the first edition of Camden's *Britannia* contained what may be the first archaeological illustration published in an English book (Kendrick, 1950, 151). In the 1594 edition there is the earliest record of crop-marks (Jessup, 1961, 185) when, in describing Richborough, the Roman Saxon shore fort in Kent, he writes, 'But now age has eras'd the very tracks of it; and to teach us that Cities dye as well as men, it is at this day a corn-field, wherein when the corn is grown up, one may observe the draughts of streets crossing one another, (for where they have gone the corn is thinner) and such crossings they commonly call S. Augustine's cross.' Undoubtedly Camden's greatest achievement is his collection of Romano-British inscriptions gleaned from the northern counties. Notwithstanding, sites and monuments, lacking from Leland's records, find a place in his well-planned pages. Thus there is mention in successive editions of, among others, Stonehenge, Silbury Hill, Bartlow Hills, the Boscawen-un circle, Kits Coty House, Jullieberrie's Grave and Maiden Bower. For example Silbury Hill is described as '. . . a round hill, riseth to a considerable height, and seemeth by the fashion of it, and by the sliding down of the earth about it, to be cast up by men's hands.'

Two contemporaries of Camden, who both helped and corresponded with him, were George Owen, of Henllys, Pembrokeshire, and Richard

Carew of Antony, Cornwall. Owen's *Description of Pembrokeshire* (Kendrick, 1950, 160) contains a reasonably accurate drawing of Pentre Ifan, which is considered as one of the county's wonders. Carew's *Survey of Cornwall*, published in 1602, is considered by many as perhaps the best of the county surveys of the early seventeenth century. He had contributed to the Cornwall chapter of the *Britannia*, but in his own book he veers away from that format to write much more discursively. Although the flair for field-work possessed by his senior Norden is lacking, he does include such features as the turf-cut figures on Plymouth Hoe (Marples, 1949, 209–12).

Within about five years of James VI of Scotland becoming James I of England, an account of Scottish antiquities was compiled based, in some measure, upon actual inspection of them. Commissionary Maul (Crawford, 1949, 97–98) would seem to have recorded monuments long since destroyed, such as barrows at Barry and a cist-burial near the Cross of Camus. James I also has the distinction of beginning what Atkinson (1956, 186) has defined as the new and more active period of interest in Stonehenge. While staying at Wilton House as guest of the Earl of Pembroke, he was taken by his host to view the monument. James was inspired to instruct the Surveyor of the King's Works, Inigo Jones, 'the Vitruvius of his age', to plan and investigate the remains. As Jones died in 1651, the results of his labours were published in 1655, by his son-in-law, John Webb, under the title *The Most Notable Antiquity of Great Britain, vulgarly called Stone-henge, on Salisbury Plain, Restored by Inigo Jones, Architect-General to the late King*. This *Restoration* is, perhaps, best summarised by Aubrey (Powell, 1948, 78): 'There is a great deal of learning in it, but having compared his scheme with the monument itself, I found he had not dealt fairly, but had made a Lesbian's rule, which is conformed to the stone; that is, he framed the monument to his own Hypothesis, which is much differing from the thing itself.'

Something of the activities, albeit curious ones, of those steeped in the early seventeenth-century approach to field monuments, an attitude of mind formed, before all else, by Camden's *Britannia*, can be seen in the church of Trelleck, in Monmouthshire, where there is a stone sundial with carved and incised panels, dated 1639. One face carries a depiction of the nearby Norman motte (*Magna mole*), another of three standing stones (Crawford, 1925, 209) (*Maior saxis*), which are close by with their heights indicated, and the third a well (*Maxima fonte*). Indeed, the antiquary, in a loose sense, was fast becoming an established character, as witnessed by Earle's chiding account in his *Microcosmography* (Evans, 1956, 16) although Shackerley Marmion in 1641 put prescient words into his antiquary's mouth: 'Antiquities . . . are the registers, the chronicles of the Age they were made in, and speak the truth of history better than a hundred of your printed commentaries.' William Camden had done his work well.

An analogous interest in field monuments, particularly stone-built long barrows and other chamber tombs, was abroad, at about this time, on the mainland of Europe. Stuart Piggott (1956, 107) has cited Ole Worm's *Danicorum Monumentorum Libri Sex* (1643) and *Danica Literatura Antiquissima* (1651) as well as Picardt's *Korte beschryvinge van eenige Vergetene en Verborgene Antiquitaten* (Amsterdam, 1660) and considers that the drawings contained in them must, in some measure, have stimulated our own antiquarians. A similar scene can be seen in France (Daniel, 1960, 13–15), an area rich in such monuments. There, as in England, early visitors carved their initials. La Pierre Levée in a suburb of Poitiers, beside which the students conducted their revels, bears the name Gerard Mercator, 1660 (Daniel, 1960, Pl 1, a).

Fussner (1962) has seen the seventeenth century as the seed-bed of the modern profession of history: a time when economic revolution coincided with a precedent seeking historical revolution, all side by side with significant developments in literature, politics, philosophy, science and religion. He argues as futile any attempt to isolate individual causes from the total historical situation. One aspect of historical intellectual development which he recognises is quantification. Cartography is seen as indicative of a general European concern with quantitative measurement, and it seems inescapable that the seeking out and recognition of field monuments is a natural corollary to this. In this formative period, however, many whose work, by the canons of the age, lay in literary, legalistic, heraldic or even ecclesiastical channels, were possessed of an antiquarian zeal which, in Douglas's (1939, 20) inimitable words, sent them 'a-whoring after antiquities.' Sir William Dugdale, at the centre of his renowned Warwickshire circle, corresponded upon barrows, visited and sketch-planned local henges and went to the Wall and Vallum, when engaged upon his Visitation of Westmorland and Cumberland (Fox, 1956, 34, 110). Robert Plot, in his *Natural History of Staffordshire* (1686, 397), makes brief mention of a promontory-sited hillfort above Shropshire. This follows his mention of the Rollright stones in his earlier *Natural History of Oxfordshire*. Elias Ashmole, an astute student of all that was curious and interesting and the recipient of the *Museum Tradescantianum*, who married Dugdale's grand-daughter, wrote in a letter an account of a stretch of Watling Street (Hamper, 1827, 323–327). The road and connected sites are described, and his field-work is charmingly illustrated when he relates how 'spying some smale trenches lately made to draine the adjacent meadow, I went to them and found many pieces of Roman brick and tyle cast up.'

Mention must also be made of Edward Lhuyd (Pl IIa) (Daniel, 1954, 149; 1966), called 'the best naturalist in Europe' by Sir Hans Sloane and, in the judgement of Sir John Rhŷs, 'in many respects the greatest Celtic philologist the world has ever seen'. Lhuyd travelled through the Celtic countries making observations on their antiquities and languages. He was the second Keeper of the Ashmolean Museum at Oxford when he died prematurely. It has been a loss to both field archaeology and Celtic linguistics that neither the Bodleian Library nor Jesus College was interested in acquiring his manuscript collection. Something of the worth of his work and unique breadth of interest—his inquiries in the Celtic realm extended to botany, geology, local dialect, folk-lore and place-names as well as archaeology and comparative philology—can be seen in the publication (Campbell and Thomson, 1963) of his Scottish Travels. Two aspects of Lhuyd's achievement are especially relevant to our theme. He drew up a sophisticated questionnaire (Jessup, 1961, 178–179) designed to elicit geographical and antiquarian information regarding Welsh parishes. It was directed to the Gentry and Clergy, who were entreated to 'communicate this Paper where they think fit, amongst their Neighbours; interpreting some Queries to those of the Vulgar, whom they judge Men of Veracity.' Two items in this comprehensive document are concerned entirely with field monuments:

VI. A Catalogue of the *Barrows*, or those Artificial Mounts distinguish'd by the several Names of *Krigeu*, *Gorsedheu*, *Tommenydh*, *Beili*, &c as also of the *Camps*, and all old *Entrenchments* whatever.
VII. Roman *Ways*, *Pavements*, *Stones* or any Underground Works; Crosses, Beacons, Stones pitch'd on (sic) end in a regular Order; such as *Meinihirion* in *Caernarvenshire*, *Karn Lhechart* in *Glamorgan* and *Buarth Arthur* in the County of Caermardhim: As also those rude Stone-Monuments distinguish'd by the several Names of *Bêdh*, *Gwely*, *Karnedh*, *Kromlech*, *Lhêch yr âst*, *Lhêch y Gowres*, *Lhêch y Wydham*, *Koeten Arthur*, *Kist vaën*, *Preseh y Vuwch Vrech*, &c.

In 1699 he travelled to Ireland as part of his plan to produce an account of the archaeology and natural history of the Celtic realm. He was the first antiquary to observe and record the discovery of the passage and chamber beneath New Grange (Ó'Ríordáin and Daniel, 1964). Two accounts written by Lhuyd are known and were cited by George Coffey (1912, 7–9). The first of these was in a letter of 1699 to Dr Tancred Robinson from Bathgate, near Linlithgow in Scotland, subsequently published in the *Philosophical Transactions* of the Royal Society (27, 503–505). The second, written some three months later in March, 1700, when Lhuyd had returned to Ireland from Scotland, was addressed to the Rev. Henry Rowlands his close friend, and was included in that writer's *Mona Antiqua Restaurata* published at Dublin in 1723. Recently copies of two letters by Lhuyd have been traced (Herity, 1967, 128–130) giving further descriptions of New Grange, previously unpublished. They are both addressed to Dr Thomas Molyneux of the Dublin Philosophical Society (Hoppen, 1970) under whose auspices Lhuyd made his Irish visits. These accounts give valuable information on the state of the monument at that time, the chamber's contents, the position of the stone basins and a standing stone on the top of the great cairn. Furthermore, he set the monument firmly in context, concluding that 'this monument was never Roman', for 'the rude carving at the entry and in the cave seems to denote it a barbarous monument.' A drawing of New Grange (Daniel, 1967, Pl 7) survives in the manuscript collection of John Anstis, the Cornish Garter King of Arms and a man much interested in field monuments, and seems to be by Lhuyd. For comparison there are two Welsh hill fort plans, probably by Lhuyd, which have recently been published (Piggott, 1965, 167–168).

Lhuyd died at the age of forty-eight with the second volume of his *Archaeologia Britannia* unpublished. This would have contained Irish material gathered in 1699 and 1700. Herity (1969, 20, *fn.* 1) has stressed the loss to the development of Irish antiquarian thought that this represents. His view, from a scrutiny of what remains, is that it would have exerted signal influence, comparable to Camden's *Britannia*, in Ireland.

Although there was, during the seventeenth century, this objective concern for field monuments, as witnessed by named categories, the hill-forts, 'camps', circles, barrows, stone chamber tombs and even chalk-cut hill-figures, the results were not separated from more general treatments; neither were they synthesised into a system of recognisable prehistory. For, while the classical writers were to some extent able to provide people who could be seen as frequenters of these field monuments, visible on every hand, provision still had to be made for some 'Ancient Britons'. These were to emerge from a marriage of the evidence of the classical writers with the new view of primitive mankind made possible by the discovery of America and its aboriginal inhabitants. Their appearance was reconstructed in a series of related drawings derived from John White, which have been detailed by Kendrick (1950, 121–125, pls. XII–XV). They would have been familiar to all from William Camden onwards, yet it remained for one man, John Aubrey, to associate positively the men and the field monuments. This he did with great effect in the introduction to his *Essay Towards the Description Of The North Division of Wiltshire* (Powell, 1949, 1–2), the significance of which has been discussed in detail by Stuart Piggott (Fox, 1956, 101). But Aubrey did not stop at this stage, for he also peopled one particular group of monuments, the stone circles, with a particular 'sect', the Druids (Piggott, 1968, 143–145), thus giving substance to a concept which, in certain quarters, is still with us. Indeed, the wheel has turned full circle, and, in the light of recent research, John Aubrey may have been closer to the mark than he ever thought when, long ago, he discussed 'our antient heathen Priests' with Edward Lhuyd and others.

John Aubrey (Pl III), striding across the seventeenth century, was undoubtedly the founder of British field archaeology and is the first to whom the appellation 'archaeologist' can be given. A man of many facets, shown by the range of his work as that is sensitively delineated by his biographer (Powell, 1948), he was possessed of an extraordinary acuteness of perception plus a powerful visual imagination. These were qualities that were deployed, equally, in his field archaeology and his biographical essays. At the same time there is within his work that systematisation which is a part of the natural philosophic methods then being developed by men whose need for the exchange and expression of ideas was to give us the Royal Society. His account of a first sight of the Marlborough Downs and Avebury (Sumner, 1931, 73–74) or, for that matter, his sketch of John Milton (Powell, 1949, 67–73) amply illustrates his power of delineative prose. Of his own approach, Aubrey wrote 'Till about the year 1649 when Experimental Philosophy was first cultivated by a Club at Oxford, it was held a strange Presumption for a man to attempt an Innovation in Learning'; continuing, 'I could not rest quiet till I had obeyed this secret call; Mr Camden, Dr Plott and Mr Wood confess the same.'

Aubrey's *Monumenta Britannica*, subtitled *A Miscellanie of British Antiquities*, remains in manuscript in the Bodleian Library, and from time to time tantalising glimpses are given when a relevant monument is reported upon (Piggott, 1962, Pl 1). The *Monumenta* set out to describe in detail field monuments from prehistoric times to the Middle Ages. As Stuart Piggott, when summarising its content, (Fox, 1956, 108) emphasied, its importance lies in that the material is assembled as a basis in itself and not merely as an adjunct to a theory or narrative. In brief (Piggott, 1956, 108), the plan of the *Monumenta* is as follows:

Part I The *Templa Druidum* contains the descriptions of Avebury and Stonehenge together with notices of other stone circles and allied sites. Here the literary sources of Druidism are introduced.

Part II treats of prehistoric and Roman forts and camps together with Roman settlements.

Part III deals with barrows, pottery, burials, linear earthworks, roads and trackways, Roman pavements and coins.

Part IV entitled *ΣΤΡΩΜΑΤΑ sive Miscellania*, was never finished but was to include the chronological sequence of architectural styles, handwriting, heraldic shields and clothing.

In his own inimitable way, Aubrey was also concerned with environment (Ashbee, 1963). The plan of his *Natural History of Wiltshire* runs from *Air and Springs Medicinall*, through *Formed Stones*, *Architecture*, *Agriculture* and *Antiquities*, to *Things Praeternatural*, in thirty-six chapters. In his famous *Description of the North Division of Wiltshire* he takes great pain to reconstruct environment, explaining 'By the nature of the soil, which is a sour woodsere land, very natural for the production of oakes especially, one may conclude that this North Division was a shady dismal wood'. Thus his approach could be considered as foreshadowing that close association of environmental science with field archaeology current today.

When one turns to the beginning of the eighteenth century, there is one particular study, based on work in the field: John Horsley's *Britannia Romana or the Roman Antiquities of Britain*, published posthumously in 1732. Horsley (Haverfield, 1924, 74), born in Northumberland in 1685, became a Presbyterian minister and teacher of natural science in Scotland, and travelled England observing Roman monuments as well as making copies of inscriptions, accurately if crudely. He knew his monuments at first hand and from his cumulative knowledge he developed the concept of Britain as a Roman province forming a part of the Roman Empire. Haverfield (1924, 75) considered the *Britannia Romana*, which is in some measure a development of Camden's basic contention, as the most scholarly narrative of a Roman province that had been produced anywhere in Europe. It stands in isolation as an early specialised undertaking which must have served as a stimulus to the young William Roy, as well as laying a foundation for subsequent development of the concept of Roman Britain.

It can be fairly said that, with the exception of Camden and Aubrey, seventeenth-century field archaeology was a by-product of the great range of historical work motivated, as Douglas (1939 *passim*) has stressed, by a continual search for precedent in ecclesiastical and political matters. During the eighteenth century other fashions and forces were at work, and their mark is writ large upon the pursuit of field archaeology, in for instance the contemplation of the picturesque, an attitude of mind intertwined with the labyrinthine excesses of romantic '*Gothick*' taste (Clark, 1964, 53–77; Piggott, 1937). But there was also stern military necessity—the pacification of the barbarous Scottish Highlands after the 1745 Rising. A further factor is that by now a body of knowledge was in existence, scattered in many books or even unpublished and in letters or manuscripts. Thus there was a foundation which could be built upon or extended.

Striding across the eighteenth century, clutching drawing-board and measuring-staff, there is, before all others, William Stukeley. In the early nineteenth century Richard Gough could affirm 'If any man was born for the service of Antiquity, it was Dr. Stukeley', while a century later O. G. S. Crawford (Crawford and Keiller, 1928, 211) wrote: 'Let us once for all pay a tribute of esteem and gratitude to Stukeley's memory'. His distinctive characteristics have been elegantly expressed by his distinguished biographer (Piggott, 1950):

> . . . as a person, Stukeley emerges as one of the most curious and complex of the English eccentrics, pathetic, charming, admirable and

laughable by turns. One becomes very endeared to the Archdruid, so enthusiastic in everything he does, whether it is riding in search of antiquities, building a hermitage in his garden, watching an eclipse of the sun (postponing his morning service so that his congregation can see it too), or writing, writing away at the extraordinary fancies of his later years, where the Druids are lurking everywhere. . . .

Stukeley as a field archaeologist has been documented in detail by his biographer (Piggott, 1950, 27–91) and the journals of some of his tours have been reconstructed, the critical five years (1721–25) being set out in detail. From 1710 to 1725 he made ten or a dozen excursions of differing length, ranging from Kent to Devonshire, Wrexham to Lincolnshire, and up to the Roman Wall. Avebury and Stonehenge occupied much of his time between 1721 and 1724. In 1725 he published *Itinerarium Curiosum Centuria I*, subtitled *An Account of the Antiquities and Remarkable Curiosities in Nature or Art observed in Travels through Great Britain.* He planned a *Centuria II* of which an incomplete draft dated 1760 exists. In the event this was published posthumously in 1776. But 1740 saw the publication of *Stonehenge, a Temple restor'd to the British Druids*, and *Abury, a Temple of the British Druids*, containing the notorious falsification of the 'Sanctuary' (Piggott, 1935), appeared in 1743. It is upon his fieldwork and these publications that his reputation as a field archaeologist rests. His original intention seems to have been to write a book upon stone circles and stone-built chamber tombs, an ambition seemingly inspired by the first part of Aubrey's *Monumenta.* Yet, however much certain aspects of Stukeley's written achievements may have fallen short of his original intentions, his methods of fieldwork and the character of his observations are of considerable interest and importance.

From his earliest days William Stukeley was conscious of the importance of the visual record, and a pocket volume of his architectural pen-drawings of mediaeval buildings survives from 1708. In 1719 (Piggott, 1965, 171) he wrote in the minutes of the then newly founded Society of Antiquaries, 'Without drawing and designing the Study of Antiquities or any other Science is lame and imperfect.' His 'Prospects' are the equivalent of modern photographs while his 'Groundplots' anticipate the 'birds-eye views', or even the air-photographs, of a later age. The engravers, rarely did full justice to his sensitive style and tended to impart to his work a sense of frozen aridity, although Vandergucht (Piggott, 1950, *passim*) was able to capture the enchantment with which the halcyon days at Avebury had endowed those drawings.

Stukeley was supremely conscious of the need for, and advantages of, accurate measurement in field archaeology, and nowhere is this better illustrated than in his work at Stonehenge. He informs his readers that (Stukeley, 1740, 6) 'The notion we ought to entertain of Stonehenge is not a little enhanc'd by the discovery I made from frequent mensurations there.' His Stonehenge plan was the result of many careful measurements from which he concluded that the basic unit of the monument was a 'Druid Cubit' (Stukeley, 1740, TAB II), a length of 20·8 ins. At 'Rowldrich' (Rollright) he again used his staff, this time working in feet, and a 'Prospect' shows a figure as scale beside the 'Kistvaen' with staff suitably in hand (Stukeley, 1743, 12, Tab VII) (Pl IIb). Col. Heneage Finch, Earl of Winchelsea, wrote to Stukeley in 1723, describing how, with his measuring chain, he had recorded the dimensions of Julliberrie's Grave at Chilham, not far from his home at Eastwell in Kent. This must be the first record made of the dimensions and orientation of a long barrow. Stuart Piggott (1950, 58) has observed that the mode of work is so closely similar to Stukeley's own that he must have given Lord Winchelsea explicit directions.

Two other comments on Stonehenge show something of Stukeley's outstanding originality of mind. One is his attempt to date the monument from the known rate of change in the variation of the compass (Atkinson, 1956, 189). The other is that a sample of Stonehenge stone had been collected by Dr Halley. Halley observed from the weathering 'that the work must be of an extraordinary antiquity, and for ought he knew, 2 or 3000 years old' (Stukeley, 1740, 5). Stukeley remarks, 'But had the Doctor been at Abury, which is made of the same stones, he might well, from the like argumentation conclude, that work as old again as Stonehenge, at least much older, and I verily believe it.' These attempts at dating are of considerable interest, for they may be among the first instances of the application of science to archaeological problems.

William Stukeley for the most part thought, as a field archaeologist must, in terms of maps and plans. Such considerations are, of course, an extension of his preoccupation with visual depiction and measurement. In 1721, as he travelled from Newbury to Marlborough (Piggott, 1950, 62), he expressed the need for a geological drift map, 'I have often wished', he wrote, 'that a map of soils was accurately made, promising to myself that such a curiosity would furnish us with some new notions of geography, and of the theory of the earth, which has only hitherto been made from hypothesis' (Stukeley, 1725, 63).

Several of his observations and deductions regarding field monuments are particularly relevant to our theme. He emphasised the importance of the barrows clustering around Stonehenge (Ashbee, 1960, 32, fig 6), saying (Stukeley, 1740, 43) that 'in general, they are always upon elevated ground, and in sight of the temple of Stonehenge.' On the matter of barrow siting, he was equally explicit. 'I observe the barrows upon Hakpen hill and others here are set with great art not upon the very highest part of the hills, but upon so much of the declevity or edge as that they make app(earance) as above to thos in the valley.' Such false crest siting of barrows is not infrequent in many parts of the country and, when discussing it, Sir Cyril Fox (1943, 22) was pleased to pay tribute to the prescience of Stukeley. A further instance of his power of perception is that he saw that Roman roads cut through disc barrows on Oakley Down, Cranborne Chase (Stukeley, 1740, Tab. III) (Pl IV) and near Beckhampton, in North Wiltshire (Stukeley, 1743, 26, Tab. IX). He noticed also the evidence of early field systems: inside Ogbury, between Amesbury and Salisbury, he saw 'many little banks, carried strait and meeting one another at right angles, square, oblong parallels and some oblique . . . yet it seems never to have been ploughed' (Stukeley, 1725, 158). In Cranborne Chase, 'on the sides of hills long divisions, very strait, crossing one another with all kinds of angles; they look like the baulks or meres of ploughed lands' (Stukeley, 1725, 158). At Great Chesterford in Essex he saw, apparently from an ale-house, 'the perfect vestigia of a temple, as easily discernable in the corn as upon paper . . .' (Piggott, 1950, 52). He made a sketch plan of this outline, and this must surely be the first positive use of a cropmark in field archaeology, though the phenomenon had been noted over a century earlier by Camden (above p 42).

Chyndonax, as Stukeley was called by his friends, presided in 1743 over an assembly of the Society of Roman Knights (Piggott, 1950, 53–56) and there made a statement of policy regarding the conservation of Roman field monuments which, in view of the present-day rate of destruction, has a strangely topical ring: 'We are to fight, *pro ara et focis*, to save citys and citysens, camps, temples, walls, amphitheatres, monuments, roads, inscriptions, coyns, buildings and whatever has a Roman stamp on them . . . the motto is *Temporis utriusque vindex*, which intimates to us that we are able to be the secretarys, the interpreters and preservers of the memorials of our ancestors.' Stukeley's character was certainly complex with his notions of Druidism, his ordination, his usage of Avebury, the Bertram forgeries and much more. Notwithstanding, it is his field archaeology that we remember as we glance up at his kindly figure, to the life on canvas (Pl V), as we ascend to the library in Burlington House, Piccadilly.

Indirectly, the actions taken to maintain public peace after Culloden, in 1746, led to the convention that our Ordnance Survey maps should bear indications of antiquities, that is, as Daniel (1950, 293) has termed it, the non-functional as well as the functional aspects of the cultural landscape. Indeed, this usage, so early established, has brought about the appointment, in this century, of Archaeology Officers within the Ordnance Survey, resulting in the happy circumstance whereby our maps are a continued stimulus to the development and practice of field archaeology.

In 1791 the Society of Antiquaries (Evans, 1956, 190) accepted as a bequest the manuscript of Major-General Roy's *The Military Antiquities of the Romans in Britain*, and decided to publish it. It was prepared

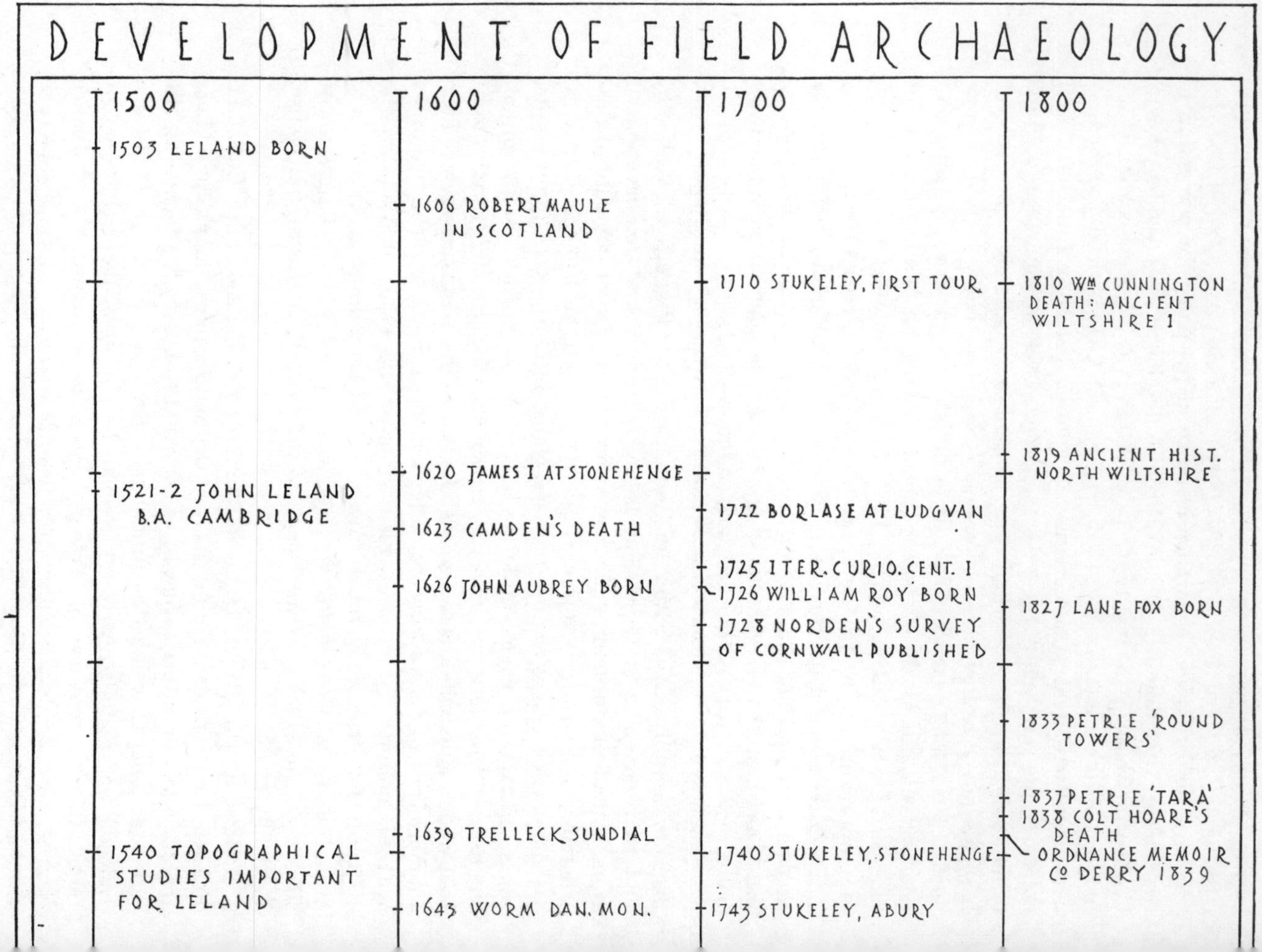

DEVELOPMENT OF FIELD ARCHAEOLOGY

1500	1600	1700	1800
1503 LELAND BORN	1606 ROBERT MAULE IN SCOTLAND	1710 STUKELEY, FIRST TOUR	1810 Wm CUNNINGTON DEATH: ANCIENT WILTSHIRE I
1521-2 JOHN LELAND B.A. CAMBRIDGE	1620 JAMES I AT STONEHENGE	1722 BORLASE AT LUDGVAN	1819 ANCIENT HIST. NORTH WILTSHIRE
	1623 CAMDEN'S DEATH	1725 ITER. CURIO. CENT. I	1827 LANE FOX BORN
	1626 JOHN AUBREY BORN	1726 WILLIAM ROY BORN	1833 PETRIE 'ROUND TOWERS'
		1728 NORDEN'S SURVEY OF CORNWALL PUBLISHED	1837 PETRIE 'TARA'
			1838 COLT HOARE'S DEATH
1540 TOPOGRAPHICAL STUDIES IMPORTANT FOR LELAND	1639 TRELLECK SUNDIAL	1740 STUKELEY, STONEHENGE	ORDNANCE MEMOIR Co DERRY 1839
	1643 WORM DAN. MON.	1743 STUKELEY, ABURY	

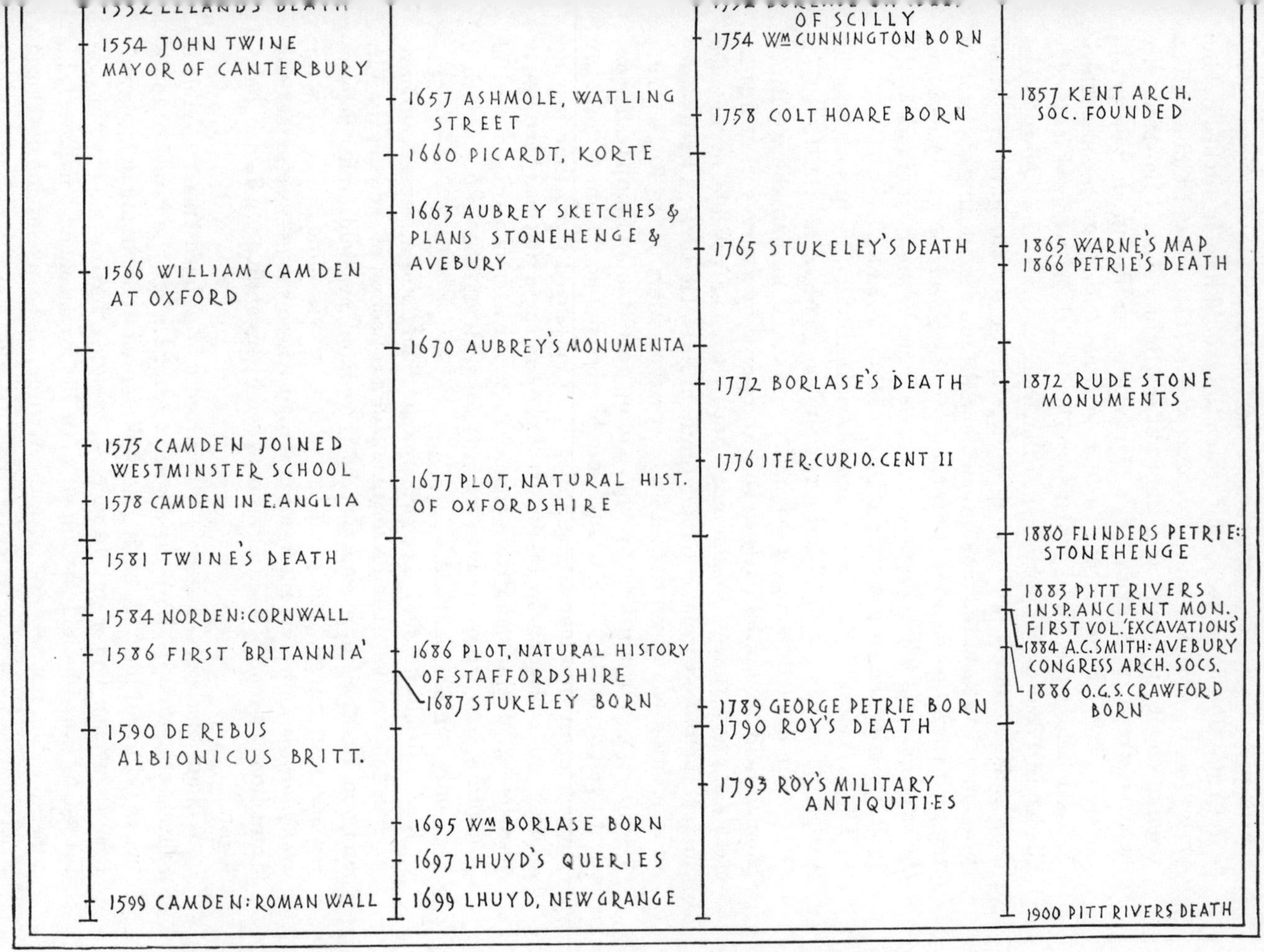

1554 JOHN TWINE MAYOR OF CANTERBURY
1566 WILLIAM CAMDEN AT OXFORD
1575 CAMDEN JOINED WESTMINSTER SCHOOL
1578 CAMDEN IN E. ANGLIA
1581 TWINE'S DEATH
1584 NORDEN: CORNWALL
1586 FIRST 'BRITANNIA'
1590 DE REBUS ALBIONICUS BRITT.
1599 CAMDEN: ROMAN WALL

1657 ASHMOLE, WATLING STREET
1660 PICARDT, KORTE
1663 AUBREY SKETCHES & PLANS STONEHENGE & AVEBURY
1670 AUBREY'S MONUMENTA
1677 PLOT, NATURAL HIST. OF OXFORDSHIRE
1686 PLOT, NATURAL HISTORY OF STAFFORDSHIRE
1687 STUKELEY BORN
1695 Wm BORLASE BORN
1697 LHUYD'S QUERIES
1699 LHUYD, NEWGRANGE

OF SCILLY
1754 Wm CUNNINGTON BORN
1758 COLT HOARE BORN
1765 STUKELEY'S DEATH
1772 BORLASE'S DEATH
1776 ITER. CURIO. CENT II
1789 GEORGE PETRIE BORN
1790 ROY'S DEATH
1793 ROY'S MILITARY ANTIQUITIES

1857 KENT ARCH. SOC. FOUNDED
1865 WARNE'S MAP
1866 PETRIE'S DEATH
1872 RUDE STONE MONUMENTS
1880 FLINDERS PETRIE: STONEHENGE
1883 PITT RIVERS INSP. ANCIENT MON. FIRST VOL. 'EXCAVATIONS'
1884 A.C. SMITH: AVEBURY CONGRESS ARCH. SOCS.
1886 O.G.S. CRAWFORD BORN
1900 PITT RIVERS DEATH

5. The life-spans and works of British field archaeologists, 16th–19th centuries.

for the press and then brought out in 1793. Fellows of the Society received a free copy, and for an extra half-crown they could have it stitched in blue paper in the manner of the *Archaeologia*. The circumstances which brought about the mapping of the Scottish Highlands, and Lowlands, are best recounted in William Roy's own words, in his introduction to *An Account of the Measurement of a Base on Hounslow-Heath*, a paper which he read before the Royal Society, and for which he received its Copley Medal, in 1785. It was published in that year in the *Philosophical Transactions*. He recounts how the difficulties of the terrain gave his friend Lt.-General Watson the notion that mapping and the ensuing exploration involved would be of prime importance to the government. As Assistant Quartermaster it fell to Roy's lot to have a share in the furtherance of the project, under the auspices of the Duke of Cumberland.

The precision of Roy's work and the adventitious circumstances of its execution have been fully described by Sir George Macdonald (1916–1917). A Roman Bath Building at Netherby awakened him to the wealth of Roman field antiquities likely to be encountered by a surveyor. At first he recorded, sometimes by sketching, but whenever possible by detailed survey, the more permanent and prominent forts. However, a fresh source of inspiration was given to him by Lt.-General Melville. In Roy's (1793, vf) own words, 'Knowing now what a temporary Roman Camp really was, he therefore during the completion of the public business formerly alluded to, in the following summer 1755 employed some time in augmenting his collection, by taking exact plans of those that had been newly discovered; at the same time that a survey was made of the wall of Antoninus, and more accurate drawings of such stations as formerly had been only slightly sketched.'

Roy's initial intention as regards Roman field antiquities seems to have extended no further than the formation of a collection of sketches (Pl VI), and one has the impression that he considered his field archaeology as secondary to his geodetic work for which he was famed. The *Military Antiquities* is, however, the work of a man whose success as a soldier and distinction as a man of science was matched by his ability as a field archaeologist.

William Borlase, whose life-span broadly paralleled that of William Stukeley, worked in the West Country. After Oxford, he returned to his native Cornwall in 1722, having been presented to the living of Ludgvan, near Penzance. Opportunities of classical study having eluded him, he turned to Cornish field monuments. In his archaeological fieldwork he adhered to the standards set by Aubrey while, like Stukeley, he developed a devotion to Druids, associating them with natural rock-basins, and, in later life, religious notions. Colt Hoare (1810, 9) greatly respected his views while Evans (1864, 6) observed Borlase's accuracy in the depiction of 'Ancient British Coins'. The significance of his contribution is obvious from the very way that Hencken in his *Archaeology of Cornwall and Scilly* (1932) relies upon Borlase in the frequent citations from his books.

The remarkable qualities and range by eighteenth-century standards, of Borlase's field work is nowhere more clearly shown than in his paper, 'Of The Great Alterations which the Isles of Scilly have undergone since the time of the Ancients', which was published in the *Philosophical Transactions* of the Royal Society (XLVIII, 1753). His knowledge of natural history and geology led him to sense something of the processes of living landscape, and as a result he was enabled to treat the submerged walls off the island of Samson and the problems of marine transgression. He explored each island, scrutinising and recording the principal monuments, with the stone-built chamber tombs looming large in his accounts. To test his field observations he even excavated the chambers of two of the tombs. An enlarged account of the Isles of Scilly (Borlase, 1756) was preceded by the monumental *Observations on the Antiquities Historical and Monumental of the County of Cornwall* in 1754, and succeeded by the searching *Natural History of Cornwall* in 1758.

William Borlase was made a Fellow of the Royal Society following the communication of a paper on 'Spar and Sparry Productions called Cornish Diamonds', only one of the nineteen contributions he made to the *Philosophical Transactions*. Shortly after 1758, he presented the whole of his collections to the Ashmolean Museum in Oxford, and in acknowledgement both of this gift, and his scholarship the University conferred upon him the degree of Doctor of Laws, in 1766. Despite his antiquarian and scientific labours, Borlase did not neglect his parish which he tended with 'the most rigid punctuality and exemplary duty'. The want of a definitive biographical study of William Borlase and his work is a lacuna in our detailing of the development of field archaeology, for he undoubtedly stands with Stukeley and Roy as one who, by his original work, exercised a formative influence as yet in great measure uncharted.

We tend, all too frequently, to think of Sir Richard Colt Hoare and William Cunnington (Sandell, 1961) in terms of their numerous excavations of barrows both long and round, subsequently described in *The History of Ancient Wiltshire* issued in 1812. Yet, these stately royal folio volumes set new standards for early earthwork observation and recording. Twelve years of persevering fieldwork were involved in their production, and, to that date, few areas had been so painstakingly explored. These volumes are essentially open-air books, as Sumner (1931) has rightly emphasised, and it is a cause for regret that their very size and weight has relegated them to the reference shelves.

Besides barrows, for which he devised a system still in some measure used today, Colt Hoare gave his attention to hill-forts and habitation sites (Woodbridge, 1970, 213). Something of his keen sense in the field emerges

(Colt Hoare, 1810, 49) when he observes the processes Nature exerted upon the physical lineaments of monuments:

> on a piece of down between Pertwood Farm and Keesley Lodge, the traces of a very ancient British settlement are marked by the unusual blackness of the soil thrown up by the moles . . . All the down adjoining Keesley is intersected by banks and other strong marks of an extensive cultivation; and the superior quality of its pasture affords another evident proof of its ancient population.

The problems of early environment did not escape him (Colt Hoare, 1810, 104), for he realised that as the bare downs were once wooded, the browsing cattle must have imposed a check upon the woodlands which had then existed.

An invaluable feature of *Ancient Wiltshire* is its maps, for Colt Hoare was fortunate in his choice of Philip Crocker as his surveyor and draughtsman. Piggott (1965, 172) points out that Crocker appears to have been in governmental employ before entering, Sir Richard's service, so that not unnaturally his maps and plans display the same quality and range of cartographic penmanship as officially practised at that time. O. G. S. Crawford (1953, 39) recalls that when he went to the Ordnance Survey he found a proof of the Wiltshire sheet of the one-inch map (dated about 1811) with corrections in Colt Hoare's own handwriting of the location and identification of antiquities. It seems that the Ordnance Survey liaised with him for, as Crawford states, there is a close resemblance between the maps in *Ancient Wiltshire* and the Ordnance Map.

Much of Colt Hoare's fieldwork appears to have been undertaken on horseback, which, as L. V. Grinsell (1953, 94) has stressed, 'has the great advantage of increased height which assists the discovery of the smaller earthworks', Grinsell adds, however, that by this procedure flints and sherds are not so readily seen. The value of Colt Hoare's fieldwork rests on the fact that our landscape has changed so dramatically during the past century and a half that many earthworks, once clear in their dereliction, no longer exist. Nowhere at the present time could we find a landscape so rich as Wiltshire was at the outset of the nineteenth century.

Colt Hoare acted also as a focus for a circle of friends bound together by their common predilection for field archaeological investigation. Thomas Leman, to whom Colt Hoare once referred as an 'ingenious brother antiquary' (Colt Hoare, 1819, 123), rode along the Roman roads. He has left manuscript notes, detailing his journeys, preserved in the Libraries of the Bath Literary and Philosophic Institution and the Wiltshire Archaeological Society at Devizes. John Skinner (Coombs and Bax, 1930), Rector of Camerton, amassed ninety-eight volumes of field notes of various kinds, mainly on monuments. He too was no mean horseman, thinking nothing of being in the saddle by six in the morning to reach Stourhead in time for

I. The Pool Farm cist-stone from Mendip, recognized as decorated by LVG, 1956.

IIA. A likeness of Edward Lhuyd, from *The Donation Book* of The Ashmolean Museum, Oxford.

IIB. The Rollright Stones, Oxfordshire, by William Stukeley (1743).

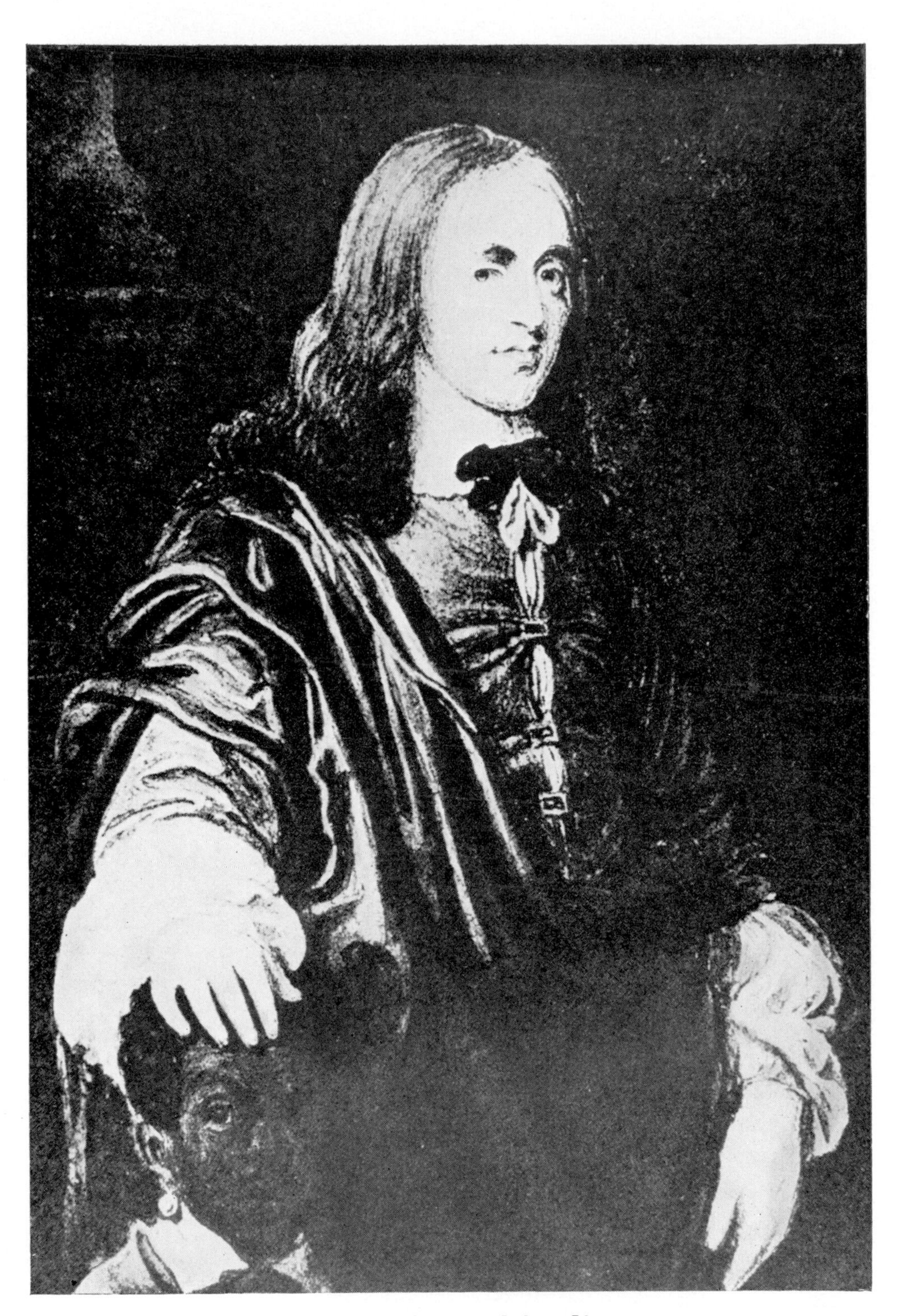

III. John Aubrey, aged about 30.

IV. Woodyates, Dorset, by William Stukeley (1740).

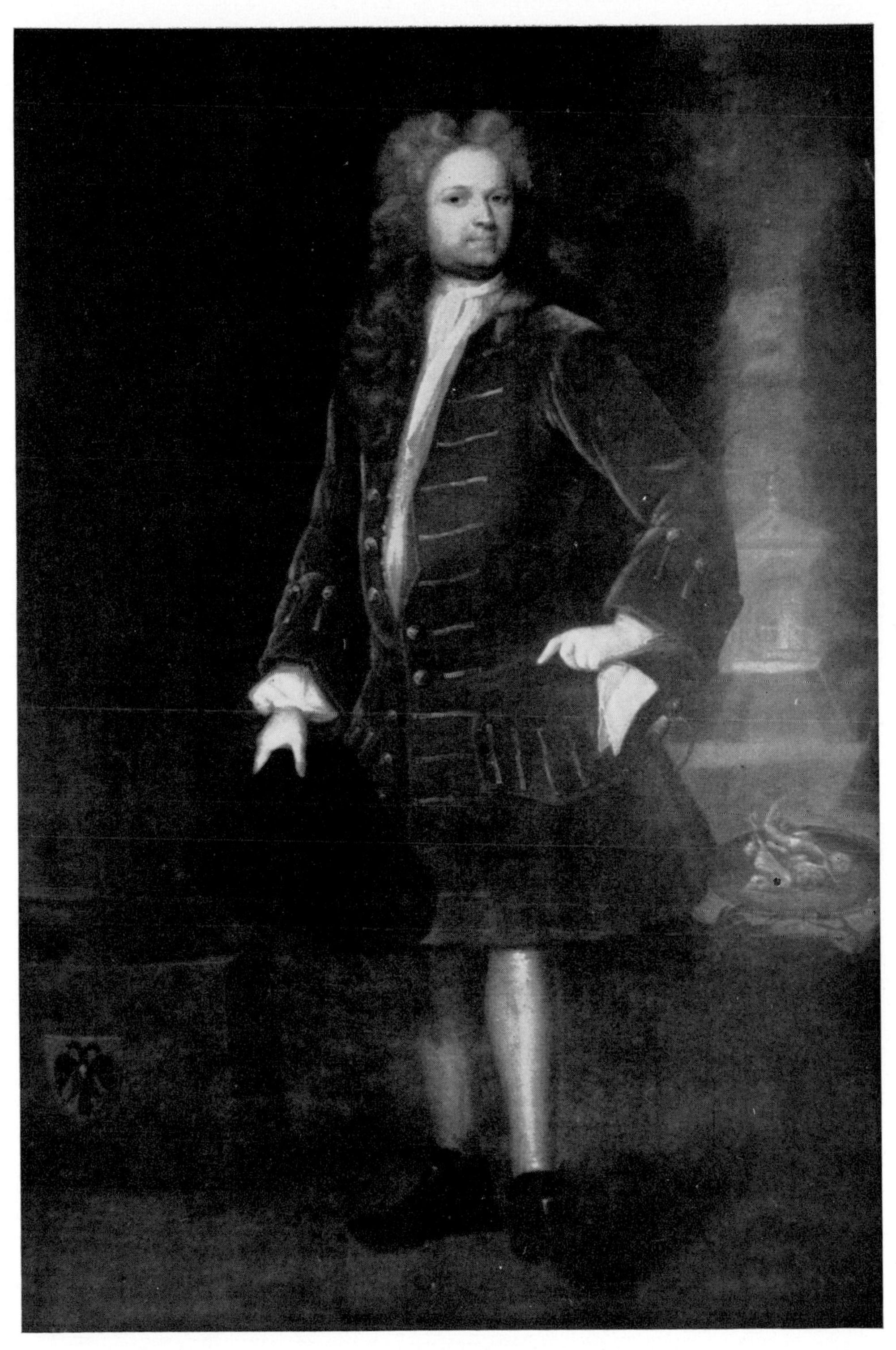

v. Portrait of William Stukeley in the possession of the Society of Antiquaries of London.

PLAN of the ROMAN STATION and adjoining CAMPS at CHEW GREEN on the HEAD of the RIVER COQUET, on the BORDER between SOUTH and NORTH BRITAIN, Supposed to be the FINES mentioned in RICHARD of CIRENCESTER. ——— September 20th 1774 –

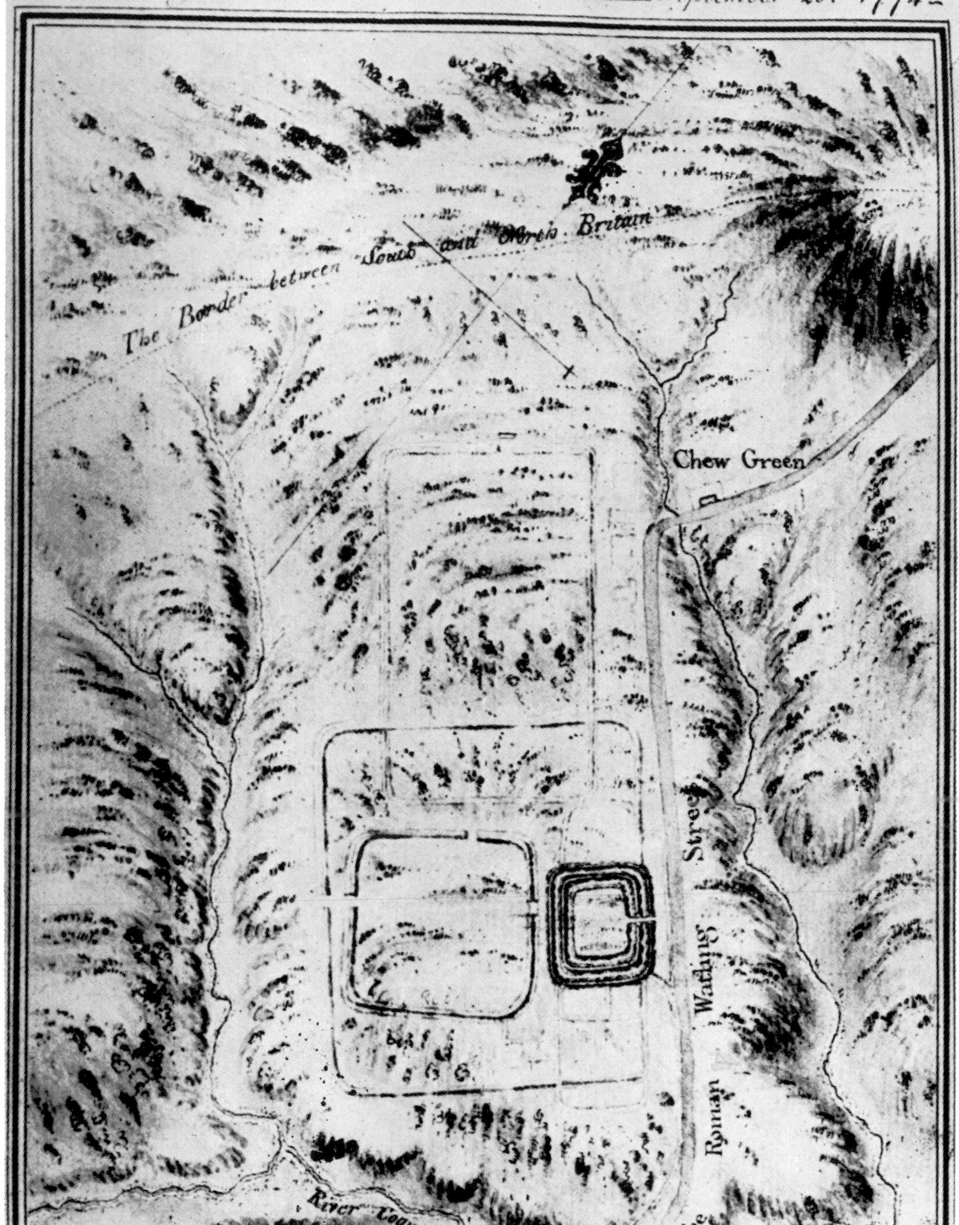

VI. The Chew Green Roman Camps by Maj-General William Roy, from *Military Antiquities. . . .* (1793)

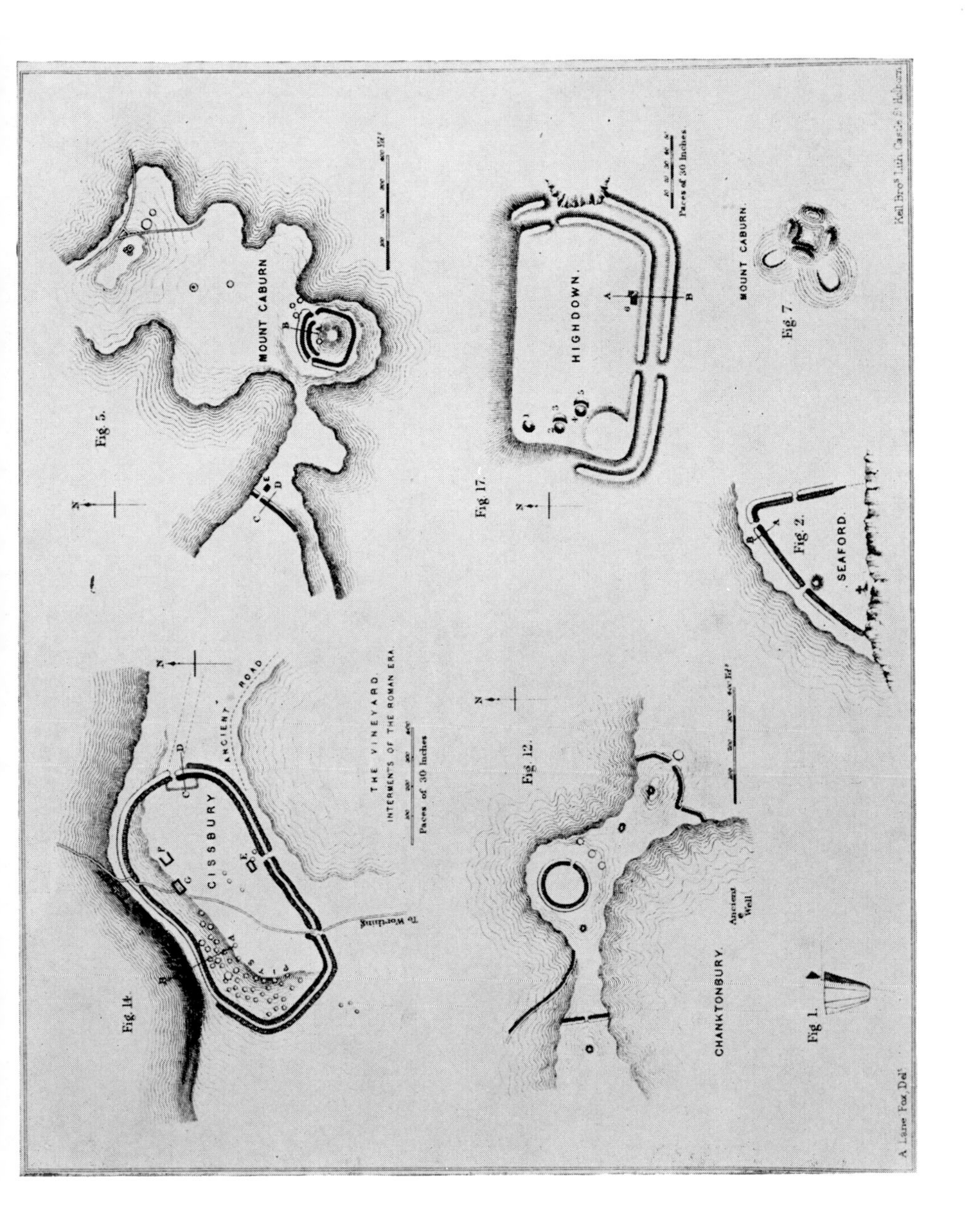

VII. The Hill-forts of Sussex by Lt-General Pitt-Rivers (née Lane Fox), from *Archaeologia* (1869).

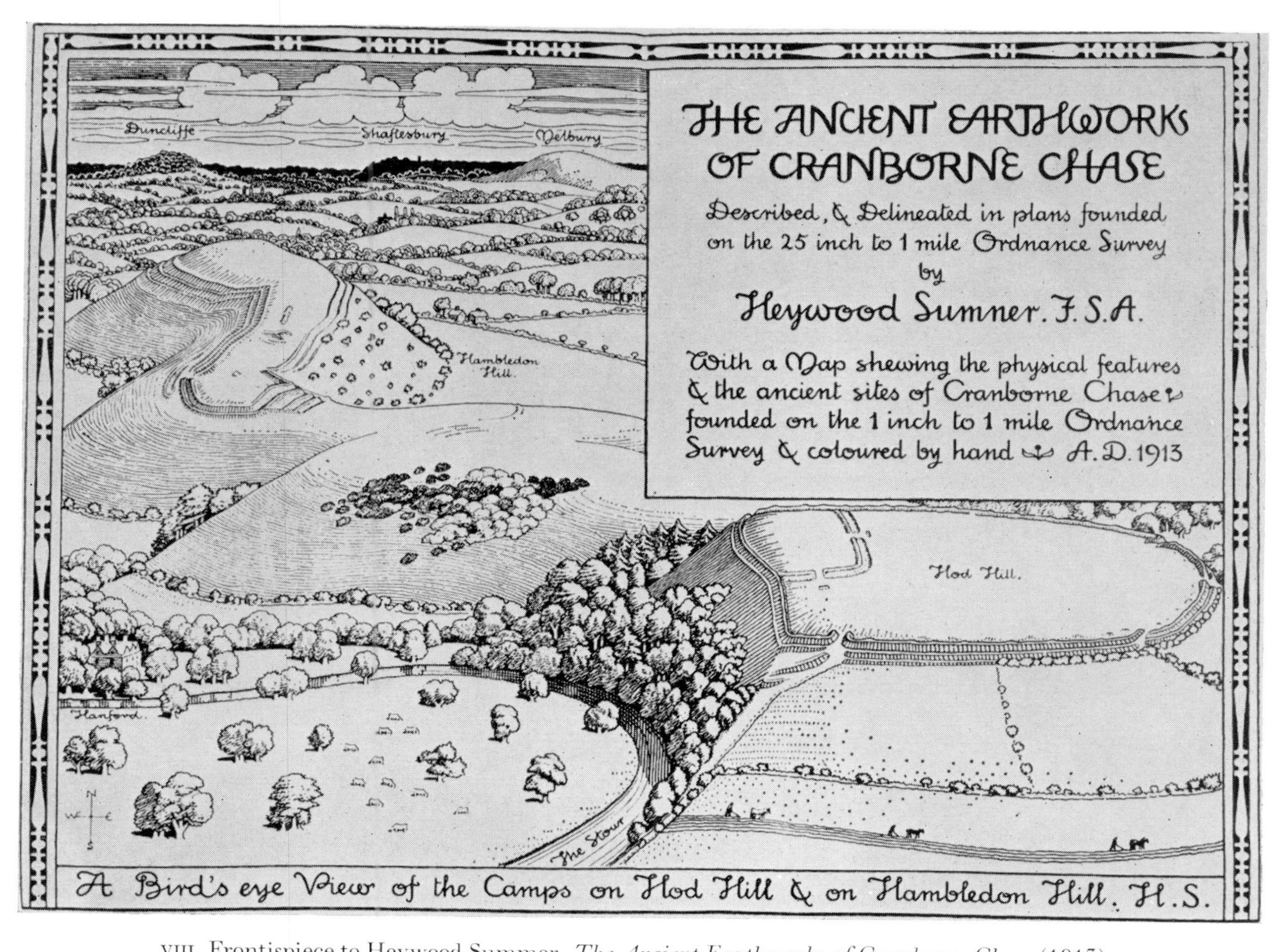

VIII. Frontispiece to Heywood Summer, *The Ancient Earthworks of Cranborne Chase* (1913).

a late breakfast, and then spending the next few days on Salisbury Plain. The value of his industry and percipience is certainly appreciated by archaeologists in north Somerset, his home-ground, and his journals, now in the British Museum, would undoubtedly repay critical publication even though his interests were extraordinarily diverse.

In the nineteenth century, as before and since, field archaeological endeavour, in terms of descriptive work or cartography, is depicted in the efforts of individuals. At the same time a new development was taking place, the formation of the institution. Enthusiasts from the semi-leisured middle classes, mobile on the new railways whose very construction had thrown up a spate of antiquities, formed themselves into all sorts of archaeological, antiquarian and publishing societies, both national and local. The activities of such societies are an integral part of the comprehensive development of archaeology in its every aspect, and some cognisance of field monuments was a feature of these activities.

Already by 1820, George Petrie (Stokes, 1868) was an established painter and draughtsman. From this time onwards, following his walk down the eastern bank of the Shannon, he had succumbed to the spell of the green countryside of raths and ivy-clad ruins. In 1833 he received the gold medal of the Royal Irish Academy for his work on round towers. The great government-sponsored and state-supported *Ordnance Topographical Survey of Ireland*, with which he became connected in that year, provided a perfect channel for his field interests. His greatest achievement in terms of field archaeology was the 'Essay on the Antiquities of Tara', presented to the Academy in 1837 and published in its *Transactions* (vol 18). This was intended to form part of the Ordnance *Memoir* for the county of Meath. Petrie collected around him a team of Irish scholars, forming a school of archaeology which produced such men as Clarence Mangan, John O'Donovan and Eugene O'Curry. Geology and natural history were directed by Captain Portlock, the local and statistical enquiries were the responsibility of Captain Dawson, archaeology was held firmly in the hands of George Petrie, while the enterprise was directed by Captain Thomas Aiskew Larcom. Another aspect of the undertaking envisaged the identification of the correct names of baronies, townlands and parishes throughout the country. Its field archaeological policy required the investigation of all existing monuments, earthwork systems, raths, chamber tombs, barrows and such early Christian remains as bee-hive houses, oratories, churches, towers, crosses and monumental stones as well as the later medieval castles and abbeys. The first volume of the Ordnance *Memoir*, covering County Derry, was published in 1839 and was regrettably the last. Governmental economy was the public explanation. This far-sighted scheme in Ireland anticipated the work carried out by disparate government departments in both England and Ireland today. By his efforts, Petrie laid the foundation for scientific field archaeology in Ireland.

Meanwhile in Dorset, Charles Warne, better known for his *Celtic Tumuli* (Warne, 1866), produced in 1865 his *Illustrated Map of Dorsetshire, its vestiges, Celtic, Roman, Saxon and Danish,* with *An Index of the Illustrated Map.* The index classified the sites, represented in different colours on the map, thus forming a useful statement of sites and earthworks then known. In Wiltshire, the Rev A. C. Smith, rector of Yatesbury, laboured for thirty years to produce his *Map of one hundred square miles round Abury*, the area that he could reach on horse back. This was published as *Guide to the British and Roman Antiquities of the North Wiltshire Downs*, by the Marlborough College Natural History Society in 1884. Smith enlarged the one-inch Ordnance Survey Map adding field names, and including additional earthworks, many of which are no longer visible. Unfortunately his omission of contour lines and field boundaries makes these maps of limited general value.

It is apposite to observe at this point that Thurnam and Greenwell were both in some measure field archaeologists as well as excavators. A compilation of the period, James Fergusson's *Rude Stone Monuments* (1872), does not appear to be based entirely upon fieldwork but is notable as a synthesis, upon a near-global scale, of a single class of field monument. He enters a plea (1872, x,fn) for a 'Megalithic Monument Publication Committee'. It would seem that, after the meeting of the Prehistoric Congress at Norwich in 1868, a committee for this purpose was formed which only foundered for lack of funds. Activities approximating to field archaeology appear also to have had a certain vogue at Oxford in the 1870s. H. J. Randall (1936, 9–15) makes mention of the activities of Freeman, Stubbs and Green, all historians of note, while Edwin Guest, known for his 'Early English Settlements in South Britain' in the Salisbury volume of the *Proceedings of the Archaeological Institute*, habitually explored the countryside, often 'with half the village in company.' Flinders Petrie, whose early essays in British field archaeology have been entirely overshadowed by his later distinction as an Egyptologist, exhibited at the Hereford meeting of the Royal Archaeological Institute, in 1877, a classified collection of thirty-six plans of British earthworks. In 1880 he laid the foundation for future research at Stonehenge (Atkinson, 1956, 192–3) by the publication of his monograph *Stonehenge; Plans, Descriptions and Theories.* This contains the most accurate plan of the monument ever likely to be made, on a scale which compels the use of a powerful lens, and introduces the system of stone numeration still in use. Wheeler (1953, 91) recalls how Petrie once visited him and spent some of his time surveying stone circles and other monuments. His instruments were a single slender bamboo pea-stick supplemented by a visiting-card: the stick gave him a line, the card a right-angle. Then at the end of the day he would reduce the contents of his notebook, aided by logarithmic tables, into a schematic diagram.

George Backhouse Witts, a civil engineer who carried out the construction of the railway which crosses the heart of the Cotswolds, published his *Archaeological Handbook of Gloucestershire* in 1883. This, by its coloured map, enumerated camps, Roman villas, long and round barrows, as well as British and Roman roads. His archaeology was couched in terms of field monuments, plans and maps, and indeed, his 1897 Presidential Address to the Bristol and Gloucestershire Archaeological Society, on the 'Ancient British Occupation of the Cotswold Hills', was delivered with a map suspended before the audience. Notwithstanding inevitable shortcomings, L. V. Grinsell (1960) was able to employ the listed barrows as a basis for his work on the county.

In 1878 a Barrow Committee, under the aegis of the Devonshire Association for the Advancement of Science, was set up, its secretary and steersman to the end of the century being R. Nigel Worth. His son, R. Hansford Worth succeeded him as secretary and carried on his work to the middle of this century (Spooner and Russell, 1953). Their sixty-nine *Barrow Reports*, plus papers on other monuments, portray Dartmoor upon a detailed basis unparalleled elsewhere until recently. Hansford Worth concentrated entirely upon the recording of observable features, avoiding speculation in the endeavour to eliminate the personal factor. Something of the potential of such fieldwork can be seen in an article on the Bronze Age Monuments of Dartmoor (Brailsford, 1938), where an attempt is made to correlate the material of that period.

General Pitt-Rivers is well known for his excavations and is not normally discussed in terms of field archaeology. Born in 1827, Augustus Henry Lane-Fox combined a distinguished military career with the practice of anthropology. In 1880 he inherited the Rivers's Rushmere estates, which entailed the surname change to Pitt-Rivers, and, following his life pattern, he thereupon began work upon the many barrows and earthworks on his own land. He retired from the army as Lt.-General in 1882 and devoted himelf to these labours almost to his death in 1900. *Excavations in Cranborne Chase* (1887–98), splendidly bound in blue and gold, recorded the results of his disciplined digging. Fieldwork, models of sites before excavation and maps, form a prelude to his detailed presentation, while his written works (Lane-Fox, 1869) reveal how he thought in terms of topographical factors (Pl VII), that is the archaeology of an area as distinct from isolated sites. M. W. Thompson (1960) has shown us something of the general as a field archaeologist at work. The title 'Inspector of Ancient Monuments in Great Britain', held by him from 1 January 1883 onwards, and used on the title-page of *Excavations*, was created by the Ancient Monuments Protection Act of 1882. Sixteen notebooks and sketchbooks, now preserved in the working records of the Inspectorate of Ancient Monuments, give details of his fieldwork in Brittany (1878–9) and tours of inspection (1883–90). The details of the sites in these notebooks are of particular importance for the earlier field archaeology of the highland regions, as this act excluded mediaeval monuments, and thus the terms of reference were largely prehistoric.

In the meantime William Copeland Borlase, the great-great-grandson of William Borlase, had become interested in the chamber tombs of Ireland. He was urged on by Max Müller of Trinity College and from 1887 onwards he explored, in summer time, region after region, visiting sites and making plans and sketches. The results of his fieldwork, together with notices of all previous literature, names and legends, anthropology and ethnology, were set down in three sumptuous green-bond volumes, bedecked with motifs culled from Lough Crew's passage graves. These books were dedicated to Sir John Lubbock, who had secured the passage of the Ancient Monuments Protection Act, and whose significant *Prehistoric Times, as Illustrated by Ancient Remains, and the Manners and Customs of Modern Savages* had appeared for the first time in 1865. Borlase's *Dolmens of Ireland* (1897) has, as de Valéra (1961, xi) stressed, served Irish megalithic studies well, for its scope has made possible the significant advances that have marked the last three decades of this century.

The emergence of archaeological societies during the nineteenth century (Haverfield, 1924, 82; Daniel, 1950, 113–4; Evans, 1951, 1; 1952, 1; 1956; 164) is a movement which has never been studied as a whole, although centenary and other volumes (Salzman, 1946; Jessup, 1956) detail, often in an intimate and entertaining fashion, their early fortunes. As a result of their activities, the Congress of Archaeological Societies (O'Neil, 1946) held its first meeting in 1889 and issued reports almost annually until 1939. Its principal and most faithful branch was the Earthworks Committee which effectively began in 1907 with a committee consisting of Professor Bertram Windle, I. Chalkley Gould, J. H. Round, W. St. J. Hope and W. M. Tapp, with power to co-opt to their number. A 'Provisional Scheme' and a 'Hints for Helpers' were issued and revised, and the classification there set out was used by the compilers of Victoria County Histories and others. The Committee's primary aim was the coordination of field research, and to this end it continued with its reports and publications, to the day of the Congress's dissolution and the formation of the Council for British Archaeology in 1945.

This Earthworks Committee depended ultimately upon spontaneous response from individuals, and this was forthcoming in various ways. In 1908, Hadrian Allcroft's monumental *Earthwork of England* appeared. He had collected a mass of material and he set it out in the categories proposed by the committee. It became a standard work and was adopted as a handbook by the Royal Commissions on Ancient and Historical Monuments, which began investigations in that year. Allcroft (1908, 8) lamented the English indifference to his subject and at the same time emphasised the vastness of the problems that lay ahead. Heywood Sumner's earthwork surveys, of Cranborne Chase (1913) and the New Forest (1917), stated that they were a result of the Committee's appeal for regional surveys. His distinctive artistic style—he was a product of the Pre-Raphaelite movement and a friend of William Morris— expressed in his maps and plans (Pl VIII), has had a far-reaching effect upon archaeological draughtsmanship (Piggott, 1965). With J. P. Williams-Freeman (1915), who carried out his work for his county society using the Committee's earthwork schedule, and who coined the very term 'field archaeology', we are upon the threshold of our own age and within the lifetimes of many of our teachers. O. G. S. Crawford (1953, 45) considered that the modern phase of field archaeology began with the Earthworks Committee, and that the growth of interest was cumulative and rapid, while stressing that he owed his own early interest to encouragement from Williams-Freeman and books such as *Earthwork of England*. All this has been inimitably recounted in his autobiography (Crawford, 1955, 76–7).

These heroic days when the century was very young saw, as side aspects of field archaeology expressed in earthworks, two minor movements. A pot-pourri of minor romantics and fervent flinters was recalled by Stuart Piggott (1963, 3–4) in his Presidential Address to the Prehistoric Society. It might be said that something of the deeper, more mystical, radix of the first seems to have been in Sussex. There, beneath an ever-shining sun, somewhere by Storrington, with the Meynells in residence, Francis Thompson at the priory and Sally gone from Ha'nacker Mill, the 'Catholic men that live upon wine' found qualities in 'the line of the Downs so noble and bare.' Arthur Beckett distilled the essence of the heady mixture in his *Spirit of the Downs* (1928) but its potency had already taken Hilaire Belloc by a not too Chestertonian route along *The Old Road* (the Pilgrim's Way) in 1904. From here Stuart Piggott has led us through these early days, by ancient and devious ways, to that *Chalk Country* (Massingham, 1936) which, between the wars, cradled much of our fieldwork. The fervent flinters banded together in 1908 to found the *Prehistoric Society of East Anglia*, and their activities, not entirely divorced from field monuments, are exemplified by W. G. Clarke's *Our Homeland Prehistoric Antiquities and how to study them* (1922) which indexes everything from anvils and arrow points to tortoise cores and truncated flakes. This particular pursuit, the results of which choke our museum vaults, had positive results from time to time. For example, the attention of H. G. O. Kendall of Winterbourne Bassett was drawn to Windmill Hill (Smith, 1965, 1) because of the quantity and variety of the flints that could be found on and about that hill.

O. G. S. Crawford modestly looked to an earlier period for the inception of the modern phase of field archaeology. For my generation it all began in October, 1920, when he joined the Ordnance Survey, to be confronted with an empty room and a table; the chair he stole from the library opposite (Crawford, 1955, 155). As Archaeology Officer, Ordnance Survey, he brought a trained and critical mind to the problems of monuments and maps, the fundamentals of field archaeology. There he produced *Professional Papers* and *Period Maps*, at the same time founding the quarterly journal *Antiquity*, from its inception a forum for ideas and discovery on a global basis. As a student at Oxford he had developed a firm sense of the part played by the environment in matters relating to man and his past. He recognised that the living landscape preserved a palimpsest of that past, and it was while flying in the First World War that he saw how air photography had to be an essential part of such archaeological field studies. His books and publications in *Antiquity* and elsewhere (Grimes, 1951, 382–6) reflect field archaeology expressed in these various dimensions. Indeed, his contributions to knowledge and method are such that they have become part of the fabric of present-day archaeology in its broadest sense. The danger is, perhaps, that their nascence and originality will not always be fully appreciated by those who have grown up to take them for granted.

Crawford, in his best-known account of air-photography (Crawford and Keiller, 1928), insisted that its first actual application to archaeology was by Col. Beazeley, R. E., who published an account in 1919 (Beazeley, 1919). Following the detection of 'Celtic' fields on air-photographs taken near Winchester, Crawford was able to map the system which, after a lecture delivered to the Royal Geographical Society setting out the principles of air-photography as applied to archaeology, he published in the *Geographical Journal* for May 1923, and reprinted in *Air Survey and Archaeology* (Crawford, 1924; 1928). A second Ordnance Survey Professional Paper, *Air Photography for Archaeologists*, was published in 1929. *Wessex from the Air* (Crawford and Keiller, 1928) resulted from Alexander Keiller's (Piggott, 1965) interest in Crawford's presentation of some of the early results of the then new and novel technique in the *Observer*. Initially Keiller anticipated the concept of overall coverage, offering to finance an air survey of Britain, and, at a later stage, even considered undertaking a such survey from the gondola of Eckener's 'Graf Zeppelin'. However, with the aid of a captured German camera. *Wessex from the Air* was begun. Crawford (1955, 172) tells of the wet summer when the sorties were flown, and considered that some of the sites were of minor importance. Notwithstanding, this book and the pattern of publication of air-photography of such sites as Woodhenge, Arminghall and many others in the pages of *Antiquity*, set the stage for all that was to follow. On the eve of the last war, Crawford, considering much of his early work out of date, allowed, after a lecture in Berlin, the publication of *Luftbild und Vorgeschichte* by Lufthansa to go forward. This particular compilation included German sites which could be scrutinised with the tinted stereoscopic spectacles which were issued with it.

Perusal of *Wessex from the Air* led Major G. W. G. Allen to emulate and develop its principles. Between 1933 and 1939, flying alone in his own aircraft, he took some two thousand air-photographs of sites in southern England. He stressed the value of oblique air-photographs, and his shots of Maiden Castle (Wheeler, 1943, *passim*) and other sites (Clark, 1941, *passim*) show the measure of this dimension. After his tragic death in 1940 his collection passed to the University of Oxford and thence to the Ashmolean Museum. The photographs were on exhibition at the end of 1948, and a summary catalogue was issued by the Museum. Following a footnote (Bradford, 1957, 4) hopes were entertained for the publication of this collection as a book to be entitled *Discovery from the Air*, for O. G. S. Crawford had set Allen's draft into order, but to date the proposal remains that footnote.

As in all matters of technology, the exigencies of war instigated advances in air-photography. These were threefold. The first is the concept of overall cover of an area, or for that matter the entire country. Indeed, as far as we are concerned, such cover now exists in large measure for our islands (Phillips, 1963, 6). The second is the general acceptance of air-photography as an essential to field archaeology, and not merely an adjunct. The third is that which was heralded by Crawford's *Luftbild and Vorgeschichte*, an appreciation of stereoscopic examination as a part of the scrutiny and usage of overlapping prints.

This military experience was put to service in the brave new post-war world. D. N. Riley (1944) detailed the geological and agricultural factors implicit in optimism result. John Bradford (1957) set out the principles of practice and purpose, buttressing his considerations with a wealth of material from Italy. At the same time, Dr J. K. S. St Joseph, now Director in Aerial Photography in the University of Cambridge, was furthering techniques, finding new sites and formulating fresh aspects of old ones, while building up a formidable collection. Since 1945 he has published numerous papers, reporting upon the progress of his work which has covered a broad time-span, while his most recent achievement is the publication of the striking results of his sorties over Ireland (Norman and St. Joseph, 1969). In the last few years a proliferation of private flying has resulted in intensive studies of specific regions (e.g. Webster and Hobley, 1964), and the beginnings of a comprehensive collection in the National Monuments Record.

An Archaeology Officer at the Ordnance Survey was the watershed between the old world and the new. For, as Stuart Piggott (1963, 5) has recounted, the middle 1930s contained the recognisable elements of the present-day archaeological scene. Something sterner than downland mysticism had been astir in Sussex and can be seen in the contents of the first issue of the *Brighton & Hove Archaeologist*, published in 1914 and continued in subsequent issues. Nowhere is this more explicit than in E. Cecil Curwen's *Prehistoric Sussex* (1929) with its striking air-photographs and Robert Gurd's plans and maps, as well as a chapter upon the detection and mapping of earthworks. Indeed, it was in *Sussex Notes and Queries* that Leslie Grinsell published his first barrow paper (1930), on the *Sussex Bell-Barrows*, although *Surrey Archaeological Collections* saw the first of his formidable barrow surveys (Grinsell, 1932).

Sir Cyril Fox's geographical study of prehistory, *The Archaeology of the Cambridge Region* (1923, 1949), strikes back to the *Steppenheide theorie* set out by Schliz (Daniel, 1963, 8); the area chosen involved the distance of a comfortable cycle-ride from his base, for field monuments were a part of the scheme. This led to the *Personality of Britain*, initially a lecture to the first International Congress of Pre- and Proto-historic Sciences held in London during August, 1932 (London, 1934, 27–9) and then published by the National Museum of Wales as an illustrated monograph. Crawford had already discussed and demonstrated the function of the distribution map, it was Fox, with a wealth of data processed by Miss L. F. Chitty, who exploited this medium as never before. Side by side with his developing geographical considerations, Sir Cyril must be always remembered for his field archaeological studies of linear earthworks, the Cambridgeshire dykes (Fox, 1923, 1925, 1926), Offa's Dyke and Wansdyke (Fox, A & C. F., 1958). The sectional reports on Offa's Dyke, initially published in *Archaeologia Cambrensis*, were collected together and issued as a British Academy monograph (Fox, 1955). His unparalleled experience of the dimensional problems pertaining to such works lay behind the Society of Antiquaries recommendations for research upon them (Fox, O'Neil and Grimes, 1946), and all who have wrestled with their quirks and paradoxes are indebted to him.

It may seem almost invidious to select and cite work illustrative of the progress of field archaeology during the 1930s, for during that decade so much was achieved by so many. During the later 1920s H. O'Neil Hencken worked in Cornwall and the Isle of Scilly compiling a reasoned statement of their archaeology from monuments as well as the material available in museums and publications. The subject had been suggested by O. G. S. Crawford who had previously visited the Isles of Scilly: the first paper in the first issue of *Antiquity* had been entitled 'Lyonesse', treating the problems of monuments and marine transgressions. As well as this, he had spent considerable time in making plans of the characteristic chamber tombs. Hencken's initial study was undertaken as a Cambridge doctoral dissertation but subsequently it matured to become *The Archaeology of Cornwall & Scilly* (1932), in Methuen's *County Archaeology* series, progeny of the *Victoria County Histories*. No serious work can be conducted in the region without reference to it.

A long barrow in Lincolnshire had been suspected, following O. G. S. Crawford's revision of the relevant Ordnance Survey sheets in 1924. C. W. Phillips undertook a revision of Lincolnshire antiquities on the 6-inch sheets in the autumn of 1929 and was able to add no fewer than nine examples of long barrows (Phillips, 1933, 1934). Further work led to 'The Present State of Archaeology in Lincolnshire', in which the results of fieldwork, material in museums and literature were dovetailed into a detailed account of this distinctive region. During the 1930s W. F. Grimes (1936, 1963) carried out his field-survey of megalithic monuments in Wales, following the proposals of the British Association Megalithic Committee (the Research Committee on Rude Stone Monuments). In common with C. W. Phillips's Ordnance Survey *Map of the Trent Basin*, the South Wales portion of Grimes's survey was employed in the compilation of the *Map of South Wales showing the Distribution of Long Barrows and Megaliths*, and both were envisaged by Crawford as forerunners of a general 'period map' of Neolithic Britain (Grimes, 1963, 94). Between 1933 and 1940 Glyn Daniel carried out his field survey, listing all the known and alleged stone-built burial chambers in southern Britain, together with their documentation and the material from them preserved in numerous museums. Aspects of the work were published in various journals, but the full range was only set out in his *Prehistoric Chamber Tombs of England and Wales* (Daniel, 1950).

During the 1930s of course, Leslie Grinsell continued his work on barrows. Indeed, by the outbreak of war he had studied not only those of Surrey (Grinsell, 1932, 1934a) and Sussex (Grinsell, 1934b), but also those of Berkshire (Grinsell, 1935), Hampshire (Grinsell, 1938–40) and the Isle of Wight (Grinsell and Sherwin, 1940), as well as aspects of Wiltshire (Grinsell, 1934c, 1941) and Somerset (Grinsell, 1939). In addition he had produced the first edition of the now classic *Ancient Burial-Mounds of England* (1936) with its wise words on the use of maps and fieldwork. Yet it should be remembered that all the fieldwork involved in these prodigious detailed area surveys was carried out on foot. Mention must also be made of Sir Mortimer Wheeler's (1957) eve-of-war task-force foray into France in search of hill-forts. This appropriately brought to an end the decade which began with C. F. C. Hawkes's (1931) article on 'Hill-forts' in *Antiquity*, to be given greater precision a year later (Kendrick and Hawkes, 1932, 161–7): the momentous decade which saw the birth of a concept of the Iron Age, which has until recently held the field.

It may be premature to attempt any assessment of field archaeology in the post-war period. However, it is possible to suggest certain patterns and trends. While individual work has continued with brilliant results, there has also been seen the development of institutional field archaeology through the appointment to state bodies, the Ordnance Survey, the Royal Commissions on Ancient and Historical Monuments and the Inspectorate of Ancient Monuments, of field archaeologists to carry out detailed fieldwork appropriate to their various objectives. On another front learned societies bring combined and critical views to the monuments of specific regions. A further development has been the sophistication of so-called scientific aids. All this is being enacted against a backcloth of progressive destruction on an unprecedented scale, coupled with the uneasy realization that our overall palimpsest of sites and monuments is more dense than had ever been dreamed.

In terms of the individual contributions which result from, or stimulate, fieldwork or field archaeology, we must look first of all to L. V. Grinsell's work in Wiltshire, the great *Victoria County History Vol. I, Pt. I.* This led to his refreshing and realistic *Archaeology of Wessex* (1958), while continuing his barrow study of Dorset (1959), Gloucestershire (O'Neil and Grinsell, 1960), Somerset (Grinsell, 1969a, 1971) and North Devon (Grinsell, 1969b). Roman roads, both major and minor, have been the subject of search for at least two centuries. In recent years the problems of field determination and authentication have been approached afresh by I. D. Margary (1950, 1967). Ancient fields, a subject for observation, record and discussion since the days of Stukeley, have been the subject of an analysis by H. C. Bowen (1961), following the formation of a British Association Research Committee in 1958. S. P. Ó'Ríordáin's *Antiquities of the Irish Countryside* (1953) put the field archaeological potential of Ireland on paper as never before and established traditions which have gone from strength to strength. *A Guide to the Prehistoric & Roman Monuments in England & Wales* (Hawkes, 1951) followed by *Guides* to *Prehistoric England* (Thomas, 1960), *Scotland* (Feacham, 1963) and *Ireland* (Killainin and Duignan, 1962; Evans, 1966) have taken their place as basic aids to field archaeology, allowing rapid identification and location of principal monuments in unfamiliar terrains. Progress towards the full publication of some of the basic evidence for British prehistory has been made by the first volume of *The Chambered Tombs of Scotland* (Henshall, 1963). The precision of this work will allow for the first time an assessment which takes into consideration all the available material. A similar policy has been pursued by the *Megalithic Survey* of the Ordnance Survey in Ireland. Volumes treating *County Clare* (de Valéra and Ó'Nuálláin, 1960) and *County Mayo* (de Valéra and Ó'Nuállián, 1964) have been issued, and another covering the northern midland counties is in preparation. Something of the advances made possible by the detailed documentation of all aspects of chamber tomb research can be seen in *Megalithic Enquiries in the West of Britain* (Powell *et al* 1969).

The Archaeology Division of the Ordnance Survey, steered since the war and until recently by C. W. Phillips, has made and kept up to date as full a record as possible of the topography of British archaeology. To this end it has issued the modestly titled *Field Archaeology, some notes for beginners* (1963). This work is perhaps the most detailed textbook on the problems inherent in the field archaeology of all periods. At about the same time a fresh start has been made with prehistoric period maps by the publication of the *Map of Southern Britain in the Iron Age* (1962). It is perhaps not too much to say that the pre-eminence of this country in matters of field archaeology, a happy state of affairs which today is nearly taken for granted, is due to the Ordnance Survey and its succession of distinguished Archaeology Officers. Something of the superlative quality of the fieldwork carried out in Dorset for the Royal Commission on Historical Monuments (England), building on the foundations laid in particular by Warne, Hutchins, Shipp and Grinsell, was seen on the occasion of the Prehistoric Society's Dorset Conference in 1962. The results for the south of the county have now been magnificently published (RCHM, 1970). Further undertakings are current in Wiltshire, Cambridgeshire, Yorkshire and the Cotswolds at the time of writing, and the Scottish and Welsh Commissions are similarly and invaluably active. The several staffs are at the forefront of their subject, but the slow pace of official publication bedevils their efforts. Here one can add little to the comments made a decade ago (Ashbee, 1960, 198). Field archaeology in the broadest sense is the basic business of the Inspectorate of Ancient Monuments as it applies itself to the monuments in its charge. Largely unsung and often trenchantly criticized, its corporate effort can be evaluated by the discerning in terms of the quality of the publications by its officials.

Since their earliest days some learned societies, both regional and national, have held meetings to study specific regions. This particular aspect of field archaeology is now perhaps best illustrated by the summer meetings of the Prehistoric Society which, since the war, has met in various regions in conjunction with local societies, to the advantage of both. The *Guides*, delineating the details of monuments, are now a formidable series demonstrating the essence of the field archaeology of each region visited.

The scientific aids to field processes which, in recent times, have won a measure of usage, are either methods of magnetic location (Aitkin, 1961, 7–59) or resistivity surveying (Aitkin, 1961, 60–78). Soil resistivity measurement has been an integral aid to geology and civil engineering since the First World War, but its first archaeological application was to the location of ditches and pits at Dorchester-on-Thames (Atkinson *et al* 1951, 4; 1953, 31–9) which were clearly visible from the air but not convenient from any particular point of reference on the ground. The method, because of ideal conditions, met with considerable success. Even within the restricted ambit of field aids there has, during the past decade, been rapid refinement coupled with ever more sophisticated usages. The inbuilt and nettle danger is that the proliferation of scientific methodology can become and end in itself and the ultimate objectives of archaeology lost to sight (Hawkes, J., 1968).

Controlled experiment, however, designed to record with precision the processes of change and decay of earthworks, is another recent innovation in field archaeology. In 1960 a ditch was dug, and a bank constructed, on the chalk of Overton Down, in Wiltshire (Jewell, 1963), simulating a simple prehistoric earthwork. During the past decade the denudation of the bank and the silting of the ditch have been periodically observed and excavated. Much has emerged already which can be brought to bear upon comparable field situations (Jewell and Dimbleby, 1966). In this context it is apposite to recall that two similar experiments, designed to elucidate field archaeological phenomena, took place in Scotland during 1937. Here certain forts had long been known, the ramparts of which could be seen as stones fused together to form a solid mass. These *vitrified forts* seemingly resulted from the burning of timber-laced stone walls. To test this hypothesis, Professor V. G. Childe and Wallace Thorneycroft (1938) had built sections of such walls and fired them, producing a scaled but successful version of the field phenomenon.

This essay is subjective in that it has involved the selection of individual achievements, conclusions and trends which, conjoined and in their entirety, comprise the entity that we can term the development of field archaeology. Inevitably, any conclusions will undoubtedly share that subjectivity. Notwithstanding, these have a certain validity, even if only to serve as a spur to deeper insight and more detailed discriminations.

One possible general pattern that emerges could be termed the *primus inter pares* principle, that is to say that almost every advance in method and knowledge has been the result of the enterprise of particular persons who have then stimulated others to work along the same lines. It may be said that, from Camden to Crawford, before and beyond, this canon obtains, for they, and others like them, modified beyond all measure ideas previously held, and gave new direction to field archaeology. Only detailed research can resolve the mechanism of the infinite inherent cross-currents involved.

Another prominent pattern is the relationship of developing field archaeology to the shifting emphasis of the thought and purpose (Collingwood, 1951, 309–15) of the day. Something of the factors involved in such a process has already been noted. Leland's vocation was that of the 'Elizabethan Discovery of England' described so sensitively by A. L. Rowse (1951, 31–65), while Camden wanted to give England its place in the councils of Europe. In Aubrey, Lhuyd, Stukeley, striding busy by Avebury's stones, and Roy, we sense that application of nascent scientific order combined with empiricism, the qualities inherent in the embryo Royal Society which numbered antiquaries in its ranks (Evans, 1956, 26). Colt Hoare's fieldwork was an aspect of his melancholy and many-faceted life with its detail and discipline setting it firmly beside that of his scientific predecessors earlier in the eighteenth century. He spoke 'from facts not theory', yet, leavening his melancholia and adorning his first great folio, there is a tinge of contemporary romanticism (Piggott, 1937, 36): beads and arrowheads festoon an archaistic *Auncient Wiltescire* on his title-page. In Pitt-Rivers we see evolutionary order as expressed in the parallel work of Darwin and Huxley, while with Williams-Freeman and the beginning of our own century we still sense something of a more spacious and leisurely age, lingering on the threshold of things to come. It was O. G. S. Crawford and the application of air-photography to field archaeology that epitomized the century of World Wars and revolutions. Albeit on a broader front, it fell to Gordon Childe, in the dimension of his *Dawn* and *Danube*, to shake us from that insidious insular torpor that still stultifies certain limbs of the body politic. Field archaeology in this tradition developed in the decade of the 1930s, that depressed economic and political prologue to catastrophe, and into the present era of exploitation and consumption. The dilemmas encountered in field archaeology are bound up with the fate of England's 'green and pleasant land'.

REFERENCES

Aitken, M. J., 1961. *Physics and Archaeology* (New York).

Alcock, L., 1967–70. 'A Reconnaissance Excavation at South Cadbury Castle, Somerset, 1968; *Antiq. J.* **47** (1967), 70–76; 'Excavations at South Cadbury Castle, 1967,' *Antiq. J.* **48** (1968), 6–17; 'Excavations at South Cadbury Castle, 1968,' *Antiq. J.* **49**, (1969), 30–40; 'Excavations at South Cadbury Castle, 1969,' *Antiq. J.* **49** (1970), 14–25.

Allcroft, A. H., 1908. *Earthwork of England* (London).

Ashbee, P., 1960. *The Bronze Age Round Barrow in Britain* (London).

Atkinson, R. J. C., 1953. *Field Archaeology* (London).
1956. *Stonehenge* (London). *et al*, 1951. *Excavations at Dorchester, Oxon*, Oxford, 1951.

Beazeley, G. A., 1919. 'Air Photography in Archaeology', *Geogr. J.* **53**, 330–335.

Beckett, A., 1928. *The Spirit of the Downs* (London).

Borlase, W., 1756. *Observations on the Ancient and Present State of the Islands of Scilly* (Oxford).

Borlase, W. C., 1897. *The Dolmens of Ireland, their distribution, structural characteristics and affinities in other countries; together with the folk-love attaching to them; supplemented by considerations on the anthropology, ethnology and traditions of the Irish People* (London).

Bowen, H. C., 1961. *Ancient Fields* (British Association for the Advancement of Science, London).

Bradford, J., 1957. *Ancient Landscapes, Studies in Field Archaeology* (London).

Brailsford, J. W., 1938. 'Bronze Age Stone Monuments of Dartmoor', *Antiquity* **12**, 444–463.

Campbell, J. L. and Thomson, D. (Eds.), 1963. *Edward Lhuyd in the Scottish Highlands*, 1699–1700 (Oxford).

Childe, V. G. and Thorneycroft, W., 1938. 'The Experimental Production of the Phenomena Distinctive of Vitrified Forts', *Proc. Soc. Antiq. Scotland* **72**, 44–55.

Clark, G., 1941. *Prehistoric England* (London).

Clark, K., 1964. *The Gothic Revival* (Harmondsworth).

Coffey, G., 1912. *New Grange and Other Incised Tumuli in Ireland* (Dublin and London).

Collingwood, R. G., 1951. *The Idea of History* (Oxford).

Colt Hoare, R., 1810. *The History of Ancient Wiltshire, Part I* (London).
1819. *The Ancient History of North Wiltshire* (London).

Coombs, H. and Bax, A. N. (Eds.), 1930. *Journal of a Somerset Rector* (London).

Crawford, O. G. S., 1924, 1928. *Air Survey and Archaeology* (Ordnance Survey Professional Papers, New Series No. 7. Southampton, 1924, second ed., 1928).
1925. *The Long Barrows of the Cotswolds* (Gloucester).
1949. *Topography of Roman Scotland* (Cambridge)
1953. *Archaeology in the Field* (London).
1955. *Said and Done, The Autobiography of an Archaeologist* (London).

Crawford, O. G. S. and Keiller, A., 1928. *Wessex from the Air* (Oxford).

Daniel, G. E., 1950a. *A Hundred Years of Archaeology* (London).
1950b. *The Prehistoric Chamber Tombs of England and Wales* (Cambridge).
1954. 'Who are the Welsh?', *Proc. Brit. Acad.* **40**, 145–167.
1960. *The Prehistoric Chamber Tombs of France* (London).

1963. 'The Personality of Wales', in Foster, I.Ll. and Alcock, L. (eds.), *Culture and Environment, Essays in Honour of Sir Cyril Fox* (London).
1966. 'Edward Llwyd: Antiquary and Archaeologist', *Welsh Hist. Rev.* **3**, 345–59.
1967. *The Origins and Growth of Archaeology* (Harmondsworth).

De Valera, R. and Ó'Nuálláin, S., 1960. *Survey of the Megalithic Tombs of Ireland, Vol. I, County Clare* (Dublin).
1964. *Survey of the Megalithic Tombs of Ireland, Vol. II, County Mayo* (Dublin).

Douglas, D. C., 1939. *English Scholars* (London).

Evans, E. E., 1966. *Prehistoric and Early Christian Ireland, A Guide* (London).

Evans, J., 1864. *The Coins of the Ancient Britons* (London).

Evans, Joan, 1951. 'The Royal Archaeological Institute; A Retrospect', *Archaeol. J.* **106**, 1–11.
1952. 'Archaeology in 1851', *Archaeol. J.* **107**, 1–8.
1956. *A History of The Society of Antiquaries* (London).

Feacham, R., 1963. *A Guide to Prehistoric Scotland* (London).

Fergusson, J., 1872. *Rude Stone Monuments in all Countries; Their Age and Uses* (London).

Fox, A. and C. F., 1958. 'Wansdyke Reconsidered', *Archaeol. J.*, **115**, 1–48.

Fox, C. F., 1923. 'Excavations in the Cambridgeshire Dykes, I,' *Cambridge Antiq. Soc. Comn.* **24**, 21–53.
1925. 'Excavations in the Cambridgeshire Dykes, IV,' *Cambridge Antiq. Soc. Comn.* **26**, 90–129.
With Palmer, W. M., 1926. 'Excavations in the Cambridgeshire Dykes, V,' *Cambridge Antiq. Soc. Comn.* **27**, 16–35.
1943. 'A Beaker Barrow, enlarged in the Middle Bronze Age, at South Hill, Talbenny, Pembrokeshire', *Archaeol. J.* **94**, 1–32.
1955. *Offa's Dyke, a field survey of the Western Frontier-works of Mercia in the 7th and 8th Centuries* (Oxford).

Fox, L. (ed.), 1956. *English Historical Scholarship in the Sixteenth and Seventeenth Centuries* (Dugdale Soc., Oxford).

Fussner, E. Smith, 1962. *The Historical Revolution* (London).

Graham, F., 1966. *Description of Cornwall by John Norden* (London 1728, reprinted F. Graham, 1966).

Grimes, W. F., 1936. 'The Megalithic Monuments of Wales,' *Proc. Prehist. Soc.* **2**, 106–39.
(ed.) 1951. *Aspects of Archaeology in Britain and Beyond. Essays presented to O. G. S. Crawford* (London).
1963. 'The Stone Circles and Related Monuments of Wales,' Foster, I. LL. and Alcock, L. (eds.), in *Culture and Environment, Essays in Honour of Sir Cyril Fox* (London), 93–152.

Grinsell, L. V., 1932. 'Some Surrey Bell-Barrows,' *Surrey Archeol. Coll.* **40**, 56–64.
1934a. 'An Analysis and List of Surrey Barrows,' *Surrey Archaeol. Coll.* **42**, 26–60.
1934b. 'Sussex Barrows,' *Sussex Archaeol. Collect.* **75**, 216–275.
1934c. 'Bell-Barrows,' *Proc. Prehist. Soc. East Englia* **7**, 203–30.
1935. 'An Analysis and List of Berkshire Barrows,' *Berkshire Archaeol. J.* **39**, 171–91.
1936. *The Ancient Burial-Mounds of England* (London).

1938–40. 'Hampshire Barrows,' Parts I–III, *Proc. Hampshire Fld. Club Archaeol. Soc.* **14**, 9–40, 195–229, 346–365.
1939. 'Some Rare Types of Round Barrow on Mendip,' *Proc. Somerset. Archaeol. Natur. Hist. Soc.* **85**, 151–166.
1941. 'The Bronze Age Round Barrows of Wessex,' *Proc. Prehist. Soc.* **7**, 73–113.
1953. *The Ancient Burial-Mounds of England* (London, 2nd ed.).
1959. *Dorset Barrows* (Dorchester).
1969a. 'Somerset Barrows, Part I: West and South,' *Somerset Archaeol. Natur., Hist. Soc.* **113**, Supplement, 1–43.
1969b. 'The Barrows of North Devon,' *Proc. Devon Archaeol. Soc.* **28**, 95–129.
Grinsell, L. V. and Sherwin, G. A., 1940. 'Isle of Wight Barrows,' *Proc. Isle of Wight Natur. Hist. Archaeol. Soc.* **3**, 179–222.
Gunther, R. T., 1945. *Life and Letters of Edward Lhuyd* (Oxford).

Hamper, W. (ed.), 1827. *The Life (written by himself and continued to his death), Diary and Correspondence of Sir William Dugdale* (London).
Haverfield, F., 1924. *The Roman Occupation of Britain* (Oxford).
Hawkes, C. F. C., 1931. 'Hill-Forts,' *Antiquity* 5, 60–97.
Hawkes, J., 1951. *A Guide to the Prehistoric and Roman Monuments of England and Wales* (London).
1968. 'The Proper Study of Mankind,' *Antiquity* **42**, 255–262.
Hencken, H. O'Neill, 1932. *The Archaeology of Cornwall and Scilly* (London).
Henshall, A. S., 1963. *The Chambered Tombs of Scotland, I* (Edinburgh).
Herity, M. J., 1967. 'From Lhuyd to Coffey; New Information from Unpublished Descriptions of The Boyne Valley Tombs,' *Studia Hibernica* **7**, 127–145
Hoppen, K. T., 1970. *The Common Scientist in the Seventeenth Century, A Study of the Dublin Philosophical Society, 1683–1708* (London).
1956. 'The Origin and First Hundred Years of the Society,' *Archaeol. Cantiana* **70**, 1–43.

Jessup, R. F., 1961. *Curiosities of British Archaeology* (London).
Jewell, P. A., 1963 (ed.). *The Experimental Earthwork on Overton Down, Wiltshire* (London).

Kendrick, T. D., 1950. *British Antiquity* (London).
Kendrick, T. D. and Hawkes, C. F. C., 1932. *Archaeology in England and Wales, 1914–1931* (London).

Lane Fox, A. H., 1869. 'An Examination into the character and probable origin of Hill Forts of Sussex,' *Archaeologia* **42**, 29–52.
London, 1934. *Proceedings of the First International Congress of Prehistoric and Protohistoric Sciences* (London).

Macdonald, G., 1916–17. 'General William Roy and his *Military Antiquities of the Romans in North Britain*', *Archaeologia* **68**, 161–228.
Margary, I. D., 1948. *Roman Ways in the Weald* (London).
1967. *Roman Roads in Britain* (London).
Marples, M., 1949. *White Horses and other Hill-Figures* London.
Massingham, H. J., 1936. *English Downland* (London).

Norman, E. R. and St. Joseph, J. K. S., 1969. *The Early Development of Irish Society: The Evidence of Aerial Photography* (Cambridge).

O'Neil, B. H. St. J., 1946. 'The Congress of Archaeological Societies,' *Antiq. J.* **26**, 61–66.

O'Neil, H. and Grinsell, L. V., 1960. 'Gloucestershire Barrows,' *Trans. Bristol Gloucestershire Archaeol. Soc.* 79, 3–149.

Ó'Ríordáin, S. P. and Daniel, G. E., 1964. *New Grange and the Bend of the Boyne* (London).

Peate, I. C., 1961. Review of M. W. Barley, *The English Farmhouse and Cottage*, *Antiquity* 35, 249–51.

Phillips, C. W., 1933. 'The Long Barrows of Lincolnshire,' *Archaeol. J.* 89, 174–202.

1934. 'Some New Lincolnshire Long Barrows,' *Proc. Prehist. Soc. East Anglia* 8, 423.

1963. *Field Archaeology: Some notes for beginners issued by the Ordnance Survey* (Ordnance Survey Professional Papers, New Series, No **13**, London)

Piggott, S., 1935. 'Stukeley, Avebury and The Druids,' *Antiquity* 9, 22–32.

1937. 'Prehistory and the Romantic Movement,' *Antiquity* 4, 31–38.

1950. *William Stukeley* (Oxford).

1951. 'William Camden and the Britannia,' *Proc. Brit. Acad.* **37**, 199–217.

1956. 'Antiquarian Thought in the Sixteenth and Seventeenth Centuries' in Fox, L. (ed.), *English Historical Scholarship in the Sixteenth and Seventeenth Centuries* (Dugdale Society, Oxford), 93–114.

1962. *The West Kennet Long Barrow, Excavations 1955–56* (London).

1963. 'Archaeology and Prehistory: Presidential Address,' *Proc. Prehist. Soc.* 29, 1–16.

1965. 'Archaeological Draughtsmanship: Part I,' *Antiquity* 39, 165–176.

1965. 'Alexander Keiller, 1889–1955,' in Smith, I. F. (1965), xix–xxiii.

1968. *The Druids* (London).

Pitt-Rivers, Lt.-Gen., 1887–98. *Excavations in Cranborne Chase*, Vols. I–IV (printed privately).

Powell, A., 1948. *John Aubrey and his Friends* (London).

(ed.) 1949. *Brief Lives and other Selected Writings by John Aubrey* (London).

Powell, T. G. E., *et al.*, 1969. *Megalithic Enquiries in the West of Britain* (Liverpool).

Randall, H. J., 1936. *History in the Open Air* (London).

RCHM, 1970. *Dorset II: South* (London).

Riley, D. N., 1946. 'The Technique of Air Archaeology,' *Archaeol. J.* **101**, 1–16.

Rowse, A. L., 1951. *England of Elizabeth* (London).

Roy, W., 1793. *The Military Antiquities of the Romans in North Britain* (London).

Salzman, L. F., 1946. 'A History of the Sussex Archaeological Society,' *Sussex Archaeol. Coll.* 85, 3–76.

Sandell, R. E., 1961. 'Sir Richard Colt Hoare,' *Wiltshire Archaeol. Nat. Hist. Mag.* 58, 1–6.

Smith, I. F., 1965. *Windmill Hill and Avebury*, *Excavations by Alexander Keiller, 1925–1939* (Oxford).

Spooner, G. M. and Russell, F. S. (eds.), 1953. *Dartmoor by the late R. Hansford Worth, compiled from the author's published works*, 1906–50 (Plymouth).

St. George Gray, H., 1905. 'A Memoir of General Pitt-Rivers, D. C. L., F.R.S. and a Bibliographical List of his Works, 1858–1900'; in *Index* to *Excavations in Cranborne Chase* and *King John's House, Tollard Royal, Vol. V* of the *Excavation Series* (Taunton).

Stokes, W., 1868. *The Life and Labours in Art and Archaeology of George Petrie, LL.D., M.R.I.A.* (London).

Stukeley, W., 1725. *Internerarium Curiosum, Centuria I* (London).
1740. *Stonehenge a Temple Restor'd to the British Druids* (London).
1743. *Abury a Temple of the British Druids* (London).

Sumner, H., 1913. *The Ancient Earthworks of Cranborne Chase* (London).
1917. *The Ancient Earthworks of the New Forest* (London).
1931. *Local Papers Archaeological & Topographical, Hampshire, Dorest & Wiltshire* (London).

Thomas, N., 1960. *A Guide to Prehistoric England* (London).

Thompson, M. W., 1960. 'The First Inspector of Ancient Monuments in the Field,' *J. Brit. Archaeol. Assoc.* 23, 103–124.

Toulmin Smith, L., 1907–10. *The Itinerary of John Leland* (London).

Warne, C., 1866. *The Celtic Tumuli of Dorset* (London).

Webster, G. and Hobley, B., 1964. 'Aerial Reconnaissance over the Warwickshire Avon,' *Archaeol. J.* 121, 1–22.

Wheeler, R. E. M., 1943. *Maiden Castle, Dorset* (Reports of the Research Committee of The Society of Antiquaries of London 12, London).

Wheeler, Sir Mortimer, 1953. 'Adventure and Flinders Petrie,' *Antiquity* 27, 87–93.

Wheeler, Sir Mortimer and Richardson, K. M., 1957. *Hill-Forts of Northern France* (Reports of the Research Committee of the Society of Antiquaries of London 19, Oxford).

Williams-Freeman, J. P., 1915. *An Introduction to Field Archaeology as illustrated by Hampshire* (London).

Witts, G. B., 1883. *Archaeological Handbook of the County of Gloucester* (Cheltenham).

Woodbridge, K., 1970. *Landscape and Antiquity, Aspects of English Culture at Stourhead 1718 to 1838* (Oxford).

CHAPTER III

The Present Significance of Fieldwork in the light of the Cornish Parochial Check-List Survey

Charles Thomas

INTRODUCTION

The words 'Grinsell' and 'barrows' have grown into virtual synonyms, and rightly so; for Leslie Grinsell in a series of classic papers has raised the bare gazetteer of sites to a new standard, and has chosen to do so in respect of the most important class of field-monument attributable to the Bronze Age. The spectacle of a solitary fieldworker, tirelessly tramping county after county, digesting in the intervals not only tea-cakes but (it would seem) topographical literature on a scale rivalled only by Royal Commissions, is unlikely to be repeated; and it is the thoroughness, the attention to obscure detail, and the sheer magnitude of the task, that have earned him his eminent niche in this essentially British pursuit.

In dedicating the paper which follows to Leslie Grinsell, the writer, as an old friend long inspired by his example, wishes to join to himself all his fellow-Cornishmen who have at various removes shared something of that inspiration. Cornwall has not yet paraded her remaining barrows for the full Grinsell treatment, but dares to express the hope that they may still engage his interest. Meanwhile, a description of the kind of field-survey which is taking place in Cornwall, admittedly a survey not confined to barrows, but one relying heavily upon the techniques of presentation which Leslie Grinsell has taught, may constitute an apt tribute; and may form a platform for contemporary views on the place of fieldwork in British archaeology today.

Origins

The concept of a *total* list of all visible and detectable remains of the past in Cornwall and Scilly was aired several times in the present century—notably just before 1914, by a group of prominent local antiquaries (eg Jenner, 1914), and indeed at the opening of the century in a rather more nationalistic context (Duncombe-Jewell, 1902)—but it does not appear that any serious attempt was made to bridge the gulf between resolution and execution. The present scheme originated, as the best schemes usually seem to do, in the work of one person, Miss Vivien Russell, living at Sennen Cove, hard by Land's End. For many years Miss Russell had undertaken both fieldwork and the supporting documentary research in respect of the Land's End peninsula, recording her finds in note form

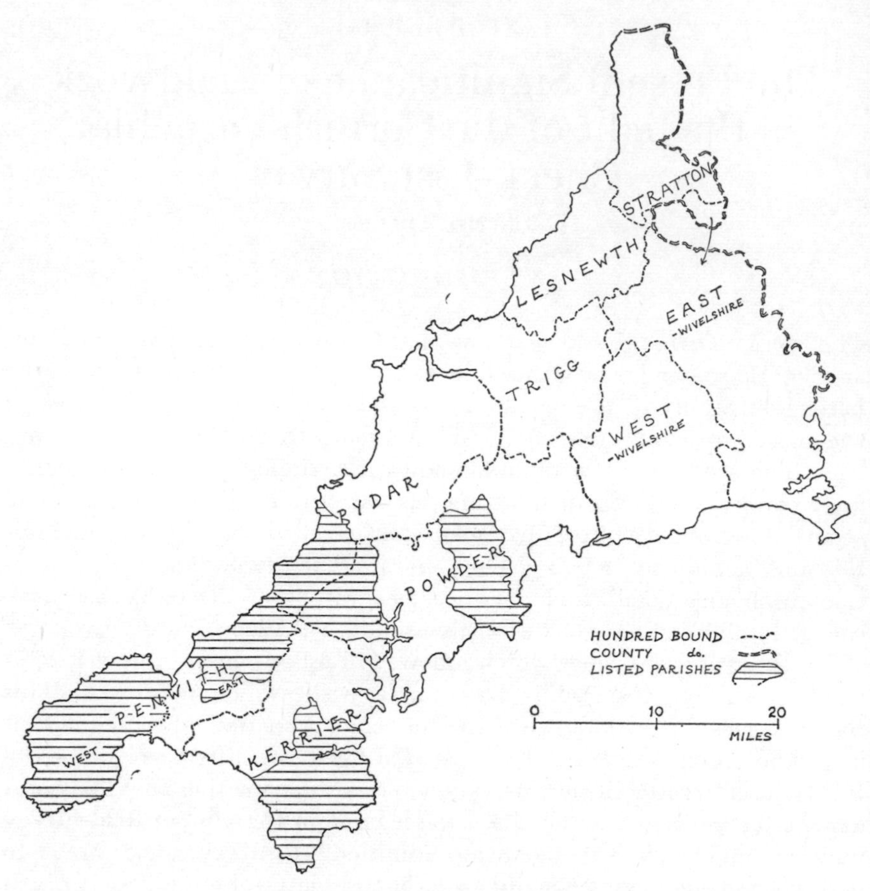

6. Cornwall, showing Hundreds and the areas covered by parochial check-lists.

and on marked-up Ordnance Survey (6 ins to the mile) sheets. She proposed in 1958 to the West Cornwall Field Club that the results of her work might be published, parish by parish (there are fourteen ecclesiastical parishes in the peninsula), and a convenient format was worked out between her, the editor of the Field Club's *Proceedings*, and the printers. The first list, which dealt with the antiquities of St Just in Penwith, was published in 1959 (Russell, 1959). With introductory notes and a list of abbreviations, it ran to nine pages in an issue which was itself only forty pages long; in other words, sufficient importance was attached to this new venture by a small club (with under a hundred members, and very limited funds) to lead it to devote almost a quarter of its journal to a gazetteer of sites.

This initial format, with the mode of classification and of references which it introduced, has with very minor adjustment proved to be the clearest and most economical way of publishing the information. When, in

1961–2, the West Cornwall Field Club enlarged itself into the Cornwall Archaeological Society, and terminated its *Proceedings* in favour of a new annual, *Cornish Archaeology*, it was able to enjoy a page text-body of 14 by 22 cms., as opposed to the older 10 by 17 cms., a change which has led to greater clarity and legibility in these check-lists.

The present position (fig 6)

At the time of writing (winter, 1970), nine issues of *Cornish Archaeollogy* have appeared, and altogether forty-three parochial check-lists (plus eight separate lists of 'Additions') (Thomas, 1969). The Cornwall Archaeological Society now maintains a membership around the five hundred mark, and in an average year may spend at least £1000 on printing (*Cornish Archaeology*, the 'Field Guide' series, circulars and notices), but the scheme of priorities accepted in 1959 still in large measure applies. In the first eight issues of *Cornish Archaeology* (1962 to 1969), averaging 110 pp. per issue, there are 118 pages devoted to check-lists—an average 14 pp. per issue, about one-eighth. In terms of crude finance, an active society, which spends up to the hilt and always has a considerable back-log of its own (and other people's) excavation reports, has set aside nearly six hundred pounds to publish compressed and formalized gazetteers of antiquities. It must be acknowledged, with gratitude, that since 1965 a continuing publications grant from the then Ministry of Public Building and Works made it feasible to maintain, and indeed in some years to increase, the number of lists published annually.

There is some doubt as to the exact number of ancient ecclesiastical parishes in Cornwall and the Isles of Scilly—quite apart from the 'new' or 'Peel' parishes of the nineteenth century, some adjustment took place—but both in these terms and in terms of square mileage, between one-fifth and one-quarter of the county has now been covered. An accelerated rate of recording and publication is under consideration.

DESCRIPTION

Aims. The aims of the parochial check-list scheme were recently defined in a circular as being:

(a) the provision of as *complete* a record as possible of antiquities (seen as a desirable end in itself); and

(b) the provision of as *reliable* a basis as possible for analytical studies of distributions, densities, cultural changes, land usage, and historical demography.

Events in Cornwall in the last few years suggest that a third aim might well be added—the provision, in advance, of appropriately full information to help to assess schemes which threaten to destroy all or any aspects of the countryside.

These aims—classificatory, academic, and conservationist, as they could be labelled—will be considered later in this essay.

Scope. The term 'antiquity' (as in 'Parochial Check-List of Antiquities') is easier to understand than to define. In this specific case, it embraces both 'field monuments' (sites, structures, and any form of remains) and 'archaeological objects' in the sense of things which possess both an academic interest and an archaeological value in excess of the intrinsic value. In practice the check-lists are meant primarily to record monuments, and only secondarily to list portable antiquities.

Monuments (standing monuments, sites, complexes of either, and industrial remains) fall into four main categories. In decreasing order of certainty, these are:

(i) Visible and widely recorded monuments, e.g., a megalithic tomb, still standing at the time of compilation, easily recognized, and marked on almost all types of map.

(ii) Monuments visible or detectable to the trained eye, but not necessarily recorded on O.S. maps and often not recorded on any known map, though probably mentioned in some MS or printed source of comparative obscurity (e.g., the majority of 'rounds' in West Cornwall).

(iii) Monuments which no longer exist, which may at best be confirmed from aerial photographs, and which have been destroyed by building, road-making, agriculture, mining, or sheer vandalism; but which are nevertheless at some point satisfactorily described in some MS or printed source, can be located, and may even be the subject of a description of their destruction.

(iv) Suspected monuments, not detectable from the air, only approximately located, but inferred with fair probability to have existed, either from some MS or printed source or from a significant place-name (such place-names are in Cornish rather than English).

In the printed check-lists these categories are not formally distinguished, though (i) and (ii) can be separated according to whether or not an O.S. entry appears in the references, and these two can be distinguished from the others by a 'Yes', 'Yes?' or merely '?' in the ANY REMAINS EXTANT column. Categories (iii) and (iv) are usually distinguished again by the absence or presence of some appropriate record in the references column (fig 7).

Units

Cornwall is a long and uneven peninsula with poor internal communications, terms like 'West Cornwall', 'mid-Cornwall', and 'North (or East) Cornwall' having very fluid interpretations. The first tier of internal division consists of the 'hundreds', which are larger than the southern English

PROVENANCE	OBJECT	PRESENT LOCALITY	REFERENCES
Miscellaneous Finds			
1 Godrevy farm	Neolithic axe	A.C.T.	Axes IV, no. 718 (Gp. I); GTY 10
2 Godrevy headland ('GB')	ditto	A.C.T.	Axes IV, no. 824 (Gp. I); GTY 10
3 Gwithian	Gold lunula	Lost	Hayle Miscellany, Dec. 1860, 2; Hencken, 70, 298, 307; DCNQ vi.102; GTY 12 (not from Paul parish)
4 Connor Downs	M.B.A. urn	?	(? From barrow no. 5); drawing of sherd, BSA fol. 23
5 Godrevy headland ('GB')	Bronze brooch	R.I.C.	Surface find 1950; Burley type A3; CA 2 ('63), 76
6 Parish church	Stocks	S. aisle	Wooden, 19th cent; GPG 16, fig. 5

HUNDRED OF POWDER

3: PARISH OF KENWYN with Tregavethan and Truro St. Mary

(10513 acs.)

RICHARD B. WARNER

PLACE	GRID REF.	ANY REMAINS EXTANT	REFERENCES
Barrows			
1 Penventinnie	79214602		Hend III 197 & 199 fig; RRIC XXIX 43
2 Chyvelah	79404521	Yes	OS LVII SE; Thomas 42; Hend III 196 & 199 fig; TA 883 'Barrow Field'
3 to 10 Gloweth	79884517 to 79854505		JRIC suppl. 1960 14-18 & figs; Hend III 196 & 199 fig; JRIC II xix; RRIC XXIX 42 & Pl. XVI; JRIC VI 171; W.B. 28.9.1866; Thomas 42; OS LVII SE; TA 'Beacon Downs'
11 Saveock Water	76584535	Yes	OS LVII SW; Thomas 42 } 'Carbittle Barrows'
12 Saveock Water	App. 766453		Thomas 42 } 'Carbittle Barrows'
13 Three Mile Stone	App. 774453		Thomas 42
14 Gloweth	?	?	Thomas 42
15 Trevaskis	App. 769465	?	Thomas 42
16 Three Burrows	74944704	Yes	OS LVII NW; Hend III 197; Thomas 42; Gilbert PH II 317
17 Three Burrows	75024705	Yes	as 16
18 Three Burrows	75074704	Yes	as 16
19 Four Barrows	76194822	Yes	OS LVII NW; Hend III 202 & 201 fig; Thomas 43; Gilbert PH II 317; H & D 358; Borlase Par Mem 93 no. 7; Redding 128
20 Four Barrows	76234822	Yes	as 19
21 Four Barrows	76204816	Yes?	Hend III 202 & 201 fig
22 Chybucca	App. 785488		Thomas 42; CA 2 ('63), 79
23 Allet Common	79504851	Yes	Hend V 82 & 84 fig; OS LVII NE; RRIC XXIX 44 & Pl. IX fig 1; Thomas 42; CA 2 ('63), 79
24 Allet Common	79524853	Yes	as 23
25 Nanteague	79024929	Yes	Hend V 82; RRIC XXIX 44; Thomas 42
26 Halgarras	79924839	Yes	Hend V 82 & 84 fig; RRIC XXIX 44& Pl. IX fig 1; Thomas 42; CA 2 ('63), 79
27 Halgarras	80074834		at centre of Henge 1. which see for refs.
28 Halgarras	80364826		OS LVII NE; Hend V 82 & 84 fig; Thomas 42; CA 2 ('63), 79
29 Whitehall	73054473	Yes	Thomas 42; Thomas Map. 'Creegbagla'

7. Specimen page from *Cornish Archaeology* of parts of parochial check-lists in published form.

hundreds, and may represent an arrangement older than the Norman conquest (Thomas, 1964). There were at one time six of these, sub-division of the two eastern hundreds having increased the number to nine. For check-list purposes, the westernmost hundred (Penwith) is split between its eastern division and its western division (West Penwith) which coincides more or less with the Land's End peninsula. The sheer volume of antiquities in the latter district justifies this procedure. Adding the Isles of Scilly, which constitute a separate unit historically, administratively, and probably ethnically, this gives us eleven first-tier groups. Check-list work is taking place in seven of these, but lists have so far been published only in respect of five of them.

Within each hundred, check-lists are numbered in order of publication —e.g. 'Powder, No. 9'—and the unit is the former ecclesiastical (Church of England) parish. This unit was chosen because the last complete and readily accessible record of field-names and tenement-names linked to a large-scale map was produced *circa* 1840 by the Tithe Apportionment Survey, the basis of which was of course the ecclesiastical parish. The present civil parishes, which are local government units, are ignored; the post-1840 'new parishes', strictly called ecclesiastical districts, are subsumed as far as possible in the older parishes from which they were formed by Orders in Council (for complete list see Henderson, 1928).

Cornish parishes differ greatly in extent, and it is now the practice to insert at the head of each printed list the estimated acreage—taken from pre-1900 Kelly's *Directories*—as a rough aid to comparison between lists.

Compilation

It would be pointless to explain in any detail how lists are compiled, and a few notes will suffice. The footslogging is left entirely to the discretion of the individual compiler, who will possess his or her own methods; and, as a large parish may require three or four years of repetitive fieldwork before a satisfactory list can be completed, it is not uncommon to tackle several parishes at the same time. The documentary sources begin with maps; the Tithe Map, a backwards survey through successive editions of all scales of Ordnance Survey maps, and a search of estate, mining, and private maps. The voluminous printed topographical literature of Cornwall is to some extent pre-digested in a list of standard abbreviations which now runs to seven foolscap pages, but over and above this material each parish will probably possess its own very localized and scarce printed matter— parish magazines (both C. of E. and Methodist), centenary programmes, church and commercial guides, and public and private pamphlets. There is a heavy burden of MS material to shoulder, most of it fortunately now gathered into one town, Truro, which starts with straight antiquarian MSS from the eighteenth century, but must go on to take in a wide range of deeds, estate papers, registers, rentals, and mining documents (Cornish *setts*, or leases of mineral rights, abound in valuable place-name evidence). What may be called 'visual documentation' includes aerial cover at different degrees of detail and reliability, nineteenth-century photographic collections, old postcard series, and all topographical views. Finally, in common with folklore collection, oral or verbal sources—traditional information gathered in a locality—though seldom reliable *per se*, can provide most useful confirmatory evidence or fruitful pointers to fresh research.

Cornwall, in common with other areas of Britain which possess or have formerly possessed a vernacular other than English, offers yet another potential source to the fieldworkers in the shape of place-name evidence. This is as tricky as it is attractive. The basic desideratum, and it is one which should be accorded a very high priority, is a corpus of all Cornish place-names (down to field-name level) with dated forms, compiled on a parish basis and cross-indexed alphabetically. A safe estimate suggests that upwards of 50,000 such names could be indexed, of which perhaps only one-fifth are now readily accessible. Quite recently, the writer recorded, largely from oral sources, 151 rock- and cliff-names from a short stretch of the north Cornish coast (Thomas, 1965), of which *only thirty-nine* appear on any form of O.S. map; and fifty-nine, in Cornish and probably all post-1500 formations, were printed for the first time.

The value of such a corpus for archaeological survey purposes would be enormous. For instance, there are over twenty words, Cornish and English, which refer to different types of field; certain of these are direct pointers to the local version of the medieval English 'open field'. The curious word *cromlech*, one of a group of Celtic neologisms which have passed into standard archaeological usage, occurs in Cornish toponymy in the corrupt form 'Grumbla'; but known cases suggest that, far from implying the remains of a megalithic tomb, this term describes a stone circle. The special case of the word *ker*, *caer*, is mentioned below. The Celtic (British) **duno-m*, latinized as *dunum*, lies behind the Irish *dún*, 'fort, fortress', and the Welsh and Cornish element *din-*, but while this is commonly found applied to major works of Iron Age date, Cornwall at least shows a series of derivatives; the semantic doublet *dinas*, a word *dinan* which is probably a diminutive, and an element '-dinnick, -dennick' (e.g., Pordennick) which suggests an adjectival **dinek*, 'fortified, possessing a rampart'. When any such name is found in a documentary source, the fieldworker can at least check the ground for an earthwork.

The check-list fieldworkers cannot be expected to possess any special linguistic knowledge, but they can at least be trained to look out for a wide series of place-name elements which are known to carry this kind of meaning. This is so even with the 1840 Tithe Apportionment Survey field-names, despite the hazards of what now looks like manuscript recording from toothless octogenarians, and typesetting from such records by alcoholics. The rich vocabulary for remains of early Christianity in

Cornwall—*lan*, *merther*, *eglos*, *sant*, etc.—still awaits analysis on these lines, even if any such analysis is to some extent a luxury which must be postponed until the survey itself is complete. Precisely similar remarks would, of course, apply to field-survey in Wales and Scotland, probably in counties like Shropshire and Hereford, and in a minor key to the very many English counties where more than one Germanic dialect or language has ben a creative place-name force in the past.

Within an individual check-list, the question of classification of monuments is one which has never been wholly resolved and is perhaps incapable of satisfactory resolution. A straight division into mesolithic, neolithic, Bronze Age (? early, middle, late), Iron Age, and so on, looks attractive, but is deceptively so. Are the late megalithic tombs of Cornwall neolithic or Bronze Age? Where would Beaker cist-graves go? Many published homestead sites in both Devon and Cornwall of the last twenty-five years, identified as Late Bronze Age (*sensu* old-style 'Deverel-Rimbury'), are almost certainly synchronous with the Wessex period and thus, if anything, Early Bronze Age. Neither field-systems with terraces and lynchets, nor isolated and unexcavated round stone huts, can be safely assigned to the pre-Roman Iron Age, as they were for so long.

The categories employed are thus fieldworkers' categories; barrows (including chambered ones), menhirs and stone circles, huts and hut-groups, hill-forts and cliff-castles, 'rounds' (univallate enclosures), souterrains, field-systems, and the major groups of visible remains that can be described without prejudice as to real date. As time has gone by, other categories, mostly of later date, have been added in parishes which appear notably rich in such; 'lans' (enclosed curvilinear cemeteries of putatively Early Christian origin), chapels, parish or manorial pounds, crosses (cross-bases, known sites of crosses), holy wells, and 'plain-an-gwaries' (the medieval open-air theatre earthworks for the performance of the Cornish miracle plays). In areas where the industrial revolution was locally important, or early, or prominent, lists of appropriate remains, sites, and standing monuments are given; these can if necessary be taken up to the end of the Victorian era.

One or two special categories deserve mention. The field-name 'Round Field' (The Round, Round Close, Round Stitch, Parc Round, Higher Round, Lower Round, etc.) is of common occurrence in most west Cornish parishes, from early maps and sources, via the Tithe Apportionment Maps, to present-day use. A minority—perhaps a third—of these do refer directly to a widespread class of small univallate earthworks, which in terms of archaeology (Thomas, 1966), seem to have been the agricultural homesteads of a section of the populace in the early centuries A.D. 'Round' here is the English equivalent of a Cornish word *ker* (older *caer*, *kaer*), which has numerous compositional guises—*Car-*, *Ker-*, *Gar-*, *-gar*, *-gear*, and (plural) *kerrow*, *garrow*, even 'Cairo' (*sic*). Frequently such a site will have given its name to the farm or tenement—Carlenno ('Laianou's enclosure') —and the actual field containing the 'round' will repeat this in some Cornish form—Gerrier (*an ger hyr*, 'the long enclosure')—or an English one ('The Round'); or worse still, attached to adjoining fields, in both languages. Exactly what is signified by the very large number of 'Round Fields', where no visible or detectable remains of any sort of monument can be located today, is a mystery. By no means all of these fields are necessarily surrounded, either by other fields or by uncultivated waste (locally, 'croft'). But, as we know only too well, smaller 'rounds' can be totally eroded through deep ploughing, even to the point of invisibility from the air, in less than a century, and all forms of hut-circle could be demolished with much less effort. 'Round Fields' are thus listed as a special *potential* category.

Again, it might be wondered why it appears desirable to devote so many inches to the stone crosses of Cornwall, since several corpora of crosses already exist in print (Langdon, 1896; *Old Cornwall* 1926–; *Devon Cornwall Notes Queries*). The answer, which would have pleased Pitt-Rivers, is that the crosses are important just because there are so many of them—probably more than a thousand, estimating the proportion of lost ones. These crosses (the majority of granite) come in all different sizes, shapes, and weights, and are field-monuments in one sense (i.e. if still demonstrably *in situ*), portable antiquities in another (i.e. if moved around once, twice, thrice, or more times, as regrettably so many have been). A fieldworker with an intimate knowledge of a locality, with access to private or obscure sources, and the ability to interpret muddled records in the light of detailed acquaintanceship with what is being described, can time and time again discover an 'original' cross-location which is not that recorded in the published corpora.

Nor can crosses readily be separated from cross-*bases*, which often remain put when the cross is removed, or cross-*sites*, frequently commemorated in specific place-names or in specific accounts (and views) which arise because of the prominent nature of these objects, (Thomas, 1967). The majority of all Cornish crosses, in this writer's view, date from the eleventh or later centuries A.D.—only a handful are certainly older than A.D. 1000—but it is abundantly clear that they possessed at least half a dozen quite separate functions, and that they constitute a rich and only partially tapped source for the history of the medieval Church in a Celtic-speaking area. The check-lists should, as far as is humanly possible, note all extant and (where this can be reliably done) destroyed crosses in a parish, and note their original locations as well as their subsequent individual wanderings.

Consolidation

It is beyond the resources of most county societies, and certainly far beyond those available in Cornwall, to contemplate the consolidated issue of check-lists in the splendid format employed by the *Victoria County History of Wiltshire*, vol I, part 1—itself another monument to the industry of L. V. Grinsell. On the other hand, one can cut one's coat in accordance with the cloth available, and the idea of producing consolidated check-lists (revised, expanded, and slightly re-classified) for a given area is by no means out of the question. The Cornwall Archaeological Society will in fact publish, in 1971, the first of such a series, using the now-completed check-lists for the Land's End peninsula; this will be Miss Vivien Russell's *West Penwith Survey*. Should the project be a success, and there is every reason to suppose that with careful costing it can be, it will be followed by other, similar, monographs as and when the material comes to hand.

AIMS

(i) *Classification*

To revert to the three aims mentioned briefly above (p 77), the first was stated to be 'the provision of as complete a record of antiquities as possible'. It might be argued that, in an ideal world, total and effective listing of all the visible and detectable remains of past human activity would be undertaken by the State, as a duty so obvious as to be past any need for social or financial justification, and moreover as a duty on all fours with the work of the National Monuments Record or the Historical Manuscripts Commission. In practice, this would mean recruiting, training, and maintaining throughout the British Isles about five hundred highly paid field staff. But there are more subtle arguments, by no means out of place in a volume of essays on fieldwork, which can be adduced to suggest that, while the overall social *duty* to list all remains of the past still stand, it is not so obvious that the *burden* need be pushed on to the State.

In the second half of this century, the greater social benefits (despite inflation) enjoyed by the retired, the extended periods of leisure (notably at week-ends), the slow rise in the general level of education, the prestige so inexplicably attached to all forms of archaeology, and—at last—the awakening of some rudimentary national conscience where matters of polution and conservation are concerned, have all been reflected in the growth of local archaeological societies and in the pronounced shift of emphasis in those societies' activities. Meetings, lectures, and social gatherings apart, the emphasis is heavily upon the provision of archaeological excavations; and this is true even when no obvious need to dig has arisen, when smaller groups quite clearly do not possess the resources to cope with unforeseen expansion of an opened site, and (worst of all, perhaps) when a fully qualified director is lacking. These are common enough sentiments, but there are related points not always made; for example, that the pitifully small cadre of full-time archaeological students who man our universities and national agencies are now patently unable to digest the results of so much excavation, perhaps not even capable of scanning all the necessary literature each year despite abstracts and news-letters; and that a five-year moratorium on excavation would be heartily welcomed by many.

Again, the constant rise in the cost of printing, paper and postage means that the scientific duty which still forms the inescapable converse of an excavation (or of any such unrepeatable field experiment), namely publication and circulation at an acceptable international minimum standard, cannot today be met by bodies which fall below certain horizons of membership and income. As these horizons, it could be argued, are those of three or four hundred members paying at least £1.50 each per year, a disturbingly high proportion of societies or 'research groups' in the British archaeological scene are evading this duty. They share an unusual privilege, in that the backwardness of our national antiquities legislation permits them to excavate sites—not infrequently scheduled sites for which permission is granted—which, in almost every other country, would be the subject of some state-controlled licence involving standards of directorship and firm undertakings as to publication and the disposal of finds.

Where, in this melancholy picture, does fieldwork enter? The answer is that fieldwork is non-destructive, generally (unlike old-fashioned 'flinting') non-competitive, within limits repeatable or subject to later verification, and of enormous scholastic value. It is true that, over some centuries, our most productive fieldworkers have preferred to work on their own, or for survey purposes in very small teams, but this does not negate fieldwork as a planned activity for a local society. Rather does it imply that untapped resources of individual members, in a wide range of directions, can be given purpose and effectiveness if they are co-ordinated into something on the lines of the Parochial Check-List Survey. Nor need this mean the end of excavation, whether for rescue or research; and the lacunae in our always-imperfect knowledge of our past, to which we so often delude ourselves that specific excavations are slanted, are given much greater precision, and are accorded a proper scale of priorities, if they are derived from analyses of large-scale fieldwork results. The pragmatist's complaint, that excavation can attract financial grants while fieldwork cannot, is far from justifiable; for (as the various committees which allot such grants in aid know all too well) properly-planned requests for financial aid to field-work schemes are hardly ever laid before them.

In short, the provision of as complete as possible a record of antiquities in a given area is at the moment, and in the foreseeable future, something that will only be done by archaeological societies in that area. No one else will do it. The various Royal Commissions, excellent as their investigators and architects are, work slowly within the confines of their Treasury allocation, and work to closely defined ends. Nor (it might be argued) is it always possible to extract the most from a district unless one has a lifetime's experience of it. This may sound like a counsel of perfection, but one of the earlier premises of the Cornish scheme was that, where possible, field-workers should commence with their native or home parishes, and work outwards from them. Can the compilation of such lists in any area be elevated to the rank of a positive social and scientific duty, incumbent upon those in that area whom society has provided with the education and leisure to undertake the work? Is it, in the light of the advancement of knowledge altogether, less of a duty than those of public service, charitable endeavour, and local government? These are deep issues, to which no ready answer can be given; but they go well beyond the old parlour game of seeking a moral justification for archaeology altogether, because the pressures upon what still remains of the British countryside mean that we can no longer sit still and chop logic. Will there be any field archaeology in the year 2050? Will there be any field, apart from national pleasure-parks?

(ii) *Advancement of Knowledge*

The second aim was defined as the provision of as *reliable* a record as possible to form 'a basis for analytical studies of distributions, densities, cultural changes, land usage, and historical demography'. As we approach the end of the twentieth century, some four millennia after an advanced stage of the first agricultural settlement of our land, no record can hope to be complete in the historical sense; we must try, therefore, to ensure that it is at least reliable. This means not only the recording of classes of field monument to which absolute dates cannot yet be assigned, but the inclusion in our records of instances which no longer exist, and which can be shown to have existed with an acceptable degree of certainty.

In terms of the Cornish survey, it will be possible to engage in 'studies in depth' when (say) a hundred parishes have been recorded. At the moment, with over forty, it is possible to draw certain tentative conclusions, because most of these parishes are joined, block-like, to each other and thus make up whole areas of survey. Hypotheses constructed on the basis of ten parishes in west Cornwall can be checked against another ten in mid-Cornwall, and in a preliminary mode against unsurveyed parishes in the east of the county, using either Tithe Maps or O.S. 6-inch sheets. Such hypotheses refer, at the moment, to crude distribution densities. The most striking thing that emerges from what has so far been done is not just that there are many more monuments than those recorded on O.S. or Tithe maps; it is that, in a number of classes, the totals are much greater than anyone had previously supposed, and the real (i.e., the unattainable, true, historical) totals must be larger still.

This is particularly so in respect of the broad period from the early second millenium B.C. to the early first A.D.—the Bronze Age, and the Iron Age in the enlarged south-western sense of the Early Iron Age and the Roman period together. Barrows, the vast majority of which must surely have been built within what we now call the Early and Middle Bronze Age, will have to be numbered not in hundreds but a thousand or more. It is not uncommon to list twenty barrows for a parish, of which a good half were destroyed before 1800 and appear on no maps, except rare estate maps of the early eighteenth century, and of which not one is visible today. Moreover, as far to the west as mid-Cornwall, it is clear that barrows occurred in small and large clusters, could be strung out along ridgeways, and even constituted linear and arc-shaped cemeteries, reproducing conditions normally associated with Wessex.

For the Iron Age, there have been several demonstrations of great interest, referring primarily to land-usage. Miss Russell's pioneer work in West Penwith showed, some time ago, that field-systems of the type known to be attached to the Chysauster courtyard-house village were in fact quite common in the peninsula, and despite much more intensive agriculture it is certain that the remnants of such exist in east Penwith as well. The demonstration, at Gwithian (Megaw *et al*, 1961), that complexes of small rectilinear terraced and lyncheted fields were present in Cornwall far back in the Bronze Age demands a cautious approach to the question of absolute date, and the fact that many of the Land's End fields occur in meaningful association with hut-circles or groups of huts does not of itself imply that these are all Iron Age.

The 'rounds', to which allusion has already been made, were given a preliminary airing in 1966 (Thomas, 1966), when it was suggested that, allowing for blank areas of high granite moorland, the all-Cornwall total might well turn out to lie between 750 and 1000. Subsequent work in no way makes it necessary to change this estimate, and perhaps the nearest analogy would be the proliferation of the very similar raths and ring-forts in Ireland.

These are the remains—barrows, fields, farms—directly associated with the life and the death of a predominantly agricultural population, confined in a long narrow peninsula, and with their distributions to some extent governed by considerations of geophysical background (Fox, 1964, ch. 1). Even with what V. G. Childe used to call 'the long chronology'—the extended temporal setting for past events accorded to us by C14 dating—they carry direct implications as to population density, and therefore secondary implications as to the rate of cultural change, the impact upon wild fauna and the importance of domesticated animals, internal 'trade' (if one can use this loose term), and pressure upon favoured lands. All ideas, however vaguely held or poorly formulated, about absolute numbers of people present in Cornwall during phases of prehistory now require a sharp upward revision. Concepts of 'innovations', based on solitary excavated sites, may well be abandoned, particularly if checked later at similar sites. It was (for example) supposed as early as 1960 that the remarkable seven-acre field-system of the Wessex period found at Gwithian, complete with plough-marks, lynchets, manure, spade-marks and terraces, implied a long tradition in south-west (if not in southern) Britain, of which this was merely a mature case recovered in exceptionally favourable circumstances. This was before the discovery of the plough-marks below the South Street (Wilts.) long barrow (Fowler and Evans, 1967), but—more appositely—the first (1970) season on the neolithic settlement on Carn Brea, some five miles from Gwithian, may provide a neolithic forerunner far closer to home (Mercer, 1970b). What is now required is a full examination of all the little complexes of huts and fields on the Cornish moors, as on Dartmoor, on the assumption that some at least of these are Early and Middle Bronze Age in time; as inded the Dartmoor pottery now seems to indicate.

In the Iron Age, the isolation of the 'rounds' as a major component of the settlement-pattern raises about a dozen queries of real importance. What is the meaning of a common pattern; two rounds only a few hundred yards apart (or closer)? Were the round-dwellers apart, in social or economic terms, from the inhabitants of unenclosed huts or hut-groups which can be shown archaeologically to be contemporary? Since rounds appear to have only a few huts inside them, what was the rest of the enclosed area? A farmyard, or seed-plots, or a cattle corral? When modern (and medieval) farms are sited directly upon rounds, does this imply continuity from the early centuries A.D.? Why are most rounds found between 250 and 450 feet O.D., and so often on the shoulders of valleys? Here one feels that, in addition to unidimensional studies of distribution, with or without the (perhaps only partly relevant) geographical factors, modern techniques of spatial analysis, developed within the so-called 'new geography' and hardly yet applied to archaeological evidence (but *cf.* Newcomb, 1968, 1970, in relation to Cornish results), offer far and away the greatest promise of an advance in understanding.

These are selected instances, and there is no room to describe others of equal fascination—the multiplicity of Early Christian chapels and cemeteries in Cornwall, surely awaiting analysis along the lines of Marstrander's work (1937) in the Isle of Man, or, for the industrial archaeologist, the extraordinary and little-known archaeology of tin-streams and tin-stamps in the last three or four centuries. Enough has been said, perhaps, to bear out the claim that this survey—the direct outcome of planned and co-ordinated fieldwork—can advance our knowledge of the past at a fraction of the cost of a large excavation and, albeit on a broad canvas, at a much faster rate than excavation. If we seek an academic justification, we need not look very far. Nor does this imply a cessation of all excavation; for, as in Cornwall, it clarifies the whole problem of where, after the magnifying glass, one can best bring the microscope to bear.

(iii) *A Conservationist's Weapon*

It is sometimes supposed—by farmers whose lands are encumbered with scheduled ancient monuments, or by local councils forced to provide houses and roads that everyone wants but wants elsewhere—that British archaeologists would like to preserve all remains of the past indefinitely. If this impression has been given in the past, archaeologists are to blame, and an extreme conservationist view on these lines has of course been voiced.

A more sensible outlook, rapidly gaining ground as a compromise with contemporary social and political pressures, is that the present generation (*scil.* of archaeologists) does have the duty to preserve a proportion of the British archaeological heritage for future study, analysis, excavation or re-excavation, and even enjoyment; but that consistent with such a duty is our right to press for *selective* preservation. While the (then) Ministry of Works' policy in the late 1940s and 1950s, of digging a very large number of partly-ruined sites, notably southern English round barrows, was thought justifiable at the time, a subsequent opinion—wise with hindsight—is that much of the money could have been better spent, and that many of the results were uninformative or, because of the dearth of qualified excavators, possibly suspect. In any case, archaeology as a discipline has now moved much closer to ecological studies and to certain of the natural sciences, and the emphasis has also moved, from individual sites regarded in isolation to a new concept of the site-in-its-environment, or of whole *areas* of prehistoric activity. The whole is seen as more important, in every sense, than the sum of its components. The field-system, or better still the field-system together with the huts in and around it, must replace the solitary excavated hut, or the single surveyed field, for the purposes of inference and analogy; and there is a further tendency to see the long-term investigation of 'area sites' justified in terms of time and money only when these are examined throughout their chronological ranges—from neolithic to Victorian, if need be. This has rarely happened; examples might be Cranborne Chase (perhaps too wide an area for this), the Lough Gur area (Ó Ríordáin and others), Gwithian (Thomas and others), Fyfield and West Overton (Fowler and others), Goodland (Case and others), and to some extent South Cadbury (Alcock). Lough Gur, Gwithian, and Fyfield have involved totals of sites well into double figures, set in well-defined and fairly well-preserved environments.

In conservationist circles, this has come to mean that we must be prepared to cut our inevitable losses, and to concentrate our efforts on that which experience suggests is almost certainly important, sacrificing that which (by its partial nature) could never yield the same degree of knowledge. If this smacks of compounding bargains with local authorities or of selling-out to motorway and gravel-digging interests, it may still constitute tactical good sense. To give a specific example, ploughed-out barrows now detectable only from the air or under certain crops are admittedly ancient monuments, but not of the same order as prehistoric field-systems fully visible on non-arable uplands which can be shown to have been untouched since the Middle Ages. The excavation of the former might reveal a primary interment and something of any feature rooted below the old land surface; but today our interest in barrows is as much in mound-construction (with its wealth of ecological evidence) and in supra-burial features or secondary use as in the primary or the bare ground-plan. A field-system, particularly if finite, fully detectable, and associated with any form of homestead, is likely to shed more light on life in the Bronze or Iron Age than a dozen or more destroyed tumuli.

The further implication is that, if we decide to endorse a policy of conserving selected representative sites and selected site-complexes or archaeological areas, instead of urging the wholesale protection of everything regardless of condition or potentialities, we must have full and supportable grounds for such selectivity. There is a great deal to be said for the selective policy, not least because it brings archaeological strategy much closer to that encountered in neighbouring interests—nature reserves, areas of special scientific interest, coastal and national parks, and the proposed new countryside 'recreation areas'.

It is at this point that we find, once more, the crucial relevance of intensive field-survey schemes. It is also appropriate here to state that the publications grant made by the Ministry of Public Building and Works for the Cornish lists is neither an instance of regional favouritism nor some unprecedented support for a worthy project. The Ancient Monuments Inspectorate, however hard-working its inspectors and architects, simply does not possess and probably never will possess enough staff to cover British antiquities at the level desirable in an ideal world. Field surveys of adequate detail not only cut down the actual working-time of the few inspectors; they should show at once whether a given monument still exists, whether it is unique or common, what is the overall context in which it should be seen, and (on a wider scale) what rates of destruction have affected specific districts. Such surveys are, in short, of genuine assistance to those who must carry out or enforce the Ancient Monuments legislation.

What, then, is meant by 'A Conservationist's Weapon'? This question can be answered by the real events of the post-war decades. Threats to ancient monuments, like threats to rural amenities, to historic towns, and to the very landscape, now take the form of hundred-mile motorways, new towns the size of Solent City or Milton Keynes, and gravel-extraction spanning a couple of counties. These are not matters of a small farmer nibbling away at an earthen long-barrow or some ambitious shopkeeper altering a Tudor façade, even if these perils in a minor key persist. The archaeological society or pressure-group, often necessarily represented today at national level by the Society of Antiquaries or by the Council for British Archaeology, must be prepared to make a very strong case, to make it forcefully, to make it in close collaboration with ecological or scientific groups; but above all to make it in abundant and convincing detail. This is rarely done at the right time because the detail is not to hand; a hundred square miles of New Town may be designated, a ten-thousand-acre airfield chosen, and only later is the relevant survey in depth carried out, *after* the inquiries have been held and the contractors have begun to move in. One must not underrate the very notable stimulus to fieldwork and field-survey provided by such gigantic schemes—as Fowler (1969) has commented, apropos of the M5/M4 motorway scheme, 'In Gloucestershire and Somerset generally, more fieldwork was carried out in 1969 than in the last few decades put together'—or the immediate gains to knowledge which follow such stimuli: 'the steady addition of new Romano-British settlements on the clay lowlands down the line of the M5 will leave an ineradicable mark on future distribution maps' (Fowler, 1969; see also Fowler, 1970). The fact remains that such co-operative campaigns as the advance field-checking of 75 miles of projected motorway route in the spring of 1969 have not been a feature of many such post-war exploitations on this scale, and can only be undertaken in regions where skilled direction and a dense reserve of competent local workers are available. The success of the M5/M4 scheme, archaeologically speaking, stresses again the need to have field-survey cover of this calibre ready *in advance*, and over as much of Britain as possible.

To return to the Cornish check-lists and the area surveys which they represent, the practical value of such knowledge in advance has been amply shown in several recent contexts. Pool (1970) has provided a telling summary of events in the Land's End peninsula, now wholly surveyed, where threats to an area peculiarly rich in complexes of visible remains and still to a large extent open, uncultivated, granite moorland have assumed extensive proportions. These threats have included the sporadic revival of cliff-top metalliferous mining, a proposal for massive open-cast mining on the central ridge, the extension on a scarcely acceptable scale of existing granite quarries, the acquisition of land for a naval helicopter exercise-area, and an entirely new china-clay extraction scheme. The peninsula itself is very largely designated (1959) as 'an area of outstanding natural beauty', contains an unusually heavy holding of scheduled ancient monuments (including some guardianship specimens, like Chysauster and Carn Euny), and is fringed with a generally unspoilt coastline, numerous stretches of which are National Trust property.

There is no place to enlarge on the sorry fact that the County Council's attitude has ranged, as Pool bluntly states, 'from the scandalous to the equivocal' and has only now come out on the side of conservation; or that the local authority, the West Penwith R.D.C., has been 'a supporter of every scheme in the past ten years calculated to ruin its own unique area' (Pool, 1970, 9). Cornwall holds deep and well-grounded fears about unemployment, and many Cornishmen—perhaps the majority—would prefer to see a landscape filled with working mines than with tourists. In the broader setting of a vanishing British countryside, and the long-term context of the value of such areas as this peninsula to all future branches of field studies—not just to archaeology—the case for conservation is an exceptionally strong one. It is therefore appropriate that at the relevant inquiries all the amenity interests have tended to speak together, with common representation, and that in this joint pressure it has been possible to produce at once highly detailed maps, backed with evidence already in print, to show the precise nature and extent of any archaeological threat.

In mid-Cornwall, where a great tract of land is now a near-lunar landscape of gigantic conical tips of white gravel, abandoned pits filled with turquoise water, and active clay-pits hundreds of feet deep, the china-clay (kaolin) industry has an apparently unlimited life and is moreover expanding. The industry is becoming rapidly mechanized and provides a major export market. Areas equal to half-a-dozen parishes have gone for ever, and a new tip can seal a whole archaeological complex in a matter of months. Special priority has therefore been given to check-list work in the relevant Hundred (Powder), particularly all around the southern and western fringes of the china-clay district. To some extent, archaeological pressure here will take the form of rescue work rather than attempts at permanent conservation, but surveys have reached the point where it is possible to say, in a way which could not have been done ten years ago, exactly what will be disturbed or destroyed by any fresh pits or by the proposed pipelines from the pits down to the south coast loading-points. The outcome has been an increasingly fruitful liaison between the industry itself (now almost entirely English China Clays Ltd), the Cornwall Archaeological Society, and the Ancient Monuments Inspectorate. Instead of mere objection for objection's sake, the archaeologists are able to put forward reasoned and detailed suggestions, and to offer views as to the comparative values of sites and complexes likely to be threatened or destroyed. The industry in its turn has facilitated Ministry-sponsored rescue digging (Mercer, 1970a), has provided advance planning information (and access to its superior and continuous air-photographic cover), has evinced a real interest in the archaeology of its area, and has now (1970) gone so far as to lend earth-moving equipment for a CAS excavation right outside the clay-pit district. This whole experience, which could at its worst have degenerated into a stagnant impasse, shows that attention will be paid to archaeological conservationism provided that there is evidence to support the views which are advanced; and comparable situations in other parts of Britain confirm this. The strongest evidence that we can offer is, and will continue to be, the evidence derived from intensive field-survey planned and executed in advance; and it is perhaps trite to add that the more often an archaeological body can adduce material of this calibre, the greater the weight that will be attached to that body's views in all such conservationist situations.

CONCLUSION

This is an essay in a volume on the theme of fieldwork, designed to do honour to a fieldworker whose own output over so many years and in so many parts of Britain must form a constant stimulus to others. It would be ridiculous to dwell on the value of L. V. Grinsell's surveys, viewed simply as a contribution to knowledge; the plain fact that they colour all our thinking about the British Bronze Age speaks for itself. But this seems to be an appropriate juncture to consider the whole matter of detailed and intensive field-survey, in a Britain which, between now and A.D. 2000, will be criss-crossed by a thousand miles of motorways, will need a dozen or so new towns and half a dozen new airports, and is already starting to import gravel from abroad, its own denuded midland river-valleys having been virtually exhausted. This is a Britain in which comparatively young archaeologists who, under the guidance of Childe or Hawkes, saw the rolling Wessex prairies of Dorset and Wiltshire still covered with Celtic fields and barrow cemeteries, cannot today guide their own pupils on similar expeditions. It is also, and perhaps fortunately, a Britain in which quite suddenly archaeologists themselves are awakening to a belated realization of their own responsibilities; to the knowledge that, if they do not take steps to preserve at least some of the archaeological countryside (the 'planned preservation of visible history', as this exercise has been called), no one else will do it on their behalf. It is, again fortunately, an era of growing leisure and wider education, in which the distinctions between the full-time and part-time archaeologists are rapidly crumbling, not least under the impact of work done in extra-mural and adult education groups. Local and regional societies, phenomena in which British archaeology has always been uniquely rich, have begun to show themselves only too willing to play a full and effective part in the face of destruction, provided that the part is made clear and meaningful to them.

The suggestions which have been put forward amount to a single message; what is most needed now is planned, co-ordinated, intensive field-survey in as many parts of the British Isles as possible. In this paper, the work of one particular society has been described, mainly by way of illustration, but the principles, the methods, the aims, and the first results will all apply to any other area or to the labours of any other society. The additions to archaeological knowledge will be profound and disturbing, and entirely fresh models of our past may eventually emerge; this is all to the good. Our responsibilities to knowledge itself, to future workers, and to the present urgencies, are in no way less than those which have already been accepted by naturalists, or geologists, or botanists, or by workers in half a dozen other disciplines. We can be sure of one thing alone—time, in our little overcrowded and over-exploited country, will be running against us for the rest of this century.

Acknowledgement: the writer is particularly grateful to Mr Charles Sparrow, Q.C., for allowing him to see the results of his (necessarily international) research into the legal definitions of 'antiquity'.

REFERENCES

Duncombe-Jewell, L. C., 1902. 'Cowethas Kelto-Kernuak,' *Celtia* (Dublin), 78–79.

Fowler, P. J., 1969. 'M5, M4 and Archeology', *Archaeol. Rev.* 4, 13–20.
1970. 'M5, M4 and Archaeology: second interim report', *Archaeol. Rev.* 5, 5–10.

Fowler, P. J. and Evans, J. G., 1967. 'Ploughmarks, Lynchets and Early Fields,' *Antiquity* 41, 289–301.

Fox, A., 1964. *South West England* (London).

Henderson, C., 1928. In *The Cornish Church Guide* (Truro), 223 (reprint, Barton, Truro, 1964), 208.

Jenner, M., 1914. 'The Ancient Monuments Consolidation and Amendment Act, 1913,' *J. Roy. Instit. Cornwall* 19, 440–55

Langdon, A., 1896. *Old Cornish Crosses* (Truro).

Marstrander, C. J. S., 1937. 'Treen og Keeill', *Norsk Tidsskrift for Sprogvidenskap* 8 (Oslo), 257–500 (English summary).

Megaw, J. V. S. *et al.*, 1961. 'The Bronze Age Settlement at Gwithian, Cornwall: preliminary report on the evidence for early agriculture', *Proc. West Cornwall Field Club* 2, 5, 200–15.

Mercer, R. J., 1970a. 'The Excavation of a Bronze Age Hut-Circle Settlement, Stannon Down, St. Breward,' *Cornish Archaeol.* 9, 17–46.
1970b. 'The Neolithic Settlement on Carn Brea: preliminary report, 1970', *Cornish Archaeol.* 9, 53–62.

Newcomb, R. M., 1968. 'Geographical Location Analysis and Iron Age Settlement in West Penwith', *Cornish Archaeol.* 7, 5–13.
1970. 'The Spatial Distribution of Hill Forts in West Penwith.' *Cornish Archaeol.* 9, 53–58.

Pool, P. A. S., 1970. 'The Battle for Penwith,' *Cornish Rev.* 15, 5–10.

Russell, V., 1959. 'Checklists of the Antiquities of West Penwith, 1: Parish of St. Just-in-Penwith,' *Proc. West Cornwall Fld. Club* 2, 3, 95–103.

Thomas, C., 1964. 'Settlement History in Early Cornwall: I, The Hundreds,' *Cornish Archaeol.* 3, 70–79.
1965. 'Coast and Cliff Names of Gwithian and the North Cliffs,' *J. Roy. Instit. Cornwall*, n.s. 1, 12–36, with additions in 3, 1967, 291–296.
1966. 'The Character and Origins of Roman Dumnonia,' in Thomas, C. (ed.), *Rural Settlement in Roman Britain* (CBA Res. Rpt. 7), 87–91.
1967. *Christian Antiquities of Camborne* (Warne, St. Austell).
(ed.) 1969. 'Parochial Checklists: a note on progress,' *Cornish Archaeol.* 8, 113–114.

CHAPTER IV

Field Archaeology in Future

Peter Fowler

> 'I am heartily sorry I did not set down the Antiquities of these parts sooner, for since the time aforesaid (1659) many things are irrecoverably lost.' John Aubrey in 1670.
>
> 'As documents of the past, field monuments are as important a form of historical material as the paper and parchment documents used by the historian' (Walsh Report, 1969, 60).
>
> 'If we want progress, history has got to go . . . progressively we have got to get rid of these ancient monuments.' Chairman of an Urban Council, *Somerset Guardian*, 16 October 1970.

John Aubrey's observation, set out again here at the end of European Conservation Year 1970, has only gained force in the intervening three centuries; and just as he was able to note the disappearance of Antiquities in the mid-seventeenth century, so in the mid-twentieth century the present generation have also seen what their elders took for granted, and the sort of field archaeology that they themselves were brought up on, largely disappear altogether. All over Europe what is left of our archaeological heritage is very much at risk: a small and unrepresentative sample could be all that is left in thirty years' time.

This situation has been reached fairly rapidly, despite Aubrey's early warning. How I envy Colt Hoare, riding across the grazed and unploughed Wiltshire Downs 150 years ago; how I envy Leslie Grinsell striding freely across the turf of the Berkshire Downs as late as the 1930s. But sentimentality about the joys of earlier fieldwork, as about the past itself, has no place in the field archaeology of the 1970s. Changes in methodology and concepts would have extinguished it in any case: the crisis of destruction in field archaeology simply allows it neither time nor place. Following the essays on the development of and the present position in archaeological field studies (*above* p 38–95), I would like here to explore some of the options open to field archaeology, its practitioners and, beyond them, British society with regard to what has been loosely called our national archaeological heritage.

My starting-point is three facts and two assumptions. Fact one is that the rate, extent and completeness of the destruction of archaeological sites of all periods is increasing so rapidly that few intact sites will remain by A.D. 2000 unless positive action is taken now. Fact two is that many more sites exist than all previous estimates have indicated, implying that the scale of current and predictable destruction is and will be absolutely greater. And fact three is that present archaeological resources are inadequate to cope with this situation.

The assumptions are that people other than myself think that it is worth while doing something about this situation. Since, however, it is a big assumption with widespread implications involving public finance, academic endeavour and personal freedom, the grounds for making it should perhaps be outlined first before discussing the second assumption and the facts stated above. It would, after all, be much easier for us, for society, simply to say 'What a pity' and move on to other things.

In the first place, but perhaps not obvious to everyone, e.g. local councillors (see above), the continuous destruction of our national archaeological heritage raises a *moral* issue. Have we in fact the right, and if so on what grounds, to destroy the evidence of our predecessors' handiwork? For the most part this survives accidentally, by unintentional good fortune rather than good planning, up to a certain point in time at which there occurs a conflict of 'space-occupancy'. The conflict is basically no more than a static version of a car accident, i.e. over what should occupy a localized piece of land and air space at a particular time. All too often the conflict, even if it is recognized, has been and still is resolved by the existing making way for the new, usually on the unstated but in fact questionable assumption that old/existing = bad, useless; new (by definition) = better, progress. But 'better' for whom and for what? And 'progress' towards what, even if the concept of 'progress' is itself valid? In fact, local expediency and finance are usually the deciding factors without reference to a moral issue, in the same way that decisions about abortion and euthenasia, for example, are also decided by particular factors despite the background of public and professional morality. The parallel is not far-fetched: field monuments, like each human life, are unique and of finite limits individually and collectively; and whereas we can replace a life with another, admittedly different, individual, we can never replace a destroyed prehistoric mound or a sixteenth-century cottage.

But to query 'Have we a right to destroy?' is negative: should not the question rather be 'Have we not an obligation to preserve?' This question was in fact answered affirmatively in 1882 with the first Ancient Monuments Act, subsequently thrice amended. Whether we like it or not, by the very nature of things we are inheritors and for a time we are responsible for an inheritance which includes our environment generally and our ancient monuments in particular. In principle, our society, like most civilised societies, long ago recognized this responsibility and accepted it. All that has gone wrong since is that the means of carrying it out have diminished in relation to the size of the problem; the moral obligation has not been reduced and the pragmatic need to act on it has in fact increased.

Of course, the flaw in the moral argument is that, just as we should not anticipate future attitudes and needs by destroying the irreplaceable now, so we cannot logically anticipate the future by assuming that it will thank us for lumbering it with remnants of the past. But, by conserving, at least we are not pre-empting the future's decision on the subject: our successors can destroy what we keep if they so wish, but they cannot do that if the past has already been destroyed by us. It seems in fact a reasonable assumption that the future will need ancient monuments and will castigate us if we continue to destroy them, just as we deprecate now the sixteenth-century reformatory zeal, the seventeenth-century bigotry and the nineteenth-century Gothic revivalist fervour which together destroyed, albeit with the best intentions, so much of what should have been our mediaeval architectural inheritance. Of course, in practice there is little to gainsay the argument that each generation must perforce do what seems best to it without too much thought for the future, and indeed to vitiate the point that, architecturally and in landscape terms, much of the interest and value of our inheritance derives from the palimpsest of successive human activities to which it bears witness; but the fundamental difference in the situation now, compared to the haphazard destruction, exploitation, alteration and preservation of our resources in the past, is that, as in the forebodings of some religious masochists, the end is in sight. This applies as much to archaeological remains, particularly those still upstanding, as to natural resources such as gravel and near-extinct species of wild life. We can presumably invent a gravel-substitute or circumvent the problem of its disappearance by a breakthrough in construction technology; in the last resort, a threatened species can be rescued by removal to a protected breeding-ground, a principle contravening that of 'natural selection' which is already acted upon. But evidence from the past is unique, the unreproduceable product of particular men in particular circumstances at a particular time, and it too is of a limited quantity which is now in danger of disappearing. This is why the moral issue is for us in the later twentieth century a real and practical one: have we the right to continue destroying our archaeological heritage when we know we are destroying it to extinction? Have we not an obligation to temper our actions by a conscious policy of conservation, so that at least a representative sample of what we inherited is passed on to the twenty-first century?

Nor are these questions idle debating points, for if European Conservation Year has achieved little else, it has articulated and rationalized the nagging doubt behind the material prosperity of the 'advanced' countries as to whether the goal of greater material prosperity is in itself sufficient immediate justification for the current rape of our environment and, ultimately, whether such a goal is in Man's own best interests. The very concept of progress, *sensu* material improvement, which has largely motivated the Western World for a century, has been, if not actually stopped in its tracks, at least queried; and the basic reason for this happening is simply that people are more than flesh and blood requiring only creature comforts. Agreed we are all consumers, but our needs embrace more than the artificial products of late-twentieth-century technology. Now the relevance of this point to archaeology in Britain over the next thirty years is two-fold: first, practically all the archaeological destruction of the last thirty years has been occasioned by pursuit of the goal 'progress', on the assumption that that in itself was sufficient reason; and second, archaeology in both obvious and subtle ways can, like the now generally accepted precepts of nature conservation and within the overall field of environmental concern, contribute towards that 'something else' which, in the final analysis, the human spirit needs. The point is now being openly made that some would prefer a conscious policy of amenity promotion even at the expense of a marginal drop in the gross national product or some such previously unquestioned materialistic yet abstract god: in practice this could mean diverting a new road around, instead of flattening, a deserted medieval village, or putting a new office block on stilts over instead of through the Roman bath-house already occupying the site. In practice such issues may seem only financial, but, at bottom, they involve moral decisions of which we should at least be aware.

My second assumption is that the nature and scope of archaeology are generally understood. In fact, as all archaeologists discover as they excavate beneath the public gaze, as they stump the country with their 'popular lectures', and as they confront local authority and commercial acumen in committee, the nature and scope of archaeology are not understood even where there is interest and goodwill. The reasons for this are not hard to seek: the dynamic nature of the subject itself (and this is not the place to explain that); the 'ivory tower' attitude of many academic archaeologists up to and including the present; the ineptitude of many local 'archaeologists' who figure in the local press; the generally misleading image of the subject diffused by so many museums with their repetitive emphasis on things as such with, if anything, overtones of aesthetics and morbidity (*cf.* Hawkes, 1951, 1); and the in many ways unfortunate involvement of the subject in those two themes, death and treasure, so dear to every journalistic typewriter and film-camera. Even in 1970 archaeology has hardly begun to present itself properly although it is nearly forty years since Wheeler was at Maiden Castle; but what can be done with a situation in which archaeology's terms of reference are predetermined and circumscribed by existing prejudices? At the end of a recent Archaeological Society lecture largely devoted to the argument being advanced here, in which I happened to illustrate a point with a slide of a crouched inhumation, the only two questions concerned the skeleton ('Why was it crouched?'—'The foetal position, madam'; 'What happens to the bones after you have found them—do you take them home?' The childish temptation to say 'Yes, the dog likes them' was duly resisted); a TV producer recently telephoned to ask if I could co-operate on a report on the destruction of archaeological sites but, despite my willingness, quickly lost interest when I could not suggest suitable film situations there and then equivalent to bulldozers charging through Stonehenge. Thus do the media shape the image.

It is indeed tragic for archaeology that at the very time when it needs to be taken seriously by non-academics, its confidence in its own rationale, in its ability to recreate a firm outline of the past, and in its methodology, has largely evaporated. It is a time of healthy self-doubt, of questioning, of seeking new orders in its field study. Academically, intellectually, this is stimulating; from the public relations point of view, from the educational point of view, it is little short of disastrous. Of course, all that is really happening is that the subject is growing up, but adolescence is doubly difficult when the world demands maturity. In all conscience, we must deny the cosy picture of the past which archaeology has largely created on the basis of the then available models, methods and material; we must deny the aims attributed to us by an interested public; but neither action alters the fact that, at the moment, archaeology cannot 'deliver the goods'. We have no substitute picture ready, cut and dried for mass consumption; and, unfortunately, neither media nor the public have the time to listen to qualified hesitation. They want to know when the Bronze Age began, not that we now have doubts about the validity of the Three Age System; they genuinely want to know what we have found, not wishing to know about the significance of the artefact-sterile soil profile we are meticulously sampling. This communication-gap is inevitable: the question is, do we try to close it, and if so, how?

The only honest solution is to persist, using increasingly the modern media of communication, in trying to put over what archaeology is really about, even if this has initially to be at the level of 'We are digging up not things but people'. But major misconceptions also exist about the role of excavation in archaeology—the two are usually regarded as synonymous—and about the scope and range of archaeology itself. When we have so recently ourselves realized that an archaeological approach is valid up to the very recent past, we cannot blame public opinion for confining our field to the Romans and the Ancient Britons before that. After all, we have still to convince many an historian of the contribution archaeology can make to medieval studies, and the claims and activities of 'post-medieval' and 'industrial' archaeologists are not above suspicion even within the profession. Yet it is surely not too difficult to grasp that the distribution and design of concrete pill-boxes of *c.* 1940 in a southern English county, or the layout of a post-Beeching deserted railway station in Northumberland, can provide information, almost certainly not written down, of the same order as a map showing Saxon shore forts or as the plan of an excavated neolithic settlement. Meanwhile, however, archaeology is confined by its popular functions to skeletons and treasure of a long time ago.

We may find this exasperating or smile wanly in a superior sort of way, but this unfortunate fact of life is much more than an academic matter which we can safely ignore as we pursue our recondite research: it is of immediate practical implication in matters of conservation. The Smitham lead-mining chimney may be only a hundred years old and it may be industrial, but because it is now the last such structure remaining on Mendip it must be maintained for the same reasons that the last undamaged Wessex barrow group must be preserved. Age is irrelevant in such matters, but archaeology will continue to be handicapped until it loses its popular pre-occupation with things that are very old. We must simply keep saying that the scope of archaeology embraces the material remains of Man's past from the earliest times to yesterday. With a receptive audience, one could add that in terms of artefacts the range is from palaeolithic to petrol pumps, and in terms of sites from chipping floors to cinemas. And, for good measure, the irrelevance of absolute age can be underlined by making the point that the pace of technological and social change, which is what after all archaeology studies so well has been so great during the last seventy years that early twentieth-century agricultural machinery and electric plant relate to us as did Roman equipment to people in 1570. Distances in time can indeed lend enchantment to the view, a spurious reason for study or preservation; but archaeology's criteria surely relate to the irregular ebb and flow of human endeavour in continuously changing circumstances rather than the metronomic measure of time.

These two assumptions—about the moral issue in, and the range of archaeology as related to, society's attitude to our past—are directly relevant to field archaeology; that is, the collection and study of primary data on and in the ground. Though, as Ashbee shows (above p 58), an early tradition of this non-excavational type of archaeology developed in Britain, it first of all declined in relative importance in the face of the artefact classificatory phase of archaeology in the later nineteenth century and subsequently almost withered away, certainly in terms of money, time and resources expended, compared with the glamorous activities of excavating. Since archaeologists themselves have unquestioningly accepted that excavation is their prime function in the field, they can hardly complain now if others accept this too. The fact that we can point to a few recent and contemporary outstanding field archaeologists—Fox, Crawford, Piggott, Bowen and, of course, Grinsell—in a way highlights the relative and absolute decline of this method of discovery and inquiry. One wonders in fact if the establishment of the Royal Commissions on Historical/Ancient Monuments sixty years ago has not had a long-term discouraging influence here, first by encouraging the belief that, eventually, 'they' will do it and, second, by setting standards of presentation and interpretation so high that they have pre-empted the field.

It is possible also that the advent of the archaeological air photograph may have encouraged the idea that superior and automatic recording had now arrived and that foot-slogging was henceforth superfluous. To be fair, however, in the last twenty-five years a great deal of fieldwork has in fact been carried out, by the Ordnance Survey, the Commission, the Ancient Monuments Inspectorate and a few individuals, and, on the other hand, the demands of rescue or salvage archaeology have absorbed the greater part of the resources available. Nevertheless, the private enterprise, part-time, amateur practice of field archaeology has waned, plausibly in imitation of the professionals and undoubtedly because of the mistaken notions that 'anyone can excavate', and that running one's own excavation was a necessary status symbol. Fieldwork, less glamorous and requiring individual effort rather than jolly communal activity, has also seemed rather pointless. Now we know better, as we make a realistic estimate of our archaeological situation, and Thomas (*above*, p 84) has already clearly defined three main reasons why fieldwork is not only required but is also a social obligation on archaeology's devotees.

The Crisis in Field Archaeology

Let us return to the three facts (above p 96) which together make a developing field archaeology imperative for the future of British archaeology. I would go further and say it is in this field that the local societies which are going to survive as more than vicarage tea-party affairs are going to find their fulfilment and make a significant contribution to archaeological knowledge. Thomas (*above* p 85) has already shown how many can no longer afford, financially or morally, to carry out their own excavations: the same is true on technical grounds, at least in terms of research excavation. A huge gap between the big professional excavation and the local group's weekend 'dig' has already opened up; each is producing different types of result, qualitatively as well as quantitatively, and it is becoming increasingly difficult to justify the latter in view of all the contrary factors. Some responsible societies have recognised this and now only undertake emergency or a professionally directed excavation; others will follow suit as their resources are seen to be inadequate and deliberate excavation is seen to be undesirable in any case. In a sense, the crisis situation therefore has been defined appositely because it offers a clear-cut role for the local society and the individual when both might have been rather at a loss: in proposing fieldwork, one is therefore not just trying to fob the part-timers off with the second-best, but suggesting the line not only that they can follow to their own advantage but also that British archaeology desperately needs developing. Often too, they are better placed, and indeed qualified, to do this than their full-time colleagues. And as a mentor, self-trained but conscientious, enjoying the task yet disciplined, we could have none better than LVG. But why does the value of his work increase with the passage of time, and why is more fieldwork so necessary now?

The reasons are basically that destruction has already overtaken many of the LVG-recorded sites, so that his field-notes are now the primary source material; and that destruction will affect the great majority of remaining sites in the next generation. It therefore falls, whether we like it or not, to the archaeologists active over the next thirty years to record what they can, because what they do will stand as the primary material thereafter. If that is not an opportunity and an obligation, to knowledge, to society and to one's own favourite area, I do not know what is. For it is a fact that 'the rate, extent and completeness of the destruction of archaeological sites of all periods is increasing so rapidly that few intact examples will remain by A.D. 2000 unless we take positive action now.' The destructive factors, all stemming from the needs to provide for a dynamic society in a group of small islands, are well known: the extractive industries such as gravel, sand, stone, coal and peat; construction works, principally town centre redevelopment, new town development, new buildings generally, new roads and motorways; and, in the country, the 'normal' processes of agriculture and forestry. Though the first may create more dramatic crises, it is undoubtedly the last two factors which have done the damage, agriculture particularly in southern and eastern England, forestry in the generally higher areas of the west and north. Apart from some larger enclosures like hill-forts, moats and motte-and-bailey castles, hardly any earthworks are now left in East Anglia; while in Wessex, Walsh (1969) provides appalling figures to bear out the evidence of one's own eyes and experience that destruction continued apace throughout the fifties and sixties as downland was brought under the plough at a cost of £12 per acre to the taxpayer. The short-term profit has now been gained—at the cost of soil exhaustion, incipient erosion and the loss of part of our European heritage of which we were the temporary caretakers.

If that sounds melodramatic, let us just glance at the most obvious of archaeological sites, and never mind the thousands of equally significant but less imposing ones. Hill-forts might be thought safe, and the way in which their ramparts still brood over the Wessex skylines almost proclaims their immunity from the surrounding arable sea of archaeological destruction. Indeed, their ramparts *do* survive and they *are* impressive, but at only a handful—Abbotsbury, Bindon, Chalbury, Hambledon, Dorset; Uffington, Berks; Beacon, Ladle and Old Winchester Hills, Hants; and Whitesheet Hill, Oldbury and Oliver's Castle, Wilts—is the interior unploughed or otherwise undamaged so that we can see on the surface the outlines of buildings and other domestic features. As current excavations, at Danebury, Hants, Pilsden Pen, Dorset, and Somerset's two Cadburys, for example, are demonstrating so clearly, our understanding of hill-forts is being immeasurably increased by large-scale and detailed work on the interiors and not just the defensive boundaries; and yet we are already down to the last ten per cent of such sites where we can both survey, teach and, if necessary, excavate with hope of success. But worse has already happened: of 'Little Woodburys', that classic of all type-sites, not a single example now exists as an earthwork in Wessex.

Or take any area, a county for example. In Somerset, in terms of visible sites, the situation generally is similar to that of hill-forts in particular, though in default of systematic fieldwork it is difficult to give precise figures, particularly of overall numbers from which percentages of surviving monuments can be stated. Once again, however, the almost inevitable LVG list of barrows for the county will shortly be fully published, so that facts will be ascertainable about them. For the rest, the hill-fort situation is similar to that already described: the ramparts survive but few interiors are intact. I know of only two Iron Age settlements other than hill-forts to which students can be taken and told 'This is what a late prehistoric settlement looks like'—a good criterion this, as teachers are realising only too well as yearly their choices for field demonstration are narrowed and they increasingly follow each other round the same few sites. Of the rural settlements of Roman Somerset, one of the most prosperous areas of Roman Britain, three or four visibly survive (Pl IX), and their agricultural background is represented by three reasonably well-preserved 'Celtic' field systems, all in the north of the county. Three examples—when tens of thousands of acres must have been cultivated in Roman and earlier times!

In Gloucestershire the picture is depressingly similar: the barrows again we know about, the hill-fort defences are impressive albeit defining ploughed or quarried interiors, and that is about all apart from outstanding freaks of preservation like Barnsley Park—which really only underlines what we have lost. For one worrying aspect of this random destruction is that we are unintentionally creating a false archaeology of a prehistoric Britain in which people only erected megaliths and hill-forts and were then buried under large mounds. The other ninety-nine per cent of people of human endeavour over some 5000 years will soon simply not be represented and will not therefore be demonstrable from the primary evidence. Prehistory will indeed then become 'the study of the incredible by the incredulous' (Hawkes, 1951, 10). But before historians roar their self-righteous approval—for we all like to hear what we 'know' to be true—may I point to Bath, self-advertised as 'Aquae Sulis of Roman Britain' and well-known gem of ('upper-class' understood) Georgian architecture. Thus the image, and so shall it be: excavations and display of the Roman baths continue, but so does the demolition of the (less important, i.e. less architecturally and aesthetically pleasing) surrounding eighteenth to early nineteenth-century buildings. About 700 houses have been destroyed in the last twenty-five years; another 600 are due to go during planned redevelopment. Inevitably (because only 'top people' exist in the history our administrators learnt?), it is the houses of the 'lower classes' which are being destroyed, and history is being falsified. Now, of course, I know that poor housing is a blight but its destruction is not the only remedy. Meanwhile, in the fullness of time, i.e. A.D. 2000, Bath in the Georgian era will appear on the face of it to have had no artisan class!

These last few paragraphs are based very much on personal experience and knowledge of but one part of England. Other areas could produce similar figures, and archaeology, to drive home its case, needs lots more facts and figures from the regions, but it also needs a national archive, both of destruction and preservation. This is in fact being built up through the grossly understaffed National Monuments Record, but details of its data are not yet published. Its parent organisation, in England anyway, has provided some of the best evidence, in general with *Monuments Threatened and Destroyed* (1963) and in particular, with reference to gravel-extraction, in *A Matter of Time* (1960). The English Commission accepted as a marginal commitment, the investigation of sites and areas notified to it as under threat. In the period 1956–1962, nearly two thousand notifications involving areas and buildings were received, nearly half of which warranted individual visits and inspections, resulting in the 1963 published list of 850 monuments threatened or destroyed. It is possible also to glean similar information running to hundreds of sites each year from the *Annual Reports* of the CBA, far and away the most comprehensive survey of what actually goes on all the time in British archaeology. Here the public façade of the publicised excavations is annually put in perspective, while the calm review of events chronicles the continuing erosion of our heritage. What fantastic scale of values in our society lies behind the relief with which, in the 1969 *Report*, it is recorded that only 266 listed buildings were destroyed in 1969 compared to 400+ in 1966, and that the annual loss of historic buildings has been reduced, according to Ministry of Housing estimates, by at least 35 per cent. Nevertheless, how long can this attrition go on? We are dealing with a wasting national asset in all respects. Of some parts the end is in sight immediately, and of others in the medium term, unless we adopt nationally and regionally a policy of conservation for visible and buried history.

The second basic fact is that many more sites exist than all previous estimates have indicated. This being so, the scale of destruction will inevitably be absolutely greater. It is of course ironic that the 'quantative revolution' in field archaeology should come about at the same time when the destructive forces are at their strongest; but it is not just coincidence that this has happened, for in large part it is the scale of current destruction, by continually turning up sites and material, that has made the realisation of the sheer quantity of archaeology on British soil inescapable (Pl.X). In a very real sense, commercial development leads inexorably to archaeological discovery. What is wrong is not so much that material is being continuously destroyed—archaeologists are not unrealistic preservationists and are not arguing that development should stop—but that proper provision for archaeological eventualities is almost never built into any

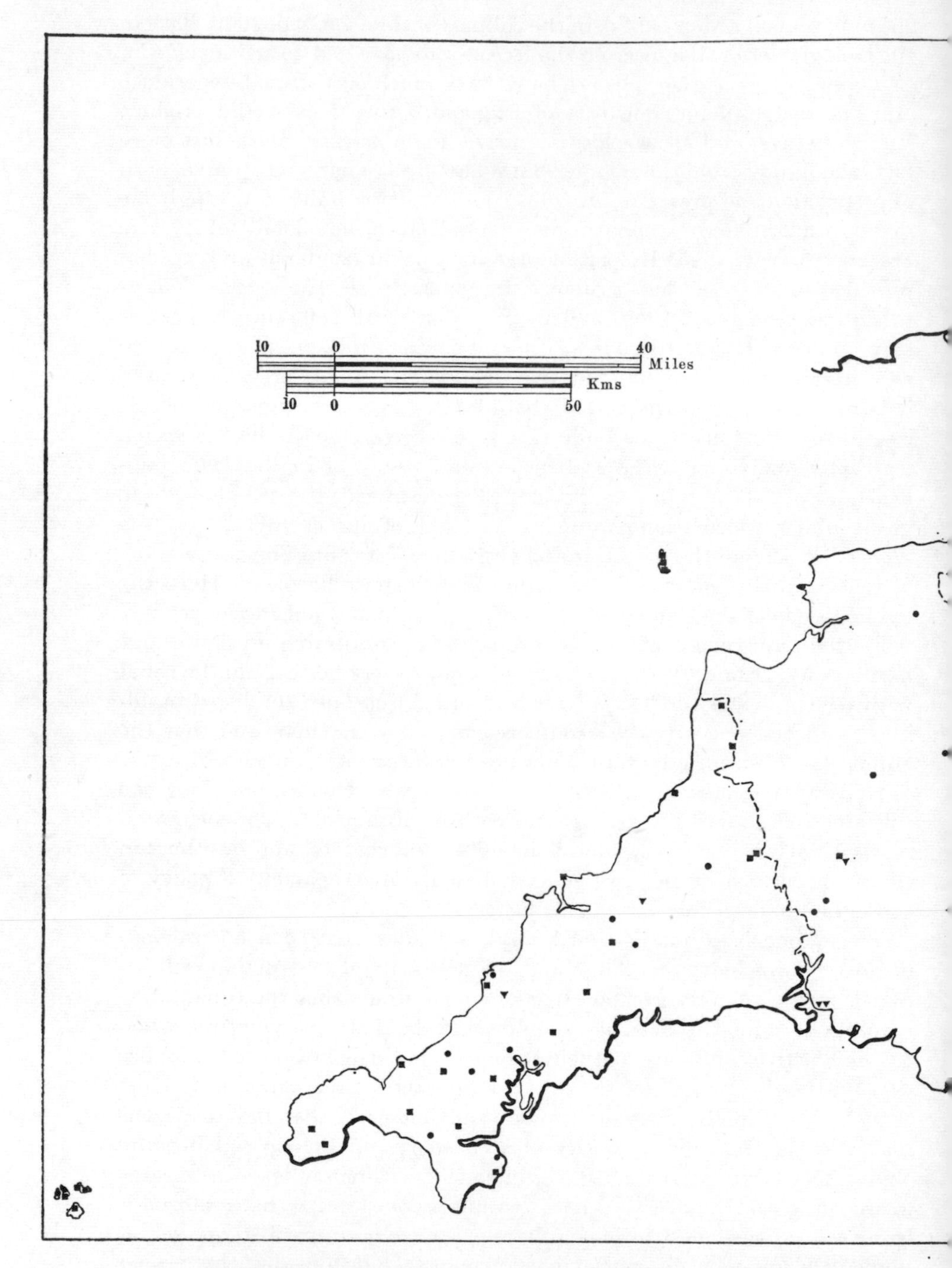

8. Archaeological fieldwork and excavation in S.W. England 1966–70, as shown by information published in *Archaeological Review*, 1966–70.

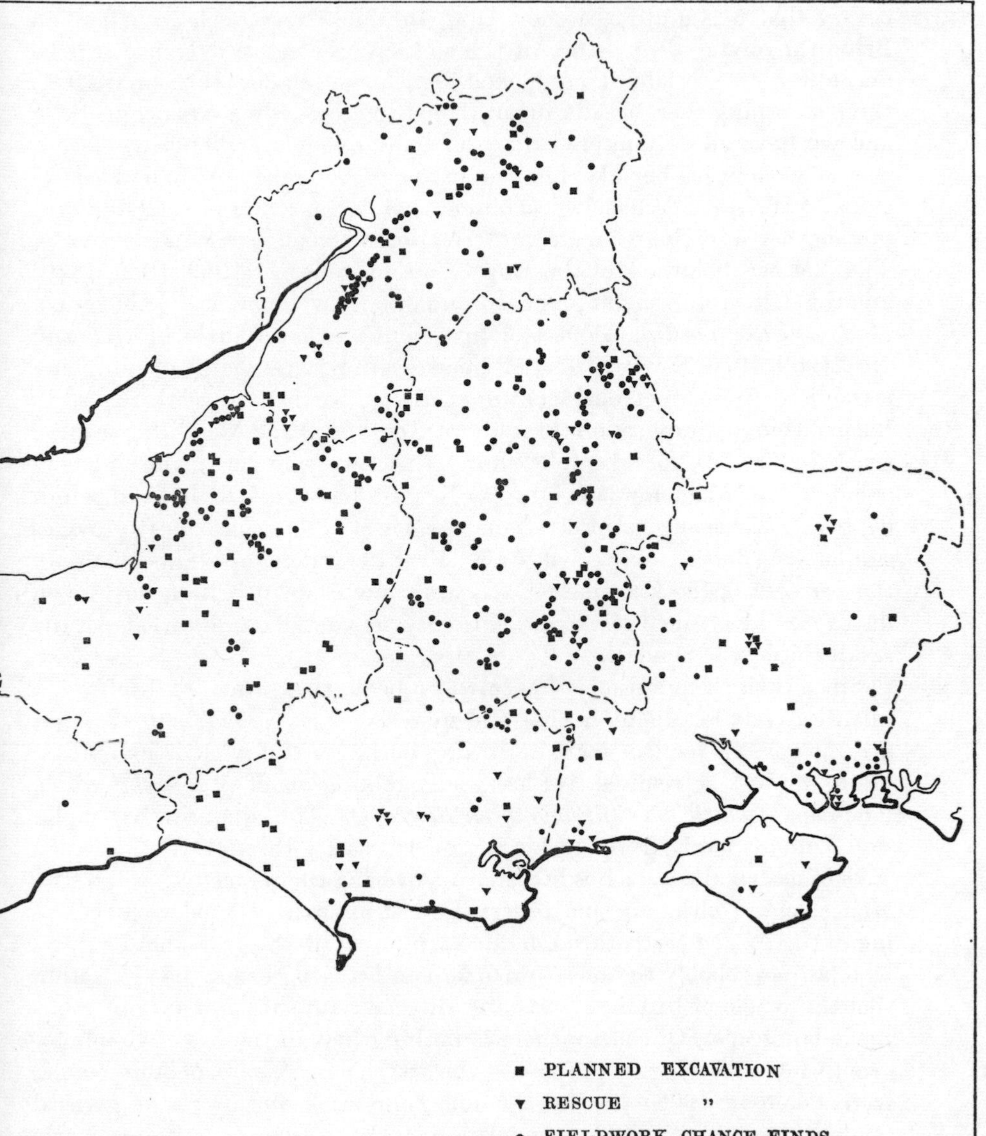
■ PLANNED EXCAVATION
▼ RESCUE "
● FIELDWORK, CHANCE FINDS
D.L.L.
P71

development plan *from the beginning*. Such has been the rate of new discovery that it is quite clear now that, in almost any work anywhere in Britain involving disturbance of the soil, archaeological evidence will be encountered, especially if it is looked for. How often does the remark 'Oh, there's nothing there' really mean, if it is not actually a downright lie—and we have all encountered that, on building sites particularly—either that no lookout has been kept or that care has been taken not to notice anything. A truism of archaeological observation is 'Look and ye shall find'; or, put another way, there is a direct correlation between search and discovery. The planned fieldwork of the Royal Commissions (esp 1960, 1969, 1970) and the deliberate watching of road and other developments in Kent (*Kent Archaeol. Rev. passim*), Gloucestershire, Somerset and Wiltshire (*Archaeol. Rev.* 1969, 1970; Fowler, 1972) all bear recent witness to this maxim, long recognised from nineteenth-century activity, particularly with regard to Palaeolithic (by implication throughout Roe, 1968) and Mesolithic studies. Clark (1968, 58), for example, shows that only one out of the fourteen examples of Maglemosian sites in Britain has come to light through deliberate archaeological excavation. Meaney (1964) unconsciously provides similar data for a later period. Analysis of her catalogue shows that only ten per cent of the known Anglo-Saxon cemeteries in Britain have been discovered by planned research, i.e. ninety per cent of our knowledge is the result initially of chance.

Since British prehistory has always been recognised as 'rich', i.e. quantitatively fortunate, in sites and material, it is reasonable to ask what are the reasons for this increase in our heritage, and what is its nature. Here, it must be realised, we are really talking about sites, even whole landscapes, *which have already been destroyed*. The 'quantitative explosion' comes mainly from their rediscovery, partly through the increased scale of destruction which is literally uncovering them, partly through the archaeological checking and observation stimilated by modern developments (fig 9), and partly through the cumulative effects of air-photography. The last is probably the most important in bringing about the realisation that the whole of Britain is virtually littered with sites and ancient man-made landscapes. Of course, there is nothing new in the use of air-photography for archaeological purposes—the first shots in Britain, of Stonehenge, were taken in 1908—but for a whole generation and more the general tendency was to exclaim in wonderment at the technique for its cleverness at capturing 'new' sites: no one went on from this to exclaim either how awful it was that so many sites had already been destroyed (and here I am thinking in particular of 'flat' sites showing up as soil- and crop-marks), to wonder about the quantitative implications, or to query whether the results, primarily from southern English chalk and gravel areas originally, could be expected on similar subsoil elsewhere or indeed on different subsoil anywhere.

Only Crawford in Wessex and Phillips in the Fens in the thirties went on conceptually, from the technical marvels of air-photography of single sites or individual complexes, to think in terms of recovering and reconstituting lost landscapes as a whole. Rather did the myth develop that much could be recovered in Wessex because there always had been a lot of human activity and consequential evidence there: everybody knew it was an exceptional area, so that the new discoveries were accepted as confirmation of its pre-eminence. A similar reaction seems to have been aroused by Allen's contemporary results just to the north in the Middle Thames area: the near-profligacy with which sites were strewn along the gravels was almost taken as what could be expected in an area so importantly situated between the centre of prehistoric Britain and Britain's best University. As with the great nineteenth century earth-moving operations, particularly railway construction and gravel-digging, which produced so much of our museum-mouldering material, the wrong deductions seem to have been drawn; or, to put the point positively, no one seems to have hazarded the interpretation that the meaning of the nineteenth-century finds and the early air photos was that the whole landscape was saturated with evidence of our predecessors' activities.

The abundance of air-photographs since taken makes the point incontrovertible, supported as it is by an unceasing flow of material wherever it is looked for in development works. The fact is that most of the British landscape has been used by men at some time or other, and often successively, and it should therefore occasion no surprise whatsoever when evidence of this is uncovered. Rather should the question be 'Why is there no evidence?' when such appears to be the case. All too often the answer will be an inadequate or non-existent archaeological presence.

This is the third fact (above p 96), the real point at issue, because we must obviously accept, in view of the second fact, that sites and evidence are going to go on being disturbed and destroyed. Even if we had the most enlightened antiquities legislation and governmental archaeological policies, material would keep turning up. As it is, the nation's archaeological resources are quite inadequate to cope with the existing situation, let alone an increasing rate of destruction. This is not the place to describe those resources which have in any case recently been examined and assessed—and, on the official side, found wanting—in a governmental Committee of Enquiry (Walsh, 1969).

Some figures not quoted in that Report are, however, relevant in considering how state archaeology is functioning. One of the statutory obligations of the Inspectorate of Ancient Monuments under the Ancient Monuments Acts is to schedule 'ancient monuments' (and when are we going to call them, as in Ireland, National Monuments? An early twentieth-century pumping station is just as valid a part of our archaeological heritage as a Wessex barrow, yet by no chronological criteria is it 'ancient').

The national total of scheduled ancient monuments is now about 8000—an impressive figure, perhaps, taken by itself but so much of it made up of wasted paperwork. Nevertheless, the process of scheduling sites proceeds with exemplary speed bearing in mind the small size of the Inspectorate's archaeological staff:

Year	1960	1961	1962	1963	1964	1965	1966	1967	1968	1969
Monuments scheduled	*c.* 300	*c.* 300	371	178	324	145	286	454	676	495

Total in 10 years *c.* 3430

Walsh (1969) recommended that the eventual number of scheduled sites should be *c.* 16,000, so at the rate practised during the sixties, it will be nearly A.D. 2000 before scheduling is completed. Even if the work is speeded up, it will still be spanning the period of greatest predictable destruction and, in itself, will provide little or no protection to the sites.

Nor is excavation the answer, if only because, without a vastly increased bugdet, there are simply not the financial resources to excavate all the scheduled, let alone the far greater number of unscheduled, sites which will be destroyed. In any case, excavation is no longer always the point: the important consideration is to conserve untouched a representative sample of the sites. In 10, 20, 30 years' time, any such site is going to be of incalculably much greater value than the results (unpublished?) of a 'smash-and-grab excavation' now. However, fortunately if meagrely, the state is committed to a circumscribed rescue excavation programme which grew quantitatively quite dramatically during the sixties, even if qualitatively and in terms of publication the improvement was not so marked:

	1960	1961	1962	1963	1964	1965	1966	1967	1968	1969
MOPBW										
excavations	45		43	48	69	90	75	83	91	98
supported schemes	15		18	21	28	36	68	47	58	51
Total	60	66	61	69	97	126	143	130	149	149
Publication	29	51	?	?	28	39	40	35	49	52

These figures reflect the rising scale of threats rather than the Inspectorate's increasing ability to cope with an improving situation. Nevertheless, given the limited amount of money for 'rescue' work, the present policy of grant-aiding self-help local schemes as far as possible is a great incentive in the regions, and means that much more is being done than if the state was acting solely on its own. The Government, nevertheless, has a statutory obligation in this matter, and it must recognise that there is a limit to how much voluntary effort can achieve and indeed is willing to do. There is no doubt that, at the moment, a lot of ostensibly state archaeology is being done on the cheap through the goodwill of, and the prompting of conscience in many, professionals and part-timers, who can become, at times, a little weary of the continuous demands on them. Their help is doubtless a constant factor but, conversely, it must never be taken for granted.

This active individual interest and involvement in our national archaeology is an almost idiosyncratic British feature, impinging on both state and public sectors as well as forming numerically the largest part of the archaeological scene, the private sector. Perhaps its very existence reflects the differences in antiquities legislation between Britain and most Continental countries. We spot-list to preserve, and only except rarities of gold and silver in certain circumstances from the landowners' possession; but in Europe generally, as well as in many ex-colonial states, the antiquities legislation is comprehensive. All sites and finds, by definition, are protected by legal obligations on citizens to report discoveries to appropriate authorities. Archaeology is much more professionalised; there is much less public involvement; yet public interest in Holland and Denmark, for example, is as great as and perhaps better informed than in Britain. Somehow, the past there seems integrated with the ways of life, the ways of thought even—a frame of mind, perhaps—whereas here it is something apart, however interesting. The popular interest is there in Britain, and has been for a long time, as Daniel (1967) demonstrates, but thinking in an historical perspective does not come naturally to the Englishman anyway despite our international reputation for 'olde worlde' attractions. Is this not perhaps the clue—that the past is a curiosity, an oddity for highways and holidays and tourists, but not part of us? 'Nowhere else does the present regard itself as less committed by what happened in history' (Plumb, 1968, 10).

Perhaps archaeology cannot be blamed entirely for this state of affairs, but it has certainly missed opportunities to prevent it arising. One reason for this is the dichotomy amongst archaeologists themselves represented by the extremes: the 'right wing' pure scholarship school of thought which holds the CBA and its doings, involved as they are with political, social and public affairs, as beneath notice, as not 'academic' (the short answer to that of course is that anyone, scholar or not, who believes that archaeology exists in a social vacuum lined only with bookshelves and museum cases inhabits an ivory tower at the entrance to a blind alley); and the 'left-wing' extreme, anarchic or just unknowing, including the growing number of people who are simply anti-establishment in any form, unaware of the existing archaeological framework, and attracted to the subject mainly for what they can get out of it.

With the second part of the phenomenon, we have a considerable sociological problem in British archaeology, fraught with potential for good and ill. Nor is it simply a matter of being for or against the CBA, though that body is naturally much concerned. Whether or not the interest in archaeology has increased relative to the increase in population over the last twenty-five years, there has been an absolute increase in the numbers of people interested in archaeology, and in particular in the number of people active out of doors, mainly in excavation. Institutionally this has been represented by the tremendous increase in the number of local societies, as already noted, and no one knows now how many of these there are or what is the total membership of all the private sector bodies. Some 230 such societies are full members of the CBA, and probably at least that number again exist in and outside the regional groups. Membership varies so much, from approaching 2000 of the large successful county Society to the half-dozen or so of the minor, immature field group, that an estimate of the numbers of people sufficiently interested and responsible to join a society is difficult to estimate. A minimum figure would be 25,000; 50,000 is likely to be more accurate and perhaps not to be greatly exceeded if an accurate count were possible. For comparison, the membership of the National Trust is now over 200,000. Beyond this threshold, however, is a non-active interest running into hundreds of thousands, if not millions, as is indicated by visitor numbers to ancient monuments—nearly half- a million at Stonehenge in 1969—and viewing figures for television programmes about archaeology. The two main problems here are how to cater for the latter and how to benefit archaeologically from the committed interest of the former, always remembering that the active field interest of a membership declines relative to the size of the total membership. Whereas, for example, in a new group of thirty-five members, perhaps fifteen will want initially to be active out of doors, in an older society with 800 members the number wanting to excavate and work in the field will perhaps not exceed fifty. Any properly established society with an active membership of ten per cent or more is lucky; a similar sort of ratio is observable in introductory extra-mural classes where, typically, perhaps only one or two out of twenty new students will wish to pursue the subject into active participation. Such a proportion would suggest a total of perhaps some 5000 active archaeologists, 95% of them part-timers, in the country, though a personal feeling is that that estimate is somewhat too high.

Nevertheless, several thousand active people, most of them excavating, organized with varying efficiency in hundreds of archaeological societies, represent a considerable asset and a considerable challenge to the structure of British archaeology. Many of the new societies have been formed where the old have done nothing or have simply failed. It could be argued indeed that each new independent group is an indictment of the existing county society—Kent and Somerset spring to mind—for failing to move conceptually and socially, quite apart from archaeologically, into the second half of the twentieth-century. The rash of new groups in and around London in particular demonstrates dramatically the problems of trying to contain the explosive nature of active fieldwork within the existing organisational structure. Yet this sociological phenomenon, occuring very often in suburbia and industrial centres, precisely where the Victorian societies with their rural roots did not operate, and bringing in many individuals with non-academic or technical backgrounds, is more than just an administrative matter: it involves matters of archaeological standards, indeed academic standards, over both field techniques and publication and, furthermore, the future direction of archaeology in this country as a developing discipline open to all who are prepared to share the discipline as well as the rewards. Because archaeology is one of the few academic subjects which still is 'open to all' on those terms, because it is widely regarded as a bridge field of study between arts and sciences, and because it is too a link subject between full- and part-timer and, further, across educational and social divisions as its adherents study a common past, this matter to standards and publication is basic. After all, any ignoramus can dig a hole in a Roman site—and many have—find some pottery, ring up the local newspaper and feature in print the following Friday. Anyone who thinks that sort of activity bears any relation to archaeological needs must be told he is wrong.

What clearly does relate to those needs now and for the foreseeable future is fieldwork, very much the poor relation of 'real' archaeology, i.e. excavation, in recent years. Yet it has never quite disappeared, partly because the state is carrying it out continuously, partly because a minority of archaeologists choose fieldwork as their method of research. Although it is of course difficult to quantify such an activity as fieldwork it is a crudely measurable element in current British archaeology. In the years 1968–70, for example, *c* 14% of the courses and other activities advertised in the CBA's *Calendar of Excavations* were primarily concerned with fieldwork. During the decade 1960–70, 33 of the 102 projects recommended by the CBA for grants from the Carnegie United Kingdom Trust went to projects primarily based on fieldwork rather than excavation; and 29% of the publication grants made by the CBA in the same decade went to fieldwork papers too. Since the CBA has a bias, and increasingly so, towards the encouragement of fieldwork, those figures can be compared with a sample of eleven British archaeological publications, examined to see how they reflected fieldwork as distinct from excavation reports, and all the other types of paper represented in the spectrum of periodical archaeological publication (*see* p 115).

Of course, all these figures cannot carry too much weight, but as an exercise they have probably been worth obtaining to give some sort of answer to the question 'How strong an element is fieldwork in British archaeology?' Overall, the figures suggest that perhaps about one-fifth of our effort goes in this direction (the next question, 'What about the other four-fifths?', cannot be pursued here).

This estimate is not in fact surprising; but if it is at all accurate, it supports the view that the proportion of our archaeological effort directed into this critical activity is inadequate in present circumstances. Britain *is* relatively well explored and very well mapped archaeologically; but what we already know is but a fraction of what is still to be recorded and made available as information. Archaeology, of course, needs the information for its own academic purposes, since it is quite clear that all distribution maps are grossly incomplete and probably very misleading; but also society in general, planners, local authorities, and the service boards (gas, water, etc) in particular, need that information too. We are all working from out-of-date and inadequate maps, and the only way to fill them is in the field. The information is not in libraries and museums, though they and Record Offices yet have much to yield. And time is not on your side (Appendix I), which adds a moral dimension, as well as a social responsibility (Appendix II), to our efforts as archaeologists in the last three decades of the twentieth century. We cannot just hope for a renaissance in fieldwork; now, with the technical skills we can bring to bear, with the support of our thousands of colleagues, and with the opportunity and duty clearly before us, we must make it happen.

Fieldwork in British Archaeology
as represented by papers published in archaeological periodicals

Journal	*Papers published*	*Fieldwork*	*Comments*
Proc. Soc. Antiq. Scot. 1962–1968	63	41	Still collecting basic data; much fldwk. on buildings, roads, etc.
Archaeol. J. 1958–1969	88	39	High % from building surveys
Wiltshire Archaeol. Natur. Hist Mag 1962–1969	79	35	Fldwk tradition
Medieval Archaeol. 1957–1968	94	30	as *Proc. Soc. Antiq. Scot.*
Cornish Archaeol. 1962–1969	79	28	Fldwk policy (*see* p 77 above)
Trans. Bristol Gloucestershire Archaeol. Soc. 1965–1969	58	28	Strong industrial archaeology and buildings interest
CBA Archaeol. Abstracts 1968–70	921 (papers abstracted)	17	Includes a few foreign, but otherwise a fair sample?
Antiq. J. 1963–1969	113	11	Tends to include excav rpts. and medieval objects
Proc. Prehist. Soc. 1957–1969	164	8	Synoptic papers, excav. rpts
Antiquity 1966–1970	109	4	Synoptic and controversial papers; fldwk tradition in quality (from Crawford) rather than quantity
Current Archaeol.	*Unclassifiable*	*Negligible*	Emphasis on topicality, excavation; fldwk apparently journalistically dull?
	1768	Average % *c.* 22	

Notes:

1. The apparent correlation: the greater number of papers/the smaller the percentage of fieldwork reports might really be accounted for by the national nature of the last 4 periodicals i.e. fieldwork is primarily a regional concern?

2. The detailed analysis behind these figures suggested a slight general increase in fieldwork in the late 1960s.

APPENDIX I

During 1970, professional and public concern about the fate of Britain's archaeological heritage came to be voiced increasingly, culminating in a public meeting in London on 23 January 1971. One of the resolutions then passed was that the Secretary of State for the Environment receive a deputation from the meeting. As part of the evidence submitted to the Department of the Environment before the deputation went to Whitehall, the following memorandum was prepared. It is printed here as the background to the above paper with the agreement of the holding committee (1971) of 'Rescue', the new Trust for British Archaeology.

The Crisis in British Field Archaeology

A. Our archaeological sites are documents of our past, stretching back into periods long before the written records that are so carefully preserved in our great libraries. If three or four ancient manuscripts were taken at random from the British Museum Library every day and burnt without record, there would be an international outcry. We should be accused of vandalism incredible in a civilized nation conscious of its long and complex development. Yet this is what is happening to our archaeological records. In towns and cities and in the countryside the obliteration of ancient settlement sites and areas progresses at an appalling rate. The implantation of new towns of unprecedented size, the proliferation of motorways (both of which in their construction require millions of tons of sand and gravel), the exploitation of peat bogs containing preserved prehistoric structures, and the afforestation of hitherto untouched marginal land where there are visible remains, all represent threats to our sites on a gigantic scale. In addition, continued ploughing of thousands of archaeological sites on arable land, and the conversion of more and more land to arable, is destroying them insidiously and irrevocably, not least now that deep ploughing is becoming common.

Some figures will illustrate the scale of the problem. At the moment there are about 8,000 scheduled monuments. Even these protected sites are being destroyed or damaged at an astonishing rate. A survey in 1964 of three different areas of Wiltshire showed that of the 640 scheduled sites of ten years previously, 250 had been completely destroyed or badly damaged, and a further 150 less badly damaged—that is, in ten years only about 240 out of 640 protected sites had remained unscathed and many had been totally destroyed. And even in well-covered areas like Wiltshire by no means all sites are scheduled. In West Dorset, for example, the Royal Commission volume (1952) recorded 280 field monuments yet 15 years later only 150 had been scheduled, and many of these have how been damaged or destroyed. In South Dorset, where the Commission (1970) recorded 871 round barrows, less than 10% were undamaged in 1963, and the undamaged number is now probably less than 5%. In other words, the prime field monuments of one of the most important areas of Bronze Age Britain have been practically obliterated in our generation. In Gloucestershire, of 75 Neolithic long barrows in the same county, half have been destroyed, while a survey in 1970 showed that only one barrow cemetery now survives intact—and that is covered by trees.

There is a similarly grim picture from Wiltshire. A survey of the 100 recorded Romano-British settlements in 1964 showed that only 10 were still well-preserved, and that figure has since been reduced. For some sorts of site we are literally down to the last one or two. Nor is the situation any the less serious for later historical periods. Some of the best authenticated figures of all are available for deserted medieval village sites. Between 1500 and 1950 about 300 were destroyed, that is in 450 years; between 1950 and 1970, that is in 20 years, another 300 were destroyed, and they are now disappearing at the rate of 20 to 30 a year.

Redevelopment in the centres of our ancient cities and towns is often removing totally the whole sequence of the history from prehistoric times to the present, and it is only rarely that adequate excavation can be carried out in advance of this obliteration. In Worcester, for example, two holes some 300 ft by 200 ft by 20 ft deep have recently been dug for redevelopment, one of them removing part of the nucleus of the city centre with its occupation and defences going back to the Late Bronze Age, the other removing a Roman suburb and the site of the medieval Blackfriars. The situation is often more serious in our smaller towns, where money and archaeologists are simply not available to record the evidence before it disappears. New towns such as Peterborough, Milton Keynes, Redditch and the rest pose problems of widespread destruction in rural areas. The Peterborough new town area, for instance, will cover about 50 square miles. The Royal Commission's survey of the site shows that miles of the river terraces of the Nene are continuous settlement and agricultural sites spanning millennia. It is estimated that between £20,000—£30,000 a year will be needed to deal adequately with the archaeology of this area alone. There seems no hope of money on this scale being forthcoming. The bulk of this vast settlement area will therefore be destroyed without record. The problem is multiplied by Milton Keynes, Northampton New Town, the new conurbation between Southampton and Portsmouth, and certainly by any third airport which is sited inland. Cublington will, if built, cover some 13 square miles. We had good reason to think that there is on average at least one archaeological site every quarter square mile in Britain. Even if this estimate is too high by 100%, about 100 sites are likely to be affected by an airfield at Cublington and the archaeological implications of one at Foulness are likewise considerable.

Our urban civilisation swallows up sand and gravel at a quite astounding rate. Motorways, urban development, housing, factory building and

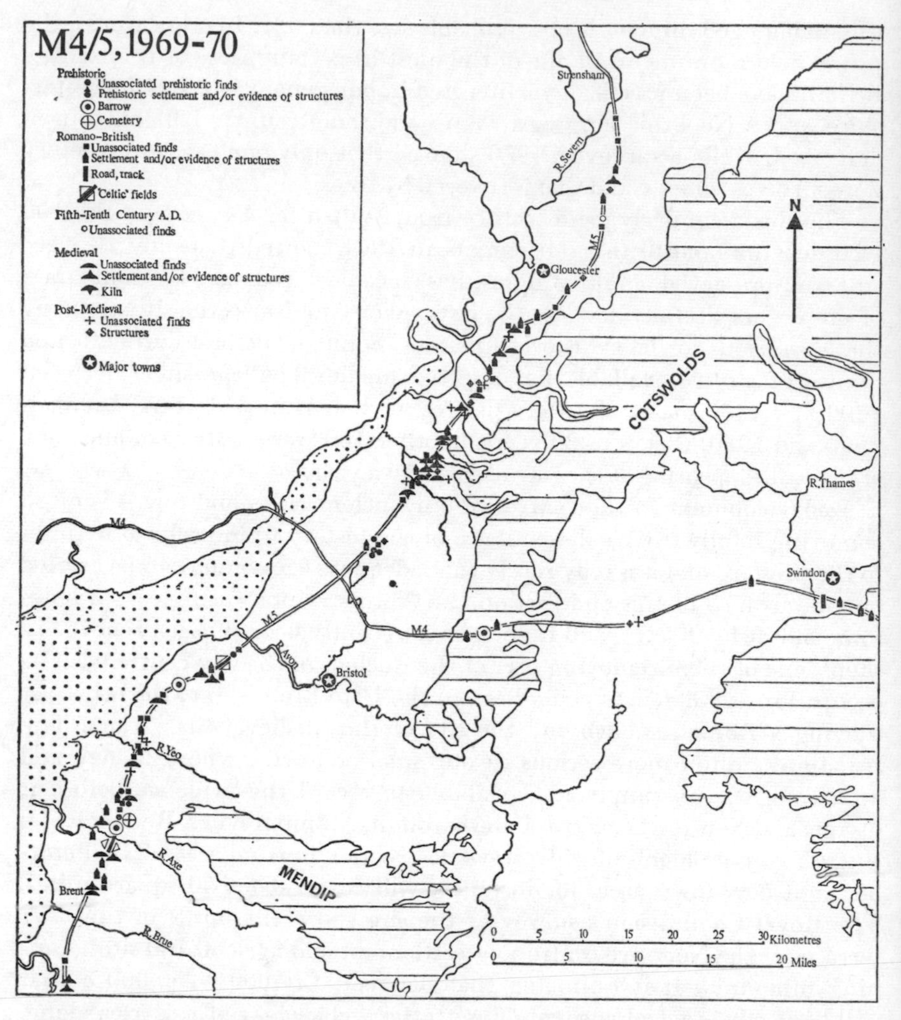

9. Sites and finds recorded, 1969–70 during construction of the M5 Motorway in Gloucestershire and Somerset and the M4 in Wiltshire.

major projects like a third airport, require sand and gravel in vast quantities. It was recently estimated that by 1980 extractors will be chewing up twelve square miles of land a year to supply the insatiable demand. Most of this sand and gravel comes from the river terraces where it was deposited at the end of the last Ice Age. The soils which developed naturally on the gravels were light and easily farmed, supporting a much less dense natural cover than, for example, the clay lands of the Midlands or the heavily-forested Weald. Early man tended therefore to settle on these river terraces, and aerial photographs taken within the last ten to fifteen years show that the valleys of many of the great rivers of lowland Britain—the

Thames, the Trent, the Severn, the Nene, the Welland and the Warwickshire Avon—together with their tributaries, form almost continuous ancient settlement sites. And all these are precisely the areas which are being removed at the rate of about two hundred million cubic yards a year.

Until recently, we have had little idea of the intensive occupation of these islands. Now the sheer quantity of antiquity buried in British soil is demonstrated not only by aerial photography and field surveys but also by the very development which destroys the sites. Again, it may be useful to quote some figures. In southern England it is now clear that there are dozens, probably hundreds, of mesolithic sites where previously only a few were known. The number of known 'sursuses' has doubled. The number of henge monuments has more than doubled. In East Anglia, where 48 round barrows were known at the beginning of 1959, at the end of that year 250 were known as the result of aerial photography in a dry summer —that is an increase of about 400%. The number of known Iron Age/Romano-British settlements round the area of Wroxeter in Shropshire is increasing annually, and there seems to be an average of about one site every quarter of a mile. Detailed fieldwork over 15 square miles of one area of Hampshire has increased the number of known sites from 5 to 95, and in the proposed new urban area between Southampton and Portsmouth, from 3 to 97. Recent work in Shropshire and Worcestershire has increased the number of known or suspected deserted medieval village sites from about a dozen to well over 200. Where we had one sub-Roman cemetery in Somerset a few years ago we now have six, and in Cornwall, where detailed checklists are being completed parish by parish, the number of enclosed Romano-British settlements has been increased tenfold, and the number of known round barrows, now somewhere near 3,000, is nearly four times what had previously been recorded. The recent extension of the M5 from north Gloucestershire to Somerset was systematically. watched by local archaeologists, both in advance of and during the construction. As a result, *c* 130 sites have so far been recorded where fewer than 10 were previously known or suspected. This is an average minimum density of about 2 sites every 1 mile along an archaeologically random line *c* 50 yards wide. Only 20 of these sites could be excavated, and only one of those completely, in advance of their destruction. The question arises—what went under the M4, the M5 in Worcestershire, the M6, the M9, the M1 and the M2? All this well illustrates the explosive quantitative nature of archaeology at the moment (fig 9).

It can of course be argued that if there are so many more sites than previously thought it will not matter too much if half of them are lost. Furthermore, would not the excavation and publication of hundreds more sites be rather embarrassing, putting a strain on our resources of manpower, of publication and on our ability to synthesise all the eventual material—perhaps it would be better to turn a blind eye, or at least a half-blind one?

Using the same analogy as before, let us think of the hundreds of thousands of documents in the Public Record Office, the British Museum, and Record Offices up and down the country. According to the above argument, it would not matter too much if half these were destroyed without being looked at—we would always have the other half. But the half we imagine being destroyed would be a random half which might include some of the most precious unstudied evidence we have—we would probably never know. Our archaeological sites and their environments are the similar raw materials of our discipline, the primary evidence for our nation's view of its unwritten past. It is this which is being eroded at a rate accelerating towards a disaster situation.

However, it is conceivable that after the next 20 or 30 years the rate of archaeological destruction will slow down, as the major road systems and new city centres are completed, when there is no need, we must hope, for more new towns on the scale of those currently planned, as the sands, gravels and peat deposit are exhausted commercially and as the surviving marginal land diminishes in acreage. For these reasons the remaining years of this century seem to us to be the most critical for the preservation, recording and exploration of a vast proportion of our sites and their environments. After this they will be gone. It seems very likely that, if we do nothing about it, these decades in which we live will be seen, from the point of view of the twenty-first century, as the period of the worst vandalism in our country's history, when we allowed thousands of archaeological sites to be obliterated without record or with little more than a passing glance. This is the scale of the problem which faces us.

B. The gravity of the situation led to a meeting of some 35 archaeologists at Barford in Warwickshire in February 1970, called by six members of the profession, to discuss ways in which the problem might be tackled both in the short and long terms. This meeting led to the formation of a working party consisting of the original six conveners of the meeting. This working party met on a number of occasions and called a further meeting in November 1970 at Newcastle-upon-Tyne, attended by about 50 archaeologists, many from the North of England, Scotland, and Northern Ireland.

By this time, therefore, a representative cross section of both full-time and some part-time archaeologists had been consulted. In addition, the ideas put forward at the Barford and Newcastle meetings had been widely canvassed among archaeological groups of all kinds.

Both meetings agreed that a public meeting should be held in London. This meeting took place on 23 January, 1971. Over 700 people attended, making this the largest archaeological meeting ever held in this country. The most encouraging feature was that the average age of those attending was about 30.

Proposals crystallized at the Newcastle meeting were put to the London meeting to sound the general body of archaeological opinion. Chief among

IX. Westmead, Butcombe, one of the last Romano-British settlements in Somerset visibly surviving as 'earthworks, (Photo 1967).

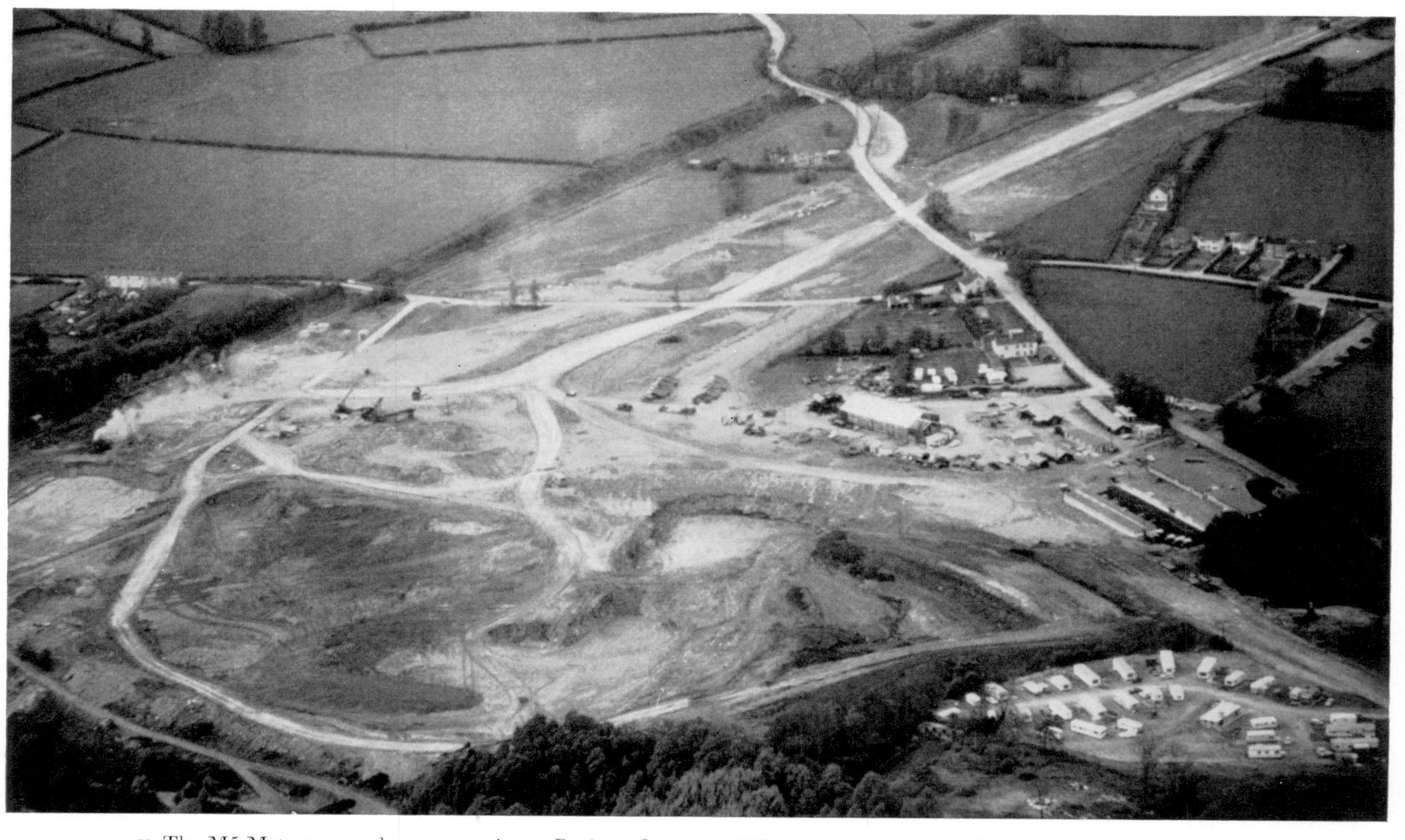

x. The M5 Motorway under construction at Puriton, Somerset, 1971. A known length of Roman road and part of a large Roman settlement were destroyed here.

XI. Conjoined ring-ditches showing as crop-marks near Preston, Gloucestershire (Preston b, c on fig 16). *Crown Copyright reserved.*

XII. Ring-ditch and settlement crop-marks near Manor Ham Barn, Kempsford, Gloucestershire (sites s–z on fig 17). River Thames in foreground. *Crown Copyright reserved.*

XIII. The Roman road (Chute Causeway) and the Grim's Ditch south of Hippenscombe, Wiltshire (*c* SU 300522). *Crown Copyright reserved.*

XIV. Charterhouse, Somerset: part of the Roman mining settlement laid out on a rough grid pattern.

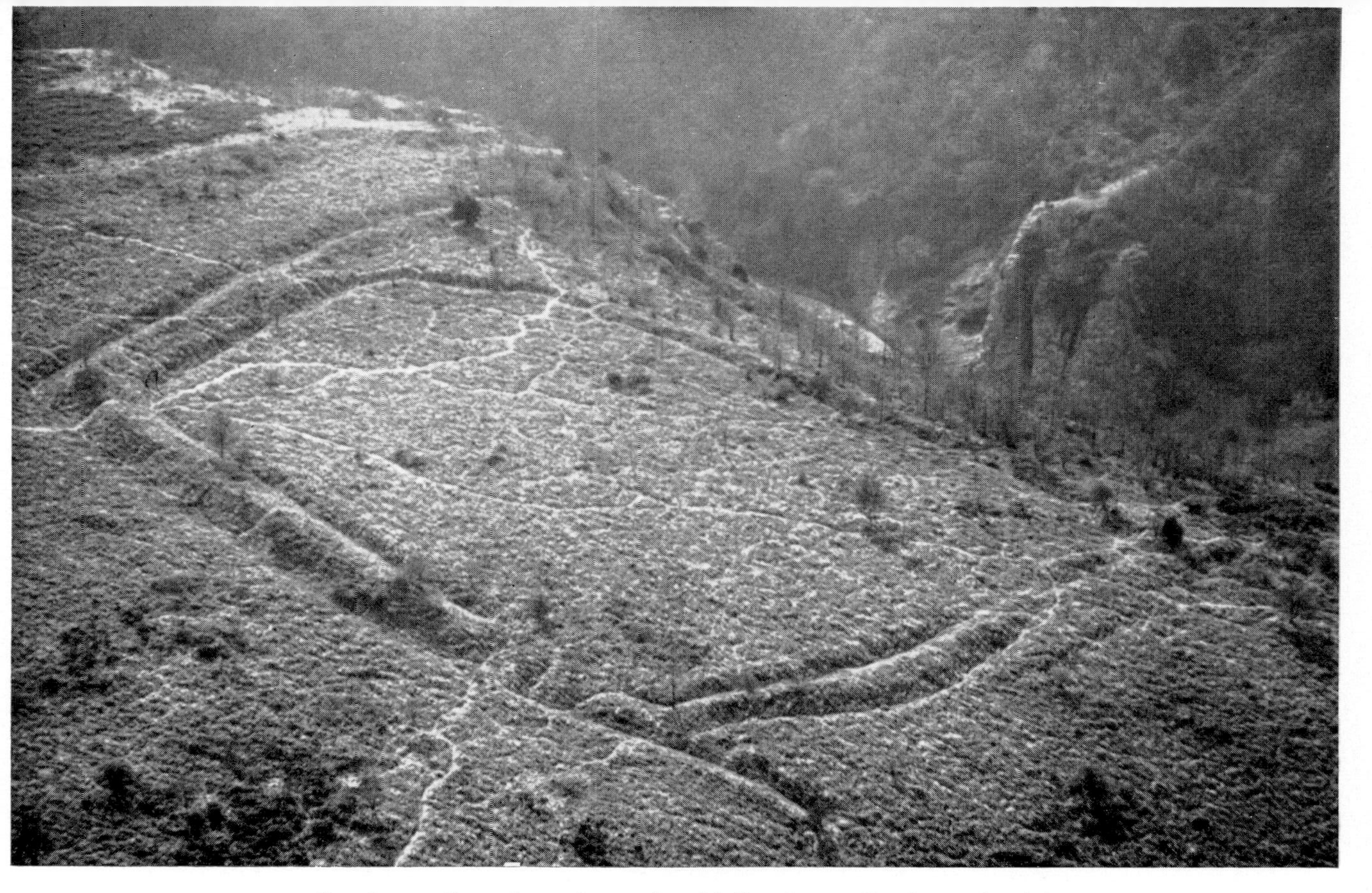

XV. Burrington Camp from the north, with Burrington Combe on the right.

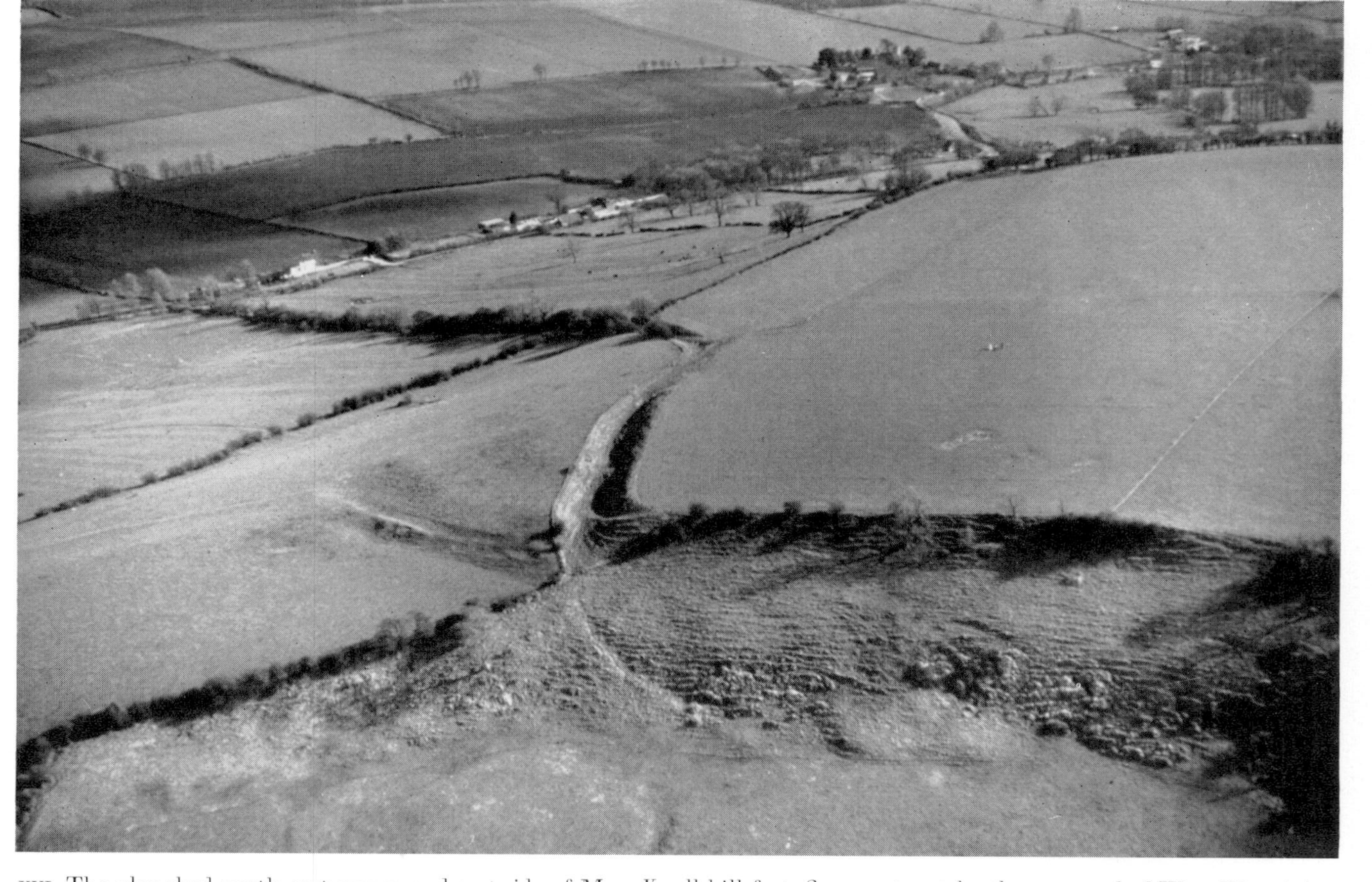

XVI. The ploughed north-east corner and east side of Maes Knoll hill-fort, Somerset, cut by the west end of West Wansdyke (hedge-line, left centre, to large ditch, centre).

these proposals were two. The first was the eventual setting up of a state Antiquities Service which would, through some 20 regional centres, and with very considerably increased funds, provide a unified and effective service, capable of dealing with emergency situations well in advance through early consultation with planners and developers. One of the prime functions of this Antiquities Service would be the creation of a national archive which would, as far as possible, store in an easily retrievable form detailed archaeological surveys of the whole country. Only in this way could threats be anticipated in time to deal with them properly.

The second and more immediate proposal put to the London meeting was the formation of an organization (to be known as RESCUE) whose aims are set out below. The meeting voted unanimously for the setting up of this body, and a holding Chairman was appointed by the meeting to form a holding Committee.

RESCUE was provisionally defined as:

an association of all interested people, with *individual* membership;

a fund-raising body, obtaining funds from subscriptions, donations, bequests and appeals.

RESCUE will use these resources:

to help make the public aware of the rapidly accelerating destruction of our archaeological heritage;

to encourage the revision and extension of existing legislation concerning archaeological remains, and to seek for new legislation where necessary;

to obtain greatly increased funds for rescue excavation and its publication;

to press for the extension and the improvement of field archaeological training at all levels;

in general to help to record and conserve the physical remains of Britain's archaeological heritage of every age, and with particular reference to the changing character of the natural environment;

specifically to support surveys, to acquire sites or areas of archaeological importance for permanent conservation, to initiate or support rescue excavations and the consequent work on the results and their publication.

The deputation, consisting of four members of the holding Committee, wishes to put to the Minister various proposals for the solution of the very grave crisis which faces British field archaeology, and to suggest ways in which the public and private sectors can co-operate to the fullest extent in providing money, manpower and expertise to rescue the evidence of Britain's past before it is obliterated.

February, 1971

APPENDIX II

The following short essay was originally written for the *Bulletin* of the Bristol Archaeological Research Group, a duplicated publication which Leslie Grinsell established on exemplary lines in the sixties, and was published in Vol. 3, no. 9, Dec. 1970, 231–3. It was of course written specifically for a local society membership in the context of an issue largely devoted to archaeology in the seventies; but as a brief personal statement relevant to field archaeology, stimulated by the long discussions, critical assessments and hopes of 1970, it might possibly be of some historical interest in A.D. 2000! Its subjective nature should at least contrast with Appendix I, which it inevitably repeats to some extent. The theme has since been elaborated in Thomas, 1971.

Archaeology in the Seventies: The Challenge

Archaeology is still young, immature: in years, but more so in its *rational*, its techiques and its organization. It has hardly changed at all in these respects over the last century, until the 1960s, and this is one of the major reasons for the convulsions within the subject and amongst its personnel now, with very wide gaps opening up over fundamental issues and between different types of self-styled archaeologists. This must be clear to anyone who thinks about the why and the how of studying the past primarily through its surviving material remains. To take one obvious example, how do we reconcile the argument that archaeology's prime justification is as public entertainment with the fundamental belief of most practising archaeologists that ultimately their responsibility is to scholarship?

For me, however, the basic challenge of archaeology in the next decade is not intellectual, but social, moral and personal. A basic choice, it seems to me, faces not only the Bristol Archaeological Research Group, not only every archaeological society, but every individual member who presumes to claim an interest in the past. Beyond us, the millions who make up our whole society have ultimately to make the same choice, and the very least we can do is to try and ensure that it is made consciously. For make no mistake about it, during the seventies, and beyond them to A.D. 2000 at the very outside, a sharply-defined issue confronts us as individuals, and our Societies, and our society: do we, or do we not, want a representative sample of our cultural history, as expressed in our formerly rich archaeological heritage, to survive into the twenty-first century? I cannot see how this question, basic to the future of archaeology and archaeologists in this country, can be sidestepped or ignored.

'What a bore,' someone says, 'B.A.R.G. has already had enough of the "crisis of destruction": Drinkwater on the now largely non-existent Gloucestershire barrows (below pp 129–56), Philip Barker at the 1970

AGM, Fowler on 'The Future of the Past' in the City Museum's 'Conservation' lectures (21 January 1970) and all that M5 drag over the last two years. Can't we now go back to real archaeology?' The answer of course is 'yes'—if you see yourself as an ostrich, B.A.R.G. as simulating Neanderthal Man, and archaeology as having the long-term growth potential of a dinosaur. The facts are that at long last we must recognize archaeology as involving social issues, because it involves people and land; as involving political issues, because it involves money and the 'freedom of the individual'; and as involving moral issues, because eventually you have to decide how you are going to spend your time and money in relation to the case outlined here. It is simply this.

The raw material of Britain's archaeological heritage, the areas and sites, structures and objects left on and in the ground by our predecessors is of finite quantity, and it is unique. It is now being destroyed so widely, so fast and so completely by industry (gravel, sand, stone, coal and peat extraction), by construction (from town development to motorways), and by agriculture and forestry, that little of it will be left intact by A.D. 2000 unless we take positive action now. The 'we' means precisely that: no-one else is going to do the job for us. Assuming that we believe the recording and conservation of our archaeological heritage to be a 'good thing' for the nation and not just a narrow sectional interest, this is where the element of social responsibility must come into our thinking and our archaeological practice. Responsible commitment is what archaeology now and henceforth requires of its practitioners and supporters.

For the situation is in fact much worse. Much more material, many more sites, actually exist than has previously been appreciated. Numerical estimates of density can be multiplied by at least five for most types of site, and by up to thirty in some cases. The present and predictable loss in numbers and knowledge is thus even greater than has been estimated; conversely, encouraging thought, anyone who undertakes to survey an area in detail, or watch a particular piece of development, can be proportionately more certain of contributing to knowledge. Among the far-reaching implications of this recent 'discovery' is the answer to those who proclaim, with regret or satisfaction as the case may be, that the day of the 'amateur' (*sensu* part-timer) is over, and to the 'academics' who fastidously avoid the crisis-in-archaeology cause, arguing that their time is better spent in 'real study' of the available evidence. Ultimately reaction to the known situation is a matter of personal choice: but I would hardly have thought there was much satisfaction in trying to complete a crossword without the 'Across' clues.

Add to the situation a third point—our frustrated awareness of the inadequacy of our present efforts—and the understandable reaction, 'I'm going to take up astrology/bee-keeping/yoga: at least that will be fun' becomes hard to counter. But is it enough to do our archaeology for fun alone, when our efforts are inefficient because we are badly organized? In the long run, such a situation is bound to be unsatisfactory, neither a credit to our subject nor fair to our material. We can distinguish two aspects of what is really a management problem, the management of our resources: reorganization at national level, and co-ordination at regional or local level. Ideally we need a National Antiquities Service embracing the whole range of state activity in archaeology, supported by adequate finances and modern legislation. Since we will not achieve that in the near future, we must set up an independent national organization—'Rescue'?—to supplement state efforts. Such an organisation would fill several obvious gaps in the existing framework: it could be an association of all interested people, offering individual membership; it could be a fund-raising organisation; it could initiate and support surveys and rescue excavations; and it could acquire archaeological areas for permanent conservation. Priorities on the last two aims would have to be established on a national basis. 'Rescue' would have to have its own full-time staff and an assured annual income, or it would have little justification for existing.

Whatever fortune attends that idea, the backbone of British field archaeology will remain the same: the skilled and dedicated part-timer who knows his own area and the people in it really well. The role of the individual operating under the aegis of a local society is crucial; in fact, it will become more important during the seventies. I do not think anyone will dispute that: the only matter for debate is how we organize ourselves so that our personal contribution through our Society, and that Society's contribution to the common cause, become as effective as possible. We are no longer antiquarians studying the local past for its own sake. Our knowledge has practical applications in planning urban and rural development, in education, in amenity, in the leisure and tourist industries, in local politics, and we must make it tell in all these fields. We cannot begin to do that, let alone cope with the actual crisis of destruction, while our organization remains fragmented. We must literally pull ourselves together, under rejuvenated, reorganized or new units, geared to the needs of the only 'real' archaeology that is going to matter for the next few decades.

I sincerely hope that the fragmentation of the fifties and sixties, largely the result of the county societies' failure to adapt to social changes, has ceased, and that the M5 operation locally marks the beginning of a new phase of collaboration. Goodness knows archaeology needs it. I believe our subject is about to grow up, as it adds social responsibility to academic discipline. The real archaeological challenge of the seventies is whether we can grow up too.

BIBLIOGRAPHY

Since few specific references are given in the above, the following list also indicates the general sources of some of the material and of the inspiration, though most of the latter comes from first-hand experience in the field and many hours of discussion with colleagues, my students and others both sympathetic and hostile. Much of the background is received from the CBA and Ancient Monuments Boards' *Annual Reports*, from *Current Archaeology*, from regional publications like the *Kent Archaeological Review, the London Archaeologist*, and the *West Midlands Archaeological News Sheet*, and from editing the *Archaeological Review* (for Wessex and the South West).

Arvill, R., 1969. *Man & Environment* (Pelican, rev. ed.).

Barford Meeting 3rd–5th February, 1970. *Proceedings* (dup. foolscap).
Barker, P. A., 1968–1969. *The Origins of Worcester* (*Trans. Worcester Archaeol. Soc.* 3: ser 2).
Barley, M. W., 1967. 'The Prospects for British Archaeology', CBA *Ann. Rpt.* **17**, 51–56.
Benson, D. and Cook, J. M., 1966. *City of Oxford Redevelopment: Archaeological Implications* (Oxford City and County Mus.).
Bowen, H. C., 1961. *Ancient Fields* (Brit. Assoc. Adv. Sci.).

Clark, G., 1968. *Archaeology & Society* (Methuen, Univ. Paperback, reprint).
Council for British Archaeology, 1948. *A Survey and Policy of Field Research in the Archaeology of Great Britain, I.*
Cunliffe, B. W., 1970. *The Past Tomorrow* (Univ. Southampton).

Daniel, G., 1967. *The Origin & Growth of Archaeology* (Penguin).

Elton, G. R., 1968. *The Future of the Past* (CUP).

Fowler, P. J. (ed.), 1968. 'Conservation and the Countryside,' *Wiltshire, Archaeol. Natur. Hist. Mag.* **63**, 1–11.
1970a. 'Museums & Archaeology, A.D. 1970–2000,' *Mus. J.* **70**, 120–121.
1970b. 'The Crisis in Field Archaeology,' *Current Archaeol.* **23**, 343–345.
1972.

Hawkes, C. F. C., 1951. 'British Prehistory half-way through the Century,' *Proc. Prehist. Soc.* **17**, 1–15.

Institute of Archaeology, London Univ. 1943. *Conference on the Future of Archaeology* (Occas. Paper 5).

McCarthy, F. D. (ed.), 1970. *Aboriginal Antiquities in Australia: their nature and preservation* (Australian Institute of Aboriginal Studies, 22).
Meaney, A., 1964. *A Gazetteer of Anglo-Saxon Burial Sites* (Allen & Unwin).

Piggott, S. 'British Archaeology and the Enemy', CBA *Ann. Rpt.* **20**, 74–85.
Plumb, J. H., 1969. *The Death of the Past* (Macmillan).

Rahtz, P., 1970. 'Archaeology in the University of Birmingham,' *Alta* (Univ. Birmingham Rev.) **11**, 261–267.
Roe, D., 1968. *A Gazetteer of British Lower & Middle Palaeolithic Sites* (CBA Res. Rpt. 8).
Royal Agricultural Society, 1970. *Agriculture & the Countryside: the needs of agriculture & forestry in relation to good conservation practice.*

Royal Commission on Historical Monuments (England)
1952. *West Dorset* (HMSO).
1960. *A Matter of Time* (HMSO).
1963. *Monuments Threatened or Destroyed* (HMSO).
1969. *Peterborough New Town: a survey of the antiquities in the areas of development* (HMSO).
1970. *South East Dorset* (HMSO).

Sheail, J. and Wells, T. C. E. (eds.), 1970. *Old Grassland—Its Archaeological & Ecological Importance* (Natur. Conservancy, Monks Wood Symposium, 5).

Thomas, C., 1971. 'Ethics in Archaeology, 1971,' *Antiquity* 45, 268–75.

Walsh, Sir D., 1966–1968. *Report of the Committee of Enquiry in the Arrangements for the Protection of Field Monuments* (HMSO, Cmnd. 3904).

PART II

Fieldwork in Practice

CHAPTER V

Barrows in Gloucestershire: Patterns of Destruction

John Drinkwater

The destruction of ancient sites is proceeding at an alarming and ever-increasing rate. Although urban development with its associated road construction and gravel workings is the most obvious agent of destruction, it is the slower, less apparent erosion of sites by the plough that will ultimately destroy much of the prehistoric and historic past of this country.

In this situation it is essential that comprehensive check lists in the Grinsell mode and accurate field surveys of all existing monuments be produced as a matter of urgency. Much of the information can be presented in the most emphatic manner by means of a 'destruction map'. Superimposition of the current physical state of each site on a normal site-distribution map will produce such a map. When re-surveyed at reasonable time intervals, the rate of destruction will become apparent and areas of intensive erosion highlighted. Further, the type and number of monuments likely to survive may be determined, and a list of representative sites, which must be preserved at all costs, can be prepared in line with the 'Recommendations for improving the existing legislation for the preservation of Ancient Monuments' (Fowler, 1968).

The use of field surveys to examine the effect of intensive agriculture on a particular group of ancient monuments can be demonstrated by studying the recent history of the barrows of Gloucestershire. This county contains approximately 450 long and round barrows, mostly situated on, or close to, arable. Field surveys of varying efficiency and magnitude have been performed, at intervals, over eighty years culminating with the publication of 'Gloucestershire Barrows' (O'Neil and Grinsell, 1960). This account was based on fieldwork performed over the previous thirty years recording all known, extant and destroyed sites. All those sites still visible in 1960 have been visited by the author during 1970.

LONG BARROWS

Previous surveys

The latest definitive account of the Cotswold—Severn group of chamber tombs, to which presumably all Gloucestershire long barrows belong, lists 95 existing or destroyed sites in the county (Corcoran, 1969). In his account, Corcoran has designated a GLO number for each Gloucestershire long barrow, both for those sites which have produced evidence of chambers/cists and those so far unexplored. This numerical system, a continuance of that first employed by Daniel (1950) in his inventory of the 37 chambered sites then recognized, is the reference system employed in this paper. Although Daniel and Corcoran give the apparent physical dimensions of sites, the major concern of both accounts is with typology, construction and finds.

It is the records of Crawford (1927) and O'Neil and Grinsell (1960) that must be examined to define those physical conditions of each site—the mound height, its situation and the adjacent land use—which will determine its future survival. In this account a direct comparison with the survey by Witts (1883) is not made. All the sites listed by him (several of which he obviously had not visited) have been considered by the later surveyors. The information which his survey provides concerning unexcavated sites is, when relevant, included in the general account.

Excluding the Sales Lot long barrow (GLO94) excavated in 1962 (O'Neil 1966), the location, dimensions and excavation records of Corcoran's 95 sites are detailed in the relevant section of 'Gloucestershire Barrows'. Using this record, and incorporating the information obtained by the 1970 re-examination of extant sites, we can subdivide the sites as follows:

(i)	Barrows fully excavated 1900–1970	8
(ii)	Barrows partially excavated or examined before 1900	15
(iii)	Destroyed sites	9
(iv)	Standing stones	9
(v)	Unexcavated unploughed sites	26
(vi)	Unexcavated ploughed sites	25
(vii)	Doubtful sites	4
		96

The above list includes one extra site, that from which the Avening Old Rectory burial chambers originated. From verbatim evidence, Daniel (1970) locates the original barrow at the Barrow Tump Cottages, Avening.

(i) *Sites fully excavated* 1900–1970

GLO	*Site*	*Year excavated*
1	Belas Knap	1927
4	Notgrove	1934
13	Nympsfield	1937
26	Ablington	1926
44	Adlestrop	1935
60	Burn Ground	1940
92	Saltway Barn	1939
94	Sales Lot	1962

Reiteration of the excavation details of the above sites is unnecessary, the subject being fully covered in previous literature (Daniel, 1950; O'Neil and Grinsell, 1960; Grimes, 1960; O'Neil, 1966; Corcoran, 1969).

Two factors of importance must be stressed. First, any attempt to order these and the other chambered tombs from the Cotswolds chronologically rests solely upon inference drawn from sites outside the area. A paucity of finds and complete lack of dateable material (radiocarbon or otherwise) emphasizes the hypothetical nature of typological schemes. Secondly, examination of the structural plans of the last four sites listed above demonstrates the individual uniqueness of each long barrow. Although all four are accepted as Neolithic funerary monuments belonging to the Cotswold-Severn group, there is a wide divergency in both chamber plan and function and in the construction and shape of the enclosing mound.

(ii) *Sites partially excavated, or examined before* 1900

GLO	*Site*	*Year of examination*
2	Poles Wood South	1874
3	Eyford Hill	1874
8	West Tump	1881
9	Hoare Stone	1806
10	Randwick	1883
14	Uley	1854
15	Gatcombe Lodge	1870
16	Windmill Tump	1839
20	Bown Hill	1863
22	Cow Common Long	1874
23	Cow Common Round	1874
24	Poles Wood East	1875
25	Lamborough Banks	1854
34	Willersey	1884
75	Avenis	1875

Most of these barrows have undergone the 'chamber clearance' style of excavation. Although with some sites (Randwick, West Tump, Poles Wood South) perimeter walls have been traced, none of the barrows has experienced the total stone by stone dismemberment practised by Grimes with the Burn Ground and Saltway Barn sites (Grimes 1960). Several of the sites have in the past suffered partial destruction by quarrying or the plough, but are at present unassailed.

Three sites, Hoar Stone (GLO9), Eyford Hill (GLO3) and Cow Common (GLO22), are most vulnerable. Overgrown, ruinous and unploughed in arable fields, they are more a nuisance to farming operations than examples of archaeological conservation. The lack of a definite boundary to the site has resulted in the Hoar Stone barrow being shortened by at least 8 metres since 1960. The Avenis (GLO75) and Willersey (GLO34) barrows have at times been ploughed and are now low, elongated mounds without visible features. Both have vague and unsatisfactory excavation reports and would repay re-examination.

Trees and undergrowth have obscured the features of most of the remainder. Randwick (GLO10) in particular, quarried and eroded, is in a poor state. West Tump (GLO8), after suffering mound damage by the collapse of dead trees, has recently been deforested. Only Uley (GLO14), a conserved 'show barrow', is worth a visit by the non-specialist wishing to 'see a megalithic tomb'.

(iii) *Destroyed sites*

In this group three sites, Westwood (GLO12), Prestbury (GLO51) and Crickley (GLO64), have been finally eradicated during this century. Througham (GLO71) is now completely covered with farm buildings. Another site in the same parish, Bisley with Lypiatt III (GLO74), is an unrecognizable mass of hummocks and hollows. The site at Dyrham and Hinton (GLO91) exists only in that portion which lies beneath a field wall built across the former barrow. The only site in this category to receive any scientific examination is Jack Barrow (GLO27), which existed until this attention in 1875. The existence of barrows at Lypiatt (GLO35) and Hirecombe (GLO37A) is supposition based on old records.

(iv) *Standing Stones*

At eight sites in Gloucestershire, the remains of a former (supposed) long barrow consist only of standing or fallen stones. Apart from the Whistlestone (GLO47), under which human remains were uncovered in the mid-nineteenth century, and the Avening Old Rectory burial chambers, their association with burial practices is rather tenuous.

Excavation of the Druid Stoke (GLO28) site, a collection of recumbent stones, produced neither finds nor information. Associated mounds were formerly recorded for the stones at Boxwell Lodge (GLO37) and Wick (GLO29). The latter site would appear to have lost at least one orthostat since the eighteenth century. The stones at Marshfield (GLO39), Horton (GLO89), Bisley with Lypiatt (GLO32), and Longstone (GLO36) have long since been the only visible remains of whatever structure originally existed.

(v) *Unexcavated, unploughed sites*

The twenty-six sites in this category are found in one of three locations: under trees, on grass or common land, or unploughed on arable. The degree of preservation afforded by each of these locations differs considerably, as does the physical condition of the individual barrows.

Barrows under Trees. Barrows with a heavy tree coverage can hardly be considered as 'protected'. Among the thirteen sites in this category, the excessive growth of large trees as found on the barrows at Leighterton (GLO18), Aston Bank (GLO53), Tinglestone (GLO31), Blackquarries Hill (GLO86) and the two College Plantation sites (GLO73, 74), must already have resulted in considerable damage to the mound and its structure. The effect of the collapse of dead trees is seen in the large cavities ripped during the last few years in the Crippetts (GLO7) and (now deforested) West Tump (GLO8) barrows.

The state of preservation amongst the sites in this group is variable. The barrows at Bourton on the Hill (GLO41), Starveall (GLO87) and Lower Swell (GLO48) survive to *c.* 2m in height. The Crippetts (GLO7) is a particularly fine mound—6·5m in height with a 'dug out' east end. Chambering is visible in the West Woods (GLO6) barrow from an unrecorded excavation. The two remaining sites, Poles Wood West (GLO46), a shapeless hummocky mound with probable quarry associations (Grinsell 1964, 27), and North Cerney (GLO48), situated on a slope, both are slightly doubtful.

Barrows under grass or on common land. Only those sites at present under grass or on common land can be considered to be in a reasonable state of preservation. Of the seven barrows which exist under these conditions, the Lodge Park Farmington (GLO5) barrow is the sole survivor. Apparently undisturbed either by ploughing or excavation, the necessity of preserving this unique site untouched needs to be stated repeatedly and loudly.

Although probably never ploughed, the Toots (GLO76) barrow was despoiled in 1880 by an 'excavation' which has bisected the mound. Norns Tump (GLO93), Whitfields Tump (GLO77), Camp North (GLO11) and the curious Camp South (GLO67) have all been mauled without record in antiquity. The denuded, featureless mound on Hawksbury Knoll (GLO88) completes this small category.

Barrows unploughed on arable. The continued survival of the six barrows, at present unploughed (and unfenced) on arable, is, to say the least, unlikely. A cautionary example is provided by the Symonds Hall Farm site (GLO85). Division by the plough of the former long mound into two discreet oval mounds continues annually.

It is usually the extremities of the site which suffer. In this manner diminution of the barrows at Lineover (GLO56), Hazelton North (GLO54) and the aforementioned Hoar Stone (GLO9) has occurred since 1960.

Although examined in antiquity, the mounds of Lechmore (GLO21) and Colnpen (GLO69) are, at present, untouched by the plough. Colnpen, a fine barrow with an attendant round barrow cemetery, should at all costs be preserved.

Coberley II (GLO62), in outward appearance 'two round barrows joined by a col' (O'Neill and Grinsell, 1960, 76), is likewise spared the plough. This site is in some respects a rather doubtful member of the 'accepted' long barrow list. Its position on the lower flanks of a hill allows it to be overlooked from higher land in the immediate vicinity—a position it shares with only one other Gloucestershire long barrow, Swell VI (GLO48). The siting of round barrows on a false crest or hill-slopes is a common feature in Gloucestershire and elsewhere, the Sezincote 1 and 2 sites being a good example.

As well as the difficulties of probably unwelcome public access, the disadvantage to the farmer of preserved, solitary barrows in the middle of ploughed fields is obvious. Unless such sites can be delimited by a fence or wall and are inspected regularly to remove weeds and vermin, conservation will be both unwelcome and ineffective, probably even if owner-compensation were granted in the form of the 'acknowledgement-payments' recommended by Walsh (1969, para 136).

(vi) *Unexcavated, ploughed sites*

The 23 sites in this category are:—

GLO	*Site*	*GLO*	*Site*
19	Grickstone Farm	*58	Leygore Manor II
30	Norbury	*59	Cheltenham Road Pltn.
33	Hazelton South	61	Furzenhill Barn
40	Snowshill	*63	Wood Barrow
42	Ganborough	*65	Pinkwell
43	Temple Guiting	66	Lad Barrow
*45	Broadwell	68	Honeycombe Farm
49	New Close	78	Buckholt Wood
*50	Condicote Lane	*80	Oldfield Wood
*52	Slade Barn	81	Avening IV
*57	Leygore Manor I	82	Kingscote I
		90	Tormarton

*sites with mounds less than 0·5m in height

Only three sites, Ganborough (GLO42), Temple Guiting II (GLO43) and Newclose (GLO49), are now over 1·2m high. The rest are in the final stages of destruction, if not already destroyed. Excavation of sites in the 'below 0·5m high' class could, even at this late stage, perhaps provide sufficient information to enable a plan of the internal features of the barrow to be made.

The Burn Ground site (GLO60), excavated by Grimes in 1940, illustrates such a possibility. The site, an 'oval mound about 2 feet high', produced a fairly complete plan of the chambers although the neolithic ground surface was dug away in many places (Grimes, 1960, 46). With such a consideration in mind, we can consider some of the listed sites in detail.

Paired Barrows. Although all sites are, in theory, of equal importance, certain barrow groupings deserve special attention. We have at present neither information nor explanation for the occasional occurrence of closely adjacent or 'paired' long barrows in the county. Excluding the groups of barrows in the Poles Wood (Swell) and Ablington areas, there are seven pairs of long barrows (or their possible remnants) in existence.

In the 'under 0·5m high' group, the two Leygore Manor sites (GLO57, 58) could well be a pair. Their destruction, however, is almost complete, both mounds having been ploughed until they are mere inequalities in the ground.

At Hazleton, of the two barrows *c.*75 m apart in the same field, only the northernmost (GLO54), a shortened but unploughed mound, remains. The southern site (GLO33), 3m high in Witts's time, is now almost flattened.

With the Newclose (GLO49) barrow an anomalous situation exists. This site is the unexcavated, ploughed half of a pair of barrows, the counterpart of which is the excavated, unploughed Eyford Hill (GLO3) barrow. Such ploughed/unexcavated, unploughed/excavated anomalies are common in the region.

The relationships and nature of the various features which cluster around Norns Tump (GLO93) can only be defined by excavation. The three ploughed mounds with which it is associated, the round barrow Avening 7, the long mound Avening IV (GLO81) and another possible long mound, become more indistinct yearly. Both these long mounds could be natural outcrops (Grinsell, 1960, 70), although their location on the edge of a hill-crest is almost identical with the partly destroyed Barrow Tumps (GLO17) site across the valley. In this context, Daniel's reference to Norns Tump as a round mound (Daniel, 1970, 262) is surprising. Although admittedly both ends of the barrow have suffered deprivation by the plough, both Crawford and Grinsell class the site as a normal long barrow.

Each of the other three possible pairs of barrows contains one doubtful member. The lesser of the two long mounds in College Plantation, Duntisbourne Rouse, is a doubtful long barrow of low profile (GLO73). Its partner (GLO72), formerly of massive proportions, now resembles two round barrows, its centre having been removed in antiquity.

The only evidence to classify the southernmost of the two Camp sites (GLO67) as a long barrow originates from Witts (1883, 76). In its present state, as both Crawford and Grinsell have commented, it resembles a (gutted) round barrow. Its practically co-joined neighbour has likewise suffered severe destruction in the past, although both sites are now under grass.

The final site in this category is the Longstone, Minchinhampton (GLO36). If this and its *in situ* smaller associate are the last vestiges of a long barrow (Grinsell, 1960, 84), this barrow would make a pair with the Gatcombe Lodge site (GLO15).

(vii) *Doubtful sites*

The only true test of authenticity for any site is by excavation. Many of the mounds included in any survey must lay claim for inclusion by virtue of their dimensions and location, rather than from evidence of burial or structure. Fewer than 25 per cent of the long barrows on the accepted list have been defined by excavation. By a reverse argument, four of the sites accepted by Corcoran appear more dubious than the rest because of their situation and associations.

The Querns barrow, Cirencester (GLO79), with its unlikely situation and close proximity to quarry workings, is, as Grinsell has commented, 'very doubtful'. The same uncertainty exists for the two long mounds, Uley II (GLO83) and Folly Wood (GLO84), the latter being associated with a large quarry-pit. The fourth site which raises some doubts is the mound at the foot of Brock Hill, Kingscote (GLO38). Its situation at the base of a steep slope, its oval shape and the presence of quarry scoops and stone tree rings in the nearby copse, outweigh the apparently orthostatic structure visible in the mound. Furthermore, it is a close neighbour of the eighteenth-century 'Bagpath Burial Circle' folly.

ROUND BARROWS

Previous Surveys

The round barrows of Gloucestershire have not been subjected to the intensive scrutiny which the chambered tombs have undergone. Apart from the records of a few localised fieldworkers only two comprehensive surveys exist (Witts, 1883, and O'Neil and Grinsell, 1960). Between these two accounts are spread eighty years of discovery and destruction which form the basis for the present study. These surveys, when combined with a re-examination of those sites still extant in 1970, enable us to make an assessment of the present state of round barrow archaeology in the county.

Witts's Survey (1883)

This account enumerates 126 sites which can, in terms of their 1970 conditions, be classified thus:

Excavated barrows	26
Destroyed since 1884	13
Untraced sites	6
Doubtful sites	12
Sites outside Gloucestershire	3
Now regarded as Long Barrows	9
Sites still extant, unexcavated	57

Unfortunately for our purposes Witts's survey is a far from satisfactory reference. Many of his listed sites he may never have visited, and with only thirty-four has he recorded the height of the mound. Of these latter, and after deduction of those either excavated since 1884 or currently unploughed, only ten remain for assessment. A further difficulty exists in the correlation of different observers' estimations of barrow height against a ploughed background. Only four barrows, Witts 50 (Sezincote 4), Witts 6 (Avening 1), and Witts 33, 34 (Bembro group), have suffered height reduction that cannot be explained in this way. Apart from the Sezincote 4 site, which must have undergone deliberate removal (8 feet of height lost in eighty years), the losses of the other sites are between 0·5m and 1·2m.

The remaining six barrows have lost less than 0·5m in height over the same period. One further site, Witts 47 (Donnington 1) (not traced by Grinsell), was recorded as being 3½ ft high by Witts. From this limited selection of sites there is evidence of sporadic intensive destruction.

O'Neil and Grinsell's Survey (1960)

In tabulated form, the location, dimensions, and site history of 357 possible round barrows are given by this survey. Separation of these sites into classes based on their 1960 conditions gives the following breakdown.

(i)	Excavated sites	56
(ii)	Destroyed unexcavated sites	72
(iii)	Doubtful sites	47
(iv)	Unexcavated extant sites	182

Some general comments follow on each of classes (i)–(iii) with a detailed examination of category (iv).

(i) *Excavated Sites*. In the relevant section of 'Gloucestershire Barrows', Leslie Grinsell has in his usual diligent manner detailed and dissected all the pre-1960 barrow excavation information. All phases of the Bronze Age are represented by barrow interments within the county. Only the 'Wessex culture' with its characteristic barrows is poorly represented. Burial mounds of this type have been encountered only on the fringes of the Cotswolds (O'Neil and Grinsell, 1960, 17). It is therefore most rewarding that the only round barrow excavated since 1960 should, from its structure and associations, help fill one of the chronological 'gaps' for this period.

The barrow, Temple Guiting 8 (Witts 32), had lost 2 ft of height since 1884. The mound, its external features obscured by the plough, was found on excavation to be a stone-built ditched bell barrow (O'Neil, 1967). The primary burial, an unaccompanied cremation in a pit, is one of a series of similar burials recorded by Grinsell (1960, 25). Five satellite cremations associated with the primary burial were enclosed in an inner stone capped turf mound. Five secondary inurned cremations had been deposited in the south-east quadrant after the construction of the cairn. The excavator has suggested a period in the late middle Bronze Age for the primary phase of the monument, with a later date for the secondary cremations, one of which was enclosed in a rusticated biconical urn (O'Neil, 1967, 24).

The contrast between the Bevans Quarry unaccompanied cremation and the celebrated Wessex grave group inhumation from Snowshill 5 (only 3 miles distant) is seen by the excavator to be 'due to a lapse of time and custom'. In the light of Burgess's (1969, 208–15) recent review of the Bronze Age, this contrast is more sharply drawn. A re-examination of the traditional Bronze Age pottery sequence and its associations has indicated a broad contemporaneity of the Wessex culture with a host of urn types (including biconical urns), all in existence in the Early Bronze Age. The Bevans Quarry and Snowshill sites can therefore be contemporaneous, both belonging to an early phase of the Bronze Age.

It is obvious that a reappraisal of the Late Neolithic—Early Bronze Age period in this region is necessary. The Cotswolds have been regarded as an area in which the Neolithic culture continued for some time after the Bronze Age was established in the surrounding regions. The apparent imbalance in the long/round barrow ratio is often quoted to support this delayed entry/emergence (Grinsell, 1960, 31). This ratio, however, depends entirely on the number of barrows assumed to have existed in the county. With less than twenty-five per cent of the long barrows defined by excavation, the possibility exists that some of those on the accepted list should not be included. Further, the number and distribution of round barrows may well be affected by an intensive air and ground survey. The preponderance of barbed and tanged flint arrowheads (an established Bronze Age artifact) over the leaf-shaped (Neolithic) forms, together with their high occurrence (2500 from the Swell region alone, Grinsell, 1964, 9) is additional evidence that the Coltswolds were not the cultural backwater previously envisaged. There is little doubt that a Neolithic-Bronze Age transition period exists—the survival of traditions of stone-working and funerary practices are evidenced by a number of barrows (Cranham 1, Coberley 1a, Hawling 10a). The complete absence of dateable material, however, other than a few ceramics, and lack of excavation of undestroyed possible transitionary sites, must render hypothetical any arguments as to relationships or date.

(ii) *Destroyed, unexcavated sites.* Information regarding destroyed barrow sites in Gloucestershire has been derived from three main sources:

(*a*) Documentary evidence.

Research into Saxon land charters and 'barrow-indicative' local names has provided at least fifteen possible barrow locations, though in the absence of tangible remains the authenticity of these sites is of course unproven. Some, like the Bishops Cleeve 1 reference, are completely unprovenanced, whereas others, such as Babbas Barrow (Adlestrop 3), have approximate locations.

(*b*) Early 'Histories' and surveys.

Of the seventy-two sites in the destroyed category, the majority are derived from references to previously extant barrows mentioned in the works of earlier historians or surveyors. Thirteen of the sites listed by Witts (1884) have, since his time, been removed, mostly by ploughing.

Witts	*Reference*
54	Donnington 4
94, 95	Wotton-under-Edge 1, 2
96–98, 113	Hawkesbury 1, 2, 3, 5
118	Alveston 1
121–6	Hawling 5–10

The Waste Group (Hawling 5–10) has been reduced to shapeless masses by quarrying and subsequent ploughing. Only a single barrow (Hawling 7) is now clearly defined.

The only evidence we have for many destroyed sites are the reports by earlier surveyors (Crawford, Mrs M. Crook, Rev R. Jowett Burton) of 'stony patches' in arable fields. The following are sites of possible barrows, the last visible traces of which were recorded in the 1920s:

Bisley with Lypiatt	12a–e
Bourton on the Hill	1
Temple Guiting	6
Swell	13
Oddington	1a
Hawling	11a

(*c*) Air-photography

By reason either of its terrain or from the lack of suitable coverage and study, the number of Gloucestershire barrow sites discovered by air-photography before the 1970 publication is surprisingly small. This is even more surprising if we remember that many Gloucestershire round barrows have a high proportion of stones in their make-up which can produce obvious stony patches when ploughed. The potential of this source of information is currently being realised by the Royal Commission's work in the county, and elsewhere in this volume (pp 157–67) Dr Isobel Smith discusses first results dealing with 'ring-ditch' sites, at least some of which are likely to have been ditched round barrows.

(iii) *Doubtful sites*. By virtue of their wide variation in size and location the authenticity of individual round barrows is difficult to establish other than by excavation. A number of ambiguous mounds, often with associated hollows, are probably the remains of stone quarries—shallow scoops made into the underlying rock to obtain stone for drystone walling and road repairs.

Mounds possibly of this origin are Bibury 3, Brimpsfield 3, 4, Chalford 1, Cirencester 3a, 4, 5, Dowdeswell 2, Horsley 3, and Minchinhampton 8. Some indication of the true nature of a site may be gained by studying the local field names, Slatepit Copse and Quarry Ground being not uncommon occurrences in the Cotswold region (Grinsell, 1964).

A possible confusion between round barrows and the remnants of hillfort and non-prehistoric earthworks can occur. The mounds at Cranham 4, Condicote 2, Oxenton 1, 2, and Southam 1 may all be of later, non-funeray origin. Doubts exist as to the nature of certain large barrows (over 4m high) which occur in the county. Grinsell has suggested that mounds of this size such as Coberley 2, Miserden 1, and Weston Birt with Lasborough 1 could be castle mounds. Some barrows of similar dimensions have, however, produced material indicating a probable Roman origin (Cirencester 6, Minchinhampton 4).

The other sites which are included in this doubtful category are those destroyed prior to 1960 for which only vague information is available. Bristol 11, Lechlade 1, 2, Nympsfield 2, Sevenhampton 2, and Swell 20, 21, are of this class.

(iv) *Unexcavated, extant sites.* We can divide the 182 sites which form this category into three groups, based on their heights as given in the 1960 publication.

Height in metres	*Number of barrows*
over 1	75
0·5–1	39
below 0·5	68

The sites in each group were examined during 1970. The physical condition of each barrow was recorded and an assessment made of its height. Further subdivision of each group into categories based on their physical condition produces the following table:

1960	1970					
Height in metres	under trees	under grass	un-ploughed on arable	ploughed	un-traced	total
over 1	33	14	11	16	1	75
0·5–1	7	8	—	20	4	39
under 0·5	—	14	—	54	—	68
Total	40	36	11	90	5	182

It is immediately apparent that half the unexcavated sites remaining in 1970 are under plough, and the majority of these are in the 'under 0·5m high' class.

Unexcavated ploughed sites

The rate of destruction. Ten years' ploughing has had an appreciable effect on the 'under 0·5m high' sites, and it is among these that the highest rate of destruction is apparent. Of the fifty-four ploughed sites in this category at least thiry-one can be considered either in the last stages of removal or beyond archaeological recovery. The sites to which this description applies are:

Avening 1, 4, 4a
Bisley with Lypiatt 3 (1, 2, 4 gone)
Broadwell 1
Chedworth 5
Coln St Dennis 1, 2, 3 (Colnpen group)
Didmarton 3, 5
Hawling 6
Naunton 1
Snowshill 6a
Swell 6, 10, 15, 16, 17, 18
Temple Guiting 1, 2, 4, 5, 7, 12, 13, 14, 15
Upper Slaughter 2, 3

Four (Horsley 5, Coberley 1, Brodwell 2, Beverston 3) of the 0·5–1m high group have suffered severe depredation, and are now all in the lower group. A further ten of the twenty ploughed sites in this group have shown appreciable height reduction over the last ten years, although they can still be included in this group.

As the height of the barrow decreases, the apparent rate of destruction increases. Even among the 'over 1m high' group, diminution and destruction have occurred during the last decade. One site (Wotton-under-Edge 1) is now untraceable and the barrows Temple Guiting 18, Pucklechurch 1, and Bisley with Lypiatt 5 are all considerably reduced.

The need for constant surveillance is illustrated by the Warren Tump (Cherington 2) site. Ploughing has reduced the formerly 1·3m high barrow to below 1m. When it was examined during January 1971 a stone slab *c.* 0·6m by 0·45m, possibly ploughed out from the barrow, was found resting against the dry-stone wall which crosses the site. The plough soil over the barrow produced a handful of flint and a human tooth, possibly from a disturbed burial.

This serves to emphasise that no site which undergoes regular ploughing can be considered safe, whatever its present height. The practice of ploughing furrows well over 0·3m deep is common in the fields on the

Cotswolds. Gashes of this depth across barrows were recorded from the following sites during 1970:

Cow Common	Swell 6–10
Eyford Hill	Upper Slaughter 2–4
Farmcote	Temple Guiting 18, 19
Salters Pool	Upper Slaughter 1

Ploughing to this depth on any barrow with a mound-height of less than 0·5m must result in disturbance or destruction of its basal layers. Since the conservation of such meagre mounds would be considered unprofitable we must either be prepared to 'write-off' the fifty-four sites in the 'below 0·5m high' category or undertake a rapid excavation programme.

When faced by a large number of sites requiring examination, an assessment of individual site priority is necessary. The basic requirement before the excavation (or conservation) of any site is undertaken is that it will provide (now or in the future) evidence of dating or structure which will actively contribute to the sum total of knowledge for its class. Since we are dealing with amorphous mounds of earth, usually without external indication of their internal features, we have to assess their importance against some other criteria. In this area any site which may further define the interrelationship between adjacent round barrows or round barrow-long barrow associations must come high on the priority list. An equal importance must also be placed on any barrow which, from its disturbance, exhibits unusual structural features.

We can therefore examine the fifty-four sites already in a state of near-extinction and the thirty-six progressing steadily towards it against three criteria:

(*a*) their association with other round barrows; (*b*) their association with long barrows; and (*c*) their exhibition of any unusual structure.

(*a*) *Associations with other round barrows.* This century has seen the eradication, usually with minimal excavation, of all but one of the major groups of round barrows in the county. Admittedly the groups at Burn Ground (Hampnett) and Netherhills (Frampton on Severn) were scientifically examined, but only after advanced destruction had rendered portions of each site past archaeological recovery. Out of the total of twenty-nine sites in the final stage of destruction in the groups at Parkwood (Didmarton 3–6), Four Barrow Field (Temple Guiting 1–6), Bembro (Temple Guiting 12–15), Nashend Farm (Bisley with Lypiatt 1–4), Lasborough Farm (Kingscote 1a–d), and Marshfield Down (Marshfield 1–8), only four barrows have been subjected to rescue excavation. Providing prompt action is taken, sufficient remains of the Parkwood, Bembro and Four Barrow Field groups to repay excavation. Destruction is, however, almost complete for the others.

We are left with a single unploughed group, that in Hull Plantations (Longborough 1–9). The importance of this group lies in its good condition, its situation, and its proximity to the henge monument at Condicote, so far the only such site defined on the Cotswolds. The nine barrows are divided between two walled plantations (Grinsell 1960, 122), with eight mounds of varying size in the western and a single large ditched round barrow in the eastern. Apart from a light covering of trees, the group appears reasonably safe. An additional important feature of the group is that the inter-barrow area is unploughed, as is the valley bottom and land to the south, the only situation from which the group is fully visible. During 1970, the ploughed hill slopes above the plantations revealed several stony areas and a scatter of flints, possibly the sites of destroyed barrows.

Confluent round barrows. Apart from the larger groups, occasional pairs of round barrows (two mounds in close association) occur in the county. Sites at which the two mounds are discrete (situated some distance apart) are well represented. The unploughed pairs of barrows at Court Hill (Standish 1, 2), Randwick Hill (Randwick 1, 2), and Heath Hill (Wyck Rissington 2, 3), are good examples which should be fully protected. The formerly well-preserved barrows Sezincote 2, 3 have suffered damage since 1959: the southernmost barrow has plough gashes in it and is now below 1·3m. The barrows at Ebworth Lodge (Cranham 1, 2), Stumps Cross (Stanway 1, 2), and Chavenage Sleight (Avening 5, 6) are all plough-reduced but still extant; whereas the sites at Farbarrow (Hawksbury 2, 3) and Fosseway (Broadwell 1, 2) have been levelled.

None of the above sites could be considered truly confluent, as with each pair the two mounds are adjacent but discrete. The lack of confluent round barrows in the Cotswold region can be explained by such mounds (often indefinite by reason of advanced destruction) being usually considered to represent the remains of a long barrow. Grinsell has expressed his doubts on the authenticity of such sites and included them in both the long and round barrow inventories. Sites of this nature at Snowshill (GLO40), Condicote Lane (GLO50), Cheltenham Road (GLO59), Coberley II (GLO62), Oldfield Wood (GLO80) and Tormarton (GLO90) have been labelled 'multiperiod' long mounds by Corcoran (1969) and included in his long barrow inventory. Such a classification, in view of the existing evidence, needs reappraisal. We now have a Wessex-type barrow (Bevans Quarry) in the heart of the Cotswolds and a suggestion that other obscured barrow types of this culture may exist. Co-joined round barrows have previously been encountered in the groups at Burn Ground, Marshfield, Cow Common and Charmy Down (Somerset). The last group, examined by Grimes (1960, 220) consisted of one large, bermed round barrow with three adjacent small mounds. The ditch constructed around the large barrow partly enclosed the two small barrows nearest to it.

(*b*) *Round barrows with long barrow associations.* Grinsell has previously discussed in detail the occurrence and implications of the siting of round barrows in immediate proximity to long barrows (1960, 15, 31). If we examine the nine sites illustrated by him, we find that not one is now untouched by the plough, and only one, the Burn Ground (Hampnett)

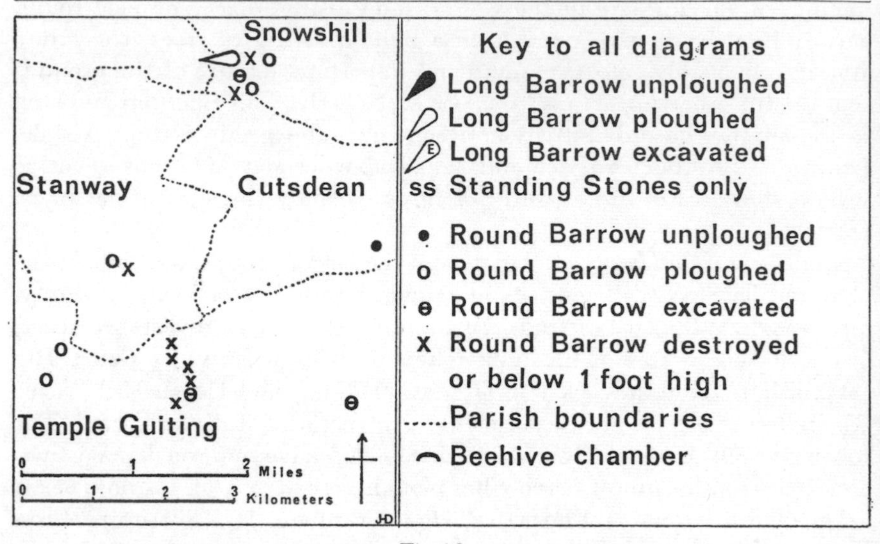

Fig 10

Temple Guiting

Of the two round barrows situated north of the hamlet of Farmcote, the northernmost, Ewes Leasowe (Temple Guiting 18), is a denuded, oval mound with a second, unrecorded possible barrow in the same field. The site to the south, Temple Guiting 19, a deeply ploughed mound, is that from which a possible cist slab was dislodged during 1970 (below p 150).

The Four Barrow Field Group, is a roughly N–S linear cemetery, a grouping less common in Gloucestershire than the nucleated assemblages. These barrows (Temple Guiting 1–6), reputed to have been 4–6 ft high in 1900, have been levelled by 1970. Only one site has been excavated.

Snowshill

The type features and inter-relationships of the barrows in this area are now indefinite due to continued ploughing. Excavation during the nineteenth-century revealed features which must give a high priority to the re-examination of the group as a whole. Since the account of Dryden's explorations in 1850 is now lost, the significance of the stone 'cistvaen' found in barrow 1, and its relevance to barrow 2, is not clear. Grinsell has suggested the two mounds are remnants of a long barrow and it is classified as such by Corcoran (GLO40). Likewise no details survive concerning a second cistvaen found by Dryden in barrow 4. The importance of the cemetery is emphasized by the renowned Wessex Culture grave group from Greenwell's CCXCVII (presumably Snowshill 5), and stresses the need to examine the almost extinct mound Snowshill 3, and the nearby pair of barrows Snowshill 6 and 6a.

If ploughing continues at its present rate only a single barrow Cutsdean 1, a bush-covered mound on arable, will eventually survive in the area illustrated.

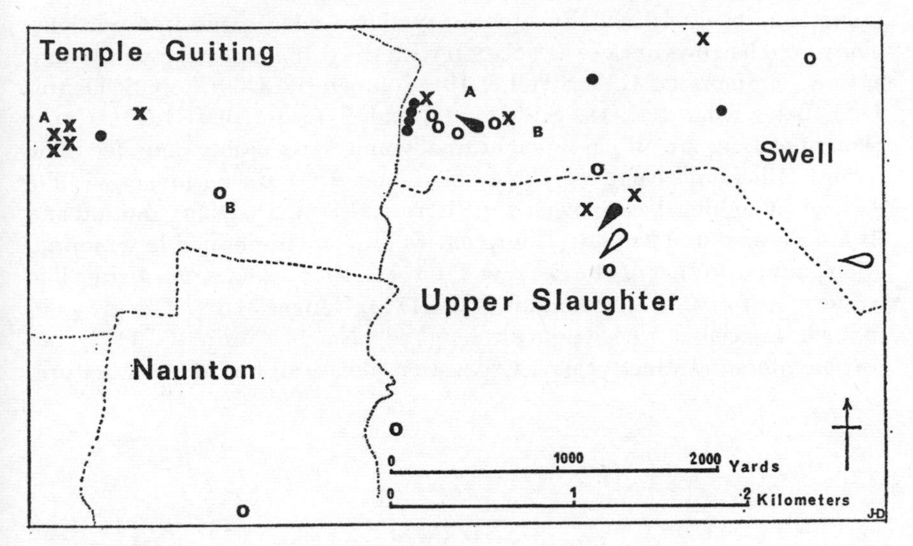

Fig 11

Temple Guiting

The Bembro group (A), Temple Guiting 12–15, the remains of which are at present under grass, has been virtually destroyed since Witts time. The nearby oval mound Temple Guiting 16 is unploughed on arable and worth conserving, as is Temple Guiting 10(B), annually ploughed but still over 1m high.

Swell

The considerable occurrence of worked and waste flint in and around the Cow Common barrow group (A), together with the high barrow density, indicates an area of intense prehistoric activity. Time, however, has not served the group well. The 'excavated' round barrows Swell 1–4 and the long barrow GLO22, although essentially unploughed, are unfenced and plough 'bites' into their perimeters are frequent. The high intensity of ploughing on the common is reducing the unexcavated sites Swell 6–10 and the excavated Swell 5 to patches of scattered stone from which flint scrapers and flakes may be gleaned. This loss is especially unfortunate in that the long barrow (GLO22) can be considered to be late in Grimes typological series, and its relationship to the closely adjacent round barrows, Swell 8–10, is of particular interest.

Although no record exists of the occurrence of barrows to the east of the hedge that crosses the common, deep ploughing during the 1970 season exposed several areas of stones in the field from which a considerable amount of flint was recovered (B).

Upper Slaughter

A parallel situation exists between the Eyford Hill group and the Cow Common cemetery. The only excavated barrow in the group (GLO3), although overgrown, is unploughed, whereas its two adjacent round barrows and the nearby Newclose long barrow (GLO49) and its associate are unexcavated but ploughed. Urgent action is needed to protect this latter group and the fine round barrow, Swell 12, a 1·50m high ploughed mound, just to the north.

Note: the long captions for fig 10–14 all work from SW-NE.

group, has been defined by any excavation under modern conditions. The round barrows in close association with the (unploughed) long mounds at Cow Common (GLO22: Swell 8–10), Colnpen (GLO69: Coln St Dennis 1–4), Belas Knap (GLO1: Sudeley 1), and Eyford Hill (GLO3: Upper Slaughter 2, 3), are all ploughed annually and considerably denuded. The Eyford Hill round barrows (Upper Slaughter 2, 3) are no longer visible. Annual ploughing has merged the Barrow Hill GLO61 long mound and its associated round barrow (Hampnett 7) into one ill-defined low mound, a fate similar to that of the Barrow Tumps GLO17/Cherington 1 site. The western half of this long barrow (GLO17) no longer exists. The group of mounds associated with the (unploughed) Norns Tump (GLO93) has become more indistinct yearly. Excavation alone can define their nature.

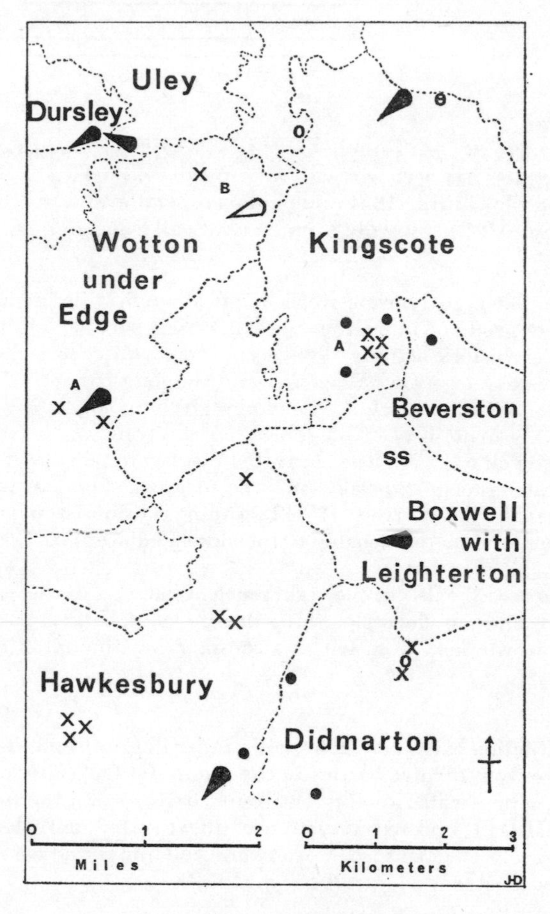

Fig 12 (caption facing)

Bown Hill (GLO20) and the nearby round barrow (Woodchester 1) have both undergone excavations—the latter site only when devastated by ploughing, by which time the only remains were a cist containing a piece of human skull. The long barrow at Newclose GLO49 and its attendant round mound (Upper Slaughter 4) are both under plough, but sufficiently extant to be worthy of attention.

Long/round barrow associations, other than those illustrated by Grinsell (1960, 15), also exist. One possible pair is that made by Wood Barrow (GLO63) (now almost extinct) and the nearby Royal Oak barrow (Chedworth 6), an oval mound, now featureless, which previously exhibited upright stones. A possible round barrow, presumably Grinsell's Brimpsfield 2, was located after an extensive search during December, 1970. This site, an overgrown stony mound, roughly sixteen paces in diameter and 0·6m

---

Hawksbury

The barrows situated in this parish have a poor survival rate. Six of the seven recorded round barrows (Hawksbury 1a–c, 2, 3, 5) have been finally levelled by ploughing during this century. The seventh (Hawksbury 4) remains isolated but unploughed, following the removal of hedges and field walls. The farmer has considerately left a margin of unploughed land around the barrow giving a protective false berm 0·60m high. Land reclamation has similarly isolated the nearby Starveall long barrow (GLO87), filling in the quarry scoop formerly close to the eastern end. The mound is overgrown with trees and surrounded by a ruined drystone wall.

Wotton under Edge

Only the Clump long barrow (GLO86) now remains of the Blackquarries Hill Group (A), the two adjacent round barrows, Witts 94 and 95 (Wotton under Edge 1, 2) having been removed by ploughing since his time. The tree-clad long mound must, by its quarrying association, be slightly doubtful.

The second pair of barrows (B) near to Symonds Hall Farm are both affected by the plough. The long barrow (GLO85) has become dissected into two separate mounds, and the round barrow (Wotton under Edge 3) is now only 0·30m high.

Kingscote

Apart from the levelled Lasborough Farm barrows (Kingscote la-d), to which authenticity is lent by their inclusion on the 1828 OS map, a degree of uncertainty exists for members of Group A. Kingscote 3 is now a heap of stones surrounding a telegraph pole in an arable field and suggests field stone clearance rather than a burial mound. Kingscote 6, a low, oval, gutted mound, is now difficult to find under grass, and the third site an overgrown oval mound at the base of Brock Hill, is Corcoran's GLO 38 (previously considered, p 136).

Didmarton

Nan Tows Tump (Didmarton 1), a 2·70m high mound densely covered with living and dead trees, and the Tump Barn (Didmarton 2) barrow, unploughed at the edge of an arable field, are both worthy of (effective) conservation. With the possible triple barrow NE of Parkwood, only the centre mound (Didmarton 4) still survives the annual ploughing. Its two outliers have now been eroded.

high, is located some sixty paces S.W. of West Tump (GLO8). If authentic—other ridges and hollows are present in the surrounding wood—this represents a further member of this category. We might also add the two barrows in Lodge Park Farmington (long barrow (GLO5) and round barrow Farmington 3), both under grass. Norbury (GLO30) and the nearby round mound, Northleach 1, are both on arable and in the final stages of removal.

(c) *Round barrows containing stone structure.* Cists or cist-like chambers, totally enclosed within the mound structure, are a feature of those Cotswold long barrows regarded as late in the typological sequence outlined by Grimes (1960, 92). The survival of this form of chamber for burial purposes, together with a technique of stone-working later applied to the construction of oval (Adlestrop, GLO44) and round (Chedworth 1) mounds, can be demonstrated. A continuity of building methods and possibly funerary tradition was shown with the Burn Ground (GLO60) long barrow and its associated round barrows Hampnett 1–4 (Grimes,

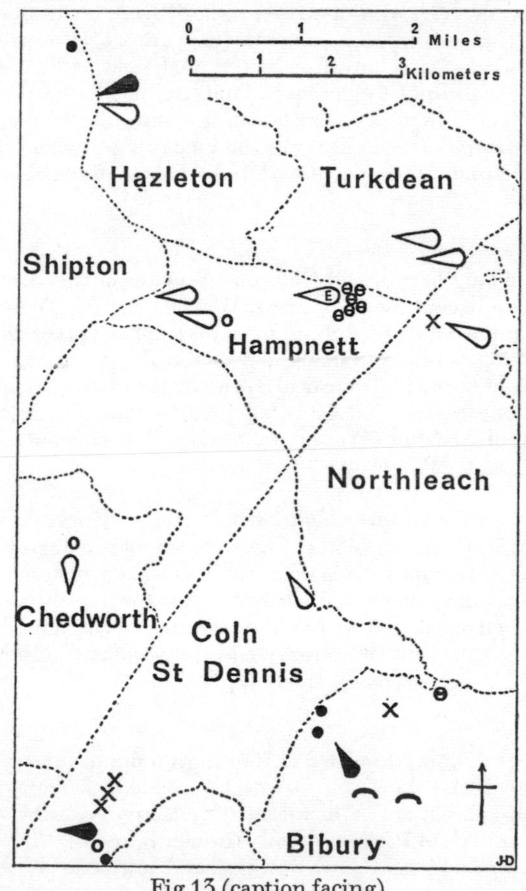

Fig 13 (caption facing)

Chedworth

The almost completely destroyed Wood Barrow (GLO63) has an oval mound (Chedworth 6) at its northern extremity, still of sufficient size to repay investigation.

Coln St Dennis

The Colnpen long barrow (GLO69) and its satellite round barrows (Coln St Dennis 1–5) form one of the last long-round barrow complexes still in a conservable condition. Action on this site must be immediate, since the three round barrows in a line to the north are of low profile and ploughed annually.

Crickley barrow (GLO64) on the boundary with Northleach has been finally eradicated in the last decade.

Bibury

The sites of Saltway Barn (GLO92), the Ablington beehive chamber (GLO26) and a third, possibly similar site, Hole Ground, lie just south of the Lamborough Banks long mound (GLO25). The particular function of such sites and the reason for their concentration in a limited area has yet to be defined. The Lamborough Banks barrow, disturbed in the previous century, now exists as an overgrown grass covered mound. Of the two round barrows to the NW, the Gambra Hill site (Bibury 1) is in good condition (unploughed on arable) but its neighbour (Bibury 2), still crowned by a sycamore tree, has been severely 'trimmed' by the plough. Ploughing has removed the doubtful mound Bibury 3 formerly situated between Gambra Hill and the excavated Oldwalls Shed barrow.

Hampnett

Continual ploughing has masked the type features of the Cheltenham Road Plantation barrow (GLO59) and the nearby Barrow Hill long barrow (GLO61) and its attendant round mound Hampnett 7. Excavation alone can define their true nature and relationship. The excavated group to the east is the Burn Ground cemetery.

Northleach

The long barrow (GLO30), within Norbury hill fort, now a low, featureless, mound, has a similarly denuded round barrow, Northleach 1, as a close neighbour.

Hazleton

Ploughing has almost completely destroyed the southernmost of these two long barrows and (although essentially unploughed) has reduced the other in both width and length.

Turkdean

The two Leygore Manor sites (GLO57, 58), both presumably long barrows, are now less than 0·25m high and virtually destroyed.

1960, 111). Evidence for a possible Neolithic-Bronze Age transition in funerary practices is shown by the apparent fusion of burial rituals revealed in the barrows Dry Heathfield (Coberley 1a), Hungerford (Cranham 3) and the Waste (Hawling 10a). Later in the Bronze Age the use of cists or slab-lined graves has become a notable feature in the county. Grinsell listed seventeen sites each having a centrally situated or primary stone-delimited burial structure (1960, 34). To this list we can add a further four sites from which a stone structure (not necessarily primary) has been recorded: Withington 1, Haresfield 4, Charlton Kings 1, and possibly Horsley 1.

The 1970 re-examination has added another two possible sites. During ploughing in 1970 a 1·3m by 0·6m by 0·45m slab was disturbed from the centre of the Farmcote (Temple Guiting 19) round barrow. Apart from a few waste flint flakes no finds were present in the plough soil. The Warren Tump (Cherington 2) site, which produced a 0·6m by 0·45m slab, has previously been considered (above p 141).

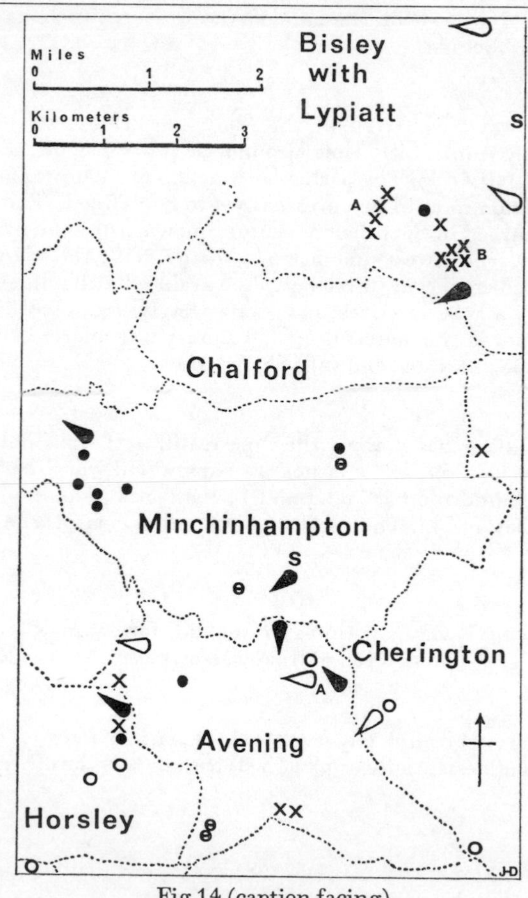

Fig 14 (caption facing)

Horsley

A string of barrow sites lie along the Avening Horsley border in a north-south line.

The southernmost site (Horsley 2) is a denuded earthern mound placed on a false hill crest. Very little flint was apparent in the surrounding field, a non-occurrence parallelled by a nearby site Horsley 3. This 'barrow' can only be regarded with the utmost suspicion, since it is now undistinguishable from many other stoney mounds and hollows, all probably derived from the adjacent quarry.

The next barrow in line is Horsley 4, a grass covered, stoney mound 1·5m high with an unrecorded excavation trench cut into the centre from the south. This site with its structure and location 'a few hundred yards south' of the Lechmore long barrow (GLO21), suggests itself as Witts No 8, a barrow he excavated in 1869 (Witts, 1883, 96).

A doubtful, now vanished, mound (Horsley 5) may have existed between this site and the long barrow.

The chambering from the Lechmore barrow has long since made its way into the surrounding field walls, leaving a featureless, grass covered long mound in an arable field. In contrast to the other sites, flint appears abundant in the surrounding area.

Avening

Due north of the Lechmore site lies the round barrow Avening 1, now a vague undulation in an arable field. The nearby Oldfield Wood site (GLO80) has suffered similar depredation and is now an ill-defined spread of small stones, only prompt excavation of which may determine its true nature. To the SE the gutted Oven round barrow (Avening 3) survives as a bush-covered mound on arable. The group of Sites A, around Norns Tump (GLO93), have been discussed previously (p 135).

Cherington

The long barrow GLO17 and its companion round barrow Cherington 1 are almost totally obliterated and survive only as indecipherable low mounds on fallow.

Minchinhampton

A false impression is given by the apparently high level of barrow survival in the western portion of this parish. Although all these sites lie on common land and are unploughed, most have either suffered unrecorded exploration, or have an element of doubt by their association with old quarry workings. Whitefield's Tump (GLO77), a damaged, short, long barrow, lies on the northern edge of the common.

Bisley with Lypiatt

Only Money Tump, a grass-covered mound 1·20m high, remains out of the twelve possible round barrows formerly present in this parish. Its nearby companion Bisley with Lypiatt 6 and the Nashend Farm Group (A) and Bournes Green Group (B) have all been reduced to patches of scattered stone in arable fields. The long barrows have fared little better. Avenis barrow (GLO75) remains as a featureless, grassy mound of low profiles. Proceeding northwards, the Limekiln Lane (GLO74) is an unrecognisable mass of hummocks and hollows, two megaliths are all that remain of the Grants Stone barrow (GLO32), and the final site (GLO71) has been destroyed by farm buildings.

Even allowing for the non-authenticity of some of these sites, we have a remarkable number of round barrows with evidence of stone structures. Four sites in this category where disturbance has indicated the presence of such structures need further investigation, namely Roel Farm (Hawling 2), Warren Tump (Cherington 2), Farmcote (Temple Guiting 19), and Barnsley Wold (Barnsley 1).

Unexcavated unploughed sites

Of the seventy-three unploughed barrows over 0·50m high, a mere thirteen exist which do not have either excessive tree cover or evidence of an earlier unrecorded examination. These thirteen sites, which must at all costs be conserved, are:

Bibury 1	Miserden 2
Bisley with Lypiatt 1	Sezincote 1, 2
Bitton 1	Standish 1, 2
Didmarton 2	Temple Guiting 16
Guiting Power 1	Willersey 1
Hawksbury 4	

A further twenty sites with a partial or total cover of trees are

Cirencester 2	Farmington 2
Cutsdean 1	Prestbury 1
Didmarton 1	North Cerney 2
Donnington 2	Randwick 1, 2
Dowdeswell 3	Shipton 1
Duntisbourne Rouse 1	Swell 11, 14, 19
Guiting Power 2	Temple Guiting 17
Hatherop 1	Upper Slaughter 5
Fairford 2	Wyck Rissington 1

The condition of the individual sites in the above list varies considerably. Cutsdean 1 and Wyck Rissington 1 are bush- or lightly tree-covered whereas Didmarton 1 has a dense tree growth, completely obscuring the mound. Conservation of these sites must include action to curtail excessive overgrowth. Evidence of a previous unrecorded opening is visible on a number of unploughed barrows. Sites in this category, for which a decision to excavate or conserve is difficult, include:

Beverston 1	Horsley 4
Coberley 2–4	Miserden 1
Elkstone 1	Sezincote 5
Haresfield 1	Withington 2

Prompt action is required if we are to save those barrows which are at present in a reasonable condition even though ploughed annually.

The barrow at Wellhead Copse (Cirencester 1) demonstrates the destructive action of the plough. Although still approximately 1·7m high, repeated ploughing has disrupted the outer structure of the mound. A number of small boulders, apparently from the inner core of the barrow, were evident in the plough soil during the winter 1970–1971. Similar disturbance of the inner structures of barrows over 1m high has been observed at Chedworth 6, Cherington 2 and Temple Guiting 19.

Other barrows in the ploughed category which are worth conserving are:

Cranham 1, 2	Swell 12
Guiting Power 1	Temple Guiting 10, 18
Rodmarton 1	Upper Slaughter 1

(The Barrington 1 Hill Barn barrow could not be located at the reference given (Grinsell, 1960, 103). If still extant, it may be included in this category).

Excavation

With a large number of sites in the county in process of destruction, and a limited budget for excavation, we can afford to examine only those sites which, by virtue of their type, location, and condition, can actively contribute to our knowledge of their particular period. Quite simply, the bulk of the barrows of Gloucestershire (and other areas) at present under plough will have to be 'written off' unless a radical, urgent change is made in the attitude to and financial provision for archaeology. If, as is certain, irreplaceable evidence of our prehistory is to be knowingly destroyed, what must we attempt to salvage? Each of the two classes of field monuments previously examined has its own criteria of importance and needs separate consideration.

With the long barrows of the Cotswold Severn culture, a special priority can be argued. The individuality of each barrow must lend emphasis to the necessity of recovering the ground plan of *every* site before its destruction. Any one of these monuments could represent a link in the typological sequence of the group that could be lost for ever by the barrow's destruction. A further objective must be the establishment of a true distribution pattern for the group. Attempts should be made, by excavation or geophysical means, to establish the nature of dubious confluent round barrow/long barrow sites to verify the existing assumed pattern.

Finally the serious lack of datable material hinders our appreciation of the Cotswold Severn group of tombs and their relationship to other monuments of the Neolithic period. The provision of such material, both organic and inorganic, should certainly be an important requirement for any excavation programme.

The impossibility of examining any but a few of the ninety round barrows at present under plough has already been stated. The two sites which must figure high in any order of priority for excavation are the groups at Cow Common (fig 11) and Snowshill (fig 10). With each group the unexcavated barrows are 'too far gone' for conservation, and sufficient details exist of earlier explorations to make definition by modern techniques profitable. At Cow Common the prolific occurrence of worked and waste flint, both from the environs of the long barrow and the neighbouring field, indicates an area of intensive prehistoric utilization. A similarly high priority must be given to those rare sites where a round barrow is situated immediately in front of the forecourt of a long barrow. The sites of Barrow Hill (GLO61)/Hampnett 7 (fig 13) and Avening Court (GLO17)/Cherington 1 (fig 14) are both badly denuded examples of this type that require attention. For the remainder, at both the possible triple barrow Didmarton 3–5 (fig 12) and the cluster of mounds around Norns Tump, Avening (fig 14), at least one barrow of reasonable height is left and requires excavation to define the nature of the monuments.

Conservation

The conservation of barrows in groups, together with their interstitual ground surface, is preferable to the practice of leaving isolated mounds as unploughed islands in a sea of corn. Although this latter process affords a degree of protection to the individual mounds, isolation destroys their continuity and interrelationship. Selection of a site for conservation must, however, depend on its physical condition, as well as the location. The probability of considerable basal disturbance in any mound below 0·5m high must render it unsuitable for conservation. Selection has to be made from those sites at present of sufficient height to have preserved internal features. The only exception to this rule are those sites of low profile, which are members of groups or associations in which the majority of barrows are of reasonable height and condition. With both long and round barrows the problems of conserving sites 'preserved' under trees has to be faced. To obtain a cessation of ploughing over those mounds still in reasonable condition is a still more difficult task.

Most long barrows at present under plough are too badly eroded to be worth conserving. A few sites like Ganborough (GLO42), Oak Piece (GLO43) and Newclose (GLO49) are still sufficiently extant to repay conservation *if immediately applied*. What is more important is that proper conservation be applied to those sites at present unploughed, especially those in arable fields. The barrows at Symonds Hall Farm (GLO85) and Lineover (GLO56) will eventually cease to be viable monuments if their annual attrition does not cease. Only the long/round barrow complex centred on Colnpen (GLO69) (fig 13) remains as an example of its class, in a state of (partial) preservation. Although badly denuded by the plough, two of the attendant round barrows still stand over 0·6m high; the three small barrows along the edge of the combe to the NE are now stony patches in the arable field.

With round barrows, a single nucleated group now remains unploughed in Gloucestershire, that in Hull Plantations, Longborough. Effective conservation will only be obtained if excess tree-growth can be curtailed. Other smaller assemblages, and those single barrows still in reasonable condition, have been detailed in previous sections. Two sites in particular deserve attention. Attempts should be made to stop ploughing over the pair of barrows at Ebworth Lodge (Cranham 1, 2) and to prevent further damage to the formerly perfect Sezincote 2 and 3 round barrows.

The provision of conserved sites which are both accessible and intelligible to the general public is an essential function of any conservation policy. Gloucestershire has four 'show' barrows—Uley, Belas Knap, Nympsfield, and Notgrove—at which the dimensions and structure of a megalithic tomb may be seen. Uley alone is the site at which a visitor can experience the earthfast, womblike atmosphere of the chamber tomb. The musty odour, muddy floor and dark recesses, especially if experienced by flickering candle-light, evoke an aura much closer to reality than the aseptic, gravelled, reconstructed grandeur, of West Kennett. Uley, perhaps above all other sites, epitomizes the trust placed with us to preserve for future generations those monuments which past generations, albeit unknowingly, have left in our care. The existence of unploughed sites is due more to the good auspices of past and present farmers and landowners than a strong conservation policy. We cannot afford to think that this 'protection' given to these sites will last forever—they remain inviolate by good fortune rather than by effective conservation. Unless action is taken immediately, then the internationally famous Cotswold barrows will have been virtually destroyed in the lifetime of the man who, more than anyone else, has done so much to record them for scholarship and posterity.

REFERENCES

Burgess, C., 1970. 'The Bronze Age,' *Current Archaeol. II*, no. 8, 208–215.

Corcoran, J. X. W. P., 1969. 'The Cotswold-Severn Group' in Powell, T. G. E. (ed.), *Megalithic Enquiries* (Liverpool UP).

Crawford, O. G. S., 1925. *The Long Barrows of the Cotswolds* (Bellows, Gloucester).

Daniel, G. E., 1950. *The Prehistoric Chambered Tombs of England and Wales.* 1970. 'Megalithic Answers,' *Antiquity* 44, 260–269.

Fowler, P. J. (ed.), 'Conservation and the Countryside,' *Wiltshire Archaeol. Natur. Hist. Mag.* 63, 1–11.

Grimes, W. F., 1960. *Excavations on Defence Sites* (HMSO).

Grinsell, L. V., 1964. 'The Royce Collection at Stow-on-the-Wold,' *Trans. Bristol Gloucestershire Archaeol. Soc.* 83, 1–33.

O'Neil, H. E., 1966. 'Sales' Lot Long Barrow, Withington, Gloucestershire, 1962–1965,' *Trans. Bristol Gloucestershire Archaeol. Soc.* 85, 5–35. 1967. 'Bevan's Quarry Round Barrow, Temple Guiting, 1963', *Trans. Bristol Gloucestershire Archaeol. Soc.* 86, 16–41, and Grinsell, L. V., 1960, 'Gloucestershire Barrows,' *Trans. Bristol Gloucestershire Archaeol. Soc.*, 79, Part I.

Walsh, Sir D., 1969. *Report of the Committee of Enquiry into the Arrangements for the Protection of Field Monuments 1966–68* (Cmnd 3904, HMSO).

Witts, G. B., 1883. *Archaeological Handbook of Gloucestershire.*

CHAPTER VI

Ring-Ditches in Eastern and Central Gloucestershire

Isobel Smith

Ten years ago, when publishing *Gloucestershire Barrows*, O'Neil and Grinsell (1960) suggested that a systematic examination of air-photographs might be expected to result in the discovery of a few barrows previously unrecorded. The present volume affords an appropriate occasion for the presentation in summary form of the results of examination of air-photographs covering the eastern and central parts of Gloucestershire, and it is pleasant to be able to offer these notes to Leslie Grinsell as an account of work in progress on a project stimulated by one of his invaluable inventories of barrows in the counties of Southern England.

The information has been compiled in the course of official duties for the Royal Commission on Historical Monuments (England) and represents a by-product of work done for the Commission's forthcoming survey of Iron Age and Romano-British monuments in the Gloucestershire Cotswolds. The writer is grateful to colleagues on the Commission staff, and particularly to Collin Bowen, for encouragement, assistance and stimulating discussion, but must be held solely responsible for views expressed here.

The survey covers the whole of Gloucestershire east of the Cotswold escarpment and an irregular zone along its foot in the Vales of Berkeley, Gloucester and Evesham, defined by the boundaries of civil parishes whose eastern parts extend above the escarpment. Owing to the small scale of the map, this western limit is shown schematically in fig 15.

Preparation of the Commission's inventory for this area has entailed examination of all air-photographs, both vertical and oblique, that were available up to the end of 1969. Stereoscopic inspection of the 1 : 10,000 scale and other vertical air-cover, undertaken by the writer's colleagues, produced no unrecorded barrow mounds, either long or round. The extensive series of oblique air-photographs, mostly taken by J. K. S. St Joseph, has yielded the same negative results. Only five hitherto unnoted round barrows, four of them in a group, have been recognised by Commission staff in the course of field-work carried out for other purposes. It therefore appears probable that nothing short of intensive search on the ground will add materially to the published list of barrows surviving as positive earthworks.

The oblique air-photographs have, however, shown that there is a surprisingly large number of circular crop-marks (ring-ditches) in the area: just over 150 have been counted. The existence of ring-ditches in the

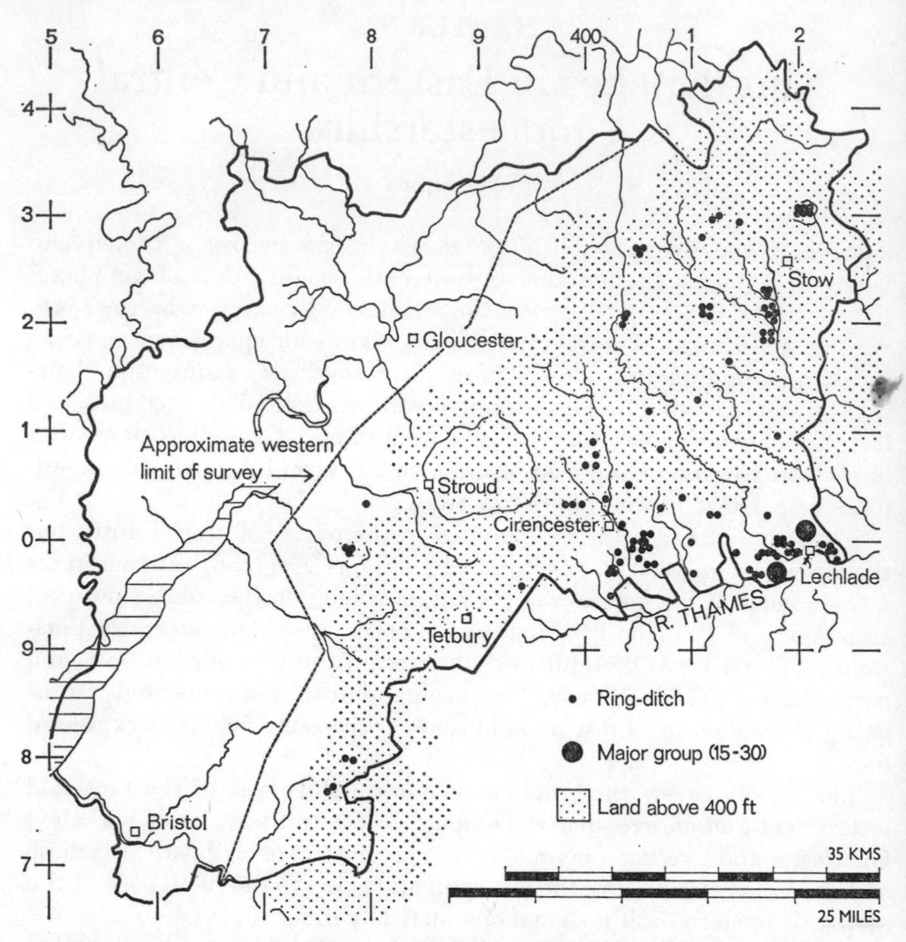

15. Distribution of ring-ditches visible as crop-marks in eastern and central Gloucestershire. *Crown Copyright reserved.*

Gloucestershire part of the Upper Thames Valley was first brought to notice by D. N. Riley (1942, 111, 113); later he plotted some three dozen on maps and reproduced a photograph of a group in Kempsford parish (Riley, 1944*a*, figs 26, 28; 1944*b*, Pl Vb). When compiling their list of round barrows, O'Neil and Grinsell (1960) adopted a cautious approach to these crop-mark sites because of the difficulty of distinguishing the marks developed by the ditches of round barrows from those made by the ditches of other circular monuments of comparable diameters. They assigned parish numbers to seven which they considered, for various reasons, to be probable or possible barrow sites and mentioned the presence of other examples.

Now that ring-ditches—whatever kinds of levelled sites they may

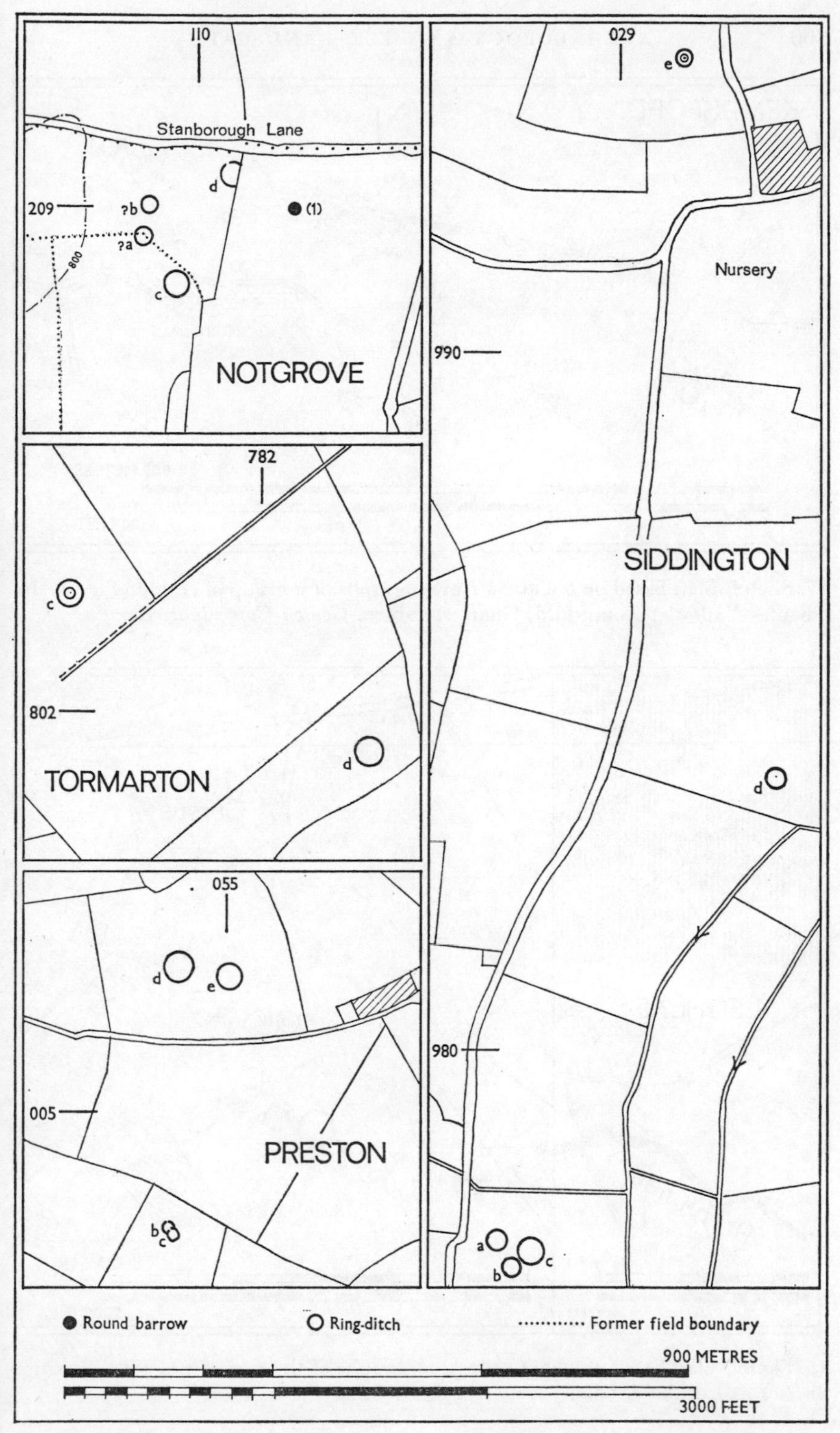

16. Sketch-plan based on oblique air-photographs of groups of ring-ditches in Gloucestershire. All are on limestone except Siddington *a–d*. *Crown Copyright reserved.*

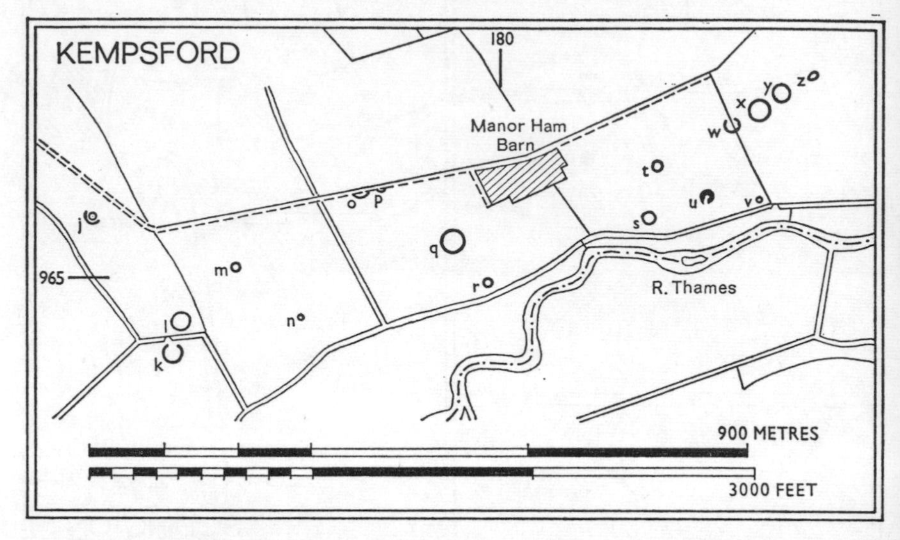

17. Sketch-plan based on oblique air-photographs of a group of ring-ditches in the Thames Valley at Kempsford, Gloucestershire. *Crown Copyright reserved.*

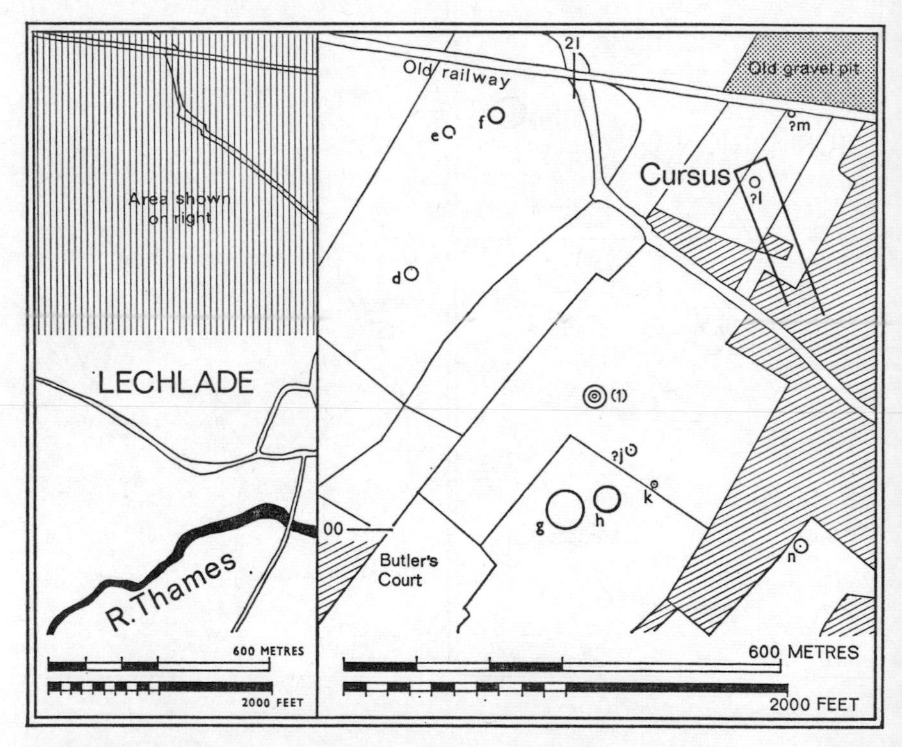

18. Sketch-plan based on oblique air-photographs of the cursus and adjacent ring-ditches at Lechlade, Gloucestershire. *Crown Copyright reserved.*

betoken—can be seen to form an important element among the field monuments of Gloucestershire, they clearly demand further attention. In view of the problems of interpretation alluded to above, all that can be offered here is a distribution map (fig 15), sketch-plans of a few groups (figs 16–18), a couple of air-photographs (Pls XI, XII), and some general comments. It is hoped that a detailed list with National Grid references and sources may be published elsewhere. As shown on figs. 16–18, individual ring-ditches within each civil parish have been distinguished by letters of the alphabet in order to avoid any possibility of confusion with barrows in the O'Neil and Grinsell list.

The seven numbered ring-ditches in that list are included on fig 15 together with the information derived from air-photographs taken over a period of nearly four decades by G. W. G. Allen, W. A. Baker, D. N. Riley, J. K. S. St Joseph and, for 1969 only, by staff of the Royal Commission's Air Photographic Service. The Allen and Riley photographs, taken *c*1932–43, are confined to the Upper Thames region, east of Cirencester. In the post-war years Baker has covered mainly areas west and north of Cirencester, while St Joseph has ranged widely over most of Gloucestershire. About one-third of the ring-ditches considered here were first recorded in 1969.

In preparing the map, fig 15, Case's definition of ring-ditches has been followed: '. . . more or less circular or oval enclosure-ditches indicated by depressions in the ground or by marks in crops or soils . . .' (Hamlin and Case, 1963, 36). Implicitly excluded from this definition are the narrower, usually penannular, drainage gullies that may enclose hut-sites; Case was not concerned with the latter. But the distinction cannot always be maintained with confidence on the evidence supplied by crop-marks. Barrow ditches of modest diameter are often penannular, and the difference between the width of a ditch and that of a gully is a matter of degree. Therefore, with the exception (it is hoped) of ploughed-out tree-rings and other irrelevant phenomena, *all* circular and roughly circular crop-marks have been plotted and a proportion of hut-sites has probably been included. Many of the ring-ditches lie amongst or near settlement crop-marks; some appear to ante-date linear ditches belonging to the settlements, but in most instances the relationship cannot be determined by inspection.

All the monuments considered here appear to have been ploughed flat; traces of mounds or banks are not visible on photographs. The negative results obtained from ground inspection of a limited number suggest that little further information is likely to be gained in this way, though ideally all ought to be visited. Many sites lie within the former open fields, and some, as mentioned above, seem to have been flattened at an even earlier date, for they are crossed by the uninterrupted crop-marks of ditches belonging to settlements of the pre-Roman Iron Age or Roman times (see

Pl XII). Similar circumstances in the Oxford region have been discussed by Case *et al* (1965, 32, 39, 55).

Most of the 151 ring-ditches are simple circles, but the number includes one triple circle, seven double circles, about two dozen penannular examples and half a dozen semi-circles. Within one ring there appears to be an inner ring of pits; in a second instance a ring seems to be composed, at least in part, of closely spaced pits. Central features (graves?) are seldom visible. Diameters, estimated for 137, range from about 30 ft to about 170 ft and may be grouped roughly as follows:

Diameter (*in feet*):	30–40	50–60	70–80	90–100	110–170
Per cent (*of* 137):	31	26	22	13	8

As will be evident from fig 15, geographical distribution is uneven. Predictably, the main concentration is found on the low-lying gravel terraces north of the Thames, where the seventy-eight ring-ditches counted include major groups in Lechlade and Kempsford parishes that are too densely clustered to be shown individually. It is uncertain whether all the 'single circles' plotted by Riley (1944*a*, fig 26) within the Gloucestershire parishes along the Thames have been included; some had not been photographed, and the list used in compiling his map (*ibid*, 66, note 6) is not to be found in the Ashmolean Museum. A further twenty-one ring-ditches occur on gravels elsewhere in the county within the limits of the area under discussion, but only one has been found west of the Cotswold escarpment in the Severn Basin. There are small groups on the more restricted deposits above 400 ft O.D. near the source of the River Coln, round the confluence of the Rivers Windrush and Dikler, and in the Vale of Moreton. In all, ninety-nine or two-thirds of the total number are on gravels.

The remaining fifty-two ring-ditches are more widely dispersed over the limestone uplands of the Cotswolds, broadly defined on fig 15 as land over 400 ft O.D. A number of those found immediately south and east of Cirencester lie on limestone above the gravel terraces but below this contour. An interesting feature of the distribution is the gradual thinning-out north-westwards from the Thames Valley as the pattern begins to merge with that of the round barrows, predominantly situated on the uplands (O'Neil and Grinsell, 1960, Map 2). This partially complementary and partially overlapping distribution may afford some support for the hypothesis that some of the ring-ditches mark the sites of former barrows.

The apparent scarcity in the Cotswolds of round barrows with ditches need not present a serious difficulty. It is true that the eight barrows excavated in Chedworth and Hampnett parishes by Grimes (1958, 102–10, 131–5) had no ditches, and that O'Neil and Grinsell (1960, 34, 61) considered barrows with ditches to be so unusual as to merit a special list. The number specified in that list does not, however, include all those described in their main inventory. Subsequent field-work and inspection of air-photographs have added another couple, and a third has been verified by excavation (O'Neil, 1967). The proportion of barrows known to have ditches remains small (around seven per cent), but this may be partially explicable in terms of the extent to which they have been ploughed and of the limited number that has been excavated by modern methods. In the circumstances, negative evidence does not provide a valid argument against the interpretation of ring-ditches as the surviving elements of completely levelled barrows.

A more positive form of support for this interpretation can perhaps be found in the location of certain ring-ditches. In six separate instances ring-ditches (numbering ten in all) lie near enough to round barrows to suggest that these last may be the chance survivors of former groups or alignments. The largest potential group (fig 16) is that at Notgrove (6 miles south-west of Stow-on-the-Wold), where a cluster, possibly comprising four rings, lies about 200 yds west of the ploughed barrow, Notgrove 1. Two of the rings, *a* and *b*, are ill-defined on the photographs and shown as doubtful on the plan. They are partially obscured by the ditches of a settlement and by marks probably of natural origin. The changes in alignment of a former field wall as it passed round *c* and through *a* may indicate that mounds existed within these ring-ditches when the open fields were laid out; but other deviations of the field boundaries cannot be explained in this way and the apparent relationship may be fortuitous.

A further eight instances occur where ring-ditches on the limestone are spaced closely enough to be considered as forming small groups, usually composed of two or three members, as in Tormarton and Preston parishes (fig 16). The pair of rings at Tormarton (12 miles S.S.W. of Tetbury) includes a double one; the diameters of the outer and inner ditches are estimated to be about 110 ft and 40 ft respectively. The two single rings, *d* and *e*, at Preston (immediately east of Cirencester) measure about 100 ft and 80 ft across, and the conjoined rings, *b* and *c*, about 70 ft and 60 ft. These last might be interpreted as confluent barrow ditches (Pl XI); it is not quite certain that *c* is penannular. The second double ring illustrated in fig 16, at Siddington (south of Cirencester), is apparently much smaller than the Tormarton example; its diameters are of the order of 60 ft and 25 ft. The inner ditch appears to enclose a central circular mark about 10 ft across. This complex ring lies on a low limestone ridge that projects southwards into the gravel-covered plain where four other ring-ditches in this parish are found.

Fig 17 and Pl XII illustrate part of a large group immediately north of the Thames in Kempsford parish, where there are in all thirty-nine ring-ditches, most of them within an area of about three-quarters of a square mile. The alignment of rings *w–z* suggests a linear barrow cemetery. The curious pear-shaped enclosure, *z*, appears to belong to this arrangement, but between it and *y* there are faint indications of other circular or semi-circular marks on the air-photographs which have not been taken into account here. A somewhat similar pear-shaped enclosure lies within an alignment at Eynsham, Oxon (Bradford and Morris, 1941, fig 13: VIII; Pl XI).

Site *u* at Kempsford measures about 80 ft across and is distinguished by an exceptionally broad crop-mark which seems to be caused by a ditch that has been recut several times or by several closely spaced ditches. It has a narrow causeway at S.S.W. Five or six similar crop-marks (50–60 ft in diameter) are known in this parish and in Lechlade; all lie amongst other ring-ditches. There is a general resemblance to some of the Class I henges of probable Late Neolithic date at Dorchester, Oxon (Atkinson *et al*, 1951, Sites V and VI), but the small diameter of the area enclosed relative to breadth of ditch is more closely matched in the pre-Roman Iron Age 'henge' at Frilford, Berks (Bradford and Goodchild, 1939, fig 5). The proportions may also be compared with those of the larger Class I henge on Sutton Common, Longbridge Deverill, Wilts (Quinnell, 1970).

Fig 18 shows the ring-ditches in the vicinity of the cursus at Lechlade. The cursus, discovered by D. N. Riley (1944*a*, 73) and hitherto unpublished, has been sketched from photographs taken by Riley and by St Joseph before the south-east end was built over. No gaps are visible within the recorded length of the side-ditches and it remains uncertain whether they extended farther S.E. This part was already inaccessible at the time of the excavation in 1965 (MU.C.O.PBW, 1966; further information kindly supplied by Mrs. F. de M. Vatcher). The ring-ditches include the triple circle, tentatively identified as the site of a barrow, Lechlade *1*, by O'Neil and Grinsell. The three rings have been shown in purely conventional fashion, for the details are difficult to distinguish. Some photographs seem to suggest single causeways in each of the two inner ditches; on others there are indications of two pits within the innermost ring. Central pits or graves can also be seen within two other rings in this group. There is evidence that the largest ring, *g*, estimated to be about 170 ft in diameter, still retained a low mound or inner bank when a linear ditch was dug across it. The linear ditch, clearly defined on either side of the ring, produces a fainter crop-mark within, as if barely penetrating the surface of the natural gravel there. The three rings marked as doubtful are represented by faint or partially obscured crop-marks.

This combination—a cursus accompanied by a group of ring-ditches which may include at least one multiple ring—is recurrent and can be seen, for example, at North Stoke, Oxon, and Drayton, Berks (Riley, 1944*a*, Pls. VI, VIII), Dorchester, Oxon (Atkinson *et al.*, 1951, fig 2), Fornham All Saints, Suffolk (St Joseph, 1964) and Rudston, E. R. Yorks (Dymond, 1966, fig 2). In each instance the ring-ditches tend to cluster near one end of the cursus and one or two may lie within it. In this connection the two round barrows within the west end of the Stonehenge cursus and the barrow cemeteries near either end may be recalled, but it is difficult to tell whether the juxtaposition has the same significance in an area where barrow cemeteries are so numerous (Ashbee, 1960, fig 6).

The problems of interpretation posed by ring-ditches on gravel are well known, and it is clear, from experience gained in the Oxford region and elsewhere, that it is unsafe to attempt to interpret individual sites from crop-mark evidence alone. Ditches that appeared to produce identical crop-marks have been shown to represent a variety of circular monuments and to range widely in date. Sometimes it is impossible to recover satisfactory information about the nature of the associated earthworks or even to determine whether such has existed: indications of date may be lacking or ambiguous. The limited amount of direct information that is available from the part of Gloucestershire under discussion and from immediately adjacent areas points to a similar situation. Thus, one of the three ring-ditches at Lower Slaughter, near Bourton-on-the-Water (Dunning, 1932), may be assumed to have belonged to a barrow since a cremation in a collared urn was found inside it. The collared urn and cremation recovered from another was, however, a secondary deposit in the ditch, so that the interpretation is less certain. From the third there is no evidence. Five ring-ditches were excavated at Langford Downs, Oxon (Williams, 1947), about two miles north of Lechlade; a secondary cremation in a late pre-Roman Iron Age pot that had been inserted in the fill of one ditch offered the only evidence of date recovered from the whole group, and in no instance could the original form of the monument be established. The single ring-ditch that has been investigated at Lechlade in advance of gravel-digging proved to be of late Roman date (Anon, 1961). This ditch, several times recut on an increasingly wider radius, had surrounded a space measuring about 10 ft across; the only central feature was a post-hole. Another that is believed to be of Roman date has been excavated at Frampton-on-Severn, Glos (O'Neil and Grinsell, 1960, 114). It was one of a group of five, all of comparable size (75 to 90 ft across), which was composed otherwise of one probable prehistoric barrow and three sites of uncertain classification.

The records of 64 excavated ring-ditches on gravels in the Oxford region have been analysed by Case (in Hamlin and Case, 1963, 35–52). Not more than 17 or 18 could be shown to have been barrows, though the central inhumations or cremations within a further 8 may suggest that small mounds had vanished without trace. Thus the *surviving evidence* allows 25 or 26 at most to be classed as barrows, 40 per cent of the total number considered. On limestone or chalk, monuments that have already been reduced to the status of ring-ditches are seldom excavated, since there is usually no immediate threat of further destruction. Consequently, a fund of experience comparable with that obtained from sites on gravel is lacking, and it is customary to assume that circular crop-marks in these subsoils represent ploughed-out barrows. A warning against over-simplification is provided by Site V in the large barrow cemetery at Snail Down, Everleigh, Wilts (Thomas and Thomas, 1955, 140). Site V, tentatively identified as a saucer-barrow by the excavators, was found to have had an outer bank but yielded neither traces of a mound nor burials. Within the ditch were three 'ritual pits', and the monument is perhaps comparable with some of the non-funerary ring-ditches of Case's Type 2a, e.g., Cassington 5 and Stanton Harcourt VI, 2 (Hamlin and Case, 1963, 43–44, with references).

The purpose of this survey has been to record the existence of a large number of ring-ditches in Gloucestershire and to note the likelihood that a proportion of them represent the sites of ploughed-out round barrows. It has been possible to single out a few individual ring-ditches as probable barrows on the grounds of their proximity to extant mounds, and others have been mentioned individually because of their apparent resemblance in plan to the smaller Class I henges. This leaves a mass of sites about which it is useless to make any comment. Some may be so severely degraded that even total excavation would produce no satisfactory conclusion. But perhaps it is just worth while to attempt a reasoned estimate of the minimum number of barrows that may be involved. For this purpose it will be best to take the 151 ring-ditches as a block and to ignore any inferences that have been drawn in relation to particular specimens.

The excavated ring-ditches in the Oxford region may be taken to constitute a representative sample of those located in the Thames valley; the information was obtained during rescue operations in parishes spread along some 40 miles of the river's course. The results of Case's analysis may therefore be applied to the sites farther upstream in Gloucestershire, where situation and pattern of distribution are directly comparable; they may also be applied with some degree of confidence to those on gravels elsewhere in the county. Extrapolation to the limestone uplands can, on the other hand, only be justified because the alternative could be nothing better than an unsupported guess. On this basis, then, it may be supposed that around 40 per cent of the 151 ring-ditches, perhaps 55–65 in all, are potent ally identifiable round barrows.

REFERENCES

Anon, 1961. 'Excavations in Gravel-Pit at Lechlade,' *Archaeol. News Letter* 7, no 5, 117.

Ashbee, P., 1960. *The Bronze Age Round Barrow in Britain* (Phoenix).

Atkinson, R. J. C., *et al.*, 1951. *Excavations at Dorchester, Oxon.*

Bradford, J. S. P. and Goodchild, R. G., 1939. 'Excavations at Frilford, Berks., 1937–1938,' *Oxoniensia* 4, 1–70.

Bradford, J. S. P. and Morris, J. M., 1941. Archaeological Notes, *Oxoniensia* 6, 84–89.

Case, H., *et al.*, 1965. 'Excavations at City Farm, Hanborough, Oxon,' *Oxoniensia* 29/30, 1–98.

Dunning, G. C., 1932. 'Bronze Age Settlements and a Saxon Hut near Bourton-on-the-Water, Gloucestershire,' *Antiq. J.* 12, 279–293.

Dymond, D. P., 1966. Ritual Monuments at Rudston, E. Yorkshire, England, *Proc. Prehist. Soc.* 32, 86–95.

Grimes, W. F., 1958. *Excavations on Defence Sites, 1939–1945*. I (Ministry of Works, Archaeological Reports, No. 3).

Hamlin, A. and Case, H., 1963. 'Excavation of Ring-Ditches and Other Sites at Stanton Harcourt; Notes on the Finds and on Ring-Ditches in the Oxford Region, *Oxoniensia* 28, 1–52.

MOPBW, 1966. (Ministry of Public Building and Works) *Excavations: Annual Report, 1965.*

O'Neil, H. E., 1967. 'Bevan's Quarry Round Barrow, Temple Guiting, 1964,' *Trans. Bristol Gloucestershire Archaeol. Soc.* 86, 16–41.

O'Neil, H. E. and Grinsell, L. V., 1960. 'Gloucestershire Barrows,' *Trans. Bristol Gloucestershire Archaeol. Soc.*, 79, Part 1.

Quinnell, N. V., 1970. 'The Sutton Common Earthwork,' *Wiltshire Archaeol. Natur. Hist. Mag.* 65, 190.

Riley, D. N., 1942. 'Crop-Marks in the Upper Thames Valley seen from the air during 1942,' *Oxoniensia* 7, 111–114.

Riley, D. N., 1944*a*. 'Archaeology from the Air in the Upper Thames Basin,' *Oxoniensia* 8/9, 64–101.

Riley, D. N., 1944*b*. 'The Technique of Air-Archaeology,' *Archaeol. J.* 101, 1–16.

St. Joseph, J. K., 1964. 'Air Reconnaissance: Recent Results, 2,' *Antiquity* 38, 290–291.

Thomas, N. and Thomas, C., 1955. 'Excavations at Snail Down, Everleigh, 1953, 1955, An Interim Report,' *Wiltshire Archaeol. Natur. Hist. Mag.* 56, 127–148.

Williams, A., 1947. 'Excavations at Langford Downs, Oxon (near Lechlade) in 1943,' *Oxoniensia* 11/12, 44–64.

CHAPTER VII

Early Boundaries in Wessex

Desmond Bonney

The man-made or human landscape is in large measure the product of Man's efforts to mould or arrange the so-called natural landscape nearer to his requirements and to impose what he chooses to regard as some order upon its apparent chaos. Such efforts, especially among sedentary communities, involve in part a need to define, by demarcation and division, areas or units of the land surface to serve a variety of economic, social and political needs. These units will vary not only in size but from one society to another, and will be subject to change with the passage of time. In Britain they have found tangible expression in the form of settlements, fields, parks, woods etc., which in turn are components of larger units such as farms, estates, tithings, parishes, hundreds and counties. In spite of observable changes a marked element of stability is demonstrable in some of these units over the last one thousand years, and it is the purpose of this essay to suggest that this stability might in some instances have persisted considerably longer, particularly in the case of certain boundaries.

In Wessex clearly defined land units first appear in any abundance in the historical record in the form of estates granted, usually by royal charter, to individuals or ecclesiastical foundations during the later Anglo-Saxon period. Such grants are most numerous in the two centuries before the Norman Conquest although they begin as early as the seventh century. A high proportion of the charters include a description of the boundaries of the estates so granted, and since these bounds normally begin and end at the same point—listing in between a variable number of identification points, of which some, if not all, are recognizable by us to-day—it is quite clear that they refer to finite, circumscribed areas of land. Of some 180 extant charters relating to land in Wiltshire, for example, about half have boundaries; approximate figures for Hampshire are 150 and 84 and for Dorset 56 and 32.

The late G. B. Grundy attempted to solve, in the study alone, virtually all the charter boundaries relating to these three counties among others, and his efforts met with a surprising measure of success. Since then others have followed, generally warily, in his pioneer footsteps, and by employing a more detailed knowledge of both the field and relevant local documents have been able in some instances to arrive at alternative and more acceptable solutions; but much detailed work remains to be done. It is abundantly clear, however, that in Wessex, whatever the case elsewhere, there is a marked coincidence between the estates or land-units delineated in the charters and those in existence as late as the nineteenth century or even the present day. In the majority of cases these early estates have survived as manors or estates and/or as ecclesiastical parishes or their component chapelries—a survival of a thousand years or more. The establishment of estate churches by secular and ecclesiastical lords from about the tenth century onwards, which was gradually to supersede the earlier system of minster churches, is largely responsible for the evolution of parishes and, therefore, for the frequent correspondence of their boundaries with those of early estates (Addleshaw, 1953; 1954). Often estate and parish coincide exactly as in the charters relating to Stanton St Bernard (Sawyer 1968, Nos. 368, 647, 685) and Little Langford (Sawyer, 1968, No 612), both in Wiltshire, though the latter has ceased to exist as an ecclesiastical parish since 1934. In other instances an estate coincides with a later manor or tithing which is not itself a parish but which comprises a constituent part of a parish. Two estates in charters (Sawyer, 1968, Nos 631 and 438) relating to Burcombe, Wilts., for example, are the later manors of North and South Burcombe which together form the parish of that name. More rarely a charter grants a large estate comprising several settlements and their associated lands which continue to enjoy, as hitherto, a considerable measure of independence both economically and sub-tenurially. In time some, but not necessarily all, of these become ecclesiastical parishes or chapelries as well. The charter (Sawyer, 1968, No 899) granting the minster at Bradford-on-Avon and its lands to the nunnery of Shaftesbury is an illustration of this. It embraced what was to become the parishes of Monkton Farleigh, Westwood, Winkfield and Bradford-on-Avon itself, together with its dependent chapelries of Atworth, Holt, Limpley Stoke, South Wraxall and Winsley. Bradford and its chapelries persisted well into the nineteenth century—a huge parish covering over eleven thousand acres.

The existence of many estates for a thousand years or more should not, however, be taken to imply total stability. Within the Anglo-Saxon period itself there is, as T. H. Aston (1958) has pointed out, ample evidence of the amalgamation and also fragmentation of estates, processes which have continued throughout later centuries. But that said, the evidence in favour of continuity remains impressive and it poses the very real question, if estates or units of land have remained meaningful and viable entities since their first recorded appearance in the charters of the later Anglo-Saxon period, how much earlier some of them might be. And if it is not altogether too ambitious, is there any evidence to suggest that some boundaries have survived as other than relict features—though perhaps only in part—from pre-Saxon times, thus hinting at an element of continuity in the disposition of territories, land-units or estates?

There is some evidence that boundaries, and by implication units of land or estates, bearing some relationship to those delineated in the land charters were in existence in pagan Saxon times, as one might justifiably expect them to have been. (The adoption of Christianity by the Anglo-

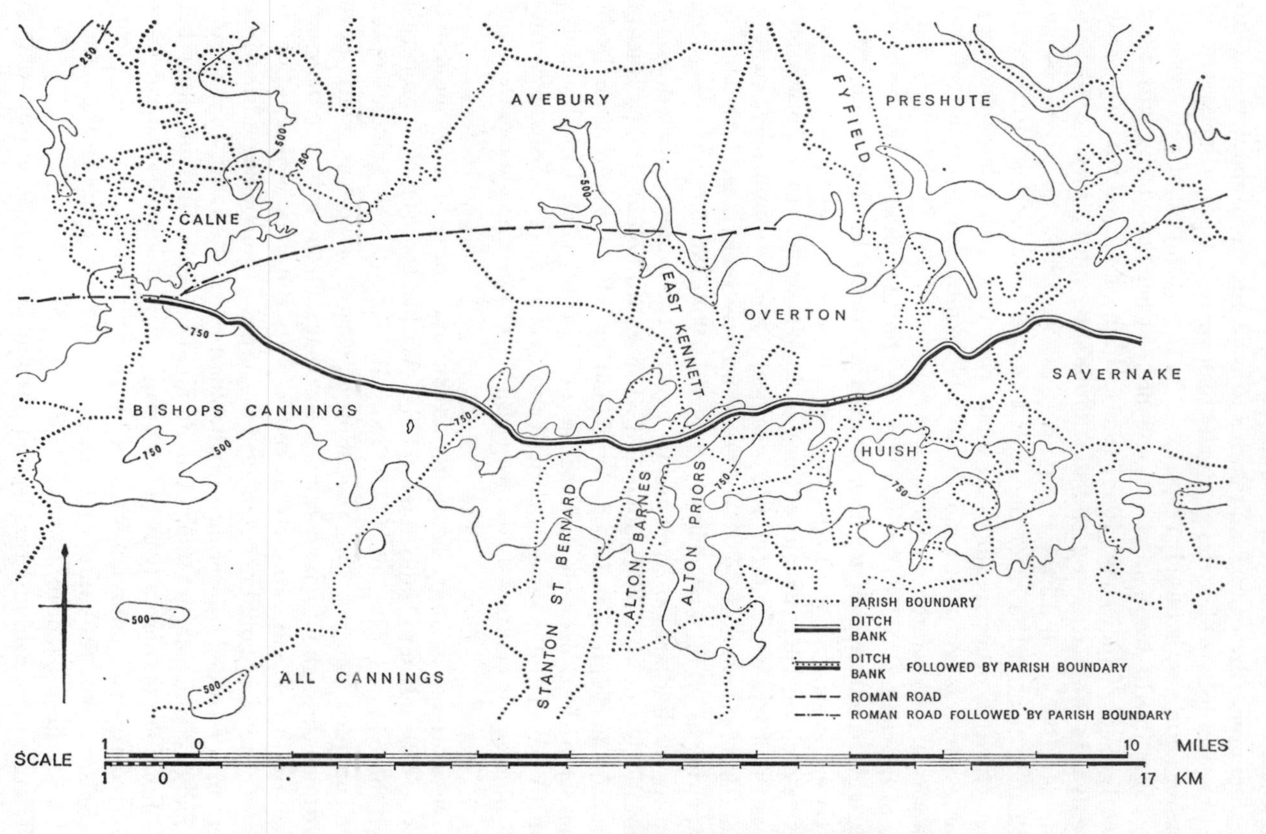

19. East Wansdyke, the Roman road and early parish boundaries.

Saxons was scarcely likely to have produced any sudden, or even slow, change in the system of land division and tenure.) For this period and topic there is some documentary evidence in the form of retrospective references in charters which appears to be of significance, but the chief source of information is the archaeological record. In Wessex the material remains of the pagan Anglo-Saxons, at least those so far known to us, consist almost entirely of burials, mostly inhumations, occuring singly, in small groups and in cemeteries, in what appear to have been flat graves and also in barrows both as primary and intrusive interments. The occurrence of grave goods with the burials characterizes them as pagan, or at least in the pagan tradition, for it is generally accepted that the custom of burying objects with the dead did not cease abruptly with conversion to Christianity. The majority of burials probably date from the sixth and seventh centuries, with some earlier and some later, but the general paucity of grave goods together with the present lack of a reliable chronology for most of them renders precise dating of most of the burials almost impossible. In this context, however, it is the distribution rather than the precise date of the burials which is important.

In Wiltshire the presence of burials of pagan Saxon date, both in cemeteries and otherwise, within or very close to medieval settlements strongly suggests that they are those of the early, if not earliest, inhabitants of those settlements. The cemeteries in particular suggest the presence of settled communities in their vicinity, and some of them include burials which appear to be as early as the fifth century. But more striking is the proportion (over 40 per cent) of burial sites (not burials), from among those which may be located with precision, which occur very close to or actually *on* parish boundaries; that is on the earliest determinable boundaries of the ecclesiastical parishes (Bonney, 1966). These parishes sometimes differ from their modern civil counterparts, usually as a result of boundary readjustments for local government purposes from the nineteenth century onwards; but in most instances the tithe maps of *c* 1840 are available to provide evidence of the earlier pattern. Such a proportion of burial sites on or close to boundaries would appear to be far too high for mere coincidence, and it is difficult to escape the conclusion that they were deliberately placed in relation to known and accepted boundaries of land-units or estates on the basis of which the later ecclesiastical parishes were formed. Again some of the burials appear to be as early as the fifth century.

Such a pattern is observable elsewhere in Wessex and beyond. In Hampshire, for example, over 40 per cent of the pagan Saxon burial sites which may be located with accuracy lie on or near ecclesiastical parish boundaries, among them the cemetery at Droxford which appears to begin in the fifth century. In Dorset, though less than a dozen certain or probable burial sites are known, nearly all occupy similar positions. For Berkshire the figure is over 30 per cent, for Lincolnshire nearly 40 per cent, and for Cambridgeshire about 25 per cent. These figures, however, take no account of any burials on or near estate boundaries which lie within parishes, i.e. where the estate does not coincide with the parish but forms a constituent part of it. Such boundaries are often somewhat more difficult to establish than those of the ecclesiastical parishes, but many have survived to be recorded on maps and some even to the present day. They are often discernible as continuous lines of hedge or fence, sometimes followed by a road or track, largely unaffected by the pattern of enclosed fields on either side which are in most cases of much more recent date. An example of a burial in such a position is that, possibly once covered by a low barrow, found during construction work in 1938 on the airfield at Netheravon, Wilts. (VCH 1957, 71). Though now in an area devoid of all but modern features, it is clear from the tithe map and award for Figheldean parish that it lay on the boundary between the manors of Choulston and Figheldean, both of them manors in Domesday Book (VCH 1955, 131, 163) and probably of much earlier origin.

Further evidence in support of this view is afforded by the Anglo-Saxon land charters. Certain terms occur in the descriptions of the boundaries of a number of estates granted by charter which suggest the presence of yet other pagan Saxon burials on such boundaries. The term 'heathen burial(s)' which occurs in charters for Wiltshire (13 times), Berkshire (8), Hampshire (7) and Dorset (1) is the most convincing of these. Grundy (1919, 166) first drew attention to it and suggested that 'these burial places were those of the pagan ages of the Saxon period'. L. V. Grinsell (1959, 61) has endorsed this view and pointed out that such burials, in so far as they are locatable at all accurately, rarely if ever coincide with a known mound or barrow. They would appear, therefore, to have been unmarked by any obvious, durable surface feature and, as has been suggested elsewhere (Bonney, 1969, 64), it is difficult to see how such burials could be earlier than pagan Saxon. Boundaries of the Saxon period, especially of the latter part of it, are scarcely likely to include reference to unmarked burials of prehistoric or Roman date. Grundy (1920, 123) has also drawn attention to the use of the terms *hlaew* (*hlaw*) and *beorg* in charter boundaries. Both normally refer to a barrow in such a context, but both have the general meaning 'a hill or natural mound', and the latter is sometimes used in this sense. Such a use of *hlaew*, however, appears to be largely unknown in southern England (Smith, 1956, 248–50). Since the terms occur in charters relating to the same general area they are hardly to be attributed to dialectal differences, and the fact that they sometimes occur in the same charter, e.g. those relating to Chalke and Stratford Tony (Sawyer, 1968, Nos 582, 861), suggests that they were used other than synonymously. Grundy believed that they indicated 'two different types of barrow', and Grinsell (1959, 61–63) has developed the idea and suggested that *beorg*, which is by far the commoner of the two, was used of prehistoric barrows and that *hlaew* was reserved for pagan Saxon barrows. Should this be so, then in Wiltshire a further ten burial sites occur on boundaries, in Hampshire five and in Berkshire thirteen. So far, however, only one barrow identified as a *hlaew* appears to have been excavated in Wessex. This, the *Posses hlaewe* of the Swallowcliffe (Wilts) charter (Sawyer, 1968, No 468) lies on the boundary of that parish and, when excavated recently, yielded evidence of a richly furnished late Saxon grave, but one which appears to have been inserted into a Bronze Age barrow. This perhaps provides some sort of answer to the question raised by Grinsell as to which term would have been used to describe a prehistoric barrow with intrusive pagan Saxon interments.

There is, then, some support for the idea of an ordered landscape in Wessex during the pagan Saxon period, especially in the chalklands where the majority of the burial sites are to be found; a landscape apparently divided on a basis similar to that discernible in the later Saxon period, whence it was to persist in large measure unaltered to the nineteenth century. To take the matter further, however, in an attempt to look beyond the pagan Saxon period, it is necessary to consider some examples of boundaries represented by obvious and durable surface remains. These comprise on the one hand linear dykes, lengths of bank and ditch often running for many miles and deliberately built as boundaries, and on the other hand Roman roads, which in most cases were not primarily constructed as boundaries, but sections of which do fulfil such a function. It is instructive to begin by looking at the most massive of the Wessex dykes, the Wansdyke—or rather at that part of it which lies in Wiltshire—and in particular at its relationship to the early estate and parish boundaries in its vicinity. For long it was thought that the Wansdyke was a single earthwork which extended, with relatively few gaps, from Maes Knoll on Dundry Hill (Pl XVI) through Wiltshire as far as the Berkshire border. East of Bath it was assumed to follow the line, and to have been built on top, of the Roman road to *Cunetio* for a distance of some fourteen miles. A recent study of the dyke (Fox, 1958), based on a detailed field survey, has shown, however, that it is in two main parts, one in Somerset extending from Maes Knoll to just south of Bath—the West Wansdyke; the other in Wiltshire crossing the high chalk downland north of the Vale of Pewsey—the East Wansdyke. Between the two sections is the Roman road, unencumbered by later additions, an observation confirmed by independent excavation (Clark, 1958). The study has also shown that a number of linear earthworks east of Savernake Forest, including the cross-valley dyke in Little Bedwyn, held to be part of Wansdkye since the early nineteenth century, do not bear that name in later Saxon documents and are very probably independent constructions.

The East Wansdyke extends for over twelve miles across east-central Wiltshire, from the edge of the main chalk escarpment on Morgan's Hill, four miles N.N.E. of Devizes, eastwards to New Buildings, two miles south of Marlborough, on the edge of Savernake Forest. The western half of its course lies across high, open chalk plateau; the eastern across lower, drift-covered land, wooded and enclosed. Like its western counterpart, the East Wansdyke faces north. On the open downland it is of massive proportions, as much as 90 ft across the rampart and ditch and reinforced in this section by a counterscarp bank. This, together with its general alignment, characterizes it as a military work designed to bar movement across open country from the north. In the more wooded country further east, however, especially in its final five miles, it is on a much reduced scale, measuring about 50 ft overall, and here, in country unsuited to early warfare, it appears to have been conceived as a territorial boundary. Essentially it bears the look of a frontier, a comment which immediately invites the questions who built it and when. Sir Cyril and Lady Fox favoured a sixth-century date for the work, suggesting that it was built by Ceawlin, ruler of the Gewisse against the Saxons of the Middle Thames Valley after his defeat at *Fethanleag* in 584. J. N. L. Myres (1964) has since expressed certain misgivings about such a date and suggested possible alternative contexts for the building of Wansdyke; that it might be a Saxon work of the mid-sixth century or a sub-Roman work of the fifth century built by the British against the well-established Saxon communities on the Upper Thames. At least it can be no earlier than the late Roman period, as General Pitt-Rivers, established by excavation as long ago as 1890 and it is most unlikely that it was built after 600. A date within the fifth or sixth centuries is scarcely in dispute and will serve for the purposes of the argument presented here.

With these facts in mind the relationship to East Wansdyke of the adjacent parishes is indeed challenging. Their boundaries, especially those of the ecclesiastical parishes derived from the appropriate tithe maps (fig 19), ignore it almost entirely. As earlier writers have observed (Taylor, 1908, 131; Young, 1940, 32–3; Shaw Mellor, 1945, 24–27), they cross it but make virtually no use of it. This might occasion no surprise towards its west end where Bishops Cannings and All Cannings, and their constituent manors, cross it to incorporate large areas of what was once upland grazing; but further east such considerations do not apply. There some of the parishes, notably the two Altons and West Overton, include only small areas of downland beyond the dyke. It can hardly be argued that these parishes, or the estates which were their forerunners, are later than the dyke, otherwise why did they not use such an obvious and well-defined feature as a boundary? Cutting off the tips of the parishes as it does, it was probably a source of annoyance rather than anything else. Saxon charters, moreover, relating to Alton Priors (Sawyer, 1968, No 1513; Grundy, 1919, 159–64), West Overton (Sawyer, No 449; Grundy, 1919, 240–44) and Stanton St Bernard (Sawyer, Nos 368, 647, 685; Grundy, 1919, 210–15)

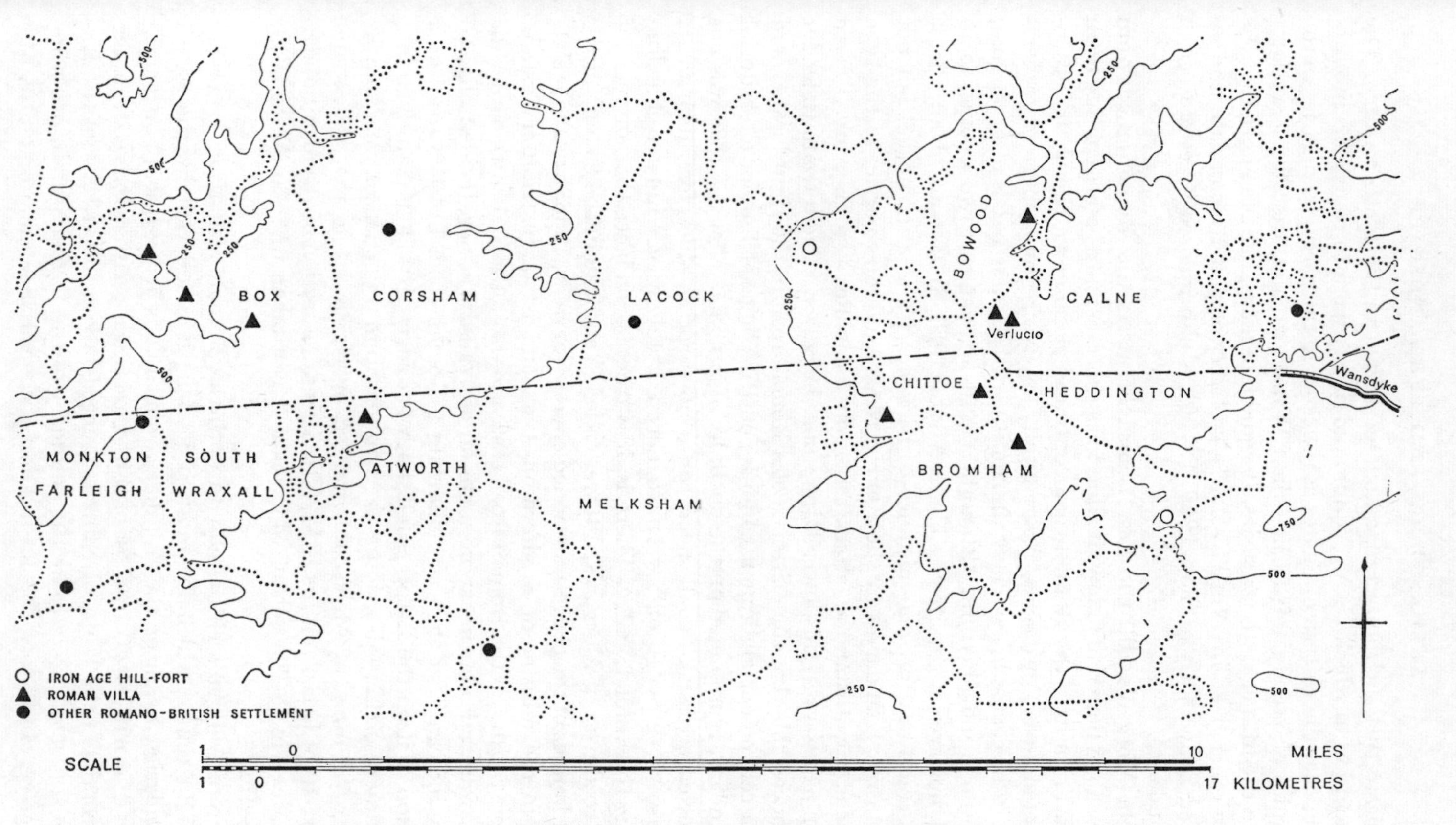

20. The Roman road and parish boundaries between East Wansdyke and Bath. (For conventions see Fig 19).

indicate that such an arrangement pertained in the tenth century. The conclusion to which G. M. Young and others were forced seems inescapable; that the pattern of estates as reflected in the parish boundaries in the vicinity of Wandyke is earlier than Wansdyke, and, therefore, not later than the fifth or sixth centuries. It should, perhaps, be noted here that the only other dyke in Wiltshire fairly certainly of post-Roman date, the so-called Bedwyn Dyke (Fox, 1959, 18–20), is also ignored by estate/parish boundaries.

On Morgan's Hill the East Wansdyke meets the Roman road from *Cunetio* to Bath and follows its line for a short distance before coming to an end. From here the Roman road continues alone down the chalk escarpment and westward across the generally low-lying ground beyond, traversing in its course heavy clays alternating with lighter bands of greensand, limestone and alluvium. Although Wansdyke as an earthwork comes to an end, however, it is quite possible, as Myres (1964, 8) has pointed out, that it was continued for some distance—in its capacity as a territorial, but not defensive, boundary—by the Roman road. A military barrier of the type needed to withstand an attack across open downland would scarcely have been necessary in this lower-lying, more heavily wooded terrain. Indeed it is conceivable that the existence of a Roman road in the right locality and on a convenient alignment conditioned the choice of line for a territorial boundary, represented on the chalk by Wansdyke. That the road was not followed across the chalk need cause no surprise, since for much of its course to the edge of Savernake Forest it follows an indefensible line along the Kennet Valley. There is, it is true, no evidence that any part of the road west of Morgan's Hill was called Wansdyke in the Saxon period. The bounds of the above-mentioned charter (Sawyer, 1968, No 899), relating to the minster of Bradford-on-Avon and its large tributary estate, follow the line of the Roman Road eastwards from the Wiltshire border for over four miles but make no mention of Wansdyke; nor, incidentally, do they indicate that they are following a Roman road. But the road, or a section of it on the Lacock/Melksham boundary, is called Wansdyke in a document of 1259 describing the boundaries of a portion of woodland in the royal forest of Melksham granted by Henry III to the Abbess and Convent of Lacock (Wilts IPM, 32). This same section of road is similarly described in the bounds of Melksham Forest taken in 1300 (VCH 1959, 446–47).

From Morgan's Hill almost to Bath the Roman road takes a notably straight course which for most of its length is followed by the parish boundaries, visible on the ground as a continuous hedge-line. (The boundaries shown in Fig **20** are those of the ecclesiastical parishes derived from the appropriate tithe maps.) Its line is ignored only in the vicinity of the Roman station of *Verlucio* by the boundary of the former parish, or rather chapelry, of Chittoe. This fossilisation of the parish boundaries on the line

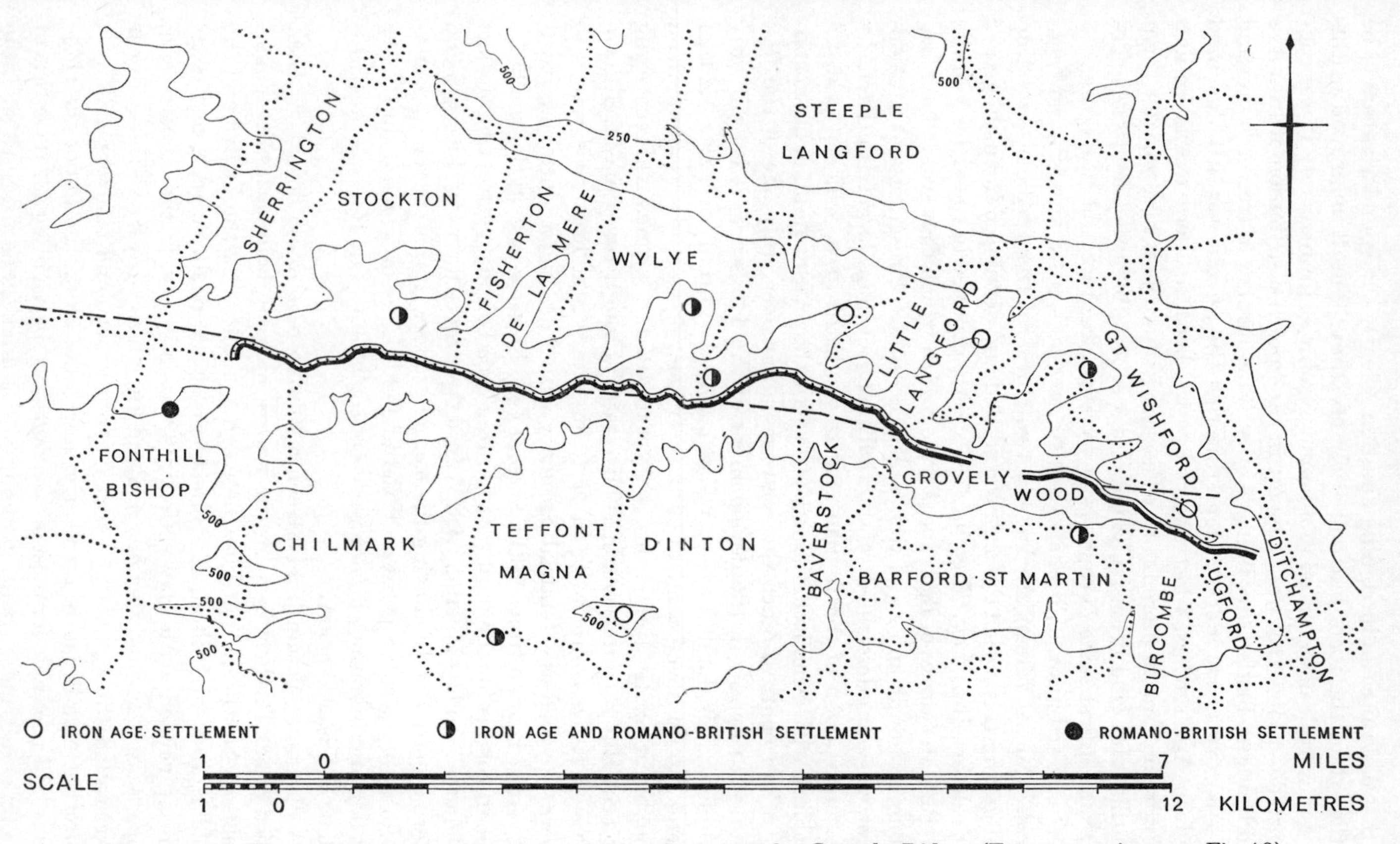

21. Grim's Dyke, the Roman road and parish boundaries on the Grovely Ridge. (For conventions see Fig 19).

of the road raises an intriguing question. Clearly the boundaries cannot be earlier than the road, but how early are they? The Roman road in this area may well have served as a boundary almost immediately it was constructed—a view that finds support in the known distribution of Iron Age and Romano-British sites in its vicinity. The number of Iron Age sites and finds is very sparse indeed, suggesting that the terrain was little favoured by Iron Age settlers. Most likely this was because there was no serious pressure on land in more favoured areas which made it necessary for them to utilise this land intensively, but also, perhaps, because they lacked adequate technical skills to cope easily with its clearance and cultivation.

The distribution of Romano-British sites presents a very different pictures. At least fifteen are known, two thirds of them villas, suggesting that during this period the area was settled and developed in an altogether more determined way. The villas are mostly grouped in the vicinity of the two Roman centres of Bath and *Verlucio* with which they would have had strong economic and social ties. This process of colonisation and development was doubtless aided substantially, and perhaps largely initiated, by the construction of the Roman road through the area, which provided a vital link with other localities, and, in particular, with a number of expanding urban centres. Since the road was almost certainly one of the first features to appear in the development of this landscape, it is eminently feasible that it should have served as a boundary from the start, and that estates should have been laid off it on either side as land was allotted and brought into cultivation. There is as yet no satisfactory means of recovering the remaining boundaries of such estates, though these may well have survived either complete or in part, but there is at least good reason to regard the road as a tenurial boundary which has had a continuous existence from Roman times to the present day. Further east on the chalk the Roman road is for the most part not used as a boundary except for a short distance beyond its junction with Wansdyke, where it crosses the downland before meeting and following the Kennet valley. In this stretch it lies unconformably across a pattern of 'Celtic' fields some of which it must have put out of cultivation, if they were not so already. The implication of this will be considered below.

A different relationship between a Roman road and a boundary dyke, which sheds further light on the nature of early boundaries, is demonstrable in Southern Wiltshire. Between the valleys of the Wylye and the Nadder, west of Wilton, is a broad flat-topped chalk ridge, much of its summit capped with clay-with-flints which, towards the eastern end, supports an extensive area of woodland known as Grovely Wood. A linear dyke, called the Grim's Dyke in tenth-century land charters, follows a somewhat erratic course for nearly nine miles along the top of the ridge and is still traceable for most of its length, as shown in fig 21. It consists of a bank, rarely more than 2 ft high, with a ditch along its north side, the

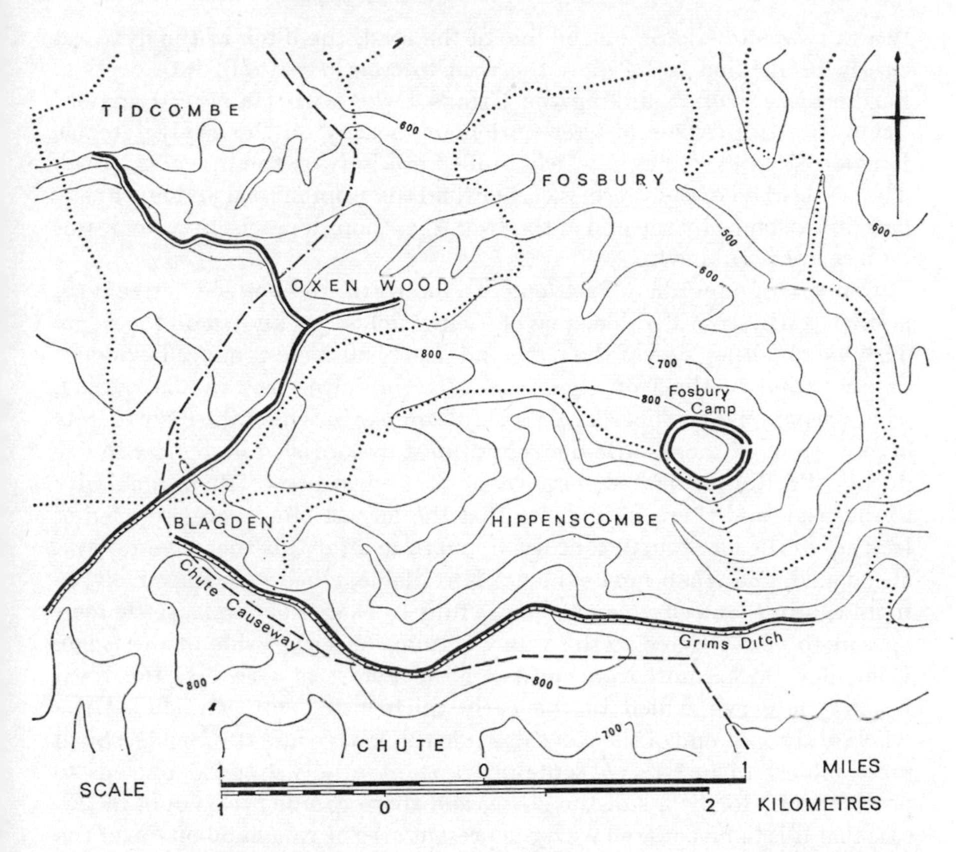

22. Grim's Ditch, the Roman road and parish boundaries south of Hippenscombe. (For conventions see Fig 19).

whole averaging some 30 ft across. It is clearly not of defensive proportions like Wansdyke, and its dimensions suggest that it fulfilled a peaceful purpose delimiting territories or units of land held by different communities or individuals. Also following the top of the ridge on a similar, but inevitably straighter, line is the Roman road from Old Sarum to the Mendips, built probably soon after the Conquest, in part to assist the transport of lead from the Mendip mines, which were in operation by A.D. 49. The road appears never to have been more than a slight earthwork, as excavation has tended to confirm (Musty, 1957–8), and to-day it survives only intermittently. It is particularly difficult to detect where it runs close to the Grim's Dyke, but its line is sufficiently established to show that it interesects the dyke at a number of points. Most of these are obscured by later disturbances or thick undergrowth, but at the extreme southern end of the parishes of Steeple Langford and Wylye, in the vicinity of their junction with Dinton, the evidence is clear. Recent fieldwork has shown that at two points here, on the line of the road, the ditch of the dyke has clearly been filled in to allow the road to cross it without interruption. Furthermore a ditch linking the Grim's Dyke with Hanging Langford Camp, the Iron Age and later settlement nearby on the Wylye/Steeple Langford boundary, has also been infilled precisely on the line of the road. The Grim's Dyke, therefore, is earlier than the Roman road and must have been in existence by the end of the Iron Age, though precisely when it was built remains unknown.

Remains of a number of settlements, mostly of undefended native type, associated with considerable areas of 'Celtic' fields, are known on the ridge. They lie on either side of the dyke and nearly all have produced evidence of occupation in the Iron Age, especially the latter part of that period. This, perhaps, is the apparently peaceful context in which the dyke had its origins. Some of these settlements continued to flourish and to grow in size during the Roman period, largely no doubt because of their proximity to the road, and there is evidence that the largest ones were occupied at least up to the late fourth century. Some time after this the ridge-top was abandoned, and when next evidence is available, albeit very selectively, in tenth-century land charters, and more fully in Domesday Book, settlement appears to be restricted to the valley bottoms on either side of the ridge. Domesday Book, moreover, speaks of the Forest of Grovely, the royal hunting preserve which in the early thirteenth century included the whole of the east end of the ridge down to the Wylye and the Nadder. Such areas subject to forest law contained a substantially wooded nucleus to provide cover for beasts of the chase, and there can be little doubt in this case that it is to be equated with the present area of woodland on top of the ridge. The presence of the earthworks of settlements and 'Celtic' fields within the present woodlands makes it clear that, when they were flourishing, the wooded area must have been much less extensive, if it existed at all. Substantial regeneration, therefore, appears to have taken place between the abandonment of the settlements and the later eleventh century.

This area was one chosen as an example by O. G. S. Crawford (1928) to demonstrate his contention, based almost entirely on the distribution of settlement in the two periods, that 'in this part of Wessex, at any rate, the break between the Roman and Saxon periods was the most complete in our history'. Such a simple view of the matter no longer finds very ready acceptance and has been questioned elsewhere (Fowler, 1966; Bonney, 1968). It remains true, however, that there is now, as when Crawford wrote, virtually no evidence of Iron Age or Romano-British settlement in or near the bottoms of the valleys flanking the Grovely ridge. But the abandonment of the hill-top settlements and the emergence of others in the valleys need by no means imply a complete break between the two. With the decline of centralised government in the fifth century and the accompanying weakening of communications, the Roman road, like many others, no doubt declined in importance. There was less incentive for people to live near it, and in unsettled times it was probably a decided advantage to be further away from it. A movement into the valleys might well have taken place then—with or without the unwelcome assistance of Saxon settlers—such as had begun in neighbouring areas at an earlier date. Certainly a change in the settlement pattern need not imply a total breakup of the traditional territorial and tenurial structure. In fact such evidence as there is implies the reverse. The tenth-century charters incorporating descriptions of the boundaries of estates centred on some of the valley-bottom settlements (Sawyer, 1968, Nos 469, Wylye; 612, Little Langford; 631, Burcombe; 766, Sherrington; 1010, Ditchampton) make it clear that the Grim's Dyke is always followed on the ridge-top. Although it is ignored by the *parish* boundaries in the heart of the wooded area, the former Extra-Parochial Place of Grovely Wood, it still marked the boundary between the *manors* of Barford St Martin and Great Wishford (VCH 1959, 432). Only for a short distance at its extreme eastern end, where it descends towards the Wylye, is it disregarded as a boundary.

The Roman road here, unlike its fellow west of Wansdyke, is totally ignored as a boundary, probably because it came not as an initial feature but as a later intrusion into an area already densely occupied and with an established layout of territorial and tenurial units. The evidence for substantial continuity of the Iron Age settlement pattern into the Roman period suggests that this system of land division suffered no serious rearrangement after the Conquest. The road was driven through the area probably in much the same way as in the nineteenth century railways were driven cross country—cutting, but certainly not altering, the boundaries of most estates—though perhaps with rather less regard for the rights of individuals and communities. It is also possible in this instance that the road was deliberately made to follow, as closely as it could, the line of the Grim's Dyke, thus observing, and perhaps reinforcing, its continuing validity as an important boundary. It is not unreasonable to conclude that in the Grim's Dyke we are looking at a boundary which served to divide at least two Iron Age land units, one to the north and one to the south, themselves perhaps further divided by boundaries from the dyke to the rivers in the manner of the present parishes, though not necessarily coinciding with them. Once built, it appears to have functioned continuously as a land division, even to this day.

A comparable relationship between an early boundary dyke and a Roman road is observable in eastern Wiltshire near the border with Hampshire. Here the road from Winchester to *Cunetio* is forced to abandon temporarily its north-westerly course in order to avoid a deep, steep-sided dry valley in the chalk known as Hippenscombe. It swings westwards in a broad curve following the high ground and resumes its original alignment after a break of over two miles. South of Hippenscombe the road survives as a substantial agger, nearly 30 ft across and up to 4 ft high, known as Chute Causeway, on which the modern road is still carried. Just north of this section of the road, following a somewhat more irregular course along the shoulder of the slope overlooking Hippenscombe, is a bank and ditch nearly three miles long and of similar proportions to the Grovely Grim's Dyke. Its size and the fact that its ditch is on the southern, uphill, side suggest that it was not intended primarily as a defensive work but rather as a land boundary in relatively peaceful circumstances. It is, however, by no means an insignificant earthwork, as Pl XIII shows, and it is curious that it has apparently gone unrecorded—it is absent from the Ordnance Survey maps for example—until recently observed and photographed from the air (fig 22).

The earthwork is not mentioned in any Anglo-Saxon charter, but it is almost certainly the ditch referred to in a document of 1330 describing the boundaries of the bailiwick of Hippenscombe, one of the constituent units of the royal forest of Chute at that time but formerly partly in the adjacent forest of Savernake to the north (VCH 1959, 425, 452–53). The southern boundary of the bailiwick runs 'by the bottom of Grim's Ditch' which surely refers to the dyke and not to Chute Causeway as has been claimed (VCH 1959). It is common for a boundary, where marked by a bank and ditch, to follow the ditch rather than the bank, as perusal of large-scale (1/2500) maps will show. Moreover it is clear from the relevant tithe maps that the southern boundary of the Extra-Parochial Place of Hippenscombe followed the dyke and not the Roman road, as the parish boundary does to this day. But how much earlier than 1330 is the dyke? The appellation Grim's Ditch suggests that it is fairly certainly as old as the Anglo-Saxon period (Gelling, 1961, 13–14), but ground inspection takes the matter further. It shows that the dyke has been built on top of 'Celtic' fields, but also that the cultivation of these fields, in particular those uphill of the dyke, continued after it had been built. Moreover, where the dyke and the Roman road run close to each other for some distance there are traces of poorly developed 'Celtic' fields laid out between the two. Such observations suggest that the dyke can scarcely be later than the Roman period and that it might well be earlier. It seems unlikely that a boundary dyke which follows a line so close to that of the Roman road, and eventually meets it at a very acute angle, would have been laid out once that road had been built and was still in use. The road is a conspicuous earthwork and would have provided an obvious boundary. Unfortunately the relationship of the dyke to the road cannot be determined where the two meet, as here the evidence has been largely obliterated by a modern track which makes it impossible to arrive at a firm conclusion from surface inspection alone. Certainly the dyke does not appear to have cut the road, neither does it run under it and appear on the far side. It could meet the road and stop, and therefore be contemporary or later, but it seems most likely that it continues for a short distance under the road, which overlies and obscures it, to meet a second dyke. The latter, which is of comparable dimensions, runs from south-west to north-east across the line of the Roman road and is certainly earlier than it. At the point of crossing, a fragment of the agger of the Roman road, preserved on the verge at the east side of the modern road, may be seen overlying the dyke. On balance an Iron Age date for the construction of these dykes would seem most likely, and some relationship to the large, multivallate hill-fort of Fosbury nearby is strongly implied. The so-called Grim's Ditch, however, appears to have remained a viable boundary since that time and to have been preferred to the Roman road. But beyond the point where it cuts the second dyke the road has superseded the earlier boundaries and has itself been used as a boundary.

Two further examples of early boundary earthworks utilized by subsequent boundaries, and which suggest the possibility of continuous usage, may be noted from Dorset. In Cranborne Chase the greater part of the late Roman defensive earthwork, Bokerly Dyke, survives as a massive bank and ditch facing north-east. It was built to block access from that direction across the gently rolling chalk downland, and in particular to control movement along the Roman road from Old Sarum to Badbury Rings. For the whole of its length south-eastward from the Roman road it constitutes the boundary between the parishes of Pentridge and Cranborne in Dorset and Martin in Hampshire (until 1893 in Wiltshire). There is reason to believe that the dyke may have survived into the post-Roman period as some form of territorial boundary or frontier between the Romano-Britons of Cranborne Chase and the Saxon settlers of south-east Wiltshire and the lower Avon valley. Certainly the paucity of pagan Saxon finds from the former area and their relative abundance in the latter supports such a view. A tenth-century charter (Sawyer, 1968, No 513) shows that the dyke formed part of the boundary of a large estate including the whole of the later parish of Martin. Again there is a suggestion that the dyke has served continuously as a boundary since it was built, but that it shed its military significance at a relatively early date and became primarily a civil boundary. A second example from further south-west in Dorset is Coombs Ditch a formidable defensive work nearly three miles long, which also faces north-east and traverses the summit of the downland between the Stour and the North Winterborne. Excavation has shown that it had a complex structural history, beginning as a small boundary bank and ditch, probably in the Iron Age, and undergoing successive enlargement to reach its present proportions, perhaps in the late Roman period (Fowler, 1973). This apparently continuous period of use as a boundary may well have been perpetuated to the present day. In a tenth-century charter (Sawyer, 1968, No 490) a section of the ditch constitutes part of the boundary of a neighbouring estate, and today it serves as a parish and estate boundary for the whole of its length except the extreme ends.

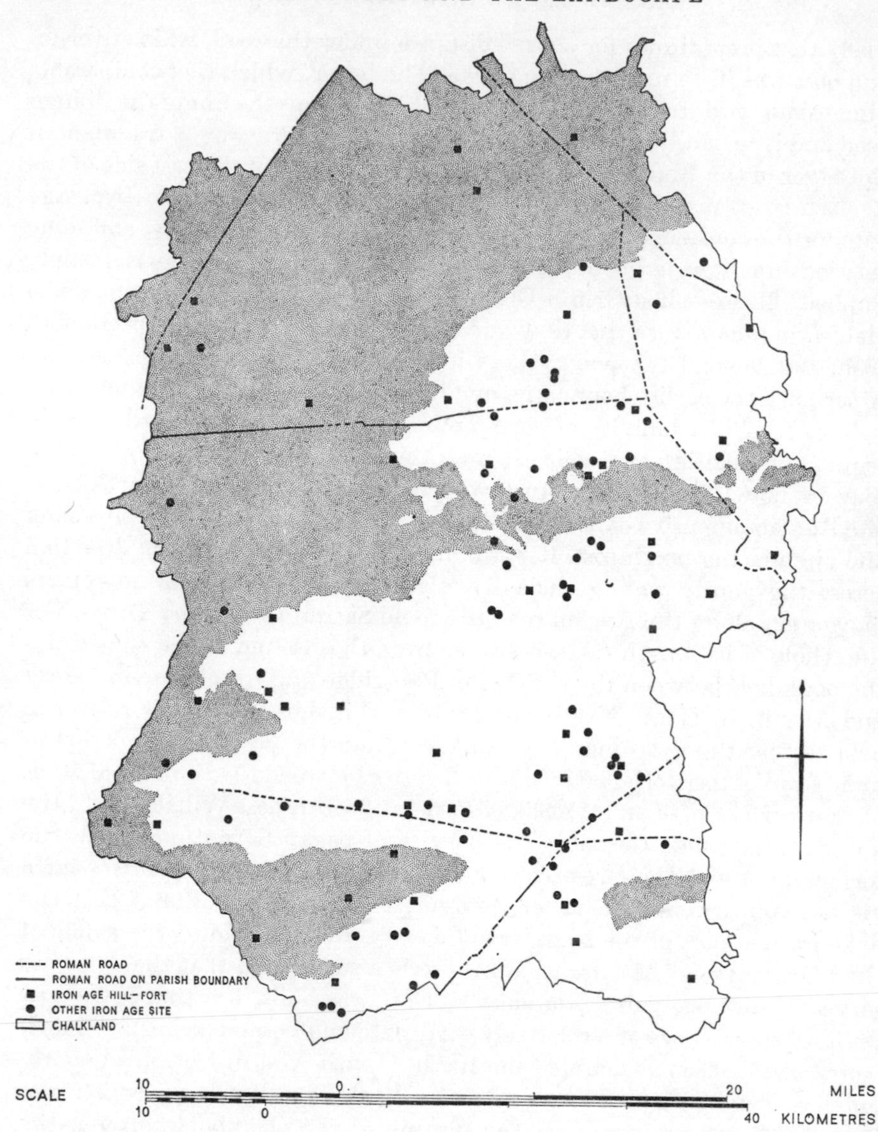

23. Pre-Roman Iron Age settlements, Roman roads and parish boundaries in Wiltshire.

Though it would be unwise to attempt to formulate any general conclusions from the above examples, they do hint at the possibility that some boundaries, and therefore even estates or land-units, have had a continuous existence since Roman and earlier times. Moreover, the use or non-use of Roman roads by later boundaries would appear, in Wiltshire at least, to bear some relationship to the density of pre-Roman settlement. The accompanying map (fig 23) shows that the Roman roads are used much

XVII. South Cadbury, hill-fort, Somerset, from the east.

XVIII. Line-and-wash drawing of Beeston Berrys earthwork, Bedfordshire, before its destruction in the mid-nineteenth century.

XIX. D-shaped earthwork at Church Spanel, Shillington, Bedfordshire, from the north (*cf.* fig 30). *Crown Copyright reserved.*

XX. Circular earthwork enclosure at Howbury, Renhold, Bedfordshire, showing its steep internal bank.

XXI. Circular earthwork enclosure at Howbury, Renhold, Bedfordshire, from the air. *Crown Copyright reserved.*

XXII. Moat at Caxton Pastures, Cambridgeshire. A large Valley-type moat in the bed of a small stream.

XXIII. Moat at Park Wood, Borough Green, Cambridgeshire. Probably built *c*. 1330.

XXIV. Moats at Croydon, Cambridgeshire. The right-hand moat is medieval. The site of the sixteenth-century house lay to the left of it, and the 'moat' beyond is part of the contemporary garden.

more as parish, and by implication early estate, boundaries in areas where evidence of Iron Age settlement is sparse or absent than in areas where it is relatively abundant. In the former areas it would seem reasonable to suppose that the roads came, or were already there, in the initial or early stages of their colonization and development which, if it took place in the Roman period rather than later, the roads doubtless did much to stimulate. Once there, the roads provided, if needed, ready-made boundaries off which other boundaries could be laid and land allotted—a commonsense matter which need not even occasion mention of the abused term 'centuriation'. In areas where Iron Age occupation was relatively dense—essentially the chalklands with their long history of early settlement—an established pattern of land allotment, of territories and estates, was already in existence when the Roman roads were laid out. They came as intrusive features into this pattern and appear to have been absorbed into it rather than to have modified it to any great extent. The Fosse Way is, perhaps, a special case. It is followed by later boundaries for considerable distances, sometimes in areas of Iron Age settlement, but the fact that it was intended as a frontier in the initial stages of the Roman occupation of Britain may well mean that any existing pattern of territories and estates was severely disrupted by its line.

The matters touched on in this essay are directly related to the question of continuity. Recent years have witnessed a renewed interest in the arguments for and against the continuous existence of certain phenomena—settlements, estates, administrative units, etc.—from the Roman period into later times. The narrow legalistic approach to the problem so often adopted in the past, while not invalid, is so obviously incomplete, and it is increasingly clear that progress can be made only by a consideration of all the available forms of evidence—historical, archaeological and toponymical. As Professor H. P. R. Finberg (1959, 4–5) has so rightly enjoined, this can best be accomplished by detailed local investigation which cumulatively in the course of time will enable a more reliable general picture to be built up. In this the study of boundaries, and the units of land they define, takes its place. Such units have a survival value almost certainly higher than that of settlements upon which, perhaps, rather too much reliance is placed as an indicator of continuity, or its lack. Abandoned settlements for which there is only archaeological but no historical record too easily give the impression of a complete break in the cultural pattern, whereas, in fact, their inhabitants, far from fleeing the locality or meeting an unsavoury end, need have moved only locally, keeping within their own territory or land unit. The latter need not in any sense have lost its identity, and short of wholesale disruption in the locality it would, in a fully occupied landscape, remain defined by its neighbours. Indeed, it is this interlocking of land units which contributes so much to their stability and makes them an indispensable object of study in any attempt to determine continuity.

REFERENCES

Addleshaw, G. W. O., 1953. *The Beginnings of the Parochial System* (St. Anthony's Hall Publications, No. 3, York).

Addleshaw, G. W. O., 1954. *The Development of the Parochial System from Charlemagne* (768–814) *to Urban II* (1088–1099) (St. Anthony's Hall Publications, No. 6, York).

Aston, T. H., 1958. 'The Origins of the Manor in England,' *Trans. Roy. Hist. Soc.* (5th series) **8**, 59–84.

Bonney, D. J., 1966. 'Pagan Saxon Burials and Boundaries in Wiltshire,' *Wiltshire Archaeol. Natur. Hist. Mag.* **61**, 25–30.

Bonney, D. J., 1968. 'Iron Age and Romano-British Settlement Sites in Wiltshire,' *Wiltshire Archaeol. Natur. Hist. Mag.* **63**, 27–38.

Bonney, D. J., 1969. 'Two Tenth-Century Wiltshire Charters Concerning Lands at Avon and at Collingbourne,' *Wiltshire Archaeol. Natur. Hist. Mag.* **64**, 56–64.

Clark, A. J., 1958. 'The Nature of Wansdyke,' *Antiquity* **32**, 89–96.

Crawford, O. G. S., 1928. 'Our Debt to Rome?', *Antiquity* **2**, 173–188.

Finberg, H. P. R., 1959. *Roman and Saxon Withington* (2nd ed. Occasional Paper No. 8, Dept. of English Local History, University of Leicester).

Fowler, P. J., 1966. 'Romano-British rural settlements in Dorset and Wiltshire: the distribution of Settlement', in C. Thomas (ed.), *Rural Settlement in Roman Britain* (CBA Research Report 7, London), 54–67.

Fowler, P. J., 1973. 'Combs Ditch, Dorset,' *forthcoming*.

Fox, A. and C. F., 1958. 'Wansdyke Reconsidered,' *Archaeol. J.* **115**, 1–48.

Gelling, M., 1961. 'Place-Names and Anglo-Saxon Paganism,' *Univ. Birmingham Hist. J.* **8**, 7–25.

Grinsell, L. V., 1959. *Dorset Barrows* (Dorchester).

Grundy, G. B., 1919; 1920. 'The Saxon Land Charters of Wiltshire,' *Archaeol. J.* **26**, 143–301; **27**, 8–126.

Musty, J. W. G. *et al.*, 1957–1958. 'The Roman Road from Old Sarum to the Mendips. The Grovely Wood—Old Sarum Section,' *Wiltshire Archaeol. Natur. Hist. Mag.* **57**, 30–33.

Myres, J. N. L., 1964. 'Wansdyke and the Origin of Wessex,' in H. R. Trevor-Roper (ed.), *Essays in British History* (Macmillan, London).

Sawyer, P. H., 1968. *Anglo-Saxon Charters, An Annotated List and Bibliography* (Roy. Hist. Soc., London).

Shaw Mellor, A., 1945. 'Parish Boundaries in Relation to Wansdyke,' *Wiltshire Archaeol. Natur. Hist. Mag.* **51**, 24–27.

Smith. A. H., 1956. *English Place-Name Elements* (English Place-Name Soc. **25**, and **26**, Cambridge).

Taylor, C. S., 1908. 'The Date of Wansdyke,' *Trans. Bristol Gloucestershire Archaeol. Soc.* **27**, 131–155.

VCH, 1955, 1957, 1959. *Victoria County History Wiltshire*, II, II, i, IV, ed. R. B. Pugh and E. Crittall (Instit. Hist. Res., London).

Wilts IPM, E. A. Fry (ed.), *Abstracts of Wiltshire Inquisitions Post Mortem* 1242–1326 (Index Library **37**).

Young, G. M., 1940. 'Saxon Wiltshire,' *Wiltshire Archaeol. Natur. Hist. Mag.* **49**, 28–38.

CHAPTER VIII

Somerset A.D. 400-700

Philip Rahtz and Peter Fowler

INTRODUCTION

Leslie Grinsell recently attempted a map of Somerset in this period (Grinsell, 1965, Map 7), and we offer this paper as an expansion of the framework he put forward. Its genesis was written in 1968 (Rahtz and Fowler, 1968) as a short paper which was also circulated privately. That essay was not intended to be other than a preliminary attempt to set down some of our thoughts on this subject, to stimulate discussion and to draft an agenda for future work. It aroused some interest, however, and drew constructive comment, especially from Charles Thomas (Thomas, 1968); this has persuaded us to write this more formal version, brought up to date by discoveries to the end of 1970. It is still obviously not a final statement, but rather hopes to show the potential of the archaeological evidence, unappreciated and almost ignored in the most recent historical survey (Porter 1967). Admittedly much of this evidence has accumulated only in recent years, but we would stress that what we know is only a fraction of that which is still in the ground.

This essay is limited to Somerset not because we believe that this county can be considered independently of neighbouring areas in the fifth to seventh centuries A.D., but because it is here that recent work has been so prolific and fruitful, and can be gathered together in a convenient way. Eventually such a synthesis must be attempted for the whole of the Severn Basin area, but work in different areas is at present very uneven. Wales has already been discussed in several recent papers by Alcock (e.g. 1965), whereas Devon, Herefordshire and Gloucestershire have not yet been fully surveyed. Comparable evidence should exist for these counties; in Gloucestershire it is currently being recognized at sites such as Frocester Court and Barnsley Park (Gracie, 1970, Webster, 1967; Fowler, forthcoming) and Gloucester (inf. H. Hurst). We hope the present paper will stimulate research in those areas, and enable such a wider synthesis to be made.

The paper is in two parts. The first, a survey of the evidence, will be the more useful; the second, a discussion of the historical potentialities of the evidence as we see them in late 1970, will we hope soon be out of date and redundant.

THE EVIDENCE

Geology, topography and resources (fig 27)

Somerset is a county of great contrasts. There are high, inhospitable upland areas of Carboniferous limestone such as Failand and Mendip, of Oolitic limestone such as Dundry, and of Devonian sandstone on eastern Exmoor; there are fertile and well-watered river valleys and low rolling hills, such as the Avon and Chew valleys and central Somerset. And there are the alluvial flats of the north and west central areas, the Somerset Levels, geologically of recent origin. For the purposes of this paper it is important to note that some of this last area was probably flooded or at least marshy by the middle of the 1st millennium A.D. (Cunliffe, 1966; Hawkins, 1971). If this were so, then the loss of land that had been settled could have led to migration from the coastal areas and indeed a re-orientation of the economy (a point now repeated with respect to Gatcombe in Branigan, 1971). If the sea level rose, as has been envisaged, some 3–6 metres above O.D. at its maximum height, reducing available land possibly as much as *c* 250 sq km, impeding drainage of neighbouring areas and considerably altering the coastline, then such a rise would have brought navigable waters much nearer to places like Congresbury and Glastonbury (fig 27). There is no evidence of any overall reclamation in our period though local drainage may have occurred and may even have been engineered. Even if the land below *c* 6m was not permanently flooded, it was so at times, as it has been sporadically until very recently (Williams, 1970).

Communications in the fifth to seventh century would have been easiest by water, either along the coast or by movement up or down the rivers Avon, Land Yeo, Banwell, Axe, Brue and Parrett. The first and last of these are major estuaries which were important not only as possible points of entry from the sea, but as physical barriers for the north and south of the county (though Somerset now extends south of the Parrett). Land communication was limited; Selwood was a natural barrier to the east. Major Roman roads were few; only the Fosseway and the roads traversing Mendip and the Poldens are likely to have remained important, though there were many minor roads which may have remained in use (Tratman, 1962).

The economic resources of Somerset include dairy produce and minerals. Of the latter, lead (and silver) was exploited in later prehistoric, Roman (Campbell *et al*, 1970) and medieval times (Gough, 1967), and is likely to have been available in the mid-1st millennium A.D.

Historical background

The period between the breakdown of central administration in Roman Britain and the English settlement in Somerset may cover the greater part of three centuries, from the early fifth to the later seventh. The initial expansion of Saxon political and military activity in the middle to late fifth century was supposedly checked by a 'British' revival, culminating in the battle of Mount Badon *c* A.D. 500. Opinion differs as to the location of the battle. Jackson (1958) has argued convincingly that it was around Badbury Rings, Dorset, not far from the east borders of Somerset. John Morris (pers. comm.) would argue a good case for the identification of Mount Badon with a site near Bath. The check to Saxon military penetration into Somerset is confirmed by Gildas' account of a 'golden age' of 'British' independence in the first half of the sixth century (cf Morris, 1966, 152), in which Somerset must have shared, lying as it did well to the west of the areas in which Saxon control had been consolidated.

The next important event for which there is documentary evidence is the battle of Dyrham in A.D. 577. Chronicle reference to this has been traditionally interpreted (e.g. Myres, 1936, 403 fn) as describing a victory by Saxons over the 'British' in the Avon valley, in which three British (?) kings were killed, and after which Bath, Gloucester and Cirencester were captured. The Saxons then took control of the Avon, Gloucestershire, the east coast of the Severn Estuary, and possibly even parts of Monmouthshire and Glamorgan if we may judge by references to Saxon activity there in the Book of Llandaff (inf Dr W. Davies). In this interpretation, the west was thus split in two. An alternative interpretation is that Dyrham was a more complex engagement involving Saxons on both sides. Whatever the correct interpretation, the independence of Somerset, except possibly the southern bank of the Avon, was not necessarily threatened (see below, p 198).

Whether Somerset's continuing independence after Dyrham for about three-quarters of a century was due to a Saxon pause to consolidate newly won lands, to the exigencies of inter-kingdom warfare, or to active strength on the part of the men of Somerset, is of course a difficult problem. The Chronicle reference to a battle of Bradford-on-Avon in 652 may reflect renewed Saxon pressure, but it is not until 658 that an apparently decisive reference occurs. This is the date of the battle of Penselwood, after which the Britons were driven 'back to the Parrett'. This has usually been taken to mean that the Saxons advanced westwards from Penselwood (in the Somerset/Wilts border area) through Somerset, until they reached the Parrett, beyond which the 'Britons' presumably withdrew. This would leave the Parrett nominally in Saxon control, but not necessarily the coastal plain beyond (towards Minehead), where the 'Britons' may have remained independent.

Hoskins (1960) has suggested as an alternative interpretation that the British were driven back to the Parrett from the *west*, the Saxons advancing not through Somerset but from Dorset, through the vale of Taunton on the south-east side of the Quantocks. Evison has recently (1969) reviewed the evidence for early Saxon penetration into West Dorset. Hoskins' interpretation, though not generally accepted, would imply that central Somerset could have remained independent after 658; but the respite can only have been brief, and it is usually assumed that, historically,

Saxons were politically and militarily dominant in Somerset by the end of the seventh century.

Late Roman Somerset

Somerset was essentially part of the lowland Roman province, contributing to and sharing in its prosperity. Nevertheless, it can be suggested that until the late third to fourth centuries there was little Romanization outside the towns of Bath and Ilchester, the other towns of Camerton, Combwich and Gatcombe being undistinguished industrial settlements in terms of architecture and degree of urbanization. Similarly, in the countryside there may have been only a few poor villas and many 'native' farms, like that currently under examination at Butcombe (Fowler, 1968, 1970). There were also potteries, stone quarries and lead-workings, the last apparently centred on the Charterhouse area, where the largely unappreciated remains of an extensive settlement based on an urban-looking grid layout are still visible (Pl XIV). Here may have been more Romanization.

In the late third to early fourth centuries, however, a series of luxurious villas were built, possibly using Gallic capital (Branigan, 1969; Rivet, 1969). They appear to have dominated the rural economy of Somerset. Although there is no proof of Christianity in Roman Somerset, such evidence exists in some of the Dorset villas, and possibly the late pewter industry in the Bath area was partly ministering to Christian needs. There is little convincing evidence of the destruction of villas in the raids of 367; most continued in unbroken use into the late fourth century or later, as did the numerous temples (six are now known) such as Pagans Hill (Rahtz, 1951) and the towns. Somerset in the late fourth century can therefore be seen as a landscape whose resources, both agricultural and industrial, were perhaps largely organized in a 'villa economy', interspersed with numerous native settlements, and a few market towns. Bath alone was a cosmopolitan spa, which may have drawn its wealth from external sources (Cunliffe, 1969). Whatever elements of Christianity there may have been in the villas or towns, the pagan religions flourished, and may indeed have experienced a late-Roman revival when temples were being built *de novo* in neighbouring areas as at Lydney and Maiden Castle (Wheeler, 1932, 1943).

An understanding of Somerset between A.D. 400 and 700 cannot be divorced from its background in the fourth century and earlier. Yet this is comparatively little known. Work has been concentrated largely on the more exotic and materially obvious remains of villa, town and temple, and there has been little work on the basic problems of its social and economic history. Little is really known of the rural background, social framework, or even of the architecture of wooden buildings (discussed, excluding the recent Somerset evidence, in Laing, 1969), all of which may be of crucial importance in understanding the developments of our period.

Continuing occupation of Roman sites in the fifth century or later

Until recent years there has been a curious reluctance even to think that occupation of Roman sites continued beyond the date at which the coin-range ended. Interpretation of archaeological evidence was keyed to known dates such as 367 and 410. Now it is recognised that even if the coins end at a certain date before *c.* 400, occupation not involving coin-loss may have continued; while sites whose coin-range includes the latest possible issues of the early fifth century may have continued in use into a period with a non-monetary economy. Coins, or no coins, apart, there is now some evidence, ceramic and stratigraphic, for continuance of occupation.

No 'Roman' pottery can at present be dated later than 400; with a few exceptions, such as colour-coated rosette-stamped ware, pottery even of the latest fourth century is hardly distinguishable from that of fifty years earlier (e.g. ApSimon, 1965, 250). If manufacture continued into the fifth century, styles seemed to have remained the same, though statistical differences may eventually be defined; but existing pottery must have continued in use for an indefinite time, to survive as the only ceramic material in levels of the fifth or even the sixth century (Rahtz forthcoming).

Of the towns, Bath (Cunliffe, 1969) so far shows no clear evidence of continuity, though it retained its identity as *Bathanceaster* in Saxon times (but see now *Archaeol. Rev.* 5, 1970, 36). The pottery and coin sequence extends to *c* 400, but there are no later finds to confirm its occupation thereafter, despite its documented 'fall' in 577. The baths area became waterlogged, perhaps due to lack of drain-maintenance. In silt over the temple site was Oxford-style pottery, possibly residual from the fourth or even the fifth century. Gatcombe has a coin range extending to *c* 400; its strong defensive wall is late-Roman and could have afforded protection long after 400. The need for it to do so has now been demonstrated by the structural evidence for fifth-century occupation (Branigan, 1971). At Camerton, use of the town continued, albeit 'squalidly', well into the fifth century (Wedlake, 1958, 97). The latest structures which may be of this period or later, comprise the 'fourth stone building period' (1958, 67) when dry stone walls were erected out of half-ruined buildings, unassociated with occupation materials. These Wedlake attributes to 'squatters' in the town. He also (1958, 82–93) regards the pewter industry there as being one of the latest features of the town, perhaps extending into the early fifth century. At Camerton there was also a cemetery of at least 109 graves, possible earlier than the 'Saxon' period to which it is usually attributed (see below, p 200), and perhaps including the graves of the inhabitants of Camerton in the first half of the fifth century and even later.

In the south of the county, Combwich (Rahtz, 1969) may have been flooded and abandoned by the late fourth century, its inhabitants migrating inland (below p 194). At Ilchester positive evidence of occupation in the fifth century or later comprises imported Mediterranean pottery of late fifth or sixth-century date (Rahtz forthcoming) and two Byzantine coins (below p 203). Excavation there has not yet been extensive enough to show the context of these finds.

The villas in some cases show evidence of structural changes, or stratigraphic sequences that suggest that their occupation continued into the fifth century or later. Examples are Cheddar (Rahtz, 1966, 1970) and Low Ham (Radford, 1946–7). At others such as Chew Park (Rahtz and Greenfield, 1973) there is contrary evidence, and occupation may have ceased by or before 400. Only at the Star villa (Barton, 1964, 79) and possibly at Cheddar is there any pottery (hand-made) of other than 'Roman' types in the latest levels (Rahtz forthcoming).

At least three of the temple sites continued after 400. At Pagans Hill, the wear on some of the latest coins suggests use in the fifth century (Rahtz 1951, 118); there was also an untypically reddish grass-tempered sherd (not published; in City Museum, Bristol). In the well were seventh century finds (Rahtz *et al* 1958), though there is no evidence to show that there was continuity between the early fifth and sixth–seventh centuries. The objects were a glass jar and an iron bucket. These were about two-thirds of the way down the 18m-deep well. which was on the east-west axis of the temple settlement. The well itself was of late-third century date; its lower part was filled with material extending only to *c* 350; above this was some organic material, probably representing abandonment; then came the seventh-century finds with some animal bones but without associated pottery. The glass jar, a Rhenish import of unique form, was of a class whose general distribution in this country is in the Germanic areas, especially Kent, and, with very few exceptions, from graves. At Brean Down (ApSimon, 1965, espec 211, 221, 235, 250), the temple itself was in ruins by the late fourth century, but a building was erected to the south of it, built from its material; this was 'rude but Roman' (Boon, 1961, 192); it was orientated approximately east/west, in contrast to the N.E.–S.W. orientation of the temple. It was built in *c* 400 as shown by coin evidence, and continued in use, ApSimon suggests, until *c* 425; it was then demolished, apparently to erect another building on the Down in the fifth century. A male burial in the temple ruins may have been that of the occupant of the south building; the skeleton was similar in preservation to those in the nearby sand cliff (see below p 199). At Henley Wood (Greenfield, 1963 *et seq*) the temple was certainly in use in the late fourth/early fifth century; later it was demolished and graves were cut through its ruins (see below p 199) and into the filling of the *temenos* ditch. These may be the graves of the people of nearby Cadbury-Congresbury (see below p 196).

Of the rural settlements, Butcombe has yielded hand-made pottery (Fowler, 1968, 222) which may, in its latest phase, be of later fourth or even fifth century date, associated with structural alterations.

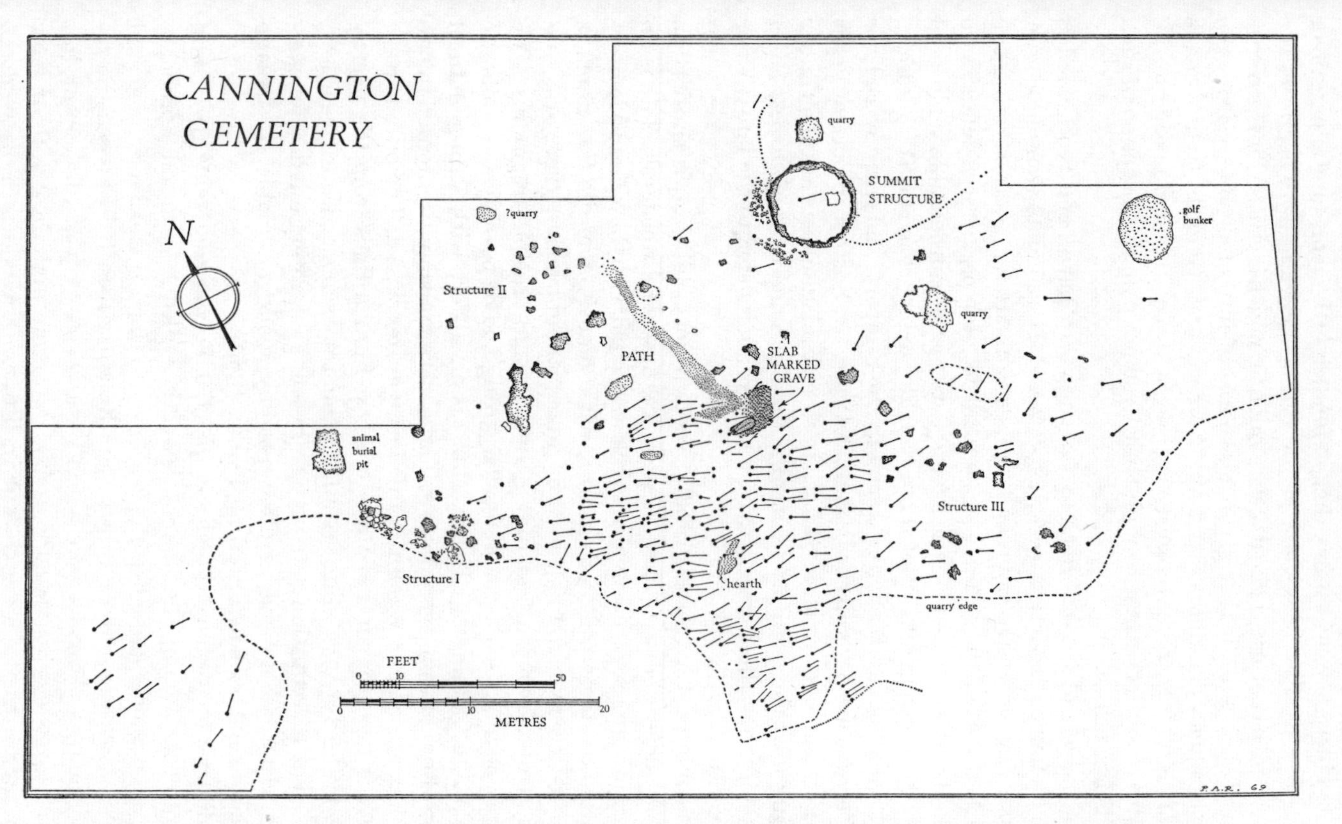

24. Schematic plan of the excavated part of the cemetery, with adjacent faetures, at Cannington, Somerset.

New or reoccupied sites

These include hill-forts or other defended settlements, and monastic or other religious sites, whose occupation can be shown to have begun in the fifth–seventh centuries. The dating evidence, which is crucial for the recognition of such sites, is that given by sherds of imported pottery from the Mediterranean (amphorae and table-ware) and Gaulish (wheel-made jars) areas (Rahtz, forthcoming). At present these are dated mainly to the late fifth or sixth century, though they need not date the inception of such sites (below p 208).

The largest of the hill-forts so far shown to have been reoccupied is South Cadbury (Pl XVII; Alcock, 1967 *et seq*). Here in late Roman or later times, a new defensive stone and timber rampart was erected round the seven hectares of the interior of the hill-fort on prehistoric defences to which the outer lines and the steep slopes gave considerable additional protection. The circuit included a tower-like structure at the SW gateway. It was dated by late Roman material in the rampart, and there were later Mediterranean sherds on the back of the rampart. Further imported sherds were found in an unweathered state in the foundation trenches of a timber building near the summit of the hill; these provide a *terminus post quem* for the filling of these trenches, which Alcock has dated to the late fifth or sixth century.

Glastonbury Tor (Rahtz, 1968b), though not a hill-fort, is similarly a naturally defensible site. There were traces of several wooden buildings on the summit; in reasonably sealed levels associated with these were Mediterranean and a few hand-made sherds, with some Roman tile fragments, a few post-Roman metal objects, and many animal bones; there was evidence of metal-working, including hearths and crucible fragments. The site may be interpreted as a defended stronghold or possibly as a monastic site (fig 28). Cannington (Rahtz, 1969) is a hill-fort with strong natural and pre-Roman Iron Age defences. These were probably augmented in late Roman or later times when the hill-fort was reoccupied. The only pottery found was late Roman, but there are post-Roman finds from the nearby cemetery (fig 24), suggesting a secular rather than a monastic site (see below, p 200). The reoccupation here may represent a migration inland of a community from Combwich, a place possibly made untenable by marine inundation and sea-borne raiding (Rahtz, 1969).

Cadbury-Congresbury (Fowler *et al* 1970, Fowler and Rahtz, 1970, and current excavation by the writers) is another hill-fort with some probably Iron Age defences and steep slopes. The site (fig 25) was reoccupied and new defensive works were built in late Roman times. It looks as if the reoccupation took place at a time when Roman pottery was still current, but only just; we suggest a date for such a transition might be *c* 450, or later rather than earlier. The ditch, cut in limestone, was over a metre deep, and provided the material for a rampart or platform of mixed stone and

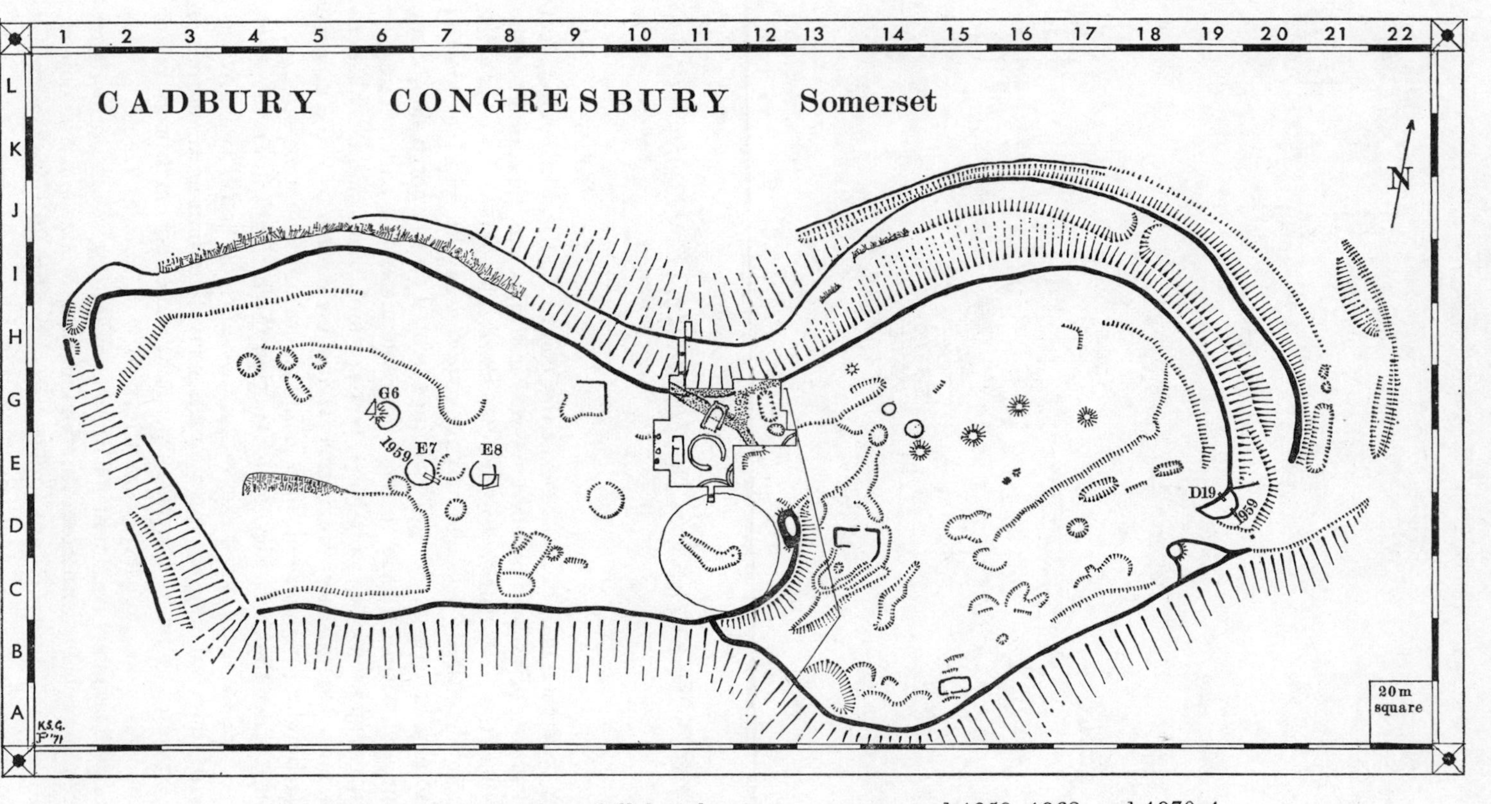

25. Plan of Cadbury Congresbury hill-fort showing areas excavated 1959, 1968, and 1970–1.

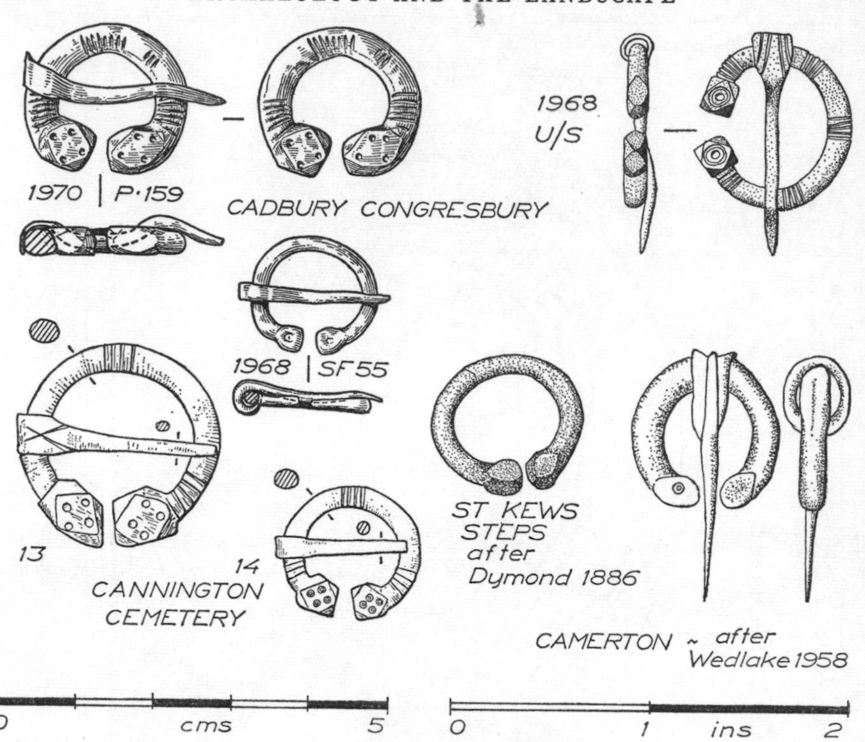

Somerset type G penannular brooches

Fig 26.

timber construction. The defences at the point examined in 1970 appear to be forming one side of an entrance-way leading up to the summit of the hill, where there is a flattish area of 0·2 hectare. This appears to have some additional defensive works and may prove to contain the principal late and post-Roman structures. Several buildings located on the north side of the summit and within the defensive works include round and rectangular structures represented by post-holes, post-pits and foundation trenches cut in the rock. One of these (Structure II in Fowler *et al*, 1970), a large circular building with an entrance facing the summit, may be a religious building rather than a living-house. Another (Structure I in Fowler *et al*, 1970, extended by the 1970 excavation) was of 'long-house' type. Associated with these buildings was an occupation layer containing thousands of animal bones; hundreds of pieces of pennant stone roof- and floor-tiles of Roman derivation, probably from the nearby temple at Henley Wood (above, p 192); many fragments of Roman and later glass and brick; glass beads, some probably imported; Roman and later bronze and iron objects, including three type G penannular brooches (fig 26); iron slag and furnace fragments; and several hundred sherds. These included some of late Roman type, but are preponderantly from Mediterranean amphorae and table-ware, with a few from vessels probably of Gaulish origin. Some indigenous hand-made sherds of grass-tempered and sandy wares also occurred. Over much of the site these types were found together, but on the back of the defences, and more particularly in the 1970 ditch section, they were separated stratigraphically. There the Roman sherds were in a primary context; they quickly gave way to a layer which is non-ceramic except for a few hand-made sherds, and it was only in the upper levels that imported sherds were found (Fowler and Rahtz, 1970).

On the basis of the 1970 sequence at Cadbury-Congresbury, imported sherds are not part of the 'late-Roman' or immediately post-Roman assemblage, but are a secondary feature in the post-Roman activity there and perhaps further afield in Somerset. A date of *c* 450 has been suggested for the refortification of Cadbury-Congresbury; it is likely that soon after that Roman ceramics went out of use, and some time later, perhaps *c* 500 or in the early sixth century, new ceramics were imported into the area. Such a date is consistent with that suggested in the areas in which this pottery was made (Thomas *et al* forthcoming).

Other hill-forts in Somerset were probably also reoccupied. There are Roman pottery and box-flue tile fragments from Brent Knoll (Taunton Museum) for example, Roman pottery from Worlebury (Dymond, 1902), and Cadbury Camp, Tickenham (Gray, 1922), and pennant roof-tiles from Dolebury. While in some cases the existence of Roman material in hill-forts may be associated with their use as temple sites within the framework of the Romanized neighbourhood, Cadbury-Congresbury shows that Roman material may well be the clue to late or post-Roman occupation in the fifth century (Fowler, 1972).

Any hill-fort or defended site, or indeed *any* site which has produced no datable material, may also prove to belong to the post-Roman centuries rather than prehistoric times. A good example of a site where an open mind might be kept is Burrington Camp (Pl. XV; Tratman, 1963b) where the absence of material (except a ?pot-cover of old Red Sandstone) led the excavator to believe that it was a prehistoric fort which has never been used (see also Fowler *et al*, 1970, 45, note 5; and generally Fowler, 1972).

Glastonbury Tor has been mentioned (above p 194) as a possible fifth–sixth-century monastic site. The only other site for which a monastic origin may be claimed is Glastonbury Abbey. Although traditions would place its origins in the fifth century or even earlier, there is no evidence from the excavations (Taylor and Taylor, 1965, 250–257, with refs, and Radford, 1968) that any structures or finds need be earlier than the mid-seventh century when reliable documentary sources begin. Notably absent are any of the classes of pottery which have been shown to characterize sites of the fifth or sixth centuries, especially the Mediterranean imports, an absence now further emphasized by the recognition of amphora sherds at the nearby Mount (Bulleid and Morland, 1926). The site may indeed have had its inception in the mid or later seventh century and may therefore be properly called 'Saxon'; or it may be pre-Saxon, and be of earlier seventh or later sixth century. The earliest features at the Abbey are the *vetusta ecclesia*, the wooden church, *c* 18 by 8m which was destroyed by fire in 1184; the oldest graves in the cemetery to the south of this, some of them slab-lined; post-holes of at least four wooden buildings, identified by Radford as oratories, one of which was 4m wide by 5·5–7·5m. long; and two rectangular structures identified by Radford as mausolea or tomb-shrines. To the east of these structures, but possibly of the early eighth century, associated with King Ine's church, was a big bank with a ditch on its east side, which Radford interpreted as the *vallum monasterii*, the boundary of the monastery. This was traced running north-south for a distance of *c* 60m. The bank was *c* 8m wide and the ditch *c* 3m deep. The ditch cut a Roman well, and the tail of the bank was overlaid by glass-working layers of the ninth century. The only other monastic site which may be earlier than the seventh century is Muchelney, where the foundations of the possibly seventh-century church are to be seen (Taylor and Taylor, 1965, 451–53, 482). Documentary evidence suggests another possibly early foundation at Congresbury, associated with St Cyngar or Congar.

Linear earthworks

The only earthwork for which a date between A.D. 400 and 700 seems probable is West Wansdyke (Fox and Fox, 1958; Myres, 1964). It consists of a substantial bank with a ditch on the north side. It extends from Odd Down, where it still forms the southern city boundary of Bath, to the east end of the Dundry ridge at Maes Knoll (Pl XVI; Tratman, 1963a). Examination of recent mechanical cuttings has shown that it is a multi-phase earthwork and was possibly stone-faced. There is no archaeological dating except a thirteenth(?)-century sherd near the ditch base, though fieldwork in the Englishcombe area suggests that it is post-Roman and pre-medieval (*Archaeol. Rev.* 2, 1967, 20 and 4, 1969, 52).

Two historical contexts have been suggested for West Wansdyke: one is that it formed the northern boundary of the 'Britons' after the battle of Dyrham in 577, when the line of the Avon was in Saxon hands (Myres, 1964); the other is that it was the northern frontier of the West Saxons after *c* 628 (Fox and Fox, 1958). Alternatively, it may relate to other crises or frontiers, e.g. in the fifth century, of which we have no documentary evidence. When Wansdyke itself is archaeologically dated, and when much more is known of post-Roman events in the territories to north and south, it should be possible to suggest its function.

The only other earthwork for which a post-Roman date has been suggested is Ponters Ball, a bank 2 km long with a ditch on its east side, which extends across the 'causeway' linking the Glastonbury 'island' to the 'mainland'. It might have been an outer boundary of the possible defended stronghold on the Tor (Rahtz, 1968b). Excavations in 1970, however, appear to date it, at least at the point examined, to the twelfth century or later (Poyntz-Wright forthcoming).

Cemeteries

Six cemeteries in Somerset other than pagan Saxon ones are likely to belong to the fifth–seventh centuries. These are of a class defined by one of us (Rahtz, 1968a) and by the Ordnance Survey (1966) as 'sub-Roman'. They are defined by being apparently post-Roman (though even less is known of late Roman cemeteries in Somerset); not pagan Saxon, i.e. there are virtually no grave-goods; and not obviously associated with later churches or with monasteries. They normally contain inhumations without grave-goods, orientated east/west, sometimes with lining slabs, and of varying posture. At Wint Hill, Banwell, were many graves, perhaps hundreds, some of which cut through the ruins of a Roman villa (Hunt, 1963, 1964). At Brean Down many graves have been seen from time to time in the sand-cliff (ApSimon *et al*, 1961, 86, 120–122, 125–27). At least ten were recorded between 1954 and 1960, and many more had previously been destroyed. One yielded a triangular knife; another had a grave lined with limestone blocks along the sides. A C14 determination is being made at Birmingham University from the leg-bone of this skeleton. There may be some connection between this cemetery and the remains around the temple described above (p 192).

At Portishead a cemetery of this type has recently been examined (*Archaeol. Rev.* 4, 1969, 51). Of 43 graves located, 27 were excavated. They were orientated east/west, and contained some residual (?) fourth century material, apparently from a nearby Roman site. At Henley Wood, Yatton, a cemetery of about 50 graves, males, females and children, was secondary to a Roman temple. Some of those in and near the temple were randomly orientated, possibly relating to the position of temple walls; most were orientated east/west, and were devoid of grave-goods. There were several double graves, and some had rough limestone slabs lining the graves. The cemetery extended eastwards from the temple entrance; most of the graves were cut into limestone bedrock, but many were dug into the filling of the rock-cut *temenos* ditch crossing the small spur on which the temple stood (it has now been quarried away). The ditch had already been filled in the fourth or possibly early fifth century, so the cemetery should be later than this. The relationship of the cemetery to the temple is clear enough and implies continuing use of a religious site for burial even though the (pagan) focus had been destroyed. It is naturally an attractive proposition to link this cemetery with the settlement on Cadbury-Congresbury hill-fort (above p 194).

The cemetery at Camerton, just outside the walls of the Roman town, is usually called Saxon (e.g. Horne, 1928, 1933; Meaney, 1964, 218—'the cemetery is of the seventh century'; Wedlake, 1958, 96–97), and possibly Christian (Hyslop, 1963, 190). Among the 109 graves, there were certainly many with grave-goods, including some apparently of the seventh century; but there were graves with finds of Roman coins, pottery and beads; fifth- or early sixth-century glass beads; beads of 'A.D. 300–600'; and many graves without finds. This may be a late Roman, sub-Roman *and* Saxon cemetery. It is usually thought of as belonging to some as yet undiscovered settlement; but the inference might more simply be drawn that it is a cemetery of the latest inhabitants of the known town itself, and therefore evidence of the town's continued occupation through the fifth, sixth and seventh centuries.

The largest known and most completely explored cemetery of this type is that at Cannington (Rahtz *in prep*). This is close to the hill-fort (above p 24), in a similar relationship to that of Henley Wood to Cadbury-Congresbury. There may originally have been several thousand graves, but most have been destroyed with little record by quarrying over the last half-century. The remaining graves, *c* 500, were excavated in 1962–3 (fig 24). Males, females and children were in due proportion; the graves were of varying depth into the rock, some lined with local or imported slabs. About a dozen were accompanied by knives. The only other grave-goods were with two infant burials; they included a silver bracelet of late Roman affinities, penannular brooches (fig 26), one with trilobe terminals possibly as late as the eighth century, an amber bead, a polychrome glass bead, and a pierced Roman coin—a mixed assemblage which well illustrates the cultural connections of the people buried there. C14 dates and residual material in and around graves, including a few imported Mediterranean sherds with hand-made pottery, some imported from Cornwall (Rahtz, forthcoming), suggest that the cemetery may have extended over several centuries, possibly from the fourth to the eighth.

Structures occurred among the graves. Two of these were important: a circular trench cut in the limestone on the summit of the hill with traces of a red sandstone revetment, possibly the site of a religious building; and a slab-marked grave of a young person. This last had evidently been a nucleus of at least part of the cemetery; a path led to it over a grave-free area, and many other graves were dug very close to it. The data from Cannington is complex and difficult to interpret, especially with the lack of comparable evidence from other cemeteries of this period. If it was the cemetery of the people who had reoccupied the hill-fort, then clearly this reoccupation was of some duration. It may have ended only when the present village of Cannington, with its church, was established, perhaps in the eighth or ninth century.

The monastic cemetery at Glastonbury has already been mentioned (p

198); and it is the only known Somerset example. The only other relevant graves are two isolated ones at Glastonbury Tor (fig 28), orientated north/south, and a few dozen pagan Saxon graves. So called because they contained 'Saxon' grave-goods, they are all towards the east or S.E. borders of the county, and may well represent early Germanic settlement, even if on a small scale. On the other hand, they may all be cemeteries of the local people who acquired and were buried with objects from neighbouring areas to the east. A provisional list is appended; a fuller consideration of the evidence is clearly needed.

Buckland Denham	3 graves (Meaney, 1964, 218; Ordnance Survey 1966, 38; Dobson, 1931, 180)
Camerton	109 graves, mostly E./W., *see* p 200 (Horne, 1928 and 1933; Hyslop, 1963, 190; Meaney, 1964, 218; Wedlake, 1958, 96–97)
Compton Pauncefoot	4 graves, E./W., ? seventh century (Taylor, 1967)
Evercreech	1 grave (Meaney, 1964, 219)
Huish Episcopi	3 graves (Meaney, 1964, 219)
Long Sutton	several graves (Meaney, 1964, 219)
Queen Camel	9 graves (Meaney, 1964, 219; Hoskins, 1960, 5; Ordnance Survey, 1966, 56)
Saltford	6+ graves (Meaney, 1964, 219; Ordnance Survey, 1966, 40)

The inscribed memorial stones at Winsford Hill on Exmoor (Rhys, 1891), and Culborne (Grinsell, 1970, 13, pl 126) may also mark the positions of graves of this period. Another possibly inscribed stone was found near Combwich (Grinsell, 1970, 105).

Finds

Apart from the finds from excavations which have already been discussed in their contexts, there are also a number of finds which are provenanced only by place or not at all.

A list is appended, but it is not exhaustive; there are doubtless others in the literature or museums:

?Bridgwater:	scramasax knife (Grinsell, 1970, 211)
Burnett:	gold pendant ?grave (*Antiq.* J. 2, 1922, 383; Dobson, 1931, 181; *Trans. Bristol. Gloucestershire Archaeol. Soc.* **59**, 1937, 244–5; in Bristol City Museum)
Camerton (fig 26):	penannular brooch (Fowler, 1964, 141; Savory, 1956, 53; Wedlake, 1958, 231, fig 54, 62)
Ham Hill:	Shield-boss ?grave (Dobson, 1931, 181; Hoskins, 1960, 5)

Ilchester:	2 disc brooches and one square-headed brooch (Dobson, 1931, 182–3, and figs 22–23)
Kewstoke (fig 26):	silver penannular brooch (Dymond, 1902, 122, Pl X, 17; Fowler, 1964, 141; Savory, 1956, 53)
	knife (Dobson, 1931, 181; Fowler, 1969, 176)
Long Sutton:	handpin (Fowler, 1964, 153)
Uphill Quarry:	perforated bone point, carved and decorated handle (Fowler, 1969, 176)
Worle:	comb (Dobson, 1931, 258; VCH *Somerset* I, 374)
	spearhead (Dobson, 1931, 258; Fowler, 1969, 176)
Worlebury:	dagger and spear-butt (Dobson, 1931, 181, 258)
Wraxall:	penannular brooch (Fowler, 1970, 177)

None of the post-Roman coins recorded are from a stratified context, nor need they be genuine ancient losses. George Boon (National Museum of Wales) has kindly listed the Byzantine coins (all AE) from Somerset in the table opposite. He does not consider that any of them are sufficiently well-established to have any validity as evidence (but see Whitting, 1961, 26–27, for a more optimistic view of at least the Ilchester pieces). The only other coin which may be earlier than the eighth century is a *sceatta* of A.D. 690–750 from Portishead (Grinsell forthcoming).

DISCUSSION

Nomenclature

So far in this paper we have avoided using at least some of the adjectives and phrases by which the period from the fifth to the seventh century is usually called, viz Dark Ages, sub-Roman, pre-Saxon, post-Roman, Arthurian, Early Christian, or Migration and Early Medieval. We suggest that no such labels are really helpful unless used in specific ways; otherwise they tend to obscure any attempt to define all historical aspects of this period. In particular, they encourage a tendency to treat these centuries as the whole of 'a period', instead of as a sequence of shorter periods each with its own characteristics. In attempting to substitute our own periods and labels we are doubtless equally guilty of subjectivity; but, as we stressed at the beginning, this discussion is meant to be overthrown by clearer thinking and more evidence as soon as possible. Our suggestions are centred in Somerset, and may only be relevant to that area.

'Dark Age(s)' or 'dark-age(s)' can certainly be dropped: however romantic it sounds, it is obscurantist by definition. 'Sub-Roman' is suitable to describe pottery, finds, buildings or even a way of life which is clearly wholly derived from that of the fourth century, usually in a devolved or debased form (Thomas, 1959); but it should not be used for a period which embraces characteristics which are neither Roman nor 'sub'. 'Pre-Saxon' may be useful in describing pottery (Rahtz, forthcoming). 'Post-Roman' is

ÆBYZANTINE COINS FROM SOMERSET

No.	Place of origin	Find-spot	Type	Circumstances of find	Present location	Source of information
1.	Cheddar	Gough's Old Cave	INVICTA ROMA XL nummi	?	Gough's Cave Museum	*Numis Chron* ser 6 xvii, 237; ibid ser 7, i, 199
2.	Ilchester	High Street	Anastasius, pierced *follis*	Found when pit dug in garden, 1930	In possession J. S. Cox	J. S. Cox
3.	Ilchester	Junction of Fosseway and Yeovil Road	Justinian, *follis* (profile type, B C$\overline{O}$N	Found by J. S. Cox in road-working trench, 1949	In possession J. S. Cox	Cox 1956, 170
4.	Chantry, near Frome	—	Justinian, *follis*	Garden digging	Taunton Museum	inf. J. D. Hallam
5.	Taunton	East Wick Road	Justinian, *follis* (pocket piece)	allotment digging 1929	Taunton Museum	inf. J. D. Hallam
6.	Watchet	St Decuman's garden	Justinian, *follis* dated A.D. 540–1, mint of Constantinople	Garden digging 1963 or 1964	Taunton Museum	inf. J. D. Hallam

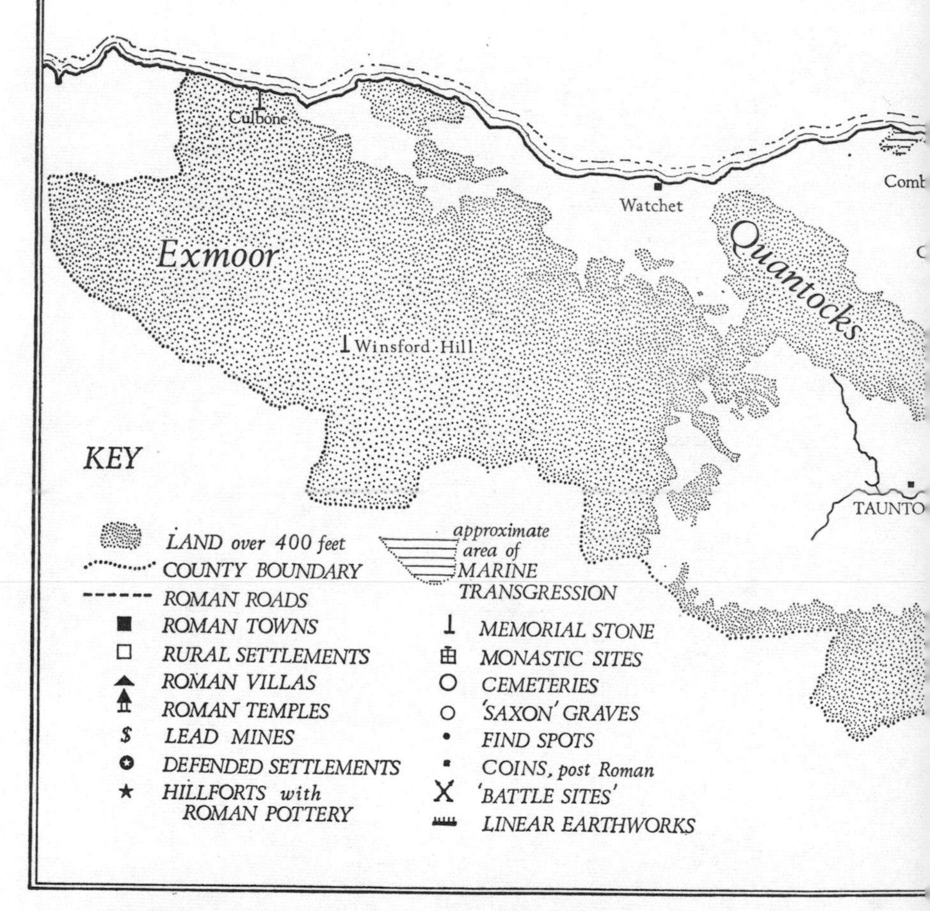

27. Somerset, showing post-Roman sites and finds as recorded to late 1970.

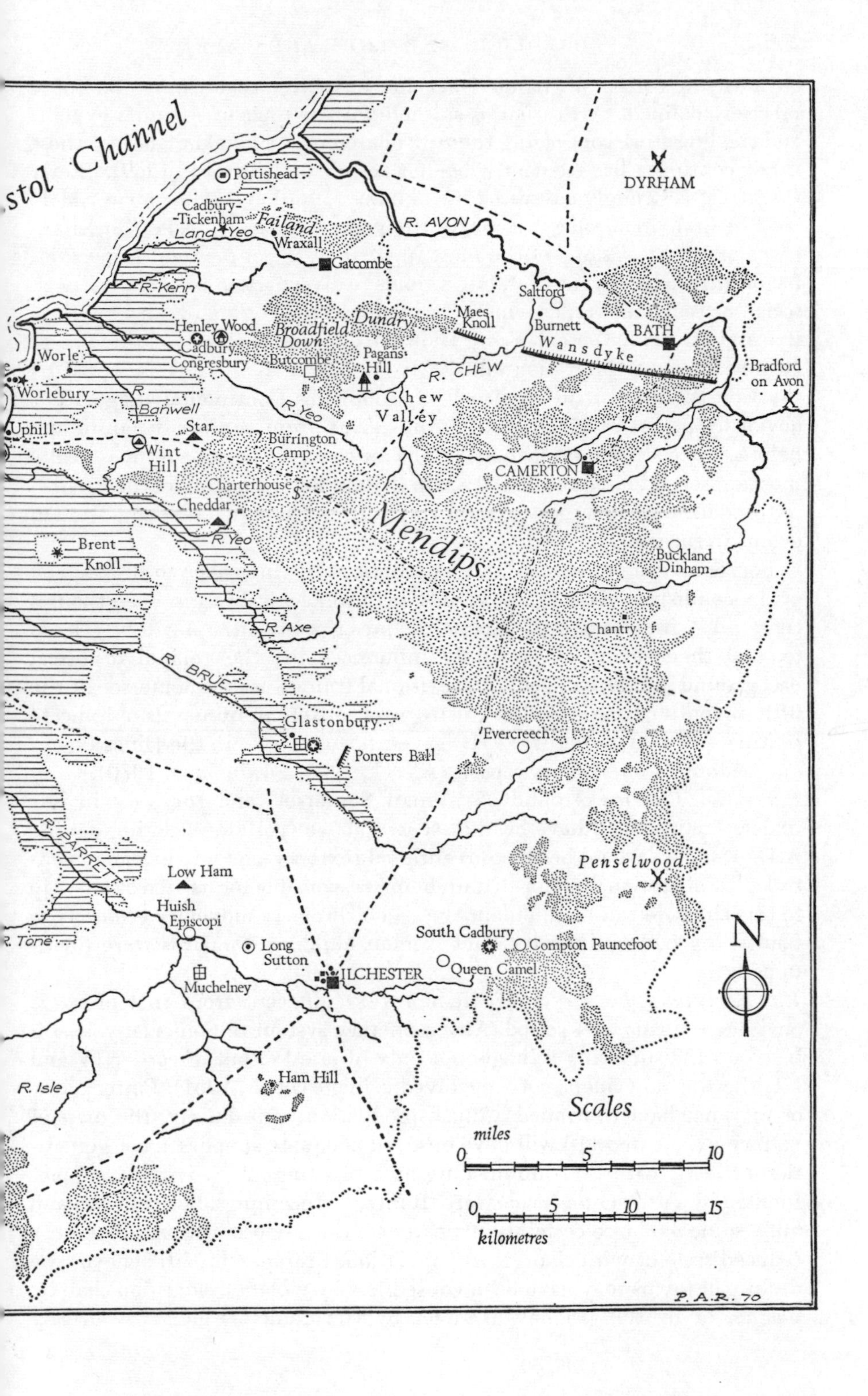

stol Channel
Portishead
Cadbury-Tickenham
Failand
Land Yeo
Wraxall
Gatcombe
R. AVON
DYRHAM
R. Kenn
Henley Wood
Cadbury Congresbury
Broadfield Down
Butcombe
Dundry
Maes Knoll
Pagans Hill
Saltford
Burnett
BATH
Wansdyke
R. CHEW
Bradford on Avon
Worle
Worlebury
R. Banwell
Uphill
Star
Wint Hill
R. Yeo
Burrington Camp
Chew Valley
Charterhouse
CAMERTON
Cheddar
R. Yeo
Mendips
Brent Knoll
Buckland Dinham
R. Axe
Chantry
R. BRUE
Glastonbury
Ponters Ball
Evercreech
R. PARRET
Penselwood
Low Ham
Huish Episcopi
R. Tone
Long Sutton
South Cadbury
Compton Pauncefoot
Queen Camel
ILCHESTER
Muchelney
N
Ham Hill
R. Isle
Scales
miles
0
5
10
0
5
10
15
kilometres
P.A.R. 70

obviously a correct if vague label for anything that cannot be more precisely defined. 'Arthurian' is suitable for the topic of Arthur's exploits and the literature concerning them; its dangers as a blanket label for these three centuries have recently been stressed by Thomas (1969). 'Early Christian' is strongly advocated by Thomas (1968) and is of course widely used in Irish archaeology; it makes the point that the spread of Christianity in the west was one of the most important, if not *the* most important, factor during these centuries, but it tends to divert attention from political, social, or economic trends which are not directly associated with Christianity, and positively obscures any thought on the survival or influence of pagan religions. 'Migration and Early Medieval' is the term adopted by the Council for British Archaeology, following Continental usage. It is obviously useful in turning our minds away from the parish pump and helping us to see Somerset in its European context. Yet the term is really most appropriate in that context, or in Britain for the history of the English settlement; only in a most general way is it useful to describe post-Roman events in the west.

For Somerset, it seems most appropriate in this paper to discuss the evidence (displayed on fig 27) wholly in chronological terms, even though these must at present be imprecise. As far as possible these will be related to, and their definition obviously influenced by, the general historical background (cf Morris 1966). A provisional framework for Somerset in the fifth–seventh centuries follows, using capital Roman numerals to indicate centuries (V=fifth century, VII=seventh century) as in the Dinas Powys and Cadbury-Congresbury reports (Alcock, 1963; Fowler *et al*, 1970).

Early V. The background of Roman Somerset, and the gaps in our understanding of it, have been discussed above (p 190). A closing date of A.D. 410 here would be the conventional textbook one for the end of central administration, and for Britain being responsible for its own affairs. Up to this time we can be confident that such things as monetary economy, a flourishing pottery industry, and Roman building standards were maintained.

Va: early-mid V. A way of life not very different from that of IV is envisaged during this period. Any monetary system in Somerset was still based on the surviving coinage, not only of late IV, but of earlier IV and III; there is no evidence of a devolved coinage (Boon, 1961). Pottery may or may not have continued in mass-production; if it did not, the mass of pottery extant in *c* 410 will have ensured adequate supplies for a generation at least, with ever-diminishing amounts thereafter, possibly supplemented by a little home-made ware (Rahtz, forthcoming). Both in town and villa, some evidence certainly indicates continuing occupation, albeit on a reduced scale or with changes in population. Branigan (1970) believes the decline of towns may have been caused less by violent destruction than by plague, or by the gradual take-over by Germanic (?) elements already present in the population in late IV or early V, or moving in from other areas. He suggests that where villas continued into V, their status may have declined to that of 'peasant farms', perhaps with a new owner. But such changes as he envisaged need not have been as early as *c* 450.

Temples also continued; there is little evidence from Somerset of the cults in vogue in IV, other than at Bath, nor of how much pagan religious practices survived, flourished or declined in early V. Were they influenced in any way by late Roman Christianity? For this last there is in any case no evidence in Somerset. Only at Brean Down is there a hint of a change, which clearly took place in our period Va. The partial destruction of the temple and the erection of an E/W orientated building hard by might be interpreted as evidence of transition from paganism to Christianity. The E/W orientation of a building is, however, no prerogative of Christianity, and there is no evidence at Brean that the new building was Christian or even religious. Its excavators regarded it as a living-house (ApSimon, 1965, 231), while admitting the drawbacks of life on the Down. Further work on the area round the temple, and on the cemetery, is obviously needed. At Henley Wood, the close relationship of the cemetery to the temple, and especially the changes in grave orientation, suggest that there is continuity here.

Vb: mid-late V. To this period we are inclined to attribute the changes which characterize what we used to call 'dark-age sites', settlements in new places, or re-occupation of old sites. This is not to say that town, villa, temple and native farm were now abandoned but, as Branigan has suggested (1970), their continuation can hardly be called Roman in any meaningful sense. Roman sites that *did* go on might be thought of as sub-Roman, except where, as perhaps at Henley Wood, the continuing use, in this case of a cemetery, was not a continuation of the site's original function. The only town with archaeological evidence which might imply continuity of function after *c* 450 is Ilchester. Like Bath, where similar suggestive evidence has recently been found (above p 191), this was a flourishing town in later centuries, which in itself may be cited as evidence of continuity. If handmade pottery in Somerset is believed to be all later than *c* 450 (and this is by no means true elsewhere, see Rahtz, forthcoming), then Star, alone among the villas, and Butcombe, may have continued as sub-Roman sites. Lack of evidence on 'villa' or other settlements does not, however, preclude continuity of occupation of villa *estates* (Fowler, forthcoming).

The new sites may be quite unrepresentative of Somerset settlements in the second half of V. They reflect excavators' interest in earthworks, and their inability to recognize undefended sites; for the new settlements that we know of were all defended by natural or man-made features. In the case of Glastonbury Tor this is possibly misleading; although the site is highly defensible, its position would also be suitable for an early monastic site, an interpretation which the excavated evidence does not contradict. But accepting for the moment that the Tor is a secular settlement, it is seen to be very small, comparable in scale with defended settlements in Wales or Scotland, such as Dunadd or Dinas Powys (*cf* Alcock, 1963). The other three sites that have been examined, the two Cadburys and Cannington hill-fort (and some of the other hill-forts whose reoccupation seems likely, above p 197), are all much larger, and represent a scale of post-Roman settlement site for which there are no parallels in areas further west (fig 29). Their size may reflect the economic wealth of Somerset relative to that of places in the 'highland zone.'

Dating these defended settlements is difficult. The evidence from Cannington is only of Roman pottery, with later material from the cemetery. There is a little Roman pottery on the Tor, but *not* in direct association with the buildings. There is late Roman pottery from South Cadbury which Alcock is inclined to regard as having nothing to do with the re-fortification, but to be earlier, perhaps of IV, and perhaps associated with a temple (Alcock in South Cadbury 1967, 72). The re-fortification of Cadbury–Congresbury is associated with the use of Roman pottery which, however, quickly went out of use. Thus Cannington and Cadbury-Congresbury perhaps began in our period Early V, or more probably Va (*c* 410–450), while the Tor and South Cadbury may have begun later in the period of currency of imported Mediterranean pottery, believed to be late V or VI. There is, however, nothing in the evidence from the Tor or South Cadbury to show that they did not originate in mid rather than later V; the imports on the Tor only give a *terminus ante quem*, and the late Roman sherds in the rampart at South Cadbury only give a *terminus post quem*, both of which could be as early as *c* 450 or even earlier.

While there is no necessity to find a common date for these settlements, it might be easier to explain their function in relation to historical events if they could be demonstrated to be broadly contemporary. Before this can be done their economic, social and political background must be discussed. The most usual interpretation is that they represent the strongholds of local rulers (e.g. Rahtz, 1968b, Alcock, 1967 *et seq*), the defended settlements of a political or military élite dominating the surrounding countryside. Their defences may have been as much for the personal protection of the élite and their retinue from hostile 'subjects' (*cf* motte-and-bailey castles), as for local strongpoints which would protect the local population against attack from outside (*cf* the Alfredian/Edwardian *burhs*). The enemy in this latter case would be sea-borne raiding parties from the Bristol Channel (especially at Cannington) or more probably Germanic groups from the east.

These are two very different concepts. The former need have no common date or cause other than the breakdown of one political system *i.e.* the Roman bureaucracy, and its replacement by 'tyrants' or 'kings' dominating small areas; such a transition might be spread over several decades and vary in time from place to place. The latter might be much more specific and contemporary in the face of a common threat. If this threat was Germanic, then the mid-V occasion is clear—the *Adventus Saxonum*, the sudden political and military take-over in the east which made such an impression on contemporary and later writers.

Who were the new ruling class who set themselves up as local tyrants or organized local defence? Were they the remnants of the ultimate Roman aristocracy, the villa-owners, the urban nobility? Or were they a new aristocracy, rising from the ranks of the peasantry, the former native farmers or villa labourers? Or were they immigrant Irish or Welsh, taking advantage of the final breakdown of the Roman system to seize land and power in a rich area? Any of these are possible, and much more evidence is needed before even a tentative choice can be made. Alcock suggests that South Cadbury was the military stronghold of an 'Arthur-type figure' who, with his retinue, commanded more than local allegiance. All of these possibilities imply that the defended settlements were those of rulers. It may be that they should be thought of more as elements of communal defence, organized either on a local or wider basis as strongpoints in times of crisis, by confederacies of local peasants or aristocrats. This may especially be true of Cannington, where the cemetery could be that of a 'normal' community of a hundred or more people. The date for the start of these new settlements may therefore be tentatively placed in mid or later V, even if their inhabitants are potentially so dramatically diverse. What have they individually in common that will demonstrate their character? This is best discussed in the next period, which we believe was in some ways the *floruit* of all these sites.

Other sites which may prove to have begun in this period include Wansdyke and some or all of the cemeteries. The suggested dates for the re-occupation of Cannington and Cadbury-Congresbury shouldap ply also to the initiation of the nearby cemeteries of Cannington and Henley Wood. The Camerton cemetery (p 200) may have been in use in IV or earlier. The others may prove to be contemporary inasmuch as they are of similar character. If it is true that these cemeteries can be identified as a group beginning at a similar time and *de novo*, as much as the four known defended settlements, then we may confidently expect to find new settlement sites in the areas around the cemeteries of Brean Down, Wint Hill and Portishead.

VIa: early-mid VI. The previous period is historically one of crisis and of reaction to crisis culminating in victory for the West at Mount Badon. A conventional date for this of A.D. 500 is adopted here as the dividing line between Vb and VIa. It represents, as defined by Gildas, not only the ascendancy of the 'British', but also the beginning of a 'Golden Age', whose decline Gildas was bemoaning *c.* 540 or a little earlier (cf Morris 1966). Mount Badon may mark the beginning of a period when the defensive works on new sites discussed in the previous section had ceased to be vitally necessary, though the sites themselves clearly continued into VI. The Germanic pressure was temporarily eased, and had possibly even retreated; it is perhaps no coincidence that this is the period when Christianity was making its most active inroads.

The new defended settlements, whatever the date of their inception and defensive works, are characterized, and indeed in most cases were initially defined, by imported Mediterranean pottery of later V–VI. The significance of this material will be discussed later; first we will compare the four sites. Their defences are variable. The two Cadburys and Cannington utilise existing Iron Age works and the natural slopes which they augmented. Cadbury-Congresbury also has a new defence of rampart, rock-cut ditch and entrance cutting across the hill-top on a previously unused line. The Cadburys both have post-Roman additions of stone and timber to the Iron Age defence—additions which seem rather crude and ineffectual by Iron Age standards. The defences of Cannington are still uncertain in character but were possibly similar. Glastonbury Tor has no need of any additional defences: its sides are so precipitous. The Tor and Cadbury-Congresbury both have evidence of metal-working, and of considerable meat-eating. At the Tor and both Cadburys there are timber buildings of some stature, based on post-hole and timber-slot construction. At Cadbury-Congresbury these include circular buildings in the pre-Roman Iron Age tradition; at Glastonbury Tor and South Cadbury all the buildings identified are rectilinear. The finds from the Tor and the Cadburys include some post-Roman metal objects and glass, but the most important finds are the imported ceramics, which very much outnumber the few indigenous handmade sherds of later V or VI.

The imports are significant not only for their value as independent dating evidence, and for what they may tell us about drinking and other habits on the sites concerned, but also for their implications on the extent of international trade and direct contact with the Mediterranean area in later V–VI (Thomas *et al* forthcoming). The range of imports has been classified by Thomas (1959). Those found in Somerset include table-ware (Class A), amphorae (Class B), and possibly Gaulish wares (for details see Rahtz, forthcoming). The Class A ware is conventionally regarded as high-quality table-ware; some of it is decorated with Christian symbols, and Thomas suggest it may have been for use in the Christian Mass. The B ware amphorae are conventionally seen as containing oil and wine, again possibly for use in Christian ritual, or for use in wealthy households with 'refined' or 'Roman' tastes; but they are often used in the Mediterranean for the carriage of a wide variety of other goods (*cf* Callender, 1965). Recently Thomas (1969, 29) has gone further in suggesting that A and B wares have an even more direct connection with Christianity in that they were originally imported for Christian use to Christian sites, and that all the material found on sites which are not specifically Christian is secondary, that is, derived from Christian sites probably merely as empty containers or just as sherds. We find it difficult to accept this view, and would prefer to see each site viewed on its own merits as a direct or indirect importer of table-ware and of amphorae complete with their contents. Nevertheless, the possible Christian associations cannot be ignored; even if the material itself is not specifically for Christian use, its occurrence shows that the sites were in direct contact with Christian influence. It may be that our period VIa is most significant in that it marks the introduction of post-Roman Christianity into Somerset. The Gaulish ware represented only at Cadbury-Congresbury suggests contacts with Gaul, possibly at a date earlier than that suggested for the A and B wares.

The pottery imports may be evidence for the ritual needs of a Christian community or for the secular needs of an aristocracy accustomed to 'Roman' luxuries. Either has yet to be proved on any of the six sites in Somerset where imports have occurred. But this pottery is presumably evidence for long-distance trade. Indeed it is virtually the only evidence for any kind of trade on any of the sites discussed in this paper: all the other features and finds could be explained wholly in terms of an independent self-sufficient economy. Yet it is unlikely that the pottery came in ships by itself; there may have been other imports for which the archaeological record is silent: silks, spices, as well as Christian ideas. Nor was it a one-way traffic. Such long-distances imports must have been highly expensive, to be paid for either by bullion (in the absence of a monetary economy) or by exports which Somerset could supply. These included perhaps local minerals—lead and silver; craft-work such as jewellery; specialised livestock such as hunting-dogs; slaves, male and female; or the more mundane surplus of rural production—cheese, leather, grain and wool.

Here we may see in period VIa hints at a stabilised society engaged in production and trade, possibly with luxurious tastes, and perhaps opening its doors to Christian influence. We are obviously receiving an unbalanced view of this society, inasmuch as the sites excavated, apart from Cannington and Ilchester, are probably exceptional and aristocratic. The three principal sites—the two Cadburys and Glastonbury Tor—with evidence of this period, especially of imports, were all defended or defensible. Were they still defended in this period of stability? The evidence from Cadbury-Congresbury hints that at the time when imports were arriving on the site, perhaps half a century after its foundation, not only had the timber and stone rampart begun to collapse, but that the ditch was almost filled up with silt and stones. We see this site as one which continued after the crisis had passed with a new phase characterized by the imports, these being secondary at a time when the defences had ceased to be a relevant aspect of the site.

Period VIa is clearly one of the most significant in our sequence, in which the exoticism of the archaeological evidence matches the documentary evidence of Gildas and the 'Age of Saints'.

VIb: mid-late VI. The lack of any material from the sites excavated which can be attributed certainly to later VI makes it difficult to say whether or not any of the places already described continued in use. The only ones where continuity can be assumed because of some dating evidence of VII or later are the Cannington and Camerton cemeteries, and they clearly show that the settlements associated with them continued too. If the conventional interpretation of Dyrham is accepted, we might expect general uneasiness as Germanic pressure was renewed, and some repairs to the defended sites, towards the end of the century. Is this the context for the possible recutting of the ditch at Cadbury-Congresbury?

We have spoken already of the lack of balance in the understanding of settlement history because of the concentration on the atypical defended (earthwork) sites. We may confidently expect to find continuity of occupation of 'ordinary' sites during this period, when we can identify them and understand their history. The same may not, however, be true of the defended sites, which may only have been founded at a time of crisis and perhaps only intermittently used in recurrent crises thereafter. If they were the settlements of 'rulers' perhaps this is less likely; much depends here on continuity of 'dynasty' or place. Potentially, both Cadburys, the Tor and Cannington may well have continued in use until later VII, but only at Cannington is there supporting evidence.

VIIa: early-mid VII. Much the same remarks can be made as for period VIb, *a fortiori*; to which we may now add that whatever memories of independence, or Badon, or a 'two-nation' state, there may have been in later VI, they are likely to have been largely lost by early VII. Probably in later VI and especially in early VII, the cultural and probably racial distinctions between the Germanic east and the 'British' west must have been become very blurred. The mixed grave-goods from the Cannington cemetery illustrate such a fusion very well. The documented events, battles, and dates may be no more than high lights or crises in a period of gradual shift of balance of power.

With a few exceptions, the only finds that can be assigned to VII are from the pagan graves. These need not represent more than the influence of eastern burial customs on the people of Somerset and the free exchange of objects throughout the area. One of the most curious finds of this period, or possibly the beginning of the next, is that of the iron bucket and glass jar from Pagans Hill (Rahtz *et al*, 1958). The iron bucket and associated animal bones make it clear that the well was in use and that there was a contemporary settlement. It is perhaps significant that there was no associated pottery: VII, and indeed VIII, may be a completely aceramic period in Somerset. The glass jar is more surprising. This was an exotic find at Pagans Hill (see above p 192) and its presence on the temple site, and the nature of the occupation there are difficult to explain. Was there continuity between V and VII, in spite of the dearth of evidence? Was there any continuation or revival of religious practices, pagan or Christian? Unfortunately, the excavation was not sufficiently comprehensive or good enough to have answered these questions, even if the evidence were there. Further work here might be very informative on what is the only known settlement of VII, other than that indicated by the continuing use of the Cannington cemetery.

VIIb: mid-late VII. In this period (if not earlier) we might expect the decline and possible abandonment of any site, such as the defended hill-forts, which owed their existence to concepts of defence against external threat, or of tryannical overlordship of local populations. Other settlements may have passed almost unknowingly into the period of Saxon domination; estate boundaries may have remained similar; major changes in land-use are still unproven. Only excavation on Saxon settlements can determine the extent to which these were on 'new' sites or on the sites of our unknown, non-defended settlements of V–VIII. No such excavation has yet been done. The only considerable work on a Saxon site has been that of Cheddar (Rahtz 1962–3), but this was atypical in being a royal site, initiated in VIII or IX. There was nevertheless some evidence of relationship between the adjacent Roman villa and the later royal and ecclesiastical complex which might imply continuity through V–VIII (Rahtz, 1962–3, 1966, 1970, and in prep).

Cannington can be cited yet again as illustrating the continuity of at least burial practice through VII even into VIII. The establishment of new settlements where they *were* new, and of churches, was not to be accomplished in a few decades of English domination.

The only other site of VII, possibly wholly of later VII, which has been extensively excavated is Glastonbury Abbey, where the monastery, with its cemetery, oratories and churches, may represent at least one aspect of English settlement which *was* new, perhaps instituted to give expression to the political power of the Saxons through this great religious centre. The traditional view is, of course, that there was continuity at Glastonbury between the English monastery and its Celtic predecessor, but, as already mentioned, this cannot be maintained from the archaeological evidence.

CONCLUSIONS

Religion

Glastonbury indeed provides the first definite evidence of Christianity in Somerset in V–VII. Historically, the origins of Christianity in Somerset would be placed in later IV or V (Radford, 1962), and we have indicated the ways in which pottery and cemetery evidence could be used, though equivocally, to support this. Indeed, as we indicated in our remarks on nomenclature, it would be rash to assume that Christianity had made extensive inroads in Somerset even by later VII. Evangelising activity there may well have been, and nominal conversion, perhaps especially at aristocratic levels; but as Bede makes it clear (though writing beyond the end of our period, and in a different context), not all of the population was converted. Many of the converted accepted the new faith only superfically and retained a duality of outlook; they were liable to recant and slip back to pagan worship at the first opportunity or temptation. Even in much later centuries elements of the 'old religion' were still to be found even in the context of Christian churches, let alone in the surrounding countryside. Our historical knowledge of the fate of late Roman paganism is uncertain indeed, mainly because of the Christian bias of the documentary sources. Archaeological evidence has no such bias (even if its exponents have), unless we give it one by using the blanket label of 'Early Christian'; and we should be prepared to interpret evidence from cemetery and settlement sites in either way.

The cemeteries we have discussed are characterised by E/W orientation and by scarcity of grave-goods; typical of Christianity certainly, but not decisively so. There is nothing Christian about the summit structure at Cannington; its position might be suitable for a 'church' focus, but equally for a temple; is this a sub-Roman temple, possibly with Christian associations? We should perhaps be prepared to think of transitional pagan/Christian structures as we would use a term like Romano-Saxon. A religious connotation is not impossible for the large penannular building at Cadbury-Congresbury; but it does not have any characteristics of a Christian church. Perhaps, in discussing these buildings, we are falling into the trap of broad dating. Both could belong to V, and not to VI, when Christianity may be assumed to be exercising more influence. On both sites the imported pottery may indeed mark the arrival of such Christian influence; or it may reflect merely aristocatic (and possibly pagan) tastes. At present, the archaeological evidence for religion in V–VII can only be described as inconclusive.

Demographic problems

Impressive though the accumulating archaeological evidence is for Somerset in V–VII, it is negligible when viewed in demographic terms. All the settlements and cemeteries we have discussed account for the lives and deaths of no more than a few hundred people—only Cannington hints at a local population of a hundred or two. This is the kind of figure that one might expect in any area equivalent to that of a later parish—or is this quite misleading? If there were even a few dozen settlements of the scale of that represented by the Cannington cemetery, where are they, and where are their cemeteries?

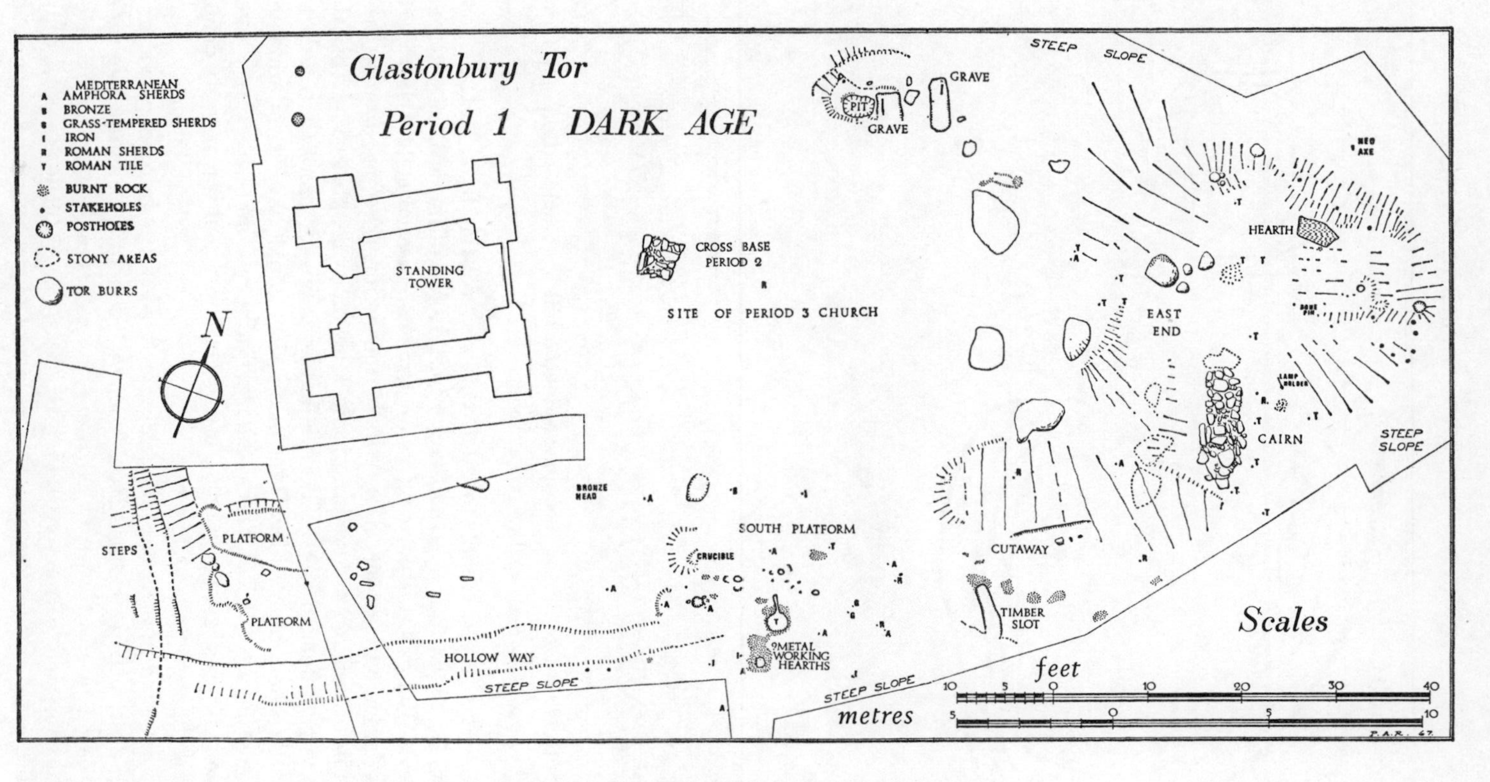

28. Glastonbury Tor: plan of the Period 1 features as excavated.

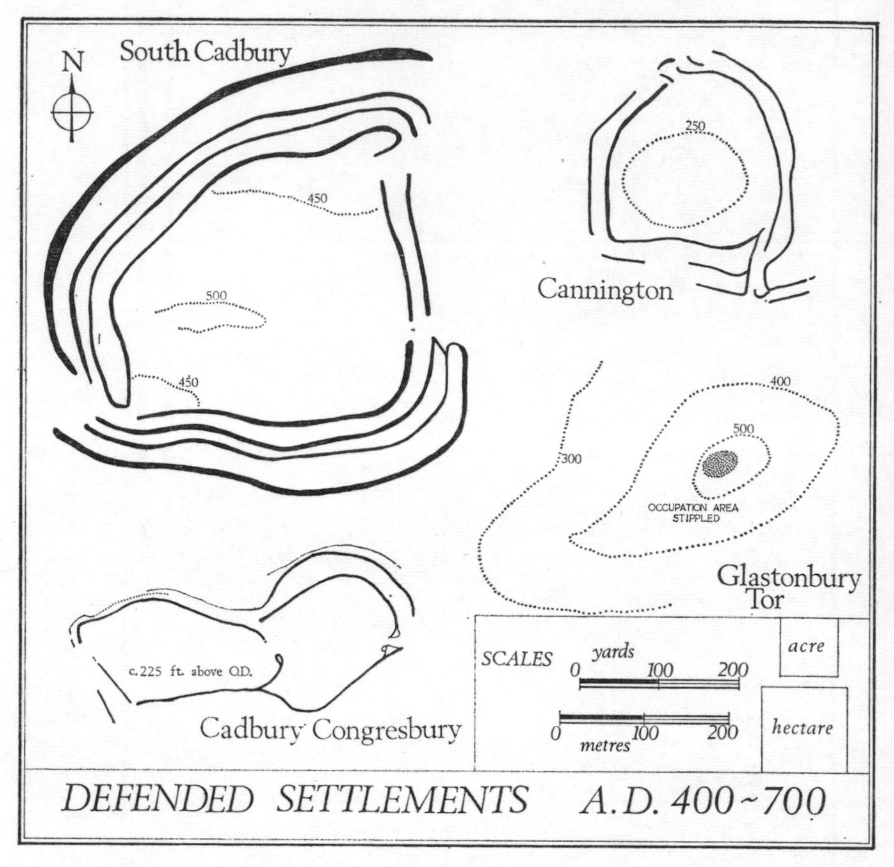

29. Outline plans of three re-occupied Somerset hill-forts and Glastonbury Tor.

The defended settlements number three or probably four. To these may perhaps be added four or five others where Roman finds are known from hill-forts. Will most hill-forts prove to have been re-occupied? If they were, we might see here a restoration (albeit unconsciously) of pre-Roman Iron Age units of territory or local kingdoms. How many people lived within the hill-forts or defended sites? There is hardly room for more than a dozen or two on Glastonbury Tor. The other sites could have accommodated hundreds (figs 28–29). Total excavation of Cadbury-Congresbury may give , positive if imprecise answer here, but if Henley Wood was its only cemetery, the inhabitants were few indeed!

Of course many more people may have lived in the immediate vicinity of such sites, sharing in their protection and economic structure. We must be prepared in the future to do more than excavate sites; whole areas must be subjected to intensive fieldwork, excavation, and documentary and environmental studies. Fortunately Cadbury-Congresbury is part of an area which is being studied in this way (Fowler, 1970, 171, and forthcoming). The demographic (or any other) problems of an area cannot be studied for a particular period without reference to earlier and later ones.

Future work

Inasmuch as it *is* based on evidence (unlike so much 'Dark Age' literature), despite our uncertainties and conjecture, this paper could not have been useful even five years ago, and would have been virtually impossible twenty years ago. This is a measure of the amount of archaeological work on V–VII that has been done in Somerset in recent years. This has been stimulated not by an overall planned research programme, but by diverse causes—rescue excavation, subsidy by private individuals or institutions, and some little deliberate co-ordinated research. It would not have been possible without the active interest of several of our professional colleagues, and of the hundreds of other archaeological workers who have borne the brunt of the digging and recording. Our gratitude must be expressed (if it is not already apparent in the text) especially for the help, albeit keenly critical, of Charles Thomas and Leslie Alcock.

Work at most of the sites mentioned has ended and now awaits definitive publication, though at Butcombe and Cadbury-Congresbury work is planned to continue in the immediate future (this paper includes results on these two sites up to the end of 1970). We hope this paper will stimulate more research, stemming from our extended Grinsell-type survey of the evidence in the first part. The second part should show how open all these problems are to further work and thought, and we can only hope that in ten years' time it will seem superficial and outdated.

REFERENCES

Alcock, L. 1963. *Dinas Powys* (Univ. of Wales).
1965. 'Wales in the Fifth to Seventh Centuries A.D. . . .' in Foster, I. Ll. and Daniel, G. E. (eds.), *Prehistoric and Early Wales* (RKP), 177–212.
1967 *et seq.* Interim rpts. on South Cadbury, *Antiq. J.* **47** (1967), 70-76, annually till **51** (1971), 1–7; *Antiquity* **41** (1967), 50; **42** (1968), 47–51; **43** (1969), 52–56.

ApSimon, A. M., 1965 (with Boon, G. C.). 'The Roman Temple on Brean Down, Somerset,' *Proc. Univ. Bristol Spelaeol. Soc.* **10** (3), 195–258.

ApSimon, A. M. *et al*, 1961. 'The Stratigraphy and Archaeology of the Late-Glacial and Post-Glacial Deposits at Brean Down, Somerset,' *Proc. Univ. Bristol Spelaeol. Soc.* 9 (2), 67–136.

Archaeol. Rev. **1**– 1966–. Annual notes and short interim reports of excavations, chance finds etc in Somerset and neighbouring counties, basic to much of this paper since so much of the material is otherwise not published at all (Dept. of Extra-Mural Studies, Univ of Bristol).

Barton, K. J., 1964. 'Star Roman Villa, Shipham, Somerset', *Proc. Somerset Archaeol. Natur. Hist. Soc.* **108**, 45–93.

Boon, G. C., 1961. 'The Roman Temple at Brean Down, Somerset, and the dating of *Minimissimi*,' *Numis. Chron.* (7th Ser) **1**, 191–197; also p 199 re Byzantine coins.

Branigan, K., 1968. 'The North East Defences of Roman Gatcombe,' *Somerset Archaeol. Natur. Hist.* **112**, 40–53.
1969. *The Romans in the Bristol Area* (Bristol Branch, Hist. Assoc.)
1970. 'The End of the Roman West,' unpublished MS kindly loaned to authors; publication forthcoming in *Trans. Bristol Gloucestershire Archaeol. Soc.*
1971. 'Gatcombe,' *Current Archaeol.* **25**, 41–44.

Bulleid, A. and Morland, J., 1926. 'The Mound, Glastonbury,' *Proc. Somerset Archaeol. Natur. Hist. Soc.* **72**, 52–54.

Callender, M. H., 1965. *Roman Amphorae* (OUP).

Campbell, J. *et al.* 1970. *The Mendip Hills in Prehistoric and Roman Times* (Bristol Archaeol. Rsch. Gp.).

Cox, J. S., 1956. *The Government of the Town* (Ilchester Hist. Monograph 8).

Cunliffe, B., 1966. 'The Somerset Levels in the Roman Period' in Thomas, C. ed., *Rural Settlement in Roman Britain* (CBA Rsch. Rpt. 7), 68–73.
1967. 'Excavations at Gatcombe . . . 1965 and 1966', *Proc. Univ. Bristol Spelaeol. Soc.* **11** (2), 126–60.
1969. *Roman Bath* (Soc. Antiqs. Rsch. Rpt. **24**).

Dobson, D. P., 1931. *The Archaeology of Somerset* (Methuen).

Dymond, C. W., 1902. *Worlebury*.

Elkington, H. D. H., 1968. *The Development of the Mining of Lead in the Iberian Peninsula and Britain under the Roman Empire* (M.A. Thesis, Univ. of Durham).

Evison, V. I., 1968. 'The Anglo-Saxon Finds from Hardown Hill,' *Proc. Dorset Natur. Hist. Archaeol. Soc.* **90**, 232–40.

Fowler, E., 1964. 'Celtic Metalwork of the Fifth and Sixth Centuries A.D.: a re-appraisal' *Archaeol. J.* **120**, 98–160.

Fowler, P. J., 1968. 'Excavation of a Romano-British Settlement at Row of Ashes Farm, Butcombe, North Somerset, 1966–1967,' *Proc. Univ. Bristol Spelaeol. Soc.* **11** (3), 209–236.
1970. 'Fieldwork and Excavation in the Butcombe Area, North Somerset, 1968–1969,' *Proc. Univ. Bristol Spelaeol. Soc.* **12** (2), 169–194.
(ed.) 1970. 'Weston-super-Mare Museum (ii),' being Pt. VIII of 'Archaeological Material in Local Museums: a checklist,' *Bull. Bristol Archaeol. Rsch. Gp.* 3 (7), 172–179.
1972. 'Hillforts, A.D. 400–700' in Hill, D. (ed.), *The Iron Age and its Hillforts* (Univ. of Southampton).
Forthcoming. 'Continuity and the Landscape . . .' in Hawkes, C. F. C. and S. (eds.), *Archaeology into History* (Dent), forthcoming.
1970 *et al. Cadbury Congresbury, Somerset, 1968* (Dept. of Extra-Mural Studies, Univ. of Bristol).
1970, and Rahtz, P. 'Cadcong 1970', *Current Archaeol.* **23**, 337–42.
Fox, C. and A., 1958. 'Wansdyke Reconsidered,' *Archaeol. J.* **115**, 1–48.

Gough, J. W., 1967. *Mines of Mendip* (2nd ed., David and Charles).
Gracie, H. S., 1970. 'Frocester Court Roman Villa,' *Trans. Bristol Gloucestershire Archaeol. Soc.* **89**, 15–86.
Gray, H. St. G., 1922. 'Excavation at Cadbury Camp, Tickenham,' *Proc. Somerset Archaeol. Natur. Hist. Soc.* **68**, 8–20.
Greenfield, E., 1963 *et seq.* Notes on Henley Wood Roman temple, *J. Rom. Stud.* **53**, 146 and **55**, 1965, 216; *Archaeol. Rev.* **4**, 1969, 47 and **5**, 1970, 28.
Grinsell, L. V., 1965. 'Somerset Archaeology 1931–65,' *Proc. Somerset Archaeol. Natur. Hist. Soc.* **109**, 47–77.
1970. *The Archaeology of Exmoor* (David and Charles).
Forthcoming. *Re* Portishead *sceatta* in *British Numis. J.* forthcoming.

Hawkins, A. B., 1971. Lecture on the Somerset Levels to the Colston Symposium, in April 1971, at Univ. of Bristol (publication forthcoming).
Horne, E., 1928. 'The Saxon Cemetery at Camerton, Somerset,' *Proc. Somerset Archaeol. Natur. Hist. Soc.* **74**, 61–70.
1933. 'The Anglo-Saxon Cemetery at Camerton, Somerset,' *Proc. Somerset Archaeol. Natur. Hist. Soc.* 79, 39–63.
Hoskins, W. G., 1960. *The Westward Expansion of Wessex* (Occ. Paper **13**, Dept. Eng. Local Hist. Univ. of Leicester).
Hunt, J., 1963 and 1964. Notes on Winthill cemetery and villa, *J. Axbridge Caving Gp. Archaeol. Soc.* 1963, 35–42; 1964, 26–28.
Hyslop, M. 1963. 'Two Anglo-Saxon Cemeteries at Chamberlains Barn, Leighton Buzzard, Beds.' *Archaeol. J.* **120**, 161–200.

Jackson, K., 1958. 'The Site of Mount Badon,' *J. Celtic Studies* **2** (2), 152–155.

Laing, L. R., 1969. 'Timber Halls in Dark Age Britain—some problems,' *Trans. Dumfriesshire Galloway Natur. Hist. Antiq. Soc.* **46**, 110–127.

Meaney, A., 1964. *A Gazetteer of Anglo-Saxon Burial Sites* (Allen & Unwin).
Morris, J., 1966. 'Dark Age Dates' in Dobson, B. and Jarrett, M. G. (eds.), *Britain and Rome* (Titus Wilson, Kendall), 145–185.
Myres, J. N. L., 1936. 'The English Settlement' in Collingwood, R. G. and Myres, J. N. L., *Roman Britain and the English Settlements* (O.U.P.). 1964. 'Wansdyke and the Origin of Wessex' in Trevor-Roper, H. R. (ed.), *Essays in British History* (Macmillan).

Ordnance Survey, 1966. *Map of Britain in the Dark Ages.*

Porter, H. M., 1967. *The Saxon Conquest of Somerset and Devon* (Brodie, Bath).

Poyntz-Wright, P., forthcoming. Ponters Ball *in prep.*

Radford, C. A. R., 1946–1947. 'The Roman Villa at Low Ham,' *Somerset Dorset Notes Queries* **25**, pts. 232 and 235.

1962. 'The Church in Somerset down to 1100,' *Proc. Somerset Archaeol. Natur. Hist. Soc.* **106**, 28–45.

1964. *The Pictorial History of Glastonbury Abbey* (Pitkin Pictorial).

1968. 'Glastonbury Abbey' in Ashe, G. (ed.), *The Quest for Arthur's Britain* (Pall Mall Press), 119–138.

Rahtz, P. A., 1951. 'The Roman Temple at Pagans Hill, Chew Stoke, N. Somerset', *Proc. Somerset Archaeol. Natur. Hist. Soc.* **96**, 112–142.

1962–1963. 'The Saxon and Medieval Palaces at Cheddar, An Interim Report,' *Medieval Archaeol.* **6–7**, 53–66; also M. A. thesis Bristol Univ. 1964; full report in prep.

1966. 'Cheddar Vicarage 1965', *Proc. Somerset Archaeol. Natur. Hist. Soc.*, **110**, 52–84.

1968a. 'Sub-Roman cemeteries,' in Barley, M. W. and Hanson, R. P. C. (eds.), *Christianity in Britain* 300–700 (Leicester Univ. Press), 193–195.

1968b. 'Glastonbury Tor,' in Ashe, G. (ed.), *The Quest for Arthur's Britain* (Pall Mall Press), 139–153; full report in *Archaeol. J.* **127**, 1970, 1–81.

1969. 'Cannington Hillfort, 1963,' *Somerset Archaeol. Natur. Hist.* **113**, 56–68.

1970. 'Cheddar Vicarage, 1970,' *Bull. Bristol Archaeol. Rsch. Gp.* **3** (9), 243–245. Full rpt *in prep.*

Forthcoming. 'Pottery in Somerset, A.D. 400–1066' in Hodges, H. and Evison, V. I. (eds.), *forthcoming* volume of essays for G. C. Dunning.

In prep. Cannington Cemetery, excavated for MOPBW 1962–1963; see *Medieval Archaeol.* **8** (1964), 237.

Rahtz, P. A. and Fowler, P. J., 1968. 'Somerset Dark Age Problems,' *Bull. Bristol Archaeol. Rsch. Gp.* **3** (3), 57–61.

Rahtz, P. A. and Greenfield, E.1973. *Excavations at Chew Valley Lake* (MOPBW Rsch. Rpt. **8**, HMSO).

Rahtz, P. A. and Harris, L. G., 1956–1957. 'The Temple Well and other Buildings at Pagans Hill, Chew Stoke, N. Somerset,' *Proc. Somerset Archaeol. Natur. Hist. Soc.* **101/2**, 15–51.

Rahtz, *et al.*, 1958. 'Three Post-Roman finds from the Temple Well of Pagans Hill, Somerset,' *Medieval Archaeol.* **2**, 104–111.

Rhys, J., 1891. 'Inscribed stone on Winsford Hill, Exmoor,' *Archaeol. Cambrensis* (ser. 5) **8**, 29–32.

Rivet, A. L. F., 1969. 'Social and Economic Aspects' in Rivet, A. L. F. (ed.), *The Roman Villa in Britain* (RKP).

Savory, H. N., 1956. 'Some Sub-Romano-British Brooches from South Wales' in Harden, D. B. (ed.), *Dark Age Britain* (Methuen), 40–58.

Solley, T. W. J., 1967. 'Excavation at Gatcombe, 1954,' *Proc. Somerset Archaeol. Natur. Hist. Soc.* **111**, 24–37.

Taylor, R. F., 1967. 'An Anglo-Saxon Cemetery at Compton Pauncefoot,' *Proc. Somerset Archaeol. Natur. Hist. Soc.* **111**, 67–69.

Taylor, H. M. and J., 1965. *Anglo-Saxon Architecture* (CUP).

Thomas, A. C., 1959. 'Imported Pottery in Dark Age Western Britain', *Medieval Archaeol.* 3, 89–111.
1968. *Somerset Dark Age Problems* 1968; *some further thoughts.* MS circulated privately.
1969. 'Are these the Walls of Camelot?' *Antiquity* 43, 27–30.
Thomas *et al* forthcoming. Paper on origins of Mediterranean imports in preparation.
Tratman, E. K., 1962. 'Some Ideas on Roman Roads in Bristol and North Somerset', *Proc. Univ. Bristol Spelaeol. Soc.* 9 (3), 159–176.
— 1963a 'Maes Knoll', *Proc. Univ. Bristol Spelaeol. Soc.* 10 (1), 11–15.
— 1963b 'Burrington Camp, Somerset', *Proc. Univ. Bristol Spelaeol. Soc.* 10 (1), 16–21.
Webster, G. 1967. 'Excavations at the Romano-British Villa in Barnsley Park, Cirencester, 1961–6', *Trans. Bristol Gloucestershire Archaeol. Soc.* 86, 74–83.
Wedlake, W. 1958. *Excavations at Camerton, Somerset* (Camerton Excavation Club).
Wheeler, R. E. M., 1943. *Maiden Castle, Dorset* (Soc. Antiqs. Rsch. Rpt. 12).
Wheeler, R. E. M. and T. V., 1932. *Report . . . Lydney Park, Gloucestershire* (Soc. Antiqs. Rsch. Rpt. 9).
Whitting, P. D., 1961. In Dolley, R. H. M. (ed.), *Anglo-Saxon Coins.*
Williams, M., 1970. *The Draining of the Somerset Levels* (OUP).

CHAPTER IX

Earthworks of the Danelaw Frontier

James Dyer

England was occupied by the Danes for more than two hundred years, yet there appear to be few visible structures to testify to their presence. Is this because the Danes constructed no earthworks, or because archaeologists have failed to identify them? The latter seems to be the answer, since the *Anglo-Saxon Chronicle* contains numerous references to Danish fortifications. In A.D. 885, for example, the Danes 'built a fortification around themselves' at Rochester. In 921 they 'built the fortress at Tempsford, abandoning the other fortress at Huntingdon'.

During the late nineteenth century it was the custom amongst British antiquaries to classify types of earthworks into neat groups suitably labelled British, Roman, Danish, Norman and so on. Roman earthworks were considered always to be rectangular and regular in proportions. Norman castles were recognised by their conical mounds and baileys. Difficulties arose in trying to distinguish between British, Saxon and Danish works. The list drawn up by the Earthworks Committee of the Congress of Archaeological Societies was based entirely on typology and could not distinguish between periods of construction of similar earthworks. In 1908 Allcroft made a valiant attempt in his *Earthwork of England* to isolate Saxon and Danish earthworks. This work achieved a certain success, but a number of sites were included which, on the basis of subsequent excavation, are no longer acceptable. The ground was cleared somewhat in 1931 when Hawkes produced his classic survey of Iron Age hill-forts, thus providing many of the fortresses and enclosures of the Earthworks Committee with a definite position in prehistory, but at the same time leaving a number of defensive works with no provenance. Could it be that there lay some of the missing Saxon and Danish sites?

Our search is made more difficult because we are uncertain of what we are looking for. We do not know what Danish earthworks in England looked like, nor have we any clear idea of the sort of pottery made by those who built them which might lead us to the identification of a site.

There seem to be two possible ways in which we may attempt to resolve the problem. In one we can consider the earthworks of the Danish homeland, and see if they suggest comparable examples in Britain. Secondly, we may start with all the known British earthworks of every period, and by a slow process of elimination reduce them to a small minority that do not seem to fit into any accepted classifications. Quite a lot of those left over may belong to the Saxon or Danish group. We must also bear in mind that any attempt to isolate such earthworks without excavation is open to many dangers. Structures of Saxon origin, as well as from the initial and final phases of Danish occupation, are liable to be lumped together without distinction, although the period as a whole can be seen as one developing through piratical raids and military occupation to one of permanent settlement. In this paper I am concerned only with attempting to define the Danish earthworks.

Details of fortified Viking Age sites in Denmark are notably lacking in the more accessible Scandinavian literature. The major towns like Hedeby and Birka were protected by massive banks supported by palisades, and surrounded by ditches. The town sites are beside water, and the defences are semi-circular in plan with the water forming the straight side of a D-shape. There is no evidence to show that these towns, unlike the fortified boroughs established in England by King Alfred, often replaced smaller camps that had offered protection to a population engaged in agriculture. Although Birka was founded *c.* A.D. 800, it was not fortified until soon after 900, and went out of use around A.D. 960. Similarly, Hedeby began *c* A.D. 800 although its defences were somewhat earlier, perhaps *c* A.D. 890. The town was destroyed by fire shortly before 1050.

Smaller defended sites were usually circular, or roughly so, Gråborg, Ismanthorp, and the smaller fortified village of Eketorp in Öland being well-known examples. Each is characterized by massive stone walls, and houses set radially inside, with further rectangular blocks of buildings in the centre. The former sites seem to have been temporary refuges, but Eketorp was permanently occupied from A.D. 450 to 750, and again from the beginning of the eleventh to the end of the thirteenth centuries. Eketorp measures only 80 metres in diameter, whilst Gråborg and Ismanthorp are about 200 metres and 120 metres in diameter respectively.

Between A.D. 950 and 1050 a series of magnificent military camps was erected in Denmark, of which four have so far been discovered. These are Trelleborg on Zealand, Nonnebakken on Funen, and Aggersborg and Fyrkat on the Jutland peninsula. These were laid out with remarkable mathematic precision, each camp being circular in plan with entrances at the cardinal points. The interior was divided into quarters by cross-roads, and in each quadrant were groups of four (at Aggersborg twelve) boat-shaped barrack houses. The whole structure was surrounded by massive timber-faced walls and minor outer ditches. It is generally accepted that the camps were created as military bases for the invasion of England by Swein Forkbeard or Cnut the Great, being paid for by the Danegeld largely extracted from English pockets (for Trelleborg see Nørlund, 1956).

Allcroft, writing in *Earthwork of England*, was probably correct when he said that 'The Danes seldom travelled far from their ships, these Danish works are commonly in riverine positions' (Allcroft, 1908, 383). At least, this must have been the case at the time of the initial settlement of England about A.D. 855. But within twenty years the Danes were strong enough to have divided into two armies, one in Northumbria and one in

East Anglia and Mercia. From the latter area they made frequent attacks on Wessex and its king, Alfred. In 886 a treaty was signed by Alfred and the Danish king, Guthrum, fixing the boundary between Wessex and the Danelaw:

> 'First concerning our boundaries: up the Thames, and then up the Lea, and along the Lea to its source, then in a straight line to Bedford, then up the Ouse to the Watling Street' (Whitelock, 1955, 380).

We do not know how strongly this Danelaw boundary was adhered to. The Lea, Ouse and Watling Street all form rigid boundaries, but what of the gap between the source of the Lea and Bedford? Two possible Roman roads cross this area and may have formed the demarcation line (Viatores, 1964, 294). Was this section marked or patrolled in any way? Assuming that it was, then perhaps in this section of Bedfordshire some clues might be gathered relating to Danish frontier works? For the purpose of this study I am, therefore, examining in detail possible earthworks close to this section of the Danelaw frontier, though occasionally considering sites from farther afield for comparative purposes.

The *Anglo-Saxon Chronicle* does not have much to tell us about the area along the Danelaw frontier. In A.D. 914 it records that a group of Danish raiders riding south towards Luton were met by the townsfolk who 'fought against them and reduced them [the Danes] to full flight and rescued all that they had captured and also a great part of their horses and their weapons' (Whitelock, 1955, 194). In 1819 a large hoard of weapons was found in the fields close to the village of Toddington (Beds), together with personal ornaments. Whilst some of the objects in the scanty descriptions are clearly of Saxon origin, others may be Danish. Toddington lies close to the minor Roman roads that may have formed the Danelaw boundary, and the objects found in 1819 may well be the remains of the 914 skirmish.

Alfred was succeeded by his son, Edward the Elder, who was responsible for bringing all the Danish settlements south of the Humber under the control of Wessex. With Aethelflæd, 'the lady of the Mercians', he built a line of forts along the northern boundary of the Danelaw from Bedford to Runcorn. The *Chronicle* tells us that in 918 Edward went with his army to Bedford and captured the town. He stayed there for four weeks and before he left ordered a fort to be built on the south side of the river. Today this semicircular area of *c* 40 acres is enclosed by a dirty, silted and weed-choked ditch, shown on Speed's map of 1610, and almost certainly a vestige of Edward's fortification. Although there is no archaeological evidence to support the antiquity of the earthwork, its artificial nature is in no doubt. It is still known by its traditional name of the King's Ditch.

In A.D. 920 a Danish army from Huntingdon and East Anglia moved to Tempsford where they built a fortress from which they hoped to gain control of Bedford and the southern Midlands. The Danes attacked Bedford, only to be repulsed with many casualties:

'Then after this, in the summer, a great force assembled . . . and all the men . . . marched to Tempsford and besieged the fortress: they attacked it until they took it by storm; and they killed the king and Earl Toglos and his son Earl Manna, and his brother and all those who were inside and chose to defend themselves; and they captured the others and everything that was inside.'

This quotation is of considerable importance since, if the fortress can be traced, then we have a decisive date for its construction. The modern village of Tempsford, Beds, lies 7 miles east of Bedford at a point where the Great Ouse and its tributary, the Ivel, join. A quarter of a mile from the river is a small, rectangular earthwork known as Gannock's Castle, measuring some 215 feet by 185 feet. It has frequently been identified as the Danish fortress and has often been quoted as a typical Danish earthwork. A careful examination of the site convinces the writer that it is a fortified manorial site of the twelfth or thirteenth century. The moat, which is not more than twenty feet wide, would not have withstood any siege, and no army of any size could have sheltered within it. Assuming a distribution of one man to every two yards of rampart, Sir Cyril Fox demonstrated that it would have held no more than 270 men (Fox, 1923, 302). Apart from this, Gannock's Castle is on the east side of the river Ivel and four hundred yards from it. The Danes are more likely to have built on the west bank, with their boats on the river behind them, ready for a hasty retreat if necessary. It may be argued that the rest of the fortress has been destroyed by ploughing, and Goddard (1904, 282) refers to the fields to the south and east being 'scored with traces of other lines . . . too faint to decipher'; but this is unconvincing when one part survives so completely. Careful examination on the ground and of aerial photographs shows no other traces of fortifications. Furthermore, the angular shape of Gannock's Castle is wrong, if Danish constructions in England are to resemble the curved outlines of those in Scandinavia.

Where, then, was the Tempsford fortress? The place-name means 'ford on the Thames' (Mawer and Stenton, 1926, 110) and indicates that the Ivel was known as the Thames in Danish times. Clearly no earthwork now exists at Tempsford that can be attributed to the Danes, so we must search further afield. It is probable that any ford on the Ivel or 'Thames' would have been known as Thames-ford. Three miles south of Tempsford, on the Ivel-ford at Beeston near Sandy, lay an earthwork which seemed to answer the problem. Five or six acres in extent, the site, known as Beeston Berrys, was composed of a great perimeter bank, irregularly D-shaped in plan, with its straight side butting on to the Ivel, and lying to the west of the river. The earthwork has now been destroyed by intensive market-gardening, but was shown on the first edition of the Ordnance Survey map dated 1835, and is the subject of a line-and-wash drawing in the Bedfordshire County Record Office (Johnson, 1959, 19; Pl XVIII). It was described in 1883 as 'opposite Galley Hill (Sandy), a ford defended by ancient ramparts called Beeston Berrys, of which there are now only faint traces to be seen'. The drawing shows a steep bank at least 10 feet high. The earthwork was large enough to have held an army, strong enough to withstand a siege, and constructed with a river navigable for boats bounding the eastern side.

Excavations in 1949 by C. F. Tebbutt at The Hillings, Eaton Socon, Hunts, showed that a pre-Norman D-shaped enclosure had existed, with the Ouse forming its eastern side (Tebbutt, 1952, 48–60). It lies 3½ miles north of Tempsford, and T. C. Lethbridge has suggested that this was the lost Tempsford site, but the writer feels that it is too small, and that the Beeston site is more likely to have held the large number of men involved.

It is worth recalling that Edward the Elder's fortification on the south bank of the Ouse opposite Bedford, the King's Ditch, was of similar but more regular D-shaped plan, butting on to the River Ouse. Perhaps, then, Saxon and Dane were both constructing semicircular or D-shaped earthworks?

Eight and a half miles south-west of Beeston lies a second D-shaped earthwork at Woodmer End, Shillington, known locally as Church Spanel (in some books Church Panel; Pl XIX). Here rising nearly 15 feet above meadows once liable to flood, is an artificially fortified gravel island, with a stream on one side and a strong D-shaped outer bank, with a wet inner ditch, and a slight inner bank surrounding the remainder. Measuring only 550 feet by 350 feet, this earthwork is decidely smaller than Beeston. Its marshy situation, taking advantage of an existing hillock, is typical of sites in the Danish homeland, as well as those chosen by the Saxons (*cf* Athelney). It is more likely to have been an outpost or refuge, rather than a base camp as Beeston may well have been. Prior to modern drainage the stream on the north-eastern side would have been navigable by boats of shallow draught, thus affording a quick 'get-away' leading into the river Ivel (fig 30).

A very similar site to Beeston and Church Spanel occurs in Wimblington parish, Cambs. On the south-western edge of Stonea island, beside Latches Fen, is a D-shaped earthwork, in which the Fen acts as the straight side and a protection, with two strong arcs of rampart and ditch jutting north-east on to the small gravel island. There are indications that the D-shaped earthworks replaced earlier banks and ditches, which are still clearly visible, and seem to have enclosed a larger area. The D-enclosure at its widest measures 1300 feet by 550 feet, its banks standing 5 feet above the ditch bottom. In describing the site, Phillips (1948, 46) drew attention to the total lack of dateable material from the camp, a feature that seems common to all the earthworks described in this paper (fig 30).

Another earthwork, again of a more irregular D-shape, occurs seven miles north of the Ouse at Bolnhurst (Beds). This site, on heavy clay land, is certainly not prehistoric as has been suggested in various local writings.

Unfortunately it has recently been badly damaged by bulldozing and ploughing. It lies on a spur at 260 feet above O.D., and is some distance from water. Drawings made in 1920 (Wadmore, 1920, 21) show the earthwork standing 10 feet high with the steep angularity that seems to characterize Danish earthworks in Denmark and northern Germany, like the Trelleborg-type camps and Danevirke which were originally shored with massive vertical timbers.

Some of these D-shaped sites may represent frontier forts of the Danelaw, and may have been constructed soon after its establishment, perhaps being the inspiration behind the plan of Edward the Elder's site at Bedford. There is reason to believe, however, that the Saxons had adopted this type of fortification even earlier, and that Alfred may have used it at Athelney (878), Lympne (892), and almost certainly at Hertford in 895, where a water-filled D-shaped enclosure still exists beside the castle, althought it has been flattened for a public park. Such forts may not always have been completed owing to the reluctance of the Saxons to give their labour for projects of that kind. At Lympne, for example, we read in the *Anglo-Saxon Chronicle* for 892 that the Danes 'stormed a fortress in the fen; inside were a few peasants, and it was only half made'. This passage stresses the frequency with which both Saxon and Danish forts were built beside or on islands in marshes and fens.

The same passage also bears out the statement frequently made by Bertil Almgren that Viking camps were often sited on islands with shelving beaches, thus enabling their shallow-draught ships to be pulled up on to dry ground well above the water-level (Almgren, 1966, 28). This also meant that Viking boats could penetrate far inland along shallow waterways, where the deeper-draught Saxon boats could not hope to reach. In view of this Almgren has suggested that harbours, as such, were not necessary. While this might often be the case in areas where the Vikings did not intend to stay for long, more permanent constructions might be required where greater concentrations of men were stationed for any length of time, as for example in the Danelaw frontier area. This same area, beside the Ouse, is liable to disastrous floods, and boats not securely harboured behind earthworks might well be washed away, as has happened on numerous occasions in the past five centuries. The destruction of their boats would leave any Viking army in an embarrassing position. Consequently, artificially constructed harbours where a few boats could be sheltered, repaired, or built might be considered in our search for Viking earthworks. To begin with, we must look at the site known as 'The Docks' at Willington, Beds, which tradition has always ascribed to the Danes (fig 31).

Willington lies on the Great Ouse, some five miles east of Bedford. The earthwork is overgrown, is partially built on, and has been somewhat damaged by a now-disused railway and market-gardening. Fortunately, sufficient remains to show, with the aid of plans made during the past

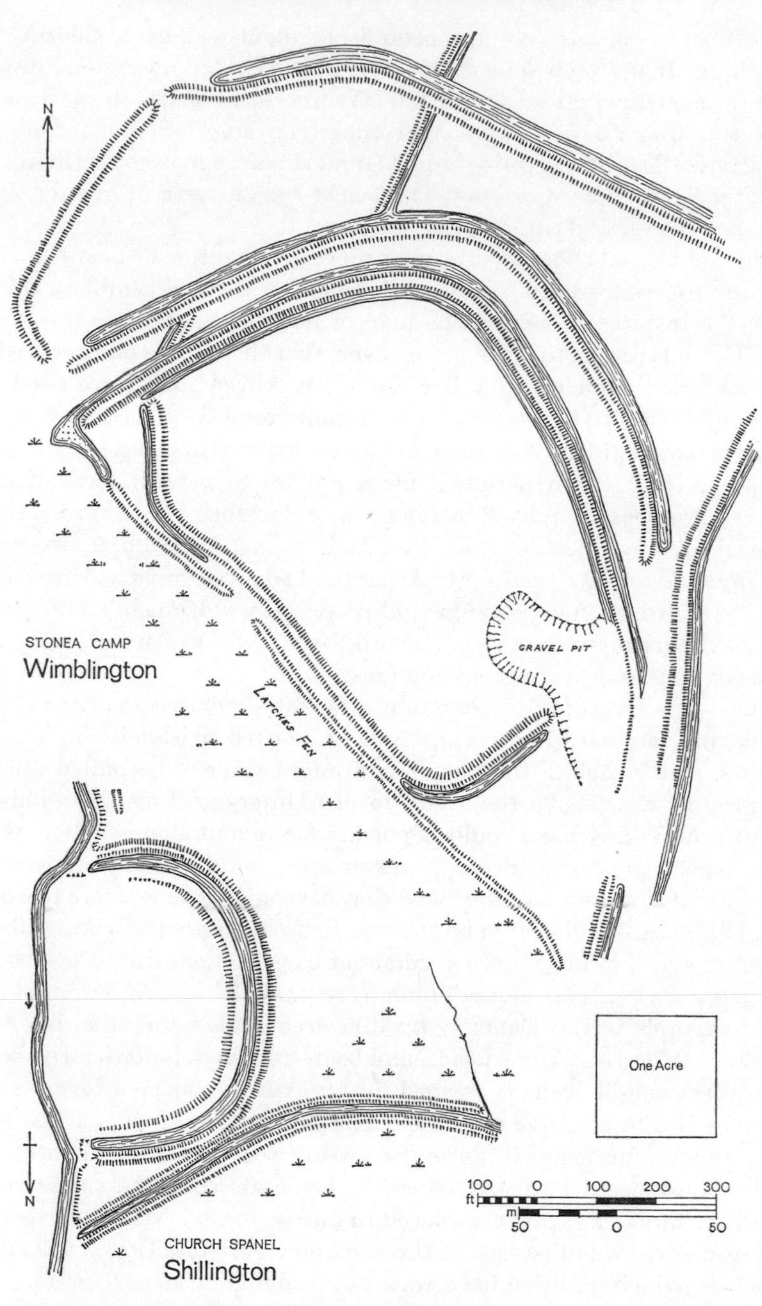

30. D-shaped enclosures (*see* p 226).

hundred years, a large rectangular harbour measuring 170 feet by 105 feet and 6 feet deep, with direct entry through a channel from the river to the north. At the southern end of the harbour is a 30-feet-wide gap leading into a smaller inner harbour measuring 110 feet by 60 feet. A third, narrower channel, 100 feet long and 15 feet wide, lies to the west, between the two harbours, and may represent a dock used for repairs or even ship-building. East of the harbours and with separate entry to the river was a channel 20 feet wide which opened out into a rectangular cutting 72 feet long, 35 feet wide and 6 feet deep. There were two sloping entrances or slipways at the northern end of this feature, each about 18 feet wide, and opposite a similar entrance at the north-eastern corner of the largest harbour. Goddard (1903, 331) likened this part of the earthwork to a *naust* or boat-house (*see* Hinsch, 1960). Such buildings had curved walls like those of the houses found at Trelleborg, but unfortunately at Willington this part of the site has now been almost totally destroyed by gardening and it is almost impossible to detect the feature at all.

West of the harbours are other inlets, some of which still hold water, including the ditch of a D-shaped enclosure fronting on to the Ouse, with a second enclosure to the south of it. These latter enclosures may represent the earliest features at the site, affording protection to those engaged in the construction of the naval works. Other outer earthworks which surrounded the harbours and D-shaped enclosures have been destroyed by building and market-gardening, although all of these features recorded by Goddard and others have been incorporated in fig 31.

The presence of the fortification beside the harbour at Willington calls to mind the reference in the *Jomsvikingasaga* (Blake, 1962) which seems to suggest that the fortress at Jomsborg was divided into two parts, an inner area containing the soldiers, and an outer section in which the harbour, large enough to hold three warships, lay. However, the description is far from clear, and it would be unwise to carry the similarity farther (Foote and Wilson, 1970, 276).

Another Bedfordshire 'harbour' site which has also suffered at the hands of the railway and road-builders, lies on the river Hiz, close to its junction with the Ivel, nine miles south of Willington, at Etonbury near Arlesey, Beds. Due to the very wide railway embankment between the site and the river there is less certainty about the layout of Etonbury. It seems certain that it was later used for manorial purposes, particularly on the eastern side (outside the area illustrated in fig 31). A rectangular harbour area is again present, measuring some 250 feet long and at least 150 feet wide, with a smaller enclosure leading off from its south-western corner. This enclosure measures 140 feet by 50 feet. The harbour is fed by a small, fast-flowing stream that runs into it from the eastern side. Exactly where the original entrance into the river Hiz was situated cannot now be determined. To the north of the harbour are two massive curved banks with

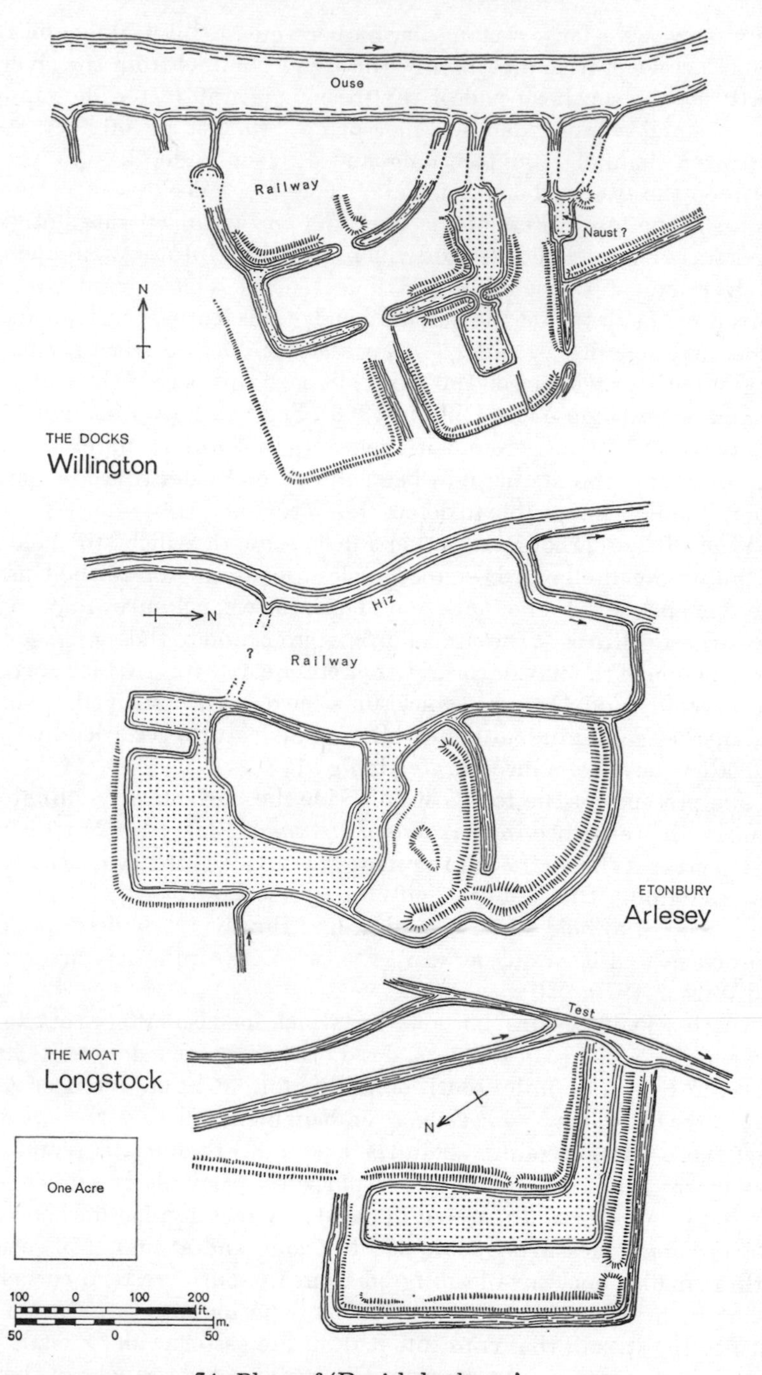

31. Plans of 'Danish harbours'.

external ditches, which enclosed a fortified area. These may originally have been D-shaped, with the straight side of the earthwork butting on to the harbour, but unfortunately too much has been buried beneath the railway enbankment to be sure. A rough sketch made by Lysons about 1800 shows an entrance linking this enclosure to the harbour area, but this is no longer visible (Lysons, *c* 1800).

Part of a third harbour site seems to have existed on the south bank of the Ouse at Clapham, Beds, two miles north-west of Bedford, where the river bank is penetrated by two silted inlets. Unfortunately this site, like the others, has been largely destroyed, this time irrevocably by gravel-digging.

R. W. Feachem has kindly drawn my attention to the similarity between these works and the earthwork at Longstock in Hampshire called 'The Moat' which has also been identified as a harbour site. Here the main harbour is more regular than the Bedfordshire examples. It measures some 300 ft by 100 ft, and is entered at right angles by a channel 250 ft long from a branch of the river Test (Williams-Freeman, 1915, 381; fig 31).

A third class of site that we can consider as a product of the Danish occupation is circular in plan, and consists of either:

(*a*) a wide, though not necessarily deep, ditch and internal bank, the latter often being very upstanding and regular in appearance, with at least one entrance through it, or

(*b*) a regular circular hollow, *c* 100 ft in diameter, the material from the flat central area having been used to provide a low bank round the perimeter of the hollow. Sited on a hill-slope, they have no external ditch, but an entrance on the lower, downhill side is present.

In both cases, due to the regularity of their layout, the sites have often in the past been identified as Roman amphitheatres. Their position on isolated hill-tops or hill-slopes, close to rivers, and often distant from known Roman sites, makes this identification unlikely. There is a greater chance of confusing these sites with Norman ring-works, and indeed only excavation is likely to establish their identity with certainty.

The best example of a work of type (*a*) is Howbury at Water End Farm, Renhold, Beds, on the Great Ouse, a mile upstream from Willington (Pls XX, XXI). This site is almost perfectly circular in plan, with a wide, water-filled ditch outside. It is 130 ft in diameter internally, with ramparts still 10 ft high. It probably had one original entrance on the west, but the old road to St Neots has cut through the site making a second on the east. This earthwork may have acted as a signal-station or small outpost. Although it would not have held many men, it crowned the highest spur east of Bedford and commanded a considerable view along the Ouse valley.

On the Hertfordshire–Buckinghamshire borders at Hawridge Court

Farm is a very regular circular ringwork with one apparently original entrance on the south-east side. Approximately 200 ft in diameter, a flat central area is surrounded by a bank 16 ft high with an external ditch still some 4 ft deep. Part of this earthwork has been destroyed by the farmhouse. The regularity of this site again suggests that it may be Danish; there is no documentary evidence to suggest a later date.

In this group, mention must once again be made of Warham Camp in Norfolk. Long considered to be of Viking construction, in recent years this bivallate earthwork has been shown to have originated in the Iron Age, largely on the excavation evidence of the defences. The fantastic regularity of the site's layout does, however, constantly remind one of the Danish Trelleborg sites (both Trelleborg and Warham are approximately 450 ft in diameter), and very serious consideration should be given to the possibility that at Warham we are considering an Iron Age 'plateau fort' adapted by the Vikings. Excavations by St George Gray (Gray, 1933, 399–413) and R. Rainbird Clarke (unpublished) showed that entrance to the camp was gained from the river on the western side, a very reasonable Viking feature. No Iron Age entrance causeways were found crossing the ditches, but these might well have been dug away in Viking times, whilst vertical timber facings to the ramparts could have been overlooked at a time when we had no Scandinavian precedents for judging what such a fort might look like. The duplication of the ramparts and ditches at Warham is unlike anything in Denmark, but again this may be explained by assuming that a more or less circular bivallate Iron Age camp was 'tidied up' by the military architects of the tenth century. Excavated finds were of the Iron Age only, but again this is in accordance with the general lack of material from British Viking occupation. Until more extensive work has been carried out on the interior of Warham the possibility of its use in the Viking period should not be dismissed.

In the same area a much smaller ringwork, similar to the Howbury type (*a*), lies in marshy ground close to the Thetford to East Wretham Heath road in Norfolk. Called Ringmere, it is circular, 104 ft in diameter with double banks and ditches bounding it. The banks still stand 4 ft high. Excavation has failed to produce dating evidence, which in itself suggests only brief occupation. Florence of Worcester describes the battle fought in A.D. 1010 between the East Anglians under Ulfcytel Snilling and Swein Forkbeard of Denmark, and records that the Danes came 'to a place called Ringmere, where they heard that Ulfcytel with his forces lay, who with a sharp encounter soon entertained them' (Clarke, 1938, 278). W. G. Clarke identified the site of the battle as either on East Wretham Heath or at Rymer, south of Thetford (Clarke, 1937, 88–89). The former seems more likely, and the earthwork described may have been Ulfcytel's temporary headquarters. If this is correct, then the East Anglian's choice of a marsh-site is not dissimilar to those which it is suggested were constructed by the

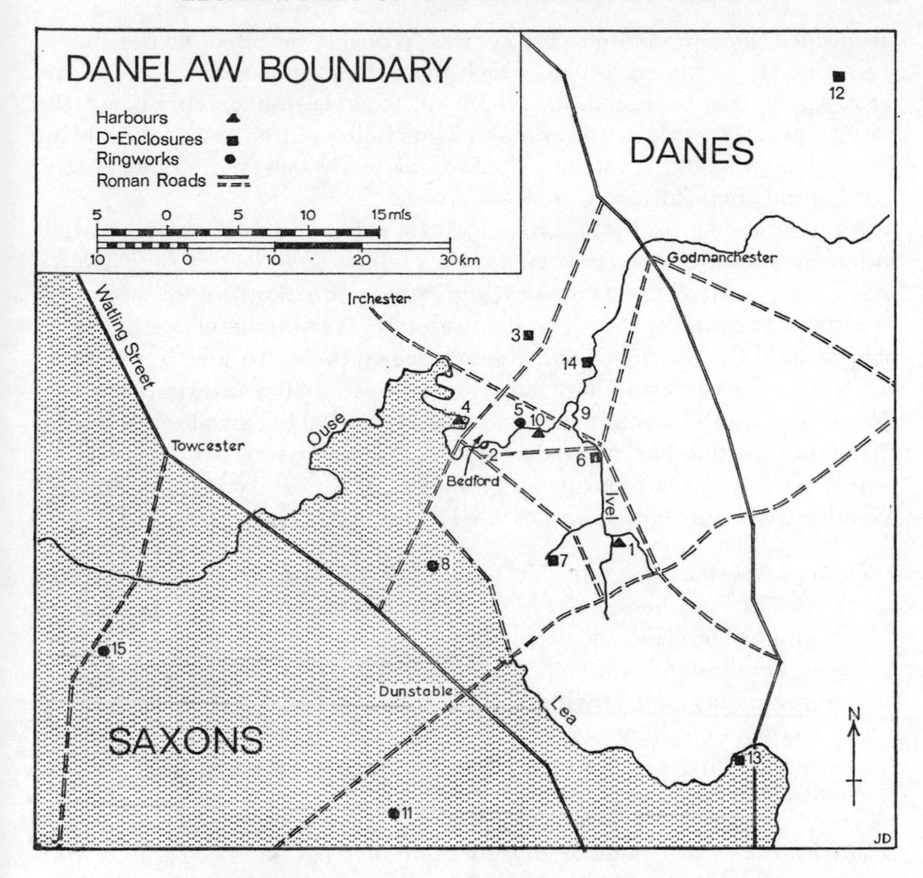

32. The Danelaw boundary (site numbers refer to the list, p. 235).

Danes in England, and bears a superficial resemblance to Swein's own great fortresses in Jutland.

It may be worth noting at this point that the Ordnance Survey marked three separate 'earthen ring' sites outside the Stonea island camp in Cambridgeshire, described above. Although no trace of these remains today, and Phillips (1948, 47) suggested that they were burial-places of probably Bronze Age date, we should perhaps consider that they may have been small ringworks of Howbury and Ringmere type.

Ringworks of the second kind (*b*) occur in Bedfordshire and Oxfordshire. Twelve miles south-west of Howbury is a site called Seymour's Mount near Steppingley, Beds. This lies at the extreme end of a short west-facing spur of greensand. A short water-filled moat cuts off the spur from the main hill-mass on the east. On the top of the spur a flat circular area 110 ft in diameter has been dug out of the hill. Some of the material removed has been used to make a very low bank round the rim of the steep-sided hollow created. Entry was probably effected at the lower, western edge of the enclosure, which butts directly on to the front of the spur. The purpose of such a site is difficult to explain, but, lying below the natural ground level, it would make a good hide-out or observation-point for a small group of men who wished to look westwards, with a moat to the east behind them for protection.

An almost identical site called Stuttle's Bank exists one-and-a-half miles north-east of Stratton Audley in eastern Oxfordshire (and twelve miles south-east of the Ouse-Watling Street junction). The earthwork consists of an amphitheatre-like depression 93 ft in diameter, with a slight bank around the perimeter and an entrance on the south side. The ground slopes from the earthwork down to a small stream half-a-mile to the north. Woods obscure the layout today, but this site probably looked south-east in the main direction of Saxon advance.

Having completed our survey of sites in the vicinity of the Danelaw boundary, we must now summarize what we have seen.

1 *D-shaped earthworks*, one side butting on to water, constructed either
   (*a*) on flat land beside rivers or navigable streams, and containing a number of acres, or
   (*b*) on small islands surrounded by marsh or fenland. These islands are upstanding and provide a good viewpoint across the surrounding countryside. The plans of the fortifications of these sites bear a superficial resemblance to the Viking town sites at Hedeby and Birka.

2 *Harbour sites*, with one or more rectangular harbours, separated from deep rivers by narrow channels, often with strong fortifications adjoining.

3 *Ringworks*, perhaps look-out posts, either
   (*a*) constructed above ground on hill-spurs, and usually not far from water, with one (or possibly two) circuits of rampart and ditch, or
   (*b*) circular hollows dug into the ground, on hill-slopes, with water fairly close. Both types of ringwork have at least one entrance. Such sites should be considered when reviewing the lineage of the major military works of Trelleborg type in Denmark.

From a local point of view the concentration of sites along the Ouse and Ivel valleys, with their ease of access to the North Sea, is of considerable significance (fig 32).

It has only been possible in this survey to scrape the surface of a most neglected subject, and if it contains only a few pointers towards an area of fieldwork which needs to be carefully considered county by county, then it will have gone some way towards serving its purpose.

GAZETTEER OF SITES DESCRIBED IN THIS PAPER

Numbers on the left refer to sites marked on the Danelaw Boundary map, fig 32:

County		*Parish and local name*	*National Grid*
Beds	1	Arlesey, Etonbury	TL: 191379
	2	Bedford, The King's Ditch	*c* TL: 055494
	3	Bolnhurst, The Camp	TL: 084597
	4	Clapham	TL: 029523
	5	Renhold, Howbury	TL: 107513
	6	Sandy, Beeston Berrys	*c* TL: 175479
	7	Shillington, Church Spanel	TL: 119350
	8	Steppingley, Seymour's Mount	TL: 001351
	9	Tempsford, Gannock's Castle	TL: 161529
	10	Willington, The Docks	TL: 113502
Bucks	11	Hawridge, Hawridge Court Farm	SP: 950058
Cambs	12	Wimblington, Stonea Camp	TL: 448930
Hants		Longstock, The Moat	SU: 362373
Herts	13	Hertford	TL: 325125
Hunts	14	Eaton Socon, The Hillings	TL: 174589
Norfolk		East Wretham, Ringmere	*c* TL: 909889
		Warham St Mary, Warham 'Danish' Camp	TL: 944409
Oxon	15	Stratton Audley, Stuttle's Bank	SP: 625283

Acknowledgement: the writer would like to thank Professor David M. Wilson for reading this paper in typescript and for making a number of valuable suggestions.

BIBLIOGRAPHY

Allcroft, A. H., 1908. *Earthwork of England.*
Almgren, B., 1966. *The Vikings.*

Blake, N. F., 1962. *The Saga of the Jomsvikings.*

Clarke, R. R., 1938. 'An earthwork on East Wretham Heath', *Norfolk Archaeol.* 26, 278*ff*.
Clarke, W. G., 1937. *In Breckland Wilds* (2nd ed. R. R. Clarke).

Foote, P. G. and Wilson, D. M., 1970. *The Viking Achievement.*
Fox, Sir Cyril, 1923. *Archaeology of the Cambridge Region.*

Goddard, A. R., 1903. 'The Danish Camp on the Ouse, near Bedford', *Saga Book of the Viking Club* 3, 331*ff*.
1904. 'Ancient Earthworks' in *Victoria County History, Bedfordshire,* I.
Gray, H. St George, 1933. 'Trial excavations in the so-called "Danish Camp" at Warham, near Wells, Norfolk', *Antiq. J.* 13, 299–413.

Hinsch, E., 1960. *Naut og hall i jernalderen,* Arbok for Universitetet i Bergen. Humanistisk serie 2.

Johnston, D. E., 1959. 'A lost Bedfordshire Earthwork', *Bedfordshire Archaeologist* 2, 19–21.

Lysons, S., *c* 1800. British Museum, Add. MS 9460, f. 25 (Arlesey).

Mawer, A. and Stenton, F. M., 1926. *Place-names of Bedfordshire and Huntingdonshire.*

Nørlund, P., 1956. *Trelleborg* (National Museets Blå Bøger, Copenhagen, English version).

Phillips, C. W., 1948. 'Ancient Earthworks', *Victoria County History, Cambridgeshire,* II.

Tebbutt, C. F., 1952. 'Excavations at "The Hillings", Eaton Socon', *Proc. Cambridge Antiq. Soc.* 45, 48–60.

Viatores, The, 1964. *Roman Roads in the South-East Midlands.*

Wadmore, B., 1920. *The Earthworks of Bedfordshire.*
Whitelock, D., 1955. *English Historical Documents, c* 500–1042.
Williams-Freeman, J. P., 1915. *Field Archaeology as illustrated by Hampshire*

CHAPTER X

Medieval Moats in Cambridgeshire

C. C. Taylor

Moated sites, or homestead moats, usually small enclosures bounded by relatively wide water-filled ditches, are one of the most common forms of medieval earthwork. It has been estimated that there are between three and four thousand in England (Emery, 1962) and this is certainly a very conservative estimate. Yet though many excavations have been and are being carried out on such sites, little work has been done using the methods pioneered by L. V. Grinsell: detailed examination of their physical characteristics and of their distribution. A valuable general statement of many of the problems of moats has been made (Emery, 1962) and Roberts (1962*a* and *b*) has written two articles, one on the distribution of Warwickshire moats and the other an excellent analysis of moated sites in the Midlands; but little else has been attempted.

In this paper the writer would like to examine moated sites in a relatively small area, that of Cambridgeshire, excluding the Isle of Ely, in terms of both their physical appearance and distribution. By these means it is hoped to show some of the problems of identifying moated sites and to suggest a possible reason for the construction of such sites which documentary evidence seems to support. The paper is based on the detailed study of a large number of moats in West Cambridgeshire, partly on subsequent work carried out by the writer elsewhere in the county, and also on the inventory of moated sites in the VCH for Cambridgeshire. Plans and descriptions of all the sites referred to here are to be found in VCH, 1948, RCHM, 1968 and RCHM, forthcoming.

The 270 or so moated sites in Cambridgeshire exhibit, as elsewhere, a bewildering variety of shape and size. Basically there is always a main enclosure, usually rectangular, sometimes circular and more rarely somewhat irregular. This main enclosure typically is or was once completely surrounded by a water-filled ditch, but sites which had a ditch on only three or just two sides are known. These moated enclosures can range in size from a few yards across to five acres in extent (Pl XXIV). Many stand alone, but there is often a variety of outer enclosures, either attached to or surrounding them. These outer enclosures may also be 'moated' or merely bounded by low banks and narrow, dry ditches. Other associated features may include ponds, water channels, mounds etc. Houses found within the moats or adjacent to them date from the fourteenth to the twentieth century, but many moats are completely devoid of standing structures. They occur within villages or hamlets, or isolated in fields or woodland, singly or in groups of up to six.

Only four Cambridgeshire moats have been excavated, two at the beginning of this century (RCHM, 1968, Barton (23) and York, 1908) and the others in the 1930s. The two last excavations were never published and only brief notes exist (Palmer, 1935 and Lethbridge, 1937). From the meagre evidence, all appear to have been built in the twelfth to fourteenth centuries, though one had evidence of earlier occupation apparently before the moat was constructed. These results are in agreement with more modern excavations from other parts of the country which seem to indicate that most moated sites were constructed as such at this period, though some have an earlier, pre-moat, occupation. In Cambridgeshire also, field evidence suggests that some moats were constructed around pre-existing buildings as at Lopham's Hall, Carlton (VCH, 1948, 20).

However, before we can use moated sites either for studies of their purpose or distribution, or indeed excavate them, we must first establish that they are in fact medieval, for a certain proportion of them are later and not true moats at all. This information cannot, in Cambridgeshire at least, be ascertained from contemporary medieval documents except in rare cases. Usually only meticulous and detailed fieldwork can establish the medieval date of moats, though sometimes post-medieval documentation can help. For example, of the 63 moated sites examined in West Cambridgeshire (RHCM, 1968) seven were not medieval moats at all but gardens of the sixteenth to nineteenth centuries, while six others had been turned into gardens later. Merely using large-scale Ordnance Survey maps is not sufficient to establish that a moated site is a garden. Their shape and moated form is often similar to true moats, and many minor details which confirm their origins as gardens, such as prospect mounds and terraces, are omitted by the Ordnance Survey. The dangers of using modern maps as a source for medieval moated sites is nowhere better illustrated than by the 'moat' at Upware in Wicken parish. All modern O.S. maps mark a moat there and show it as a normal square ditched enclosure. However the original 25-inch survey of 1886 shows it correctly as a mound with sharp angular projections at the corners. The site is in fact a seventeenth-century Civil War gun battery or Sconce, and not a moat at all.

In addition the number of moats shown on O.S. maps is quite inadequate for detailed distribution studies. Taking West Cambridgeshire again, of the 50 definitely medieval moated sites found there only 31 are marked on O.S. maps. Eight were discovered by combing local archaeological and historical literature, while eleven were found only by detailed fieldwork involving the systematic searching of all woods and copses in the area. In East Cambridgeshire (RCHM, forthcoming) in a much smaller area, the nine moats known from O.S. maps have been increased to 19 by fieldwork, while one of the former proved to be a medieval millpond which had been turned into a garden in the eighteenth century.

Detailed fieldwork can, however, do much more than merely discover new sites or disprove their medieval date. It can help to ascertain the reason for the construction of such sites and, perhaps more important, indicate some misconceptions about moats. The siting of moats is of significance, for in Cambridgeshire it shows clearly that in the majority of cases the purpose of the wide ditches round such sites was not for drainage, although this is a common explanation for them elsewhere (Dymond, 1968). Roberts (1962b) has identified three typical positions for moats. These are Level Moats, i.e. those on level ground, whose ditches are filled by seepage of water; Perched Moats, i.e. those set on valley sides, whose ditches are filled by leats linked to adjacent rivers or streams; and Valley Moats, i.e. those in valley bottoms, whose streams flow through the moat.

This threefold classification is applicable in Cambridgeshire, though in fact the majority (*c* 70%) of moats there are of the Valley type. Many moats are actually in the beds of small streams (e.g. RCHM, 1968, Caxton 22; Pl XXII), while sometimes a river forms one side of the moat itself (e.g. RCHM, 1968, Orwell 41). The examination of many Cambridgeshire moated sites shows that they are often formed by constructing a dam across an existing or diverted stream so that the water is ponded up behind it within the ditches surrounding the main enclosure. These dams are a clearly recognizable feature of the majority of the county's moats, often visible as a relatively high and wide external bank on the downstream side of the site (RCHM, 1968, Coton 13). These dams presumably had some form of sluice or weir in them to control the level of water in the ditches, and though none have survived in Cambridgeshire their positions can usually be identified. A further 12 per cent of Cambridgeshire moats which can be classified as of the Level type are almost always in permanent wet ground, even when there are drier areas only a few yards away (RCHM, 1968, Croydon 19 and 20). Those moats of the Perched type are also of significance. Especially remarkable is a group of four moated sites at Bottisham, arranged in a line 50–100 yards apart on the side of a shallow valley. Due to an accident of preservation, they still retain a complex system of watercourses linking them to each other and to the adjacent stream. In effect the whole natural drainage has been diverted to pass through all the moats (RCHM, forthcoming). All this evidence indicates that the basic idea behind the siting of Cambridgeshire moats is that of getting water on to the site, not away from it.

Perhaps the most obvious reason for moated sites would seem to be for defence. Again careful fieldwork can show that this is not so, except in a very limited sense. First, the very existence of moats with a ditch on only two or three sides would seem to make defence unlikely (RCHM, 1968, Barton 24 and Gamlingay 59 and 60). Further, the ditches around moats are never very wide, usually between 20 and 30 feet across. This, combined with the relatively small area enclosed, would have meant that the predominantly wooden buildings there could have easily been set on fire by marauding bands throwing firebrands across the ditches. Also, though not unknown, it is rare to find moats in Cambridgeshire with raised interiors. The interiors of the vast majority are level with the surrounding land and, even when they are raised, are never more than two to three feet high. In some cases where the moat is set on sloping ground, no attempt has been made even to level up the interior (VCH, 1948, 20, Lopham's Hall, Carlton). It is often difficult to see where the spoil from the ditch-digging was dumped. It was certainly not used to add to the defence of the sites by putting it inside. Most Cambridgeshire moats have no internal banks at all, and others have only low spread ones, some at least of which appear to be only spoil dumped from periodic cleaning of the ditches.

Many moats also have the remains of permanent earthen causeways across the ditches giving access to the interiors. It is often difficult to be sure, without excavation, which of the causeways that now exist are original. Nevertheless some can certainly be identified as such (e.g. RCHM, 1968, Boxworth 15). In these cases at least, defence is hardly likely to have been a prime motive in their construction.

Though therefore defence against human enemies does not seem to be important, it may be argued that the ditches provided defence against wild animals, especially in forested areas. This is theoretically possible, but leaving aside the question of whether medieval England was sufficiently well populated with such animals, one would surely expect that in a farming community stock rather than humans would have been most at risk from animal predators. And yet it is clear that at most moated sites stock was not kept within the moated enclosures but in outer yards, sometimes bounded by low banks and small ditches or by nothing that survives today. In many cases only the main house and its outbuildings seem to have been protected. On the whole, then, fieldwork shows little evidence of any real defensive motive behind the construction of moats in Cambridgeshire.

We must therefore look elsewhere for the reasons for moats. Many other ideas have been put forward at various times. It has been suggested that moats could have been built for fishponds, for water-supply, as fire-protection and as animal drinking-places, and there can be little doubt that moats were actually used for some or all of these purposes. Yet all these functions could have been achieved by constructing less complex forms of ditches. In most cases simple ponds would have done admirably. Indeed many Cambridgeshire moated sites are associated with long rectangular ponds which were probably for fish.

What therefore can our detailed field examination of moated sites tell us about their function? It appears that, in Cambridgeshire at least, they were not constructed primarily for drainage, defence, fish, etc, or any clearly defined single purpose. They may of course be the complex result of the need for some of these things in various combinations, but in the writer's view there seems to be something more than these purely material objectives.

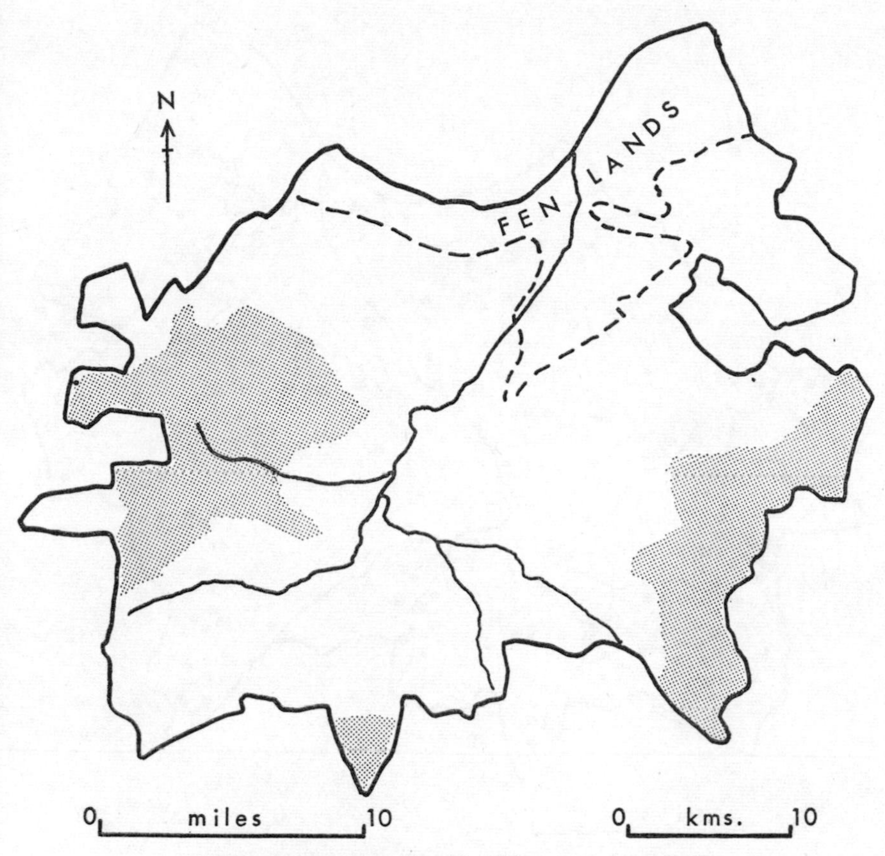

33. Cambridgeshire: Boulder Clay areas (stippled).

Before discussing this in detail we will now turn to the study of Cambridgeshire moated sites from the distributional point of view, which is another of the ways in which L. V. Grinsell has so often shed light on the problems of archaeological sites. At least two studies have been carried out by plotting the distribution of moated sites (Coles, 1935 and Roberts, 1962a). Both of these, one in Essex and the other in Warwickshire, indicated that moated sites in these areas were concentrated in formerly forested regions, and were therefore to be connected with the establishment of medieval farms in these forests at a time when the land was being cleared for agriculture. But if we use the same technique in Cambridgeshire certain difficulties appear. There are two parts of the county for which there is ample evidence for the existence of former forest—a long narrow strip of land in the S.E. and a large triangular area in the west (fig 33). In both places the underlying soil is largely based on boulder clay which would suggest the existence of a former forest cover. Archaeological and historical

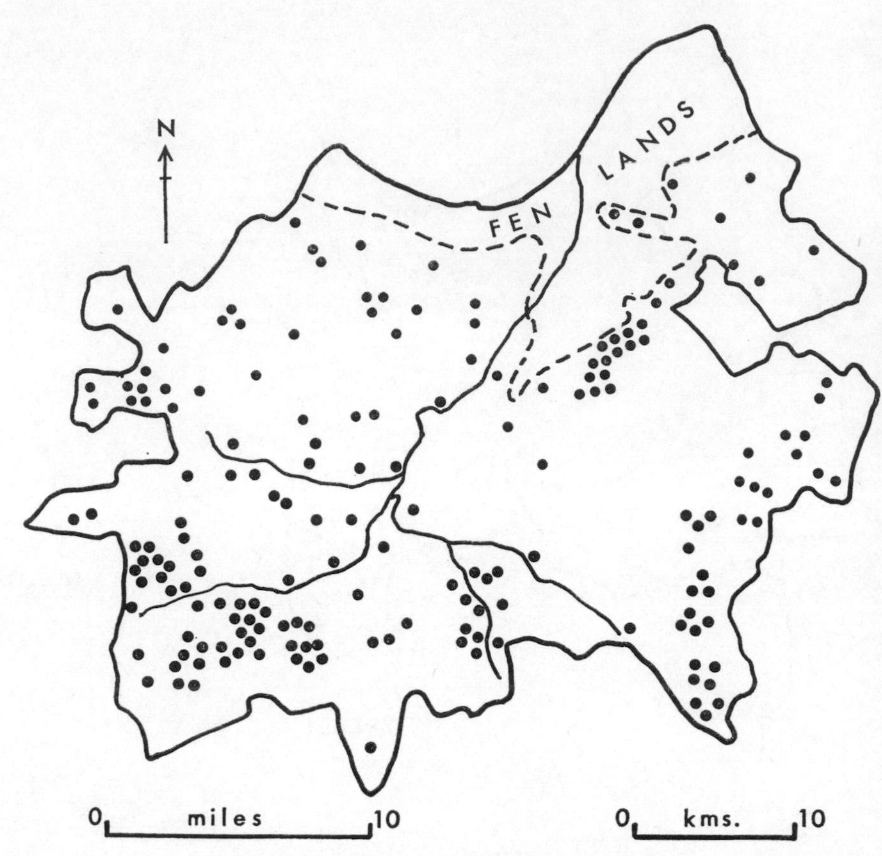

34. Cambridgeshire: medieval moated sites.

evidence also supports this. The distribution of Pagan-Saxon burials is almost entirely outside these two areas and indicates that primary Saxon settlement was lacking here (Fox, 1923). In addition the evidence of woodland in the county in the late eleventh century, as recorded in Domesday Book, is confined almost solely to the two boulder clay regions (Darby, 1957). Likewise the distribution of place-names, such as *weald* and *-ley*, also indicative of former woodland, is again confined to these two areas (Reaney, 1943). The distribution of moated sites in Cambridgeshire has no relationship at all with these formerly forested areas (fig 34). Both the areas have moated sites within them, but so do most other parts of the county. Indeed the greatest concentration of moated sites is along the fen edge in the east and within the broad open river valleys of the S.W. The only area empty of moats is the chalk upland of the S.E. along the line of the Icknield Way which has always been devoid of settlement since the Saxon period, and where there is no water to fill the ditches. However this

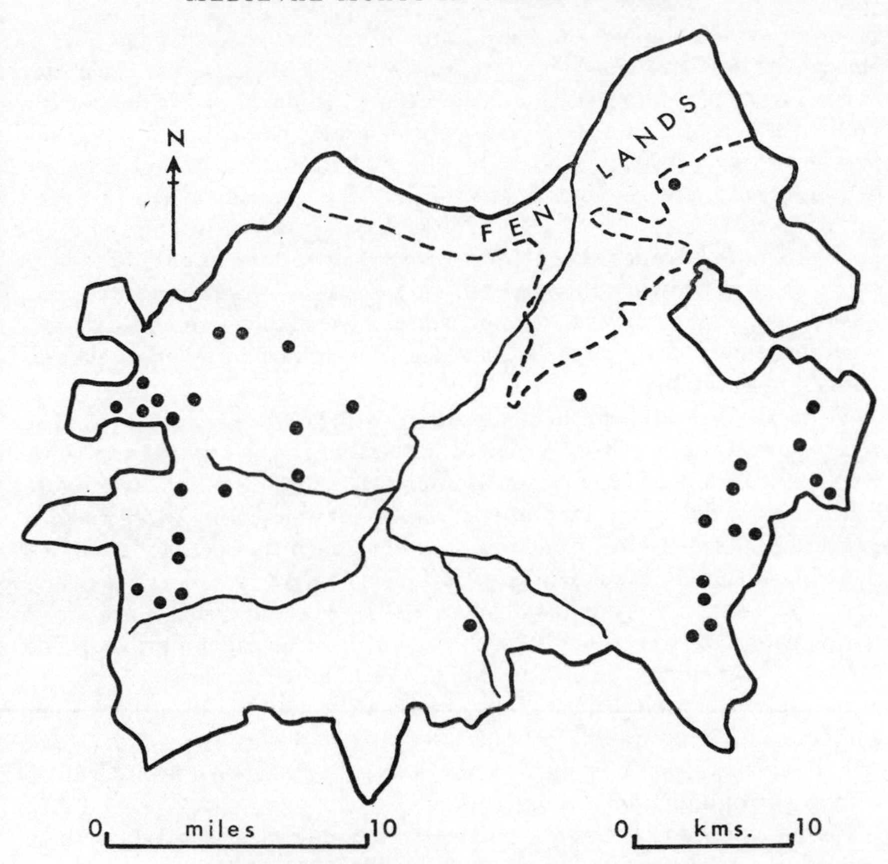

35. Cambridgeshire: isolated medieval moated sites.

apparently meaningless distribution is achieved by mapping *all* moated sites. If we are more selective in our choice we can produce a more meaningful pattern. As already noted, moated sites are found both within villages and quite remote from them. If we plot only isolated moats, that is moats not within the built-up areas of village as they were in the early nineteenth century or those not within villages now deserted, the pattern is very different (fig 35). With few exceptions isolated moats are confined to the former forested areas. Therefore these may be considered to be the sites of farmsteads set up in these forested regions as the woodland was cleared. This clearance of medieval forest associated with the setting up of isolated farms with or without moats is of course well known (Roberts, 1962a; Taylor, 1967a and b). Yet do these Cambridgeshire moats themselves actually represent part of the process of clearing the woodlands? None of the isolated moats in the county have been excavated, and so it is impossible to date any of them by these means. On the other hand documentary evidence appears to help. Many isolated moated sites have farmsteads within them whose names are of considerable antiquity. Swansley Wood Farm in Caxton parish and Papley Grove Farm in Eltisley parish, both in the centre of the West Cambridgeshire boulder clay area, are first recorded as inhabited places by the mid-twelfth and late thirteenth centuries respectively. In S.E. Cambridgeshire Derisley Farm in Wood Ditton parish is first recorded in 1239 and Barsey Farm in Shudy Camps parish in 1268 (Reaney, 1943). These and many others like them tend to support the general date for moated sites that have been excavated elsewhere, and suggest that the clearance of the woodland here and its associated settlements took place at this time. We cannot however accept this without reservation.

First, the validity of the place-name evidence itself is suspect. The occurrence in documents of a named settlement in the twelfth and thirteenth centuries does not necessarily mean that the settlement was established at that date. The kind of documents detailed enough to give such names do not themselves come into existence until that period. It is much more likely that many such isolated forest settlements are older than their first appearance in documents (Taylor, 1970). And Cambridgeshire moats are probably no exception. Indeed occasionally this can be proved. The isolated farmstead known as Yen Hall in West Wickham parish in the S.E. of the county, a typical moated site, is, by an accident of tenurial history and documentary survival, actually recorded in a document dated A.D. 974 (Reaney, 1943). This means that as an inhabited site it is much older than its surrounding moat would suggest.

More important, there is evidence which indicates that when these isolated moats were first constructed, presumably in the twelfth–fourteenth centuries, they were not in forested areas at all. For though we have pointed to the undoubted evidence that West and S.E. Cambridgeshire were *once* forested, no actual date for this was indicated. Domesday Book makes it clear that these areas were not heavily wooded by 1086, though they clearly had been at an earlier period. For the whole of West Cambridgeshire Domesday Book lists 30 places with woodland. At all but three of these the woodland is given in terms of only wood for 'making fences' or 'for the houses' (*nemus ad sepes* and *nemus ad domos et sepes*). The three other entries record the amount of woodland available for pigs (*silva x porcis*) though they are only for 10, 20 and 60 pigs respectively. This indicates that by 1086 there was very little woodland left in the area. In S.E. Cambridgeshire all the 17 entries for woodland are in terms of numbers of pigs, apart from two which record deer parks. The numbers of pigs are sometimes large, up to 450 at Wood Ditton and 511 at Camps, though they go down as low as 20 as at Silverley. This shows that, while much forest still existed here, its clearance was already under way in many places.

By the late thirteenth century the area of woodland in the county was much smaller. It has been estimated (Rackham, 1967 and 1968) that around 1300 only 2 per cent of the West Cambridgeshire boulder clay area was under woodland, that is, much less than there is even today. In fact it has been shown that, far from these years being a time of agricultural expansion in the clay areas of the county, there is evidence of an actual contraction of arable land there (Baker, 1966). Thus it seems that most of the former forested areas of the county has been largely cleared and settled by the thirteenth century, and so the construction of moats at this time around existing or new farmsteads in these places would have had little to do with defence in a thickly forested landscape. In addition we still have to bear in mind the existence of many other medieval farmsteads in these areas which never had moats round them, and also the appearance of the moated sites in villages and hamlets in the densely settled parts of the county which had never been forested in historic times. So again, from the distributional viewpoint as well as from their physical appearance, it seems that moated sites in Cambridgeshire are not the result of a need for protection.

Finally there is one more method of study which combines both fieldwork and distribution. In West Cambridgeshire the examination of moated sites led to the publication of an apparently rather complex and cumbersome classification of these sites based on a whole series of physical characteristics (RCHM, 1968). For our purposes, the most important parts of this classification were as follows. First, the distinguishing of small simple moated sites with enclosed areas of less than half an acre (Class A1a) from larger moats with interiors covering more than half an acre (Class A1b; in practice this usually means well over one acre). Secondly, the distinguishing of moats with attached enclosures bounded by low banks and narrow dry ditches (Classes A2b and c) from those with attached enclosures bounded by wide wet ditches, i.e. a form of double moat (Class A2a). In the West Cambridgeshire areas there appeared to be nearly twice as many small moats as large ones and about the same number of double moats as those with slight outer enclosures. A similar study of the moats in the S.E. Cambridgeshire area produced much the same result, but an examination of the moated sites elsewhere in the county gave a different picture. Nearly three-quarters of the moats there are over an acre in area, and while there are many double moats those with slightly defined outer enclosures are rare. This is the reverse of what one would expect if moats were primarily for defence. In the remoter, sparsely settled and formerly forested areas surely larger moats or double moats would have been built to protect not only the farmhouse but the farm buildings as well. Likewise in the more densely settled parts within large nucleated villages, small moats and moats with slight outer enclosures ought to have been sufficient to protect farmsteads. But this is not so. The fact that the larger, more sophisticated and impressive-looking moated sites are in places where the enclosed buildings would need least protection, and that the smaller, ill-defended moats are in the remoter more isolated parts once again suggests that Cambridgeshire moated sites can hardly be primarily defensive.

Why then were these moats constructed? Why was it that for a period of about two and a half centuries some, but by no means all, farmers and local lords found it necessary or desirable to enclose their existing and new houses with wide water-filled ditches? What, if protection, drainage, etc. were not the primary reasons, led people to go to considerable lengths in constructing such ditches and often build their houses in extremely unfavourable positions in order to fill these ditches with water? There may be no easy answer to these questions. It is possible that moated sites are the result not of materialistic reasons but of more intangible social ones. They may be reflecting the general prosperity of their owners and the desire to show off this prosperity by imitating the higher ranks of contemporary society as well as following in the footsteps of their ancestors. For medieval moated sites, common as they are, form only a small part of a long English tradition of surrounding houses with water. Their origins may lie in the pre-Conquest ringworks which were probably built for protection around the homes of thegns at a time when defence was a necessity. In the post-Conquest period when defence became less necessary the idea of having a water-filled ditch around one's house may have become a symbol of prestige aimed at by all who could afford it was well as for more practical reasons. The influence of the great castles in the land, with their huge defensive structures and wide moats, may also have had its effect.

Is there any evidence for such theories in Cambridgeshire? Can we see this assumed desire for ostentatious mock defensive works around houses in either documents or on the ground? This writer believes we can, at least in part. In Cambridgeshire it is possible to detect the desire for the imitation of great castles working down through most classes of society. By the twelfth century the Crown had built great fortresses such as Cambridge Castle. The major lords too had their castles. Such were the de Veres, Earls of Oxford, who constructed the largest castle in the county at Castle Camps in the centre of their extensive estates. An example further down the social scale may be seen at Cheveley Castle, which consists of a small rectangular enclosure of only half an acre surrounded by a ditch 75 feet wide and 20 feet deep. Its interior, which was not raised, was once separated from the ditch by a thin curtain wall and corner towers. It was a castle in name only and can hardly have been a great defensive structure. It is little more than a superior type of moated site. It was built in 1341 by Sir John Pulterey, a merchant-financier and four times Lord Mayor of London (VCH, 1948), and must surely represent merely a symbol of his wealth and prestige, built in imitation of his social superiors rather than from any need for protection.

Moving lower in society, the moated sites in Borough Green parish in

S.E. Cambridgeshire illustrate the kind of people who probably constructed some of the county's moated sites (Palmer, 1939 and VCH, 1948). The moat in the village itself was the centre of the main manor of the parish. From the late eleventh century this manor was held by the de Burgh family who, though owning land in Yorkshire, lived here. Until the early thirteenth century they were little more than local farmers but in the latter part of that century the family started to improve its social position. One Thomas de Burgh became involved in public life and represented the county in Parliament, and his second son, another Thomas, certainly spent money in showy additions to his estate. In 1330 this Thomas obtained a licence to make a deer-park at Borough Green and in 1334 to crenellate his Yorkshire home. Thomas's death in the latter year ended his plans, but it seems probable that one of the two Thomases constructed the moat in the village around their manor house, and the latter Thomas almost certainly built the isolated moat which exists at Park Wood in his new deer-park (Pl XXIII). A third moat in the parish was the centre of a subinfeudated estate known as Bretton's Manor. By 1234 it was held by William de Bretton who started life in a small way but ended as one of the King's Justices. He gradually acquired small pieces of land in Cambridgeshire, Essex and Northamptonshire, but Borough Green was his home. By the time he died in 1261 he had founded a county family, and his son John de Bretton became a knight and continued to increase his estates. The family lived at Borough Green until 1353 when the estate was leased. There can be little doubt that either William or John de Bretton was responsible for the moat around their house.

These examples are perhaps not typical of all the people who built moats in the county, and many must have been constructed by smaller farmers whose names are not recorded in documents. But at least one can start to appreciate some of the aims and aspirations behind the construction of moats.

Even after moated sites ceased to be constructed as such, the idea of watercourses associated with dwellings continued in the form of gardens. By the sixteenth century old moated sites in Cambridgeshire were being turned into gardens and new 'moated' gardens constructed. Some of the new gardens were almost exact copies of the earlier moats with minor refinements. At Croydon Wilds (RCHM, 1968, Croydon 14) a typical moated site was constructed around a new house in the early seventeenth century. But it was made exactly square, raised terraces or walkways were erected on two sides and small prospect mounds set up in the corners. In other places the moat was constructed purely as a façade to the main front of the house. At Haslingfield Hall (RCHM, 1968, Haslingfield 2 and 34) the moat, which is contemporary with the mid-sixteenth-century house, is merely three-sided with the main side to the front. The inner sides of the ditches are brick-lined and a pretty sixteenth-century brick bridge across the ditch gives access to the house. Of the older moated sites which were turned into gardens that at Papworth St Agnes is typical. There the rectangular medieval moat had mounds put in the corners and two outer ditched enclosures added to surround small formal gardens, all probably carried out in 1585 when the magnificent manor house within the moat was erected (RCHM, 1968, Papworth St Agnes 21). At another site at Croydon (RCHM, 1968, Croydon 12; Pl XXIV) the medieval moat was abandoned, probably in the sixteenth century, and a new house erected alongside it. Then a new 'moat' was constructed in front of the house and both old and new moats were made part of an elaborate garden.

In view of this type of 'moat' one wonders how much in the design of sixteenth- and seventeenth-century English gardens with their emphasis on ponds and moats is a direct continuation of the ideas behind medieval moated sites and not just new, continental influences. In Cambridgeshire at least, the impact of medieval moats seems to have been very great indeed.

So in Cambridgeshire, though much more work remains to be done on moated sites, there are clear indications that they were not primarily defensive structures. They seem to have been a relatively short-lived fashionable ideal constructed around houses for prestige purposes by local lords and prosperous farmers, directly imitating their social superiors. Then the basic form of the moated site was developed into part of the tradition of English garden design by later generations.

BIBLIOGRAPHY

Baker, A. R. H., 1966. 'Evidence in Nonarum Inquisitiones of Contracting Arable Land in England during the 14th Century,' *Econ. Hist. Rev.* 19, 525–528.

Coles, R., 1935. 'The Past History of the Forest of Essex,' *Essex Naturalist* 24, 115–133.

Darby, H. C., 1957. *Domesday Geography of Eastern England.*

Dymond, D., 1968. 'The Suffolk Landscape,' in L. M. Munby (ed.), *East Anglian Studies*, 42.

Emery, F. V., 1962. 'Moated Settlements in England,' *Geography* 47 (4), 378–388.

Fox, C., 1923. *The Archaeology of the Cambridge Region.*

Lethbridge, T. C., 1937. *Procs. Cambridge Antiq. Soc.* 37, xiii.

Palmer, W. M., 1935. *Procs. Cambridge Antiq. Soc.* 35, xxviii.

Palmer, W. M., 1939. 'A History of the Parish of Borough Green,' *Cambridge Antiq. Soc., Octavo Pub.* 54.

Rackham, O., 1967. 'The History and Effects of Coppicing as a Woodland Practice,' in *The Biotic Effects of Public Pressures on the Environment* (Nature Conservancy Staff Symposium), 82–93.

Rackham, O., 1968. 'Medieval Woodland Areas,' *Nature in Cambridgeshire* 9, 22–25.

RCHM, 1968. *Cambridgeshire*, Vol. I.

RCHM, forthcoming. *Cambridgeshire*, Vol. II.

Reaney, P. H., 1943. 'The Place Names of Cambridgeshire,' *English Place-Name Soc.* 19.

Roberts, B. K., 1962a. 'Moated Sites', *The Amateur Historian*, 5 (2), 34–38.

Roberts, B. K., 1962b. 'Moated Sites in Midland England,' *Trans. Birmingham Archaeol. Soc.* 80, 26–33.

Roberts, B. K., 1964. 'Moats and Mottes,' *Medieval Archaeol.* 8, 219–222.

Taylor, C. C., 1967a. 'The Pattern of Medieval Settlement in the Forest of Blackmoor,' *Procs. Dorset Natur. Hist. Archaeol. Soc.* 87, 251–254.

Taylor, C. C., 1967b. 'Whiteparish, a Study of the Development of a Forest Edge Parish,' *Wiltshire Archaeol. Natur. Hist. Mag.* 62, 79–102.

Taylor, C. C., 1970. *The Making of the English Landscape: Dorset* (London), 84–86.

VCH, 1948. *Cambridgeshire* II, 13–37.

York, A. C., 1908. 'The Round Moat at Fowlmere,' *Proc. Cambridge Antiq. Soc.* 12, 114–119.

CHAPTER XI

Bibliography of L. V. Grinsell's Publications, 1929-1971

compiled by Nicholas Thomas and Peter Fowler

The following 120 items spanning 42 years are not completely exhaustive, but we hope nothing of moment has been omitted. Suffice it to indicate the range and scale of our friend's interests.

Note: journals are placed under the year for which they were published, to avoid repeatedly quoting the year of publication (usually that immediately following). Abbreviations follow the CBA *List* (above p 37).

1929

'Lower and Middle Palaeolithic Periods in Sussex', *Sussex Archaeol. Collect.* **70**, 172–182

1930

'Long Barrows and Bell-barrows in Sussex,' *Sussex Notes Queries*, Aug., 69–71

1931

(*a*) 'Classification of Downland Tumuli', *Sussex Notes Queries*, Feb., 140–143

(*b*) 'Grave-mound Cluster on Mill Hill, Rodmell,' *Sussex Notes Queries*, Nov., 236–238

(*c*) 'Sussex in the Bronze Age,' *Sussex Archaeol. Collect.* **72**, 30–68

1932

(*a*) 'Some Surrey Bell-barrows', *Surrey Archaeol. Collect.* **40**, 56–64

(*b*) 'Sussex in the Bronze Age—Addendum and Corrigendum', *Sussex Notes Queries*, Aug., 85–86

(*c*) 'Sussex Palaeoliths—Addenda et Corrigenda', *Sussex Notes Queries*, Aug., 86

1934

(*a*) 'Bell-barrows', *Proc. Prehist. Soc. East Anglia* **7**, 203–230

(*b*) 'An Analysis and List of Surrey Barrows', *Surrey Archaeol. Collect.* **42**, 26–60

(*c*) 'Sussex Barrows', *Sussex Archaeol. Collect.* **75**, 216–275

1935

(*a*) 'An Analysis and List of Berkshire Barrows, Part I', *Berkshire Archaeol. J.* **49**, 171–191

(*b*) 'The Lambourn Long Barrow', *Proc. Prehist. Soc.* **1**, 149

1936

(*a*) 'An Analysis and List of Berkshire Barrows, Part 1—Addenda. Part II—List', *Berkshire Archaeol. J.* **40**, 20–58

(*b*) *Ancient Burial-Mounds of England* (Methuen)
(*c*) 'A Chambered Long Barrow near Lambourn', *Trans. Newbury Dist. Fld. Club* 7, 191
(*d*) 'The Lambourn Chambered Long Barrow', *Berkshire Archaeol. J.* **40**, 59–62

1937

'Some Aspects of the Folklore of Prehistoric Monuments', *Folklore* **48**, 245–259

1938

(*a*) 'Berkshire Barrows: Part III—Evidence from the Saxon Charters', *Berkshire Archaeol. J.* **42**, 102–116
(*b*) 'Hampshire Barrows', *Proc. Hampshire Fld. Club Archaeol. Soc.* **14**, 9–40

1939

(*a*) 'Berkshire Barrows, Part IV—Addenda and Corrigenda', *Berkshire Archaeol. J.* **43**, 9–21
(*b*) *The Blowing Stone* (St. Catherine Press Ltd.)
(*c*) 'Hampshire Barrows, Part I, Addenda and Corrigenda, and Part II' *Proc. Hampshire Fld. Club Archaeol. Soc.* **14**, 195–229
(*d*) 'Scheme for recording the Folklore of Prehistoric Remains', *Folklore* **50**, 323–332
(*e*) *White Horse Hill and Surrounding Country* (St. Catherine Press Ltd.)
(*f*) 'Some Rare Types of Round Barrow on Mendip', *Proc. Somerset Archaeol. Natur. Hist. Soc.* **85**, 151–166

1940

(*a*) 'The Archaeological Contributions of Richard Jefferies', *Newbury Dist. Fld. Club* **8**, 216–226
(*b*) 'Hampshire Barrows, Parts I and II, Addenda and Corrigenda, and Part III', *Proc. Hampshire Fld. Club Archaeol. Soc.* **14**, 346–365
(*c*) 'Notes on the White Horse Hill Region', *Berkshire Archaeol. J.* **43**, 135–139
(*d*) 'References to the Newbury District in Aubrey's *Monumenta Britannica*', *Newbury Dist. Fld. Club* **8**, 156–158
(*e*) 'Sussex Barrows, Supplementary Paper', *Sussex Archaeol. Collect.* **81**, 210–214
(*f*) 'Wayland's Smithy, *Beahhild's Byrigels and Hwittuc's Hlaew:* a suggestion', *Newbury Dist. Fld. Club* **8**, 136–139
(*g*) With Sherwin, G. A., 'Isle of Wight Barrows', *Proc. Isle Wight Natur. Hist. Archaeol. Soc.* **3**, 179–222

1941

(*a*) 'The Boat of the Dead in the Bronze Age,' *Antiquity* **15**, 360–370
(*b*) 'The Bronze Age Round Barrows of Wessex', *Proc. Prehist. Soc.* **7**, 73–113

1942

(*a*) 'Kivik Cairn, Scania', *Antiquity* **16**, 160–174

(*b*) 'Sussex Barrows: Supplement No II', *Sussex Archaeol. Collect.* **82**, 115–123

1943

'The Boat of the Dead', *Antiquity* **17**, 47–50

1947

(*a*) *Egyptian Pyramids* (Bellows)
(*b*) 'Folklore of Ancient Egyptian Monuments', *Folklore* **58**, 345–360

1948

'Bronze Implements in the Avalon Museum, Glastonbury', *Archaeol, Cantiana* **61**, 185

1950

With Wells, H. B., Tallamy, H. S. and Betjeman, Sir John, *Studies in the History of Swindon* (Swindon Borough Council)

1951

(*a*) 'Scandinavian Implement from Enfield', *Trans. London Middlesex Archaeol. Soc.* N.S. **10**, 308–309
(*b*) 'Shaving the Eyebrows as a Funeral Custom', *Man* **50**, No. 231, 144

1952

Letter: Authorship of *The Barrow Diggers*, *Archaeol. Newsletter* **4**, No. 10, 151

1953

(*a*) 'Early Funerary Superstitions in Britain', *Folklore* **63**, 271–281
(*b*) 'A Flint Dagger from Avebury', *Wiltshire Archaeol. Natur. Hist. Mag.* **55**, 176, 291
(*c*) 'A Socketed Bronze Adze from Somerset', *Antiq. J.* **33**, 203–204
(*d*) With Gettins, G. L. and Taylor, H., 'The Marshfield Barrows', *Trans. Bristol Gloucestershire Archaeol. Soc.* **72**, 23–44
(*e*) *Ancient Burial-Mounds of England* (2nd Ed, Methuen)

1954

(*a*) 'A Polished Flint Axe from Mendip', *Proc. Univ. Bristol Spelaeol. Soc.* **7**, 42–43
(*b*) 'A Gold Stater from Gloucestershire', *Brit. Numis. J.* **27**, (1952–4), 88–89

1955

(*a*) 'Death and the After-Life', *Nature* **176**, 809–812

(*b*) In Thomas, N., 'The Thornborough Circles, Near Ripon, North Riding,' *Yorkshire Archaeol. J.* **38,** 425–445, *opp* 442

1956

(*a*) Letter: 'Lost and Found,' *Museums J.* **55,** 220
(*b*) *Stanton Drew Stone Circles, Somerset* (HMSO)
(*c*) With Rahtz, P. A., 'Three Roman Stone Coffin Burials from Wick, Glos', *Trans. Bristol Gloucestershire Archaeol. Soc.* **75,** 193–198

1957

(*a*) 'A Decorated Cist-slab from Mendip', *Proc. Prehist. Soc.* **23,** 231–232
(*b*) 'The Ferryman and his Fee', *Folklore* **68,** 257–269
(*c*) *A History of the County of Wiltshire* **1,** i (OUP)
(*d*) 'Polished-Edge Flint Knife and a Stone Axe from Priddy,' *Proc. Univ. Bristol Spelaeol. Soc.* **8,** 44–46
(*e*) 'A Socketed Bronze Axe from Oldland', *Trans. Bristol Gloucestershire Archaeol. Soc.* **76,** 148–149
(*f*) 'An Inscribed Gold Stater of the Dobunni from King's Weston, Bristol', *Brit. Numis. J.* **28,** (1955–1957), 175

1958

(*a*) *The Archaeology of Wessex* (Methuen)
(*b*) With Selwood, P. H., 'An Early British Coin from Whitehorse Hill', *Berkshire Archaeol. J.* **56,** 63–64
(*c*) 'A Perforated Stone Axe-hammer from Challacombe', *Trans. Devonshire Ass.* **90,** 215–216
(*d*) 'Prehistoric Objects from Wiltshire in The Lukis Museum, St. Peter Port, Guernsey', *Wiltshire Archaeol. Natur. Hist. Mag.* **57,** 76
(*e*) 'Marshfield Barrows: Supplementary Note', *Trans. Bristol Gloucestershire Archaeol. Soc.* **77,** 151–155

1959

(*a*) *Dorset Barrows* (Dorset Natur. Hist. Archaeol Soc.)
(*b*) 'A Saxon Bronze Strap-end from Blaise Castle Hill', Appendix C, 168–169, in Rahtz, P. A. and Brown, J. Clevedon, 'Blaise Castle Hill, Bristol, 1957', *Proc. Univ. Bristol Spelaeol. Soc.* **8,** 147–171

1960

(*a*) 'Children and Archaeology', *Museums J.* **60,** 5–12
(*b*) 'A Palaeolith from Beckford, Worcs.', *Antiq. J.* **40,** 67–68
(*c*) With O'Neil, H., 'Gloucestershire Barrows', *Trans. Bristol Gloucestershire Archaeol. Soc.* **79,** Pt. I
(*d*) 'Evidence of Roman Ironworking on Exmoor', *Notes Queries Somerset Dorset* **27,** (1955–1960), 192–193

(*e*) 'A Round Barrow on Mendip', *Notes Queries Somerset Dorset* **27**, (1955 1960), 202–203
(*f*) 'Work at the Pool Farm Cist, Mendip, 1956–8', *Notes Queries Somerset Dorset* **27**, (1955–1960), 243–244

1961

(*a*) 'The Breaking of Objects as a Funerary Rite', *Folklore* **72**, 475–491
(*b*) *A Guide to Air Photographic Archaeology in the South-West* (Council for British Archaeology, Group XIII, Bristol)

1962

The Bristol Archaeological Research Group was founded in March. LVG was the editor of its thrice-yearly *Bulletin* until 1968, after which he was Editor (Special Publications) responsible for the *Field Guides* and *Special Publications* until 1971. Only a few of the notes, short papers, etc., that he wrote for the *Bulletin*, and only the other Bristol Archaeol. Res. Gp. publications of which he was part author as well as editor, are noted below.
(*a*) *A Brief Numismatic History of Bristol* (Bristol City Museum)
(*b*) With Rahtz, P. A., and Warhurst, A., *The Preparation of Archaeological Reports* (Bristol Archaeol. Res. Gp.). Duplicated.
(*c*) With Evens, E. D., Piggott, S. and Wallis, F. S., '4th Report of the Sub-Committee of the S.W. Group of Museums and Art Galleries (England) on the Petrological Identification of Stone Axes', *Proc. Prehist. Soc.* **28**, 209–266

1963

Stoney Littleton Long Barrow, Somerset (HMSO)

1964

(*a*) 'Numismatics in Bristol City Museum', *Spink's Numis. Circular* **72**, No. 5, 103–104
(*b*) 'Settlement in Prehistoric and Roman Times', in Monkhouse, F. J. (ed.), *A Survey of Southampton and its Region* (Brit. Assoc. Advance Sci.), 189–204
(*c*) Ed. and part author, *A Survey and Policy concerning the Archaeology of the Bristol Region* **1** (to the Norman Conquest) (Bristol Archaeol. Res. Gp.). Duplicated.
(*d*) 'The Royce Collection at Stow-on-The-Wold', *Trans. Bristol Gloucestershire Archaeol. Soc.* **83**, 1–33
(*e*) 'A Gold Stater from Kingswood, Glos', *Trans. Bristol Gloucestershire Archaeol. Soc.* **83**, 143–144

1965

(*a*) 'Somerset Archaeology, 1931–65', *Proc. Somerset Archaeol. Natur. Hist. Soc.* **109**, 47–77

(*b*) 'A Gold Stater from Pensford, Somerset', *Proc. Somerset Archaeol. Natur. Hist. Soc.* **109,** 108
(*c*) 'Primitive Currency in a Provincial Museum', *Cunobelin* II (Year Book Brit. Assoc. Numismatic Societies), 55–57
(*d*) Ed. and part author, *Survey & Policy of the Archaeology of the Bristol Region* 2 (1066 onwards) (Bristol Archaeol. Res. Gp.). Duplicated.
(*e*) 'Belas Knap Long Barrow', *Archaeol. J.* **122,** 194–195

1966

(*a*) *Belas Knap Long Barrow, Gloucestershire* (HMSO)
(*b*) 'A Bronze Torc from Winscombe, Somerset', *Notes Queries Somerset Dorset* **28,** pt. 283, 259–260
(*c*) *Prehistoric Sites in the Mendip, South Cotswold and Bristol Region* (Bristol Archaeol. Res. Gp., Field Guide no. 1)
(*d*) With Rahtz, P. A. and Warhurst, A., *The Preparation of Archaeological Reports* (John Baker)
(*e*) 1964c 2nd ed.
(*f*) 'A Palaeolithic Implement from Poole Keynes', *Trans. Bristol Gloucestershire Archaeol. Soc.* **85,** 207–208
(*g*) With James, D., 'The Royce Collection: Supplement', *Trans. Bristol Gloucestershire Archaeol. Soc.* **85,** 209–213

1967

(*a*) 'Barrow Treasure in Fact, Folklore and Legislation', *Folklore* **78,** 1–38
(*b*) 'The Bath Mint', *Spink's Numis. Circular* **75,** No. 11, 299
(*c*) With Archibald, M. M., 'A Small Medieval Coin-hoard from Maesbury', *Notes Queries Somerset Dorset* **28,** 344
(*d*) 'Silver Coins of the Dobunni from Naunton', *Trans. Bristol Gloucestershire Archaeol. Soc.* **86,** 193–194

1968

(*a*) *Guide Catalogue to the South Western British Prehistoric Collections* (Bristol City Museum)
(*b*) 'Barrows as Repositories for Coin Hoards and other Treasures', *Seaby's Coin & Medal Bull.*, No. 3, 90–91
(*c*) With Hebditch, M., *Roman Sites in the Mendip, Cotswold, Wye Valley and Bristol Region* (Bristol Archaeol. Res. Gp., Field Guide no. 2)

1969

(*a*) *Prehistoric Bristol* (Bristol Branch Hist. Assoc.)
(*b*) 'A Visit to William Cunnington's Museum at Heytesbury in 1807' *Antiquity* **43,** 62 (reprinted in *Wiltshire Archaeol. Natur. Hist. Mag.* **64,** 118–20)

(c) *The Cheddar Caves Museum: a Brief Guide, summary catalogue & bibliography* (Cheddar Caves Museum)

(d) 'Somerset Barrows, pt I: West and South', *Somerset Archaeol. Natur. Hist.* **113**, Supplement, 1–43

(e) 'North Devon Barrows', *Proc. Devon Archaeol. Soc.* **28**, 95–129

(f) 'A Note on the Rillaton Barrow', *Cornish Archaeol.* 8, 126–127

1970

(a) *The Archaeology of Exmoor* (David & Charles)

(b) 'Introduction to the Prehistoric Remains' in Verey, D., *Gloucestershire* (*The Buildings of England*, Penguin), 69–76

(c) *South Western England* (Discovering Regional Archaeology, Shire Publications)

(d) 'Prehistoric & Roman Monuments on Exmoor' in *Exmoor National Park Guide* (HMSO)

(e) *et al*, *The Mendip Hills in Prehistoric & Roman Times* (Bristol Archaeol. Res. Gp., Special Publication No 1)

1971

With Dyer, J., *Wessex* (Discovering Regional Archaeology, Shire Publications)

Forthcoming

'Somerset Barrows, pt 2: North and East', *Somerset Archaeol. Natur. Hist.* 115

'The Past and Future of Archaeology in Somerset', *Somerset Archaeol. Natur. Hist.* 115

'The Technique of Archaeological Distribution Maps' in Lynch, F. & Burgess, C. (eds), *Prehistoric Man in Wales and the West* (Adams & Dart)

'Witchcraft at Barrows and other Prehistoric Sites,' *Antiquity* **46**

The Bristol Mint: an historical outline (Hist. Assoc., Bristol)

Contributor to *Sylloge of Bristol and Gloucestershire Coins* (British Academy)

Guide-Catalogue to the Collections from Ancient Egypt (Bristol City Museum)

'The Individual Fieldworker' in *Fieldwork in British Archaeology* (CBA and Adams and Dart)

Notes on the Contributors

PAUL ASHBEE, M.A., F.S.A., is a lecturer in the Centre of East Anglian Studies, University of East Anglia. It was, however, while still a schoolmaster that he established his reputation in a series of excavations and their publication for the Ancient Monuments Inspectorate and that he carried out much of the work for his barrow books, *The Bronze Age Round Barrow in Britain* (Phoenix, 1960), and *The Earthern Long Barrow in Britain* (Dent, 1970).

DESMOND BONNEY, B.A., F.S.A., is a senior Investigator on the staff of the Royal Commission on Historical Monuments (England). He has served on the councils of the Prehistoric Society and of the Cornwall Archaeological Society and is currently on the councils of the Royal Archaeological Institute and of the Wiltshire Archaeological Society. Research interests include the evolution of settlement and agrarian patterns in the early historic period and the historical geography of Wiltshire.

JOHN DRINKWATER, L.R.I.C., is an analytical chemist employed in the tobacco industry. His main interest is the prehistory of the Bristol region with, as a direct result of being a university extra-mural student of Leslie Grinsell, a penchant for burial mounds. He has been assistant editor of the *Archaeological Review* and is currently secretary of Bristol Archaeological Research Group.

JAMES DYER, M.A., F.S.A., is Senior Lecturer in Archaeology and History at Putteridge Bury College of Education, Luton, and a Council Member of the Prehistoric Society. He has written and edited a number of archaeological guide books to regions of Britain and Denmark, and has made a special study of the prehistory of the Chilterns.

PETER FOWLER, M.A., F.S.A., is staff tutor in prehistory and archaeology in the Department of Extra-Mural Studies, University of Bristol. He was formerly on the staff of the Royal Commission on Historical Monuments (England) and is currently honorary secretary of the Council for British Archaeology and a vice-president of the Prehistoric Society. His special interests include agrarian archaeology. A frequent broadcaster, his publications include *Regional Archaeologies: Wessex* (Heinemann, 1967)

PHILIP RAHTZ, M.A., F.S.A., is Senior Lecturer in Medieval Archaeology at the University of Birmingham. He has since 1953 directed many rescue excavations in England, and has also worked in Ghana, Yugoslavia and Greece. Current research interests are mainly in the West Midlands, but he periodically returns to work in his native Somerset to dig at Glastonbury or Cadcong.

ISOBEL SMITH, B.A., Ph.D., F.S.A., is an Investigator for the Royal Commission on Historical Monuments (England), Hon. Editor of the *Wiltshire Archaeological and Natural History Magazine* and Hon. Secretary of the Implement Petrology Survey of the South-West. Editor of *Windmill Hill and Avebury: Excavations by Alexander Keiller*, 1925–1939.

CHRISTOPHER TAYLOR, B.A., F.S.A., is an Investigator for the Royal Commission on Historical Monuments (England). He has worked for the Commission in Dorset, Cambridgeshire and Peterborough and is now in Northamptonshire. His interests include almost anything to do with the history of the landscape. Author of *Dorset* (Hodder & Stoughton, 1970).

CHARLES THOMAS, M.A., F.S.A., is Director of the Institute of Cornish Studies (University of Exeter and Cornwall County Council). He was Professor of Archaeology at Leicester University, 1967–71, and is currently President of the Council for British Archaeology and of the Royal Institution of Cornwall. His research interests are mainly interdisciplinary, but include the archaeology of the early Church. Author of *Early Christian Archaeology of North Britain* (OUP 1971), *Britain and Ireland* 400–800 *A.D.* (Thames and Hudson 1971), numerous papers, and editor of *Cornish Archaeology*.

NICHOLAS THOMAS, M.A., F.S.A., F.M.A., is Director of the Bristol City Museum to which he came after service at Devizes and Birmingham City Museums. His excavations include hill-forts and barrows, and his fieldwork has embraced American museums which he visited as a Churchill Fellow. Author of *A Guide to Prehistoric England* (Batsford, 1960).

Acknowledgements

J. Mascaró Pasarius for the *Frontispiece*; Bristol City Museum for Pl. I; the Society of Antiquaries of London for permission to reproduce Pls V–VII; J. E. Hancock for Pls X, XIV–XVII; Royal Commission on Historical Monuments (England) for Pls XI and XII and figs 15–18; Dr. J. K. S. St. Joseph and University of Cambridge Committee for Aerial Photography for Pls XIII, XIX, XXI–XXIV; Bedfordshire County Record Office for permission to reproduce Pl XVIII; *Archaeological Review* for permission to reproduce figs 8 and 9; and Controller HMSO for the base maps of figs 15–18. Pages 116–21 are reproduced by permission of Rescue, a Trust for British Archaeology, and pp 122–24 by permission of the editor of Bristol Archaeological Research Group *Bulletin*.

Index

Index

Abbreviations: BA: Bronze Age; PRIA: pre-Roman Iron Age; RB: Romano-British; EM: early Medieval (*c* AD 500–1000); MED: Medieval